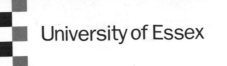

CORPORATE BORROWING: LAW AND PRACTICE

CORPORATE BORROWING: LAW AND PRACTICE

Third Edition

GEOFFREY FULLER MA (OXON), Solicitor
Partner, Allen & Overy LLP

JORDANS

Published by
Jordan Publishing Limited
21 St Thomas Street
Bristol BS1 6JS

Whilst the publishers and the author have taken every care in preparing the material included in this work, any statements made as to the legal or other implications of particular transactions are made in good faith purely for general guidance and cannot be regarded as a substitute for professional advice. Consequently, no liability can be accepted for loss or expense incurred as a result of relying in particular circumstances on statements made in this work.

British Library Cataloguing-in-Publication Data
A catalogue record for this book is available from the British Library.

ISBN 1 84661 009 5

Typeset by Etica Press Limited, Malvern, Worcestershire
Printed in Great Britain by Antony Rowe Limited, Chippenham, Wilts

To Liz

PREFACE

Part of the appeal (or, some would say, frustration) of the law of borrowings is that it embraces so many different areas of law: contract, trusts, company law, security, insolvency, tax, financial services regulation, and so forth. This book is not intended to be an exhaustive study of each of those areas but aims to bring together the elements of them that are relevant to understanding the law of corporate borrowings.

This is an unashamedly *legal* book (as can immediately be seen from the number of footnotes and case references). However, it is also intended for the interested layman, and in particular covers not just the law but also market practice, linking the two together as far as possible.

In addition to being completely updated, the book has been considerably expanded from the second edition. In particular, I have added a new chapter on structured finance, and rewritten the chapter on variation of rights and the section on corporate and directors' powers. The chapter on attracting lenders has been rewritten to take account of the Prospectus Directive, and there are new sections on electronic communications and signatures and on financial collateral arrangements. The security chapter has been updated to take account of the Enterprise Act 2002, the Insolvency Act 2000 and the impact of the *Spectrum Plus* decision, and the chapters on trustees, subordination and guarantees have all been expanded. Time, however, has not permitted me to cover borrowings by entities other than English companies. Maybe in the fourth edition ...

I am grateful to many of my friends and colleagues at Allen & Overy who have helped me in preparing this new edition. I would particularly like to thank Matt Mortimer (who reviewed the taxation chapter), Effie Chao and John Taylor (who reviewed the chapter on US selling restrictions), Beth Collett (who drafted the material on the Prospectus Directive) and Stephen Miller (who reviewed various parts of the new text). I am also particularly grateful to Denise Brett and Norma Witts, who patiently typed up the amendments, and my wife, for her advice and encouragement throughout. That said, any errors or omissions are entirely my responsibility.

I have endeavoured to state the law and practice as at 31 May 2006.

GW Fuller
One New Change
London EC4M 9QQ
September 2006

CONTENTS

TABLE OF CASES

References are to paragraph numbers

TABLE OF STATUTES

References are to paragraph number

TABLE OF STATUTORY INSTRUMENTS

References are to paragraph numbers

TABLE OF FOREIGN STATUTES

References are to paragraph numbers

TABLE OF EC LEGISLATION

References are to paragraph numbers

Chapter One

THE NATURE OF BORROWINGS

INTRODUCTION

'Neither a borrower, nor a lender be;
For loan oft loses both itself and friend,
And borrowing dulls the edge of husbandry.'[1]

1.1 Whatever truth there may be in Polonius's advice, it is a fact of life that the vast majority of people do, at some stage, borrow and/or lend money.[2] In the case of companies, borrowing, whether by loans from banks or by the issue of debt securities, is an essential feature of responsible financial management: too little, and the company does not have as much money available for capital investment and working capital as it ought; too much, and the interest burden will cause financial problems.

LOAN CAPITAL

1.2 The money borrowed by companies is often spoken of as 'loan capital'. The word 'capital' is used in many senses in relation to companies: share capital, loan capital, working capital, issued capital, paid-up capital and so forth. The common idea underlying all these terms is that of 'money obtained or to be obtained for the purpose of commencing or extending a company's business as distinguished from money earned in carrying on its business'.[3] Money earned in carrying on the business may, however, be turned into capital, or capitalised, in the sense that it may be used in some extension of the company's business or in paying off or replacing existing capital, instead of being used to pay dividends.

1.3 Loan capital is simply capital that has been borrowed.[4] It is sometimes spoken of as the opposite of working capital, but this is not a

---

[1] *Hamlet*, Act 1, scene 3.
[2] 'The human species, according to the best theory I can form of it, is composed of two distinct races, the men who borrow, and the men who lend' (Charles Lamb, *Essays of Elia*).
[3] *Lindley on Companies* (6th edn, 1902), p 543.
[4] The term has specific meanings for certain purposes: eg it is defined in s 78(7) of the Finance Act 1986 for stamp duty purposes (see further **18.20**). In normal commercial usage, though, it merely refers to capital that has been borrowed: see, eg, the definition in the *Oxford English Dictionary*: 'the part of the capital of a company or the like that is borrowed for a specified period'.

correct distinction. Working capital refers to the part of a company's capital (whether loan capital or share capital) that is used in its day-to-day business operation to meet current expenses, ie cash, debtors and other current assets.[5]

LOANS

1.4   What then is a loan?[6] Its most important characteristic is that it is a form of debt, and therefore to be contrasted with share capital. There are many types of hybrid transactions which combine characteristics of both debt and share capital,[7] but English law will generally treat a monetary obligation as either one or the other. The distinction is important for a number of reasons:

(a)   creditors rank ahead of shareholders in a winding up of the company;
(b)   creditors rarely, if ever, have any right to vote at general meetings of the company and can generally exercise control over the company only through covenants in the debt contract;[8]
(c)   interest paid by the company on a debt is usually deductible for tax purposes,[9] whereas dividends on shares are not;
(d)   interest on a debt may be payable subject to a withholding of tax,[10] whereas dividends are payable without withholding;
(e)   dividends are usually only payable if there are sufficient distributable profits, whereas interest is usually payable irrespective of profits. If the interest does vary with profits or if the lender is to receive a share of profits, the lender's claim in a winding up of the company is automatically subordinated to the claims of the company's other creditors;[11]
(f)   the repayment of share capital is subject to rules on the reduction of capital, but the payment of a debt is not;

---

[5]   In accounting practice, working capital is shown as the excess of current assets over current liabilities.
[6]   Or a borrowing: the terms are interchangeable. On loans generally, see Burgess, *Law of Loans and Borrowing*; *Chitty on Contracts* (29th edn, 2004), paras 38–223 to 38–269.
[7]   Eg preference shares with a fixed maturity date and a right to a fixed dividend, subordinated loans entitling the lender to repayment only of the amount left after payment of all other creditors (see **Chapter 8**), and convertible securities entitling the holder to receive like offers to those which the shareholders receive (see **5.38ff**). See further McCormick and Creamer, *Hybrid Corporate Securities: International Legal Aspects* (1987).
[8]   Subject, eg, to their rights to petition for the company's winding up.
[9]   See **18.1ff**.
[10]   See **18.15ff**.
[11]   Partnership Act 1890, s 3 and r 12.3(2A)(c) of the Insolvency Rules 1986, SI 1986/1925, as amended. Partnership Act 1890, s 3 applies not only to loans to individuals but extends also to loans to companies (*Re Leng, Tarn v Emmerson* [1895] 1 Ch 652; *Re Theo Garvin Ltd* [1969] 1 Ch 624; cf *Re Rolls-Royce Co Ltd* [1974] 1 WLR 1584), and applies whether the agreement to lend is written or oral (*Re Fort* [1897] 2 QB 495).

(g) shares may not be issued at a discount, but debt securities may be.[12] However, the issue price of convertible securities must not, when taken in conjunction with the conversion price, be such as to enable conversion to result in the shares being issued at a discount;[13] and

(h) the value of a shareholder's investment can increase with the capital value of the company's business, but the value of a creditor's investment generally does not.

1.5 However, not every type of debt constitutes a loan. A purchase on credit, for example, is not a loan by the vendor,[14] nor is an issue of loan stock[15] as consideration for the acquisition of property.[16] The essence of a loan is 'a sum of money lent for a time to be returned in money or money's worth'.[17] There must be both an initial advance and an obligation to repay: 'Borrowing necessarily implies repayment at some time and under some circumstances'.[18] The obligation to repay will usually be express,[19] but need not be so: any payment, in the absence of circumstances indicating otherwise,[20] imports a prima facie obligation to repay unless the payee can prove otherwise.[21]

1.6 One difficult question is whether there is still a loan if the obligation to repay is only contingent. It is common for companies to borrow money through the issue of perpetual or irredeemable securities,[22] expressed to be repayable only in the winding up of the company or at the company's option. It is also common for loans to be subordinated by expressing repayment to be contingent on the company's solvency,[23] or to be 'limited recourse' in

---

[12] *Re Anglo-Danubian Steam Navigation and Colliery Co* (1875) 20 Eq 339; *Re Compagnie Générale de Bellegarde (Campbell's Case)* (1876) 4 ChD 470; *Webb v Shropshire Railways Co* [1893] 3 Ch 307.

[13] *Mosely v Koffyfontein Mines Ltd* [1904] 2 Ch 108. On convertible securities generally, see further **5.38ff**.

[14] *Chow Yoong Hong v Choong Fah Rubber Manufactory* [1962] AC 209 at 216.

[15] Described in **Chapter 3**.

[16] *IRC v Port of London Authority* [1923] AC 507. Nor is a purchase of book debts at a discount (*Olds Discount Co Ltd v John Playfair Ltd* [1938] 3 All ER 275; *Chow Yoong Hong v Choong Fah Rubber Manufactory* [1962] AC 209), nor the discounting of bills under an acceptance credit facility (*IRC v Rowntree & Co Ltd* [1948] 1 All ER 482), nor a hire-purchase transaction (*Olds Discount Co Ltd v Cohen* [1938] 3 All ER 281n; *Transport and General Credit Corporation Ltd v Morgan* [1939] Ch 531; *Premor Ltd v Shaw Brothers* [1964] 2 All ER 583). See also *Yorkshire Railway Wagon Co v Maclure* (1882) 21 ChD 309.

[17] *Shorter Oxford English Dictionary*, quoted with approval by Walton J in *Champagne Perrier-Jouet SA v H H Finch Ltd* [1982] 3 All ER 713 at 717.

[18] *Re The Southern Brazilian Rio Grande do Sul Railway Co Ltd* [1905] 2 Ch 78 at 83 per Buckley J. See also *Chow Yoong Hong v Choong Fah Rubber Manufactory* [1962] AC 209; *De Vigier v IRC* [1964] 2 All ER 907; *MSD Speirs Ltd v Fahey* [1973] 1 NZLR 478; *Neilson v Stewart* [1990] SLT 346 (affd on other grounds [1991] BCC 713).

[19] See further **5.3–5.4**.

[20] Eg if the payment is made to a relative, thus giving rise to a presumption of 'advancement' (ie gift).

[21] *Seldon v Davidson* [1968] 2 All ER 755. Cf *Cary v Gerrish* (1801) 4 Esp 9; *Welch v Seaborn* (1816) 1 Stark 474.

[22] See further **5.1**. Perpetual securities are often issued by banks, on a subordinated basis, to improve their capital adequacy ratios: see further **8.5**.

[23] See **Chapter 8**.

nature, in that the lender is only entitled to be repaid out of a particular fund or asset.[24] Funds raised in this way are invariably designated as loan capital in companies' books, but it has been suggested[25] that, if the repayment is conditional, the fund-raising only constitutes a loan if the event on which it is conditional is bound to happen. However, it is clear[26] that it is not inconsistent with an agreement being by way of loan that the money cannot be sued for, and that the creditor must look to a fund for payment. Furthermore, securities which are expressed to be irredeemable are still loans if, on their true construction, they are irredeemable only so long as the company is in existence, and thus become repayable only on winding up.[27] An obligation to repay which is only contingent would thus appear not to be inconsistent with the transaction being a loan,[28] and it is therefore thought that perpetual, subordinated and limited recourse debts are all capable of constituting loans.[29] Further aspects of the repayment obligation are considered at **5.1 to 5.22**.

1.7 Another difficult question is whether the initial advance must be made to the person who is to repay. In *Potts' Executors v IRC*,[30] the House of Lords held that payments by a company on behalf of a director, with the director being debited with the payments in his account with the company, did not amount to loans.[31] However, certain of their Lordships made it clear that a payment by A to B at the request of C, on terms that it is to be repaid by C, can amount to a loan, and that whether it does depends upon the circumstances of the case.[32] Thus money paid by a banker pursuant to a cheque drawn on an overdrawn account is a loan to the customer[33] and, whereas an issue of loan stock[34] by way of acquisition consideration is not a borrowing,[35] a contract pursuant to which the company purchases the property at a stated sum, borrows that sum from the vendor and issues loan

---

24　Examples include securitisations and repackagings (considered in **Chapter 7**) and project finance lending.

25　In *Chitty on Contracts* (29th edn, 2004), para 38–223. See also *City of London Brewery Co Ltd v IRC* [1899] 1 QB 121 at 137–138 per Rigby LJ; *Edinburgh Corporation v British Linen Bank* [1913] AC 133 (stock redeemable at option of issuer treated as an annuity).

26　See *Mathew v Blackmore* (1857) 1 H&N 762; *De Vigier v IRC* [1964] 2 All ER 907.

27　*Re The Southern Brazilian Rio Grande do Sul Railway Co Ltd* [1905] 2 Ch 78. If they are truly irredeemable, they are not loans but perpetual annuities.

28　See also *Waite Hill Holdings Ltd v Marshall* (1983) 133 NLJ 745.

29　Though the interest payments may be treated as 'distributions': see **18.14**.

30　[1951] AC 443, followed in *Re HPC Productions Ltd* [1962] 1 Ch 466 and *Champagne Perrier-Jouet SA v H H Finch Ltd* [1982] 3 All ER 713.

31　For the purposes of the surtax provisions of s 40 of the Finance Act 1938.

32　Per Lord Simonds at 454, Lord Normand at 459, Lord Morton (dissenting) at 462 and Lord MacDermott at 465. See also *Parsons v Equitable Investment Co Ltd* [1916] 2 Ch 527; *Law v Coburn (Inspector of Taxes)* [1972] 1 WLR 1238. It was suggested in *Re HPC Productions Ltd* [1962] Ch 466 that an important factor is whether B is accountable for the money to C. The doctrine of sham is also relevant: see *Chow Yoong Hong v Choong Fah Rubber Manufactory* [1962] AC 209 at 216–217; *Welsh Development Agency v Export Finance Co Ltd* [1992] BCLC 148; *Lloyds & Scottish Finance Ltd v Cyril Lord Carpets Sales Ltd* [1992] BCLC 609.

33　See **2.2**.

34　Described in **Chapter 3**.

35　See **1.5**.

stock to the vendor in satisfaction of the obligation to repay may well be a borrowing.[36]

IMPORTANCE OF THE DISTINCTION

1.8   Whether a particular transaction is a loan can be important for several reasons:

(a) for determining whether the transaction falls within the corporate powers of the company to borrow, since, notwithstanding s 35(1) of the Companies Act 1985, the 'old' ultra vires doctrine is still relevant in certain circumstances;[37]

(b) for determining whether the transaction counts toward a limit on borrowings to which the company is subject. The limit might be imposed by the company's articles of association, by a regulatory authority or by a loan agreement or other contract entered into by the company;[38]

(c) for determining whether a default under the transaction will trigger a cross-default or cross-acceleration clause in other loan documentation,[39] (which will depend on whether the clause is expressed to relate only to borrowings or is more widely drawn); and

(d) for determining its tax and stamp duty treatment.[40]

TYPES OF COMPANY BORROWING

1.9   Borrowing by companies takes many different forms. Exact categorisation is difficult, since terminology is often used inconsistently and a number of hybrid structures have been developed, but borrowing by companies can nevertheless broadly be divided into two main types: bank loans and debt securities. These are considered in the following chapters.

---

[36] By analogy from the reasoning in *Re Harmony and Montague Tin and Copper Mining Co (Spargo's Case)* (1873) 8 Ch App 407.

[37] See **Chapter 9**.

[38] In practice, most limits will also restrict other transactions which have the same economic effect as loans, eg acceptance credits, securities issued by way of acquisition consideration, purchases on credit, finance leases etc. On contractual borrowing limits generally, see **9.17 to 9.37**.

[39] See further **5.17 to 5.19**.

[40] See further **Chapter 18**.

Chapter Two

TYPES OF BORROWING (1): BANK LOANS

GENERALLY

2.1   There are two main types of bank loans: overdrafts, and advances under loan facilities. Overdrafts are not normally regarded as part of a company's capital, but they are nevertheless considered here for the sake of completeness.

OVERDRAFTS[1]

2.2   An overdraft constitutes a loan;[2] 'a payment by a bank, under an arrangement by which the customer has an overdraft, is a lending by the bank to the customer of the money'.[3] A bank is only obliged to let its customer overdraw if it has agreed to do so[4] or if such an agreement can be implied from the pattern of their relationship.[5] Drawing a cheque where there are insufficient funds in the account to honour it amounts to a request for an overdraft, which, in the absence of prior agreement, the bank can choose to accept or to reject.[6]

---

[1]   On overdrafts generally, see *Paget's Law of Banking* (12th edn, 2002), p 176; *Encyclopaedia of Banking Law*, paras C(501) to C(522); Burgess, *Law of Loans and Borrowing*, para 3–23; Ellinger, Lomnicka and Hooley, *Ellinger's Modern Banking Law* (4th edn, 2006), pp 689–706; Ferran, *Company Law and Corporate Finance* (1999), pp 459–462.

[2]   See, eg, *Looker v Wrigley* (1882) 9 QBD 397; *Cunliffe Brooks & Co v The Blackburn and District Benefit Building Society* (1884) 9 App Cas 857; *Cuthbert v Robarts, Lubbock & Co* [1909] 2 Ch 226; *Potts' Executors v IRC* [1951] AC 443 at 455, 459 and 462; *Coutts & Co v Stock* [2000] 2 All ER 56 at 60.

[3]   *Re Hone* [1951] Ch 85 at 89 per Harman J.

[4]   *Cunliffe Brooks & Co v The Blackburn and District Benefit Building Society* (1884) 9 App Cas 857 at 864 per Lord Blackburn. See also *Bank of New South Wales v Laing* [1954] AC 135; *Barclays Bank Ltd v W J Simms Son & Cooke (Southern) Ltd* [1980] QB 677 at 699.

[5]   *Cumming v Shand* (1860) 5 H&N 95. See also *Parkinson v Wakefield and Co* (1889) 5 TLR 646 (termination of obligation).

[6]   *Lloyds Bank plc v Voller* [2000] 2 All ER (Comm) 978 at 982 per Wall J; *Barclays Bank Ltd v WJ Simms Son & Cooke (Southern) Ltd* [1980] QB 677 at 699 per Goff J; *Cuthbert v Robarts, Lubbock & Co* [1909] 2 Ch 226 at 233 per Cozens-Hardy MR. The giving of such a cheque in payment may, however, constitute a criminal offence under s 15 of the Theft Act 1968 (obtaining property by deception): see, eg, *Halstead v Patel* [1972] 2 All ER 147.

2.3 In the absence of contrary agreement, an overdraft is repayable on demand[7] and the bank is entitled to charge interest,[8] which may be compounded annually or semi-annually.[9]

LOAN FACILITIES[10]

Types of facilities

2.4 Loan facilities take many forms. The most basic ('term loans') provide that the bank is committed throughout a specified period (the 'commitment period') to make advances upon request by the company up to a maximum amount, with all the advances being repayable together, either in instalments or in one lump sum ('bullet repayment'). Alternatively, the facility may be 'revolving', in that the company can borrow for a selection of periods, repay and borrow again. The facility may be available in a single currency or in a selection of currencies with an ability to switch from one to another (a 'multi-currency option') and it may be made available by a single bank or by a group of banks ('syndicated').

---

7 *Williams and Glyn's Bank Ltd v Barnes* [1981] Comm LR 205; *Barclays Bank plc v Green and Challis* [1996] 4 JIBL N–82. The bank must, however, still honour cheques drawn on the account before repayment is demanded: *William Rouse v The Bradford Banking Co Ltd* [1894] AC 586 at 596 per Lord Herschell LC. Once the bank has demanded repayment, it must allow the borrower such time as is necessary to implement payment procedures before it can take proceedings: *Toms v Wilson* (1863) 4 B&S 442; *Lloyds Bank Ltd v Margolis* [1954] 1 All ER 734 at 738; *Cripps (Pharmaceuticals) Ltd v Wickenden* [1973] 2 All ER 606; *Bank of Baroda v Panessar* [1987] Ch 335. However, this requirement does not apply if the debtor has already admitted that he is unable to pay: *Sheppard & Cooper Ltd v TSB Bank plc* [1996] 2 All ER 654. See also *Buckingham and Co v The London and Midland (Bank) Ltd* (1895) 12 TLR 70.

8 As to which, see further **5.23ff**.

9 *IRC v Holder* [1931] 2 KB 81, affd on different grounds sub nom *Holder v IRC* [1932] AC 624; *Paton (Fenton's Trustee) v IRC* [1938] AC 341; *National Bank of Greece SA v Pinios Shipping Co No 1, The Maira* [1990] 1 AC 637. The House of Lords in the last case expressly left open the question of whether the bank (in the absence of agreement) is entitled to compound interest at intervals of less than six months (though quarterly compounding has since been approved by the Court of Appeal as being in accordance with modern banking practice: *Kitchen v HSBC Bank plc* [2000] 1 All ER (Comm) 787 at 791 per Brooke LJ). See also *Emerald Meats (London) Ltd v AIB Group (UK) plc* [2002] EWCA 460, in which the Court of Appeal held that, in the absence of agreement to the contrary, the bank was entitled to charge interest in accordance with its standard terms. The right to compound (as opposed to simple) interest terminates when the relationship of banker and customer terminates, eg because the customer dies (*Fergusson v Fyffe* (1841) 8 Cl&Fin 121; *Crosskill v Bower* (1863) 32 Beav 86; *Williamson v Williamson* (1869) 7 Eq 542) or closes his account (*Crosskill v Bower*, above), but not merely because the bank demands payment (*National Bank of Greece SA v Pinios Shipping Co No 1, The Maira*, above). Cf *Bank of Credit and Commerce International SA v Malik* [1996] BCC 15.

10 On loan facilities generally, see Wood, *International Loans, Bonds and Securities Regulation* (1995), Chapters 2–6; Tennekoon, *The Law and Regulation of International Finance* (1991), Chapter 5; Ellinger, Lomnicka and Hooley, *Ellinger's Modern Banking Law* (4th edn, 2006), pp 706–724; Ferran, *Company Law and Corporate Finance* (1999), pp 462–481; Cranston, *Principles of Banking Law* (2nd edn, 2002), pp 304–324; Rhodes, *Syndicated Lending* (4th edn, 2004); Penn, Shea and Arora, *The Law and Practice of International Banking* (1987), Chapter 6; *Encyclopaedia of Banking Law*, paras F(3150)–F(4999); Gabriel, *Legal Aspects of Syndicated Loans* (1986).

2.5   A facility may take the form either of an 'advance' facility (where the banks make cash advances to the company) or of a 'bill' or 'acceptance' facility (involving the 'drawing' of bills of exchange on the banks). A bill of exchange[11] is an order by one person (the drawer) to another person (the drawee) requiring the drawee to pay a stated sum of money to a specified payee or to his order or to the bearer of the bill. When a company 'draws' a bill under a bill facility or acceptance facility, the company (as drawer) executes the bill and delivers it to the bank (as drawee), which pays the drawer an amount less than the face value and 'accepts' the bill, ie by signing the bill, agrees to pay the bill if it is delivered to the bank on maturity. The bank then sells (or 'discounts'[12]) the bill in the market. The amount payable to the company and the amount at which the bank sells the bill are calculated by reference to the 'Eligible Bill Discount Rate', the published rate at which bills of exchange are discounted in the bill discount market. On maturity of the bill, the holder will present it to the accepting bank for payment of the face value and, under the terms of the facility, the company will be obliged to reimburse the bank for the amount which it pays out.

2.6   A further kind of facility is a 'swingline'. This is a committed facility providing for very short-term advances (typically up to seven days), and is generally put in place to support a commercial paper programme.[13] Its purpose is twofold: first, if the company has to repay a tranche of commercial paper and does not want to issue a new tranche on the repayment date because of what it sees as temporarily adverse market conditions, it can repay through the use of the swingline facility and issue the commercial paper (and thereby repay the swingline advance) a few days later; and, secondly, it reassures potential purchasers under the commercial paper programme that the company will be able to repay them on maturity regardless of market conditions.

Conditions precedent

2.7   One feature common to virtually all facilities is that the banks' obligations to make advances do not immediately arise on the signing of the loan agreement but are subject to the satisfaction by the borrower of certain conditions precedent.[14] There are two types: conditions precedent to the commencement of the commitment period, and conditions precedent to each

---

11   Defined in Bills of Exchange Act 1882, s 3(1). Bills of exchange are negotiable instruments: see further **15.3ff**.
12   Due to the fact that the bill will be sold at less than its face value.
13   See further **Chapter 4**.
14   Where the facility is to finance the cash element of a takeover offer, though, the conditionality that is acceptable is very limited. This is because the offeror's bank or financial adviser must confirm in the offer document that 'resources are available to the offeror sufficient to satisfy full acceptance of the offer' (Rule 24.7 of the City Code on Takeovers and Mergers: see also Rule 2.5(a) regarding announcement of the offer). The conditions precedent that are acceptable vary, but are often limited to the non-occurrence of events of insolvency.

advance. The former normally include receipt of any guarantees and/or security, authorisations and legal opinions, and are intended to ensure that all legal matters are in order and that the security (if any) is in place. The latter include the warranties given by the borrower on signing (in particular, the warranty of no material adverse change since the last audited accounts) being true on an updated basis and no event of default or inchoate event of default (eg a breach which would be an event of default but for a grace period) having occurred.[15] These conditions precedent are intended to ensure both that all legal matters are still in order and that the banks are not obliged to lend if the borrower has become a greater credit risk than it was when the financial terms were agreed.[16]

2.8   A typical conditions precedent clause in a syndicated facility (in this case, a revolving multi-currency facility, based on the Loan Markets Association's recommended form) reads as follows:

1.1   Initial conditions precedent

The Borrower may not deliver a Utilisation Request unless the Agent has received all of the documents and other evidence listed in Part I of Schedule [ ] (*Conditions precedent*) in form and substance satisfactory to the Agent. The Agent shall notify the Borrower and the Lenders promptly upon being so satisfied.

1.2   Further conditions precedent

(a)   The Lenders will only be obliged to comply with Clause [ ] (*Lenders' participation*) if on the date of the Utilisation Request and on the proposed Utilisation Date:

(i)   in the case of a Rollover Loan, no Event of Default is continuing or would result from the proposed Loan and, in the case of any other Loan, no Default is continuing or would result from the proposed Loan; and

(ii)   the Repeating Representations to be made by the Borrower are true in all material respects.

(b)   The Lenders will only be obliged to comply with Clause [ ] (*Change of currency*) if, on the first day of an Interest Period, no Default is continuing or would result from the change of currency and the Repeating Representations to be made by the Borrower are true in all material respects.

1.3   Conditions relating to Optional Currencies

(a)   A currency will constitute an Optional Currency in relation to a Loan if:

(i)   it is readily available in the amount required and freely convertible into the Base Currency in the Relevant Interbank Market on the Quotation Day and the

---

[15]   Often, however, the conditions precedent to a 'rollover' (which is technically a fresh advance) will be less onerous than for an advance which involves 'new' money.

[16]   On conditions precedent, see further Cranston, *Principles of Banking Law* (2nd edn, 2002), pp 312–313; Ferran, *Company Law and Corporate Finance* (1999), pp 467–468; *Encyclopaedia of Banking Law*, paras F(3224)–F(3229).

Utilisation Date for that Loan; and

(ii)   it has been approved by the Agent (acting on the instructions of all the Lenders) on or prior to receipt by the Agent of the relevant Utilisation Request for that Loan.

(b)   If the Agent has received a written request from the Borrower for a currency to be approved under paragraph (a)(ii) above, the Agent will confirm to the Borrower by the Specified Time:

(i)   whether or not the Lenders have granted their approval; and

(ii)   if approval has been granted, the minimum amount (and, if required, integral multiples) for any subsequent Utilisation in that currency.

Related definitions:

'**Default**' means an Event of Default or any event or circumstance specified in Clause [ ] (*Events of Default*) which would (with the expiry of a grace period, the giving of notice, the making of any determination under the Finance Documents or any combination of any of the foregoing) be an Event of Default.

'**Event of Default**' means any event or circumstance specified as such in Clause [ ] (*Events of Default*).

'**Optional Currency**' means a currency (other than the Base Currency) which complies with the conditions set out in Clause [ ] (*Conditions relating to Optional Currencies*).

'**Repeating Representations**' means each of the representations set out in Clauses [ ], [ ] and [ ].

'**Rollover Loan**' means one or more Loans:

(a)   made or to be made on the same day that a maturing Loan is due to be repaid;

(b)   the aggregate amount of which is equal to or less than the maturing Loan;

(c)   in the same currency as the maturing Loan (unless it arose as a result of the operation of Clause [ ] (*Unavailability of a currency*); and

(d)   made or to be made to the Borrower for the purpose of refinancing a maturing Loan.

'**Utilisation**' means a utilisation of the Facility.

'**Utilisation Date**' means the date of a Utilisation, being the date on which the relevant Loan is to be made.

'**Utilisation Request**' means a notice substantially in the form set out in Schedule [ ] (*Requests*).

Multi-currency options

2.9   Where a multi-currency option is included, this enables the borrower to select a new currency for the loan for the next interest period. It then repays the old currency and the bank advances the new currency, the amount being calculated by reference to the then current rate of exchange between the base currency of the loan (which may not necessarily be the old currency) and the new currency. If the borrower continues with the new currency for the following interest period, the amount will again be recalculated[17] against the base currency, so that the currency amount is brought back into line with the base currency at the beginning of each interest period.

2.10   A typical multi-currency option clause in a loan facility (in this example, a syndicated term loan facility based on the Loan Markets Association's recommended form) reads as follows:

1.1   Selection of currency

(a)   The Borrower shall select the currency of a Loan:

(i)   (in the case of an initial Utilisation) in a Utilisation Request; and

(ii)   (afterwards in relation to a Loan made to it) in a Selection Notice.

(b)   If the Borrower fails to issue a Selection Notice in relation to a Loan, the Loan will remain denominated for its next Interest Period in the same currency in which it is then outstanding.

(c)   If the Borrower issues a Selection Notice requesting a change of currency and the first day of the requested Interest Period is not a Business Day for the new currency, the Agent shall promptly notify the Borrower and the Lenders and the Loan will remain in the existing currency (with Interest Periods running from one Business Day until the next Business Day) until the next day which is a Business Day for both currencies, on which day the requested Interest Period will begin.

1.2   Unavailability of a currency

If before the Specified Time on any Quotation Day:

(a)   a Lender notifies the Agent that the Optional Currency requested is not readily available to it in the amount required; or

(b)   a Lender notifies the Agent that compliance with its obligation to participate in a Loan in the proposed Optional Currency would contravene a law or regulation applicable to it,

the Agent will give notice to the Borrower to that effect by the Specified Time on that day. In this event, any Lender that gives notice pursuant to this Clause will be required to participate in the Loan in the Base Currency (in an amount equal to that Lender's proportion of the Base Currency Amount) and its participation will be treated as a separate Loan denominated in the Base Currency during that Interest Period.

1.3 Change of currency

(a)   If a Loan is to be denominated in different currencies during two successive Interest Periods:

(i)   if the currency for the second Interest Period is an Optional Currency, the amount of the Loan in that Optional Currency will be calculated by the Agent as the amount of that Optional Currency equal to the Base

---

17   Except, usually, where the variation in exchange rates has been only small.

Currency Amount of the Loan at the Agent's Spot Rate of Exchange at the Specified Time;

(ii)   if the currency for the second Interest Period is the Base Currency, the amount of the Loan will be equal to the Base Currency Amount;

(iii)   (unless the Agent and the Borrower agree otherwise in accordance with paragraph (b) below) the Borrower shall repay the Loan on the last day of the first Interest Period in the currency in which it was denominated for that Interest Period; and

(iv)   (subject to Clause [ ] (*Further conditions precedent*)) the Lenders shall re-advance the Loan in the new currency in accordance with Clause 1.5 (*Agent's calculations*).

(b)   If the Agent and the Borrower agree, the Agent shall:

(i)   apply the amount paid to it by the Lenders pursuant to paragraph (a)(iv) above (or so much of that amount as is necessary) in or towards purchase of an amount in the currency in which the Loan is outstanding for the first Interest Period; and

(ii)   use the amount it purchases in or towards satisfaction of the Borrower's obligations under paragraph (a)(iii) above; and

(c)   If the amount purchased by the Agent pursuant to paragraph (b)(i) above is less than the amount required to be repaid by the Borrower, the Agent shall promptly notify the Borrower and the Borrower shall, on the last day of the first Interest Period, pay an amount to the Agent (in the currency of the outstanding Loan for the first Interest Period) equal to the difference.

(d)   If any part of the amount paid to the Agent by the Lenders pursuant to paragraph (a)(iv) above is not needed to purchase the amount required to be repaid by the Borrower, the Agent shall promptly notify the Borrower and pay the Borrower, on the last day of the first Interest Period, that part of that amount (in the new currency).

1.4   Same Optional Currency during successive Interest Periods

(a)   If a Loan is to be denominated in the same Optional Currency during two successive Interest Periods, the Agent shall calculate the amount of the Loan in the Optional Currency for the second of those Interest Periods (by calculating the amount of Optional Currency equal to the Base Currency Amount of that Loan at the Agent's Spot Rate of Exchange at the Specified Time) and (subject to paragraph (b) below):

(i)   if the amount calculated is less than the existing amount of that Loan in the Optional Currency during the first Interest Period, promptly notify the Borrower and the Borrower shall pay, on the last day of the first Interest Period, an amount equal to the difference; or

(ii)   if the amount calculated is more than the existing amount of that Loan in the Optional Currency during the first Interest Period, promptly notify each Lender and, if no Default is continuing, each Lender shall, on the last day of the first Interest Period, pay its participation in an amount equal to the difference.

(b)   If the calculation made by the Agent pursuant to paragraph (a) above shows that the amount of the Loan in the Optional Currency for the second of those Interest Periods converted into the Base Currency at the Agent's Spot Rate of Exchange at the Specified Time has increased or decreased by less than [   ] per cent. compared to its Base Currency Amount (taking into account any payments made pursuant to paragraph (a) above), no notification shall be made by the Agent and no payment shall be required under paragraph (a) above.

1.5 Agent's calculations

(a)   All calculations made by the Agent pursuant to this Clause will take into account any repayment, prepayment, consolidation or division of Loans to be made on the last day of the first Interest Period.

(b)   Each Lender's participation in a Loan will, subject to paragraph (a) above, be determined in accordance with Clause [ ] (*Lenders' participation*).

Related definitions (to the extent not defined in an earlier example):
'**Agent's Spot Rate of Exchange**' means the Agent's spot rate of exchange for the purchase of the relevant currency with the Base Currency in the London foreign exchange market at or about 11.00 a.m. on a particular day.

'**Base Currency Amount**' means, in relation to a Loan, the amount specified in the Utilisation Request delivered by the Borrower for that Loan (or, if the amount requested is not denominated in the Base Currency, that amount converted into the Base Currency at the Agent's Spot Rate of Exchange on the date which is three Business Days before the Utilisation Date or, if later, on the date the Agent receives the Utilisation Request) adjusted to reflect any repayment (other than a repayment arising from a change of currency), prepayment, consolidation or division of the Loan.

'**Selection Notice**' means a notice substantially in the form set out in Part [ ] of Schedule [ ] (*Requests*) given in accordance with Clause [ ] (*Interest Periods*).

Withholding tax

2.11   It is normally considered important that the interest is paid to the banks without any deduction of tax. Even if the banks obtain a tax credit for the deduction, this will take time and in the meantime the banks lose the use of the money. Interest payable by UK companies is payable without deduction of UK tax if it is interest on an advance from a bank and, at the time the interest is paid, the person beneficially entitled to the interest is subject to UK corporation tax in respect of the interest.[18] However, to guard against changes in the tax treatment of the loan, a grossing-up clause is included, providing that the borrower, if it is required to deduct tax,[19] will pay an increased amount, so that the net amount received by the bank after

---

[18]   See further **18.15**.

[19]   Sometimes this extends to any tax, wherever arising; but borrowers often negotiate a limitation to taxes of the home jurisdiction and of the jurisdiction through which payments are made. In contrast, a grossing-up provision in a eurobond issue normally only ever relates to tax arising in the issuer's home tax jurisdiction: see further **3.4** and **18.18**.

deduction equals the full amount of the interest intended to be received by it.[20] The grossing-up clause usually also includes an indemnity in favour of the banks as an additional protection.

2.12 In order to prevent unfairness to the borrower, the borrower will be entitled to prepay the loan (or, in the case of a syndicated facility, the part that is affected) if it becomes obliged to gross-up. The borrower will normally have a general right of optional prepayment, but this can usually only be exercised at the end of an interest period (in order to avoid 'broken funding' costs for the banks),[21] and only pro rata to all banks rather than just those affected by the withholding. The purpose of this additional right of prepayment (which usually also permits prepayment if the increased costs clause is activated)[22] is to enable the borrower to terminate the loan agreement in relation to the affected banks more quickly (eg after five business days) so long as it indemnifies the banks in question against their 'broken funding' costs.

2.13 A typical grossing-up clause in a syndicated facility (in this case, based on the Loan Markets Association's recommended form) reads as follows:

1.1 Definitions

(a)   In this Agreement:

"**Protected Party**" means a Finance Party which is or will be subject to any liability, or required to make any payment, for or on account of Tax in relation to a sum received or receivable (or any sum deemed for the purposes of Tax to be received or receivable) under a Finance Document.

"**Qualifying Lender**" means:

(i)   a Lender (other than a Lender within sub-paragraph (ii) below) which is beneficially entitled to interest payable to that Lender in respect of an advance under a Finance Document and is:

(A)   a Lender:

(1)   which is a bank (as defined for the purpose of section 349 of the Taxes Act) making an advance under a Finance Document; or

(2)   in respect of an advance made under a Finance Document by a person that was a bank (as defined for the purpose of section 349 of the Taxes Act) at the time that that advance was made,

and which is within the charge to United Kingdom corporation tax as respects any payments of interest made in respect of that advance; or

(B)   a Lender which is:

(1)   a company resident in the United Kingdom for United Kingdom tax purposes;

(2)   a partnership each member of which is:

---

20   As to the validity of gross-up provisions, see *Encyclopaedia of Banking Law*, para F(1755).

21   See further **5.7**.

22   See **2.15**.

(a)　　a company so resident in the United Kingdom; or

(b)　　a company not so resident in the United Kingdom which carries on a trade in the United Kingdom through a permanent establishment and which brings into account in computing its chargeable profits (for the purposes of section 11(2) of the Taxes Act) the whole of any share of interest payable in respect of that advance that falls to it by reason of sections 114 and 115 of the Taxes Act;

(3)　　a company not so resident in the United Kingdom which carries on a trade in the United Kingdom through a permanent establishment and which brings into account interest payable in respect of that advance in computing the chargeable profits (for the purposes of section 11(2) of the Taxes Act) of that company; or

(C)　　a Treaty Lender; or

(ii)　　a building society (as defined for the purpose of section 477A of the Taxes Act).

"**Tax Confirmation**" means a confirmation by a Lender that the person beneficially entitled to interest payable to that Lender in respect of an advance under a Finance Document is either:

(i)　　a company resident in United Kingdom for United Kingdom tax purposes;

(ii)　　a partnership each member of which is:

(A)　　a company so resident in the United Kingdom; or

(B)　　a company not so resident in the United Kingdom which carries on a trade in the United Kingdom through a permanent establishment and which brings into account in computing its chargeable profits (for the purposes of section 11(2) of the Taxes Act) the whole of any share of interest payable in respect of that advance that falls to it by reason of sections 114 and 115 of the Taxes Act; or

(iii)　　a company not so resident in the United Kingdom which carries on a trade in the United Kingdom through a permanent establishment and which brings into account interest payable in respect of that advance in computing the chargeable profits (for the purposes of section 11(2) of the Taxes Act) of that company.

"**Tax Credit**" means a credit against, relief or remission for, or repayment of, any Tax.

"**Tax Deduction**" means a deduction or withholding for or on account of Tax from a payment under a Finance Document.

"**Tax Payment**" means either the increase in a payment made by the Borrower to a Finance Party under Clause 1.2 (*Tax gross-up*) or a payment under Clause 1.3 (*Tax indemnity*).

"**Taxes Act**" means the Income and Corporation Taxes Act 1988.

"**Treaty Lender**" means a Lender which:

(i)　　is treated as a resident of a Treaty State for the purposes of the Treaty; and

(ii)   does not carry on a business in the United Kingdom through a permanent establishment with which that Lender's participation in the Loan is effectively connected.

"**Treaty State**" means a jurisdiction having a double taxation agreement (a "**Treaty**") with the United Kingdom which makes provision for full exemption from tax imposed by the United Kingdom on interest.

"**UK Non-Bank Lender**" means:

(i)   where a Lender becomes a Party on the day on which this Agreement is entered into, a Lender listed in Part [ ] of Schedule [ ] (*The Original Parties*); and

(ii)   where a Lender becomes a Party after the day on which this Agreement is entered into, a Lender which gives a Tax Confirmation in the Transfer Certificate which it executes on becoming a Party.

(b)   Unless a contrary indication appears, in this Clause a reference to "determines" or "determined" means a determination made in the absolute discretion of the person making the determination.

1.2   Tax gross-up

(a)   The Borrower shall make all payments to be made by it without any Tax Deduction, unless a Tax Deduction is required by law.

(b)   The Borrower shall promptly upon becoming aware that it must make a Tax Deduction (or that there is any change in the rate or the basis of a Tax Deduction) notify the Agent accordingly. Similarly, a Lender shall notify the Agent on becoming so aware in respect of a payment payable to that Lender. If the Agent receives such notification from a Lender it shall notify the Borrower.

(c)   If a Tax Deduction is required by law to be made by the Borrower, the amount of the payment due from the Borrower shall be increased to an amount which (after making any Tax Deduction) leaves an amount equal to the payment which would have been due if no Tax Deduction had been required.

(d)   The Borrower is not required to make an increased payment to a Lender under paragraph (c) above for a Tax Deduction in respect of tax imposed by the United Kingdom from a payment of interest on a Loan, if on the date on which the payment falls due:

(i)   the payment could have been made to the relevant Lender without a Tax Deduction if it was a Qualifying Lender, but on that date that Lender is not or has ceased to be a Qualifying Lender other than as a result of any change after the date it became a Lender under this Agreement in (or in the interpretation, administration or application of) any law or Treaty, or any published practice or concession of any relevant taxing authority; or

(ii)

(A)   the relevant Lender is a Qualifying Lender solely under sub-paragraph (i)(B) of the definition of Qualifying Lender;

(B)   HM Revenue & Customs has given (and not revoked) a direction (a "**Direction**") under section 349C of the Taxes Act (as that provision has effect on the date on which the relevant Lender became a Party) which relates to that payment and that Lender has received from the Borrower a certified copy of that Direction; and

(C)   the payment could have been made to the Lender without any Tax Deduction in the absence of that Direction; or

(iii)   the relevant Lender is a Qualifying Lender solely under sub-paragraph (i)(B) of the definition of Qualifying Lender and it has not, other than by reason of any change after the date of this Agreement in (or in the interpretation, administration or application of) any law, or any published practice or concession of any relevant taxing authority, given a Tax Confirmation to the Borrower; or

(iv)   the relevant Lender is a Treaty Lender and the Borrower is able to demonstrate that the payment could have been made to the Lender without the Tax Deduction had that Lender complied with its obligations under paragraph (g) below.

(e)   If the Borrower is required to make a Tax Deduction, the Borrower shall make that Tax Deduction and any payment required in connection with that Tax Deduction within the time allowed and in the minimum amount required by law.

(f)   Within thirty days of making either a Tax Deduction or any payment required in connection with that Tax Deduction, the Borrower shall deliver to the Agent for the Finance Party entitled to the payment evidence reasonably satisfactory to that Finance Party that the Tax Deduction has been made or (as applicable) any appropriate payment paid to the relevant taxing authority.

(g)   A Treaty Lender and the Borrower shall co-operate in completing any procedural formalities necessary for the Borrower to obtain authorisation to make that payment without a Tax Deduction.

(h)   A UK Non-Bank Lender which becomes a Party on the day on which this Agreement is entered into gives a Tax Confirmation to the Borrower by entering into this Agreement.

(i)   A UK Non-Bank Lender shall promptly notify the Borrower and the Agent if there is any change in the position from that set out in the Tax Confirmation.

1.3   Tax indemnity

(a)   The Borrower shall (within three Business Days of demand by the Agent) pay to a Protected Party an amount equal to the loss, liability or cost which that Protected Party determines will be or has been (directly or indirectly) suffered for or on account of Tax by that Protected Party in respect of a Finance Document.

(b)   Paragraph (a) above shall not apply:

(i)   with respect to any Tax assessed on a Finance Party:

(A)   under the law of the jurisdiction in which that Finance Party is incorporated or, if different, the jurisdiction (or jurisdictions) in which that Finance Party is treated as resident for tax purposes; or

(B)   under the law of the jurisdiction in which that Finance Party's Facility Office is located in respect of amounts received or receivable in that jurisdiction, if that Tax is imposed on or calculated by reference to the net income received or receivable (but not any sum deemed to be received or receivable) by that Finance Party; or

(ii)   to the extent a loss, liability or cost:

(A)   is compensated for by an increased payment under Clause 1.2 (*Tax gross-up*); or

(B)   would have been compensated for by an increased payment under Clause 1.2 (*Tax gross-up*) but was not so compensated solely because one of the exclusions in paragraph (d) of Clause 1.2 (*Tax gross-up*) applied.

(c)   A Protected Party making, or intending to make, a claim under paragraph (a) above shall promptly notify the Agent of the event which will give, or has given, rise to the claim, following which the Agent shall notify the Borrower.

(d)   A Protected Party shall, on receiving a payment from the Borrower under this Clause, notify the Agent.

1.4 Tax Credit

If the Borrower makes a Tax Payment and the relevant Finance Party determines that:

(a)   a Tax Credit is attributable either to an increased payment of which that Tax Payment forms part, or to that Tax Payment; and

(b)   that Finance Party has obtained, utilised and retained that Tax Credit,

the Finance Party shall pay an amount to the Borrower which that Finance Party determines will leave it (after that payment) in the same after-Tax position as it would have been in had the Tax Payment not been required to be made by the Borrower.

2.14   A typical tax/increased costs prepayment clause in a syndicated facility (based on the Loan Markets Association's recommended form) reads as follows:

1.1 Right of repayment and cancellation in relation to a single Lender

(a)   If:

(i)   any sum payable to any Lender by the Borrower is required to be increased under paragraph (c) of Clause [ ] (*Tax gross-up*); or

(ii)   any Lender claims indemnification from the Borrower under Clause [ ] (*Tax indemnity*) or Clause [ ] (*Increased costs*),

the Borrower may, whilst the circumstance giving rise to the requirement for indemnification continues, give the Agent notice of cancellation of the Commitment of that Lender and its intention to procure the repayment of that Lender's participation in the Loans.

(b)   On receipt of a notice referred to in paragraph (a) above, the Commitment of that Lender shall immediately be reduced to zero.

(c)   On the last day of each Interest Period which ends after the Borrower has given notice under paragraph (a) above (or, if earlier, the date specified by the Borrower in that notice), the Borrower shall repay that Lender's participation in that Loan.

1.2   Restrictions

(a)   Any notice of cancellation or prepayment given by the Borrower under this Clause shall be irrevocable and, unless a contrary indication appears in this Agreement, shall specify the date or dates upon which the relevant cancellation or prepayment is to be made and the amount of that cancellation or prepayment.

(b)   Any prepayment under this Agreement shall be made together with accrued interest on the amount prepaid and, subject to any Break Costs, without premium or penalty.

(c)   The Borrower may not reborrow any part of the Facility which is prepaid.

(d)   The Borrower shall not repay or prepay all or any part of the Loans or cancel all or any part of the Commitments except at the times and in the manner expressly provided for in this Agreement.

(e)   No amount of the Total Commitments cancelled under this Agreement may be subsequently reinstated.

(f)   If the Agent receives a notice from the Borrower under this Clause it shall promptly forward a copy of that notice to the affected Lender.

Related definitions (to the extent not defined in an earlier example):
'**Break Costs**' means the amount (if any) by which:
(a)   the interest which a Lender should have received for the period from the date of receipt of all or any part of its participation in a Loan ....
to the last day of the current Interest Period in respect of that Loan ..., had the principal amount ... received been paid on the last day of that Interest Period;
exceeds:
(b)   the amount which that Lender would be able to obtain by placing an amount equal to the principal amount ... received by it on deposit with a leading bank in the Relevant Interbank Market for a period starting on the Business Day following receipt ... and ending on the last day of the current Interest Period.

Increased costs clause

2.15   Another common feature of bank loan facilities is the increased costs clause. This reflects the fact that banks usually calculate the interest rate of the loan on the basis of a margin over the cost to them of borrowing in the inter-bank market. The clause usually provides that, if any law or official directive increases any of the banks' underlying costs of lending or of capital, the borrower must compensate them. This is seen by banks as an important protection against erosion of their return, since central bank reserve requirements, special taxes, capital adequacy rules and liquidity requirements may impose costs on them which are attributable to the loan but which are not reflected in the cost of funds. The inherent weakness of such a provision, though, is the possible difficulty of allocating certain costs to particular loans. In order to prevent unfairness to the borrower, the borrower will have a prepayment option in relation to any affected bank, which is exercisable if the increased costs clause is activated in relation to that bank.[23]

2.16 A typical increased costs clause in a syndicated facility (again, based on the Loan Markets Association's recommended form) reads as follows:

1.1 Increased costs

(a)   Subject to Clause 1.3 (*Exceptions*) the Borrower shall, within three Business Days of a demand by the Agent, pay for the account of a Finance Party the amount of any Increased Costs incurred by that Finance Party or any of its Affiliates as a result of (i) the introduction of or any change in (or in the interpretation, administration or application of) any law or regulation or (ii) compliance with any law or regulation made after the date of this Agreement.

(b)   In this Agreement "**Increased Costs**" means:

(i)   a reduction in the rate of return from the Facility or on a Finance Party's (or its Affiliate's) overall capital;

(ii)   an additional or increased cost; or

(iii)   a reduction of any amount due and payable under any Finance Document,

which is incurred or suffered by a Finance Party or any of its Affiliates to the extent that it is attributable to that Finance Party having entered into its Commitment or funding or performing its obligations under any Finance Document.

1.2 Increased cost claims

(a)   A Finance Party intending to make a claim pursuant to Clause 1.1 (*Increased costs*) shall notify the Agent of the event giving rise to the claim, following which the Agent shall promptly notify the Borrower.

(b)   Each Finance Party shall, as soon as practicable after a demand by the Agent, provide a certificate confirming the amount of its Increased Costs.

1.3 Exceptions

Clause 1.1 (*Increased costs*) does not apply to the extent any Increased Cost is:

(a)   attributable to a Tax Deduction required by law to be made by the Borrower;

(b)   compensated for by Clause [ ] (*Tax indemnity*) (or would have been compensated for under Clause [ ] (*Tax indemnity*) but was not so compensated solely because any of the exclusions in paragraph (b) of Clause [ ] (*Tax indemnity*) applied);

(c)   compensated for by the payment of the Mandatory Cost; or

(d)   attributable to the wilful breach by the relevant Finance Party or its Affiliates of any law or regulation.

Related definitions (to the extent not defined in an earlier example):
'**Mandatory Cost**' means the percentage rate per annum calculated by the Agent in accordance with Schedule [ ] (*Mandatory Cost formulae*).

---

[23]   For the form of this clause, see **2.14**.

Syndication

2.17　Where the loan facility is syndicated, each amount advanced by an individual bank constitutes a separate loan by that bank, with the banks' obligations being several and their rights divided. This is partly to avoid the creation of a partnership between the banks, partly to ensure that the banks are not underwriting each other's obligations or guaranteeing to the borrower that other banks in the syndicate will remain solvent, and partly to facilitate individual bank set-offs (since a bank may not be entitled to set off a loan due to it against a deposit with it if it owns the benefit of the loan in undivided shares with the other banks).[24]

2.18　Where the loan facility is syndicated, one of the banks will be designated as the 'Agent'. Its primary functions are:

(a)　to check the conditions precedent and to certify to the other banks when they have been satisfied;

(b)　to act as a paying bank in respect of transfer of funds between the borrower and the syndicate. When an advance is required to be made, the banks transfer their individual amounts to an account with the Agent, who then transfers the aggregate amount to the borrower. Equally, payments of interest and principal are made by the borrower to the Agent, who then apportions them among the banks in accordance with their entitlements, thus ensuring equal treatment of the syndicate members;

(c)　to perform banking duties, such as the calculation of interest rates; and

(d)　to demand early repayment (or 'accelerate') on the occurrence of an event of default, if required to do so by the requisite majority of the banks.[25] The Agent is also sometimes given a discretion to accelerate without waiting for a decision of the majority banks, in order to deal with emergencies. However, it is normal to provide that the Agent is not under an obligation to monitor whether an event of default has occurred.[26] After acceleration, however, enforcement, reflecting the divided nature of the banks' rights, is the individual responsibility of each bank.[27]

---

[24]　See further *Encyclopaedia of Banking Law*, para F(3223); Cranston, *Principles of Banking Law* (2nd edn, 2002), pp 57–61.

[25]　Usually provided to be those banks whose commitments together represent more than either 50 per cent or 662/3 per cent of the total commitments. As to the effectiveness of majority decisions, see **Chapter 16**.

[26]　Since, in the absence of such a provision, a duty to exercise due diligence in monitoring the borrower's compliance with the agreement and to keep the syndicate banks informed might arise: see *Bowstead and Reynolds on Agency* (17th edn, 2001), p 157–158; *Proudfoot v Montefiore* (1867) 2 QB 511.

[27]　Subject to the 'pro rata sharing clause' mentioned in the next paragraph, and also subject in certain cases (usually where the banks have been granted security) to the 'no action' clause, whereunder individual banks may not take enforcement action without approval by the requisite majority of banks. As to the position of the Agent, see further Gabriel, *Legal Aspects of Syndicated Loans* (1986), pp 148–181; Wood, *International Loans, Bonds and Securities Regulation* (1995), pp 98–103 and Chapter 11; Tennekoon, *The Law and Regulation of International Finance* (1991), pp 58–67; *Encyclopaedia of Banking Law*, paras F(3405)–F(3414); Ellinger, Lomnicka and Hooley, *Ellinger's Modern Banking Law* (4th edn, 2006) p 719.

2.19 In one important respect, however, the concept of the banks as independent and several lenders is not reflected, and that is in the 'pro rata sharing clause'. This usually provides that, if any bank receives a greater proportion of its share (by any of various specified means, eg by reason of set-off, litigation (though this is usually excluded where the other banks had an opportunity to participate but chose not to do so), an individual guarantee or a direct payment by the borrower) than the other banks do of theirs, it must pay the excess to the Agent, which redistributes to the other banks pro rata, and the initial bank is treated as not having received the excess. The provision is intended to ensure syndicate equality by requiring the sharing of individual receipts. One effect of the clause is that it may, depending on the circumstances, allow 'double-dipping' by the banks. If the borrower has £140 deposited with one of the banks, and owes £100 to the bank under the loan, then the bank could set off £100 of the deposit against the loan, leaving £40 of the deposit. It would then share the £100 with the other banks, as a result of which an amount would still be left owing to it under the loan, which it could then set off against the remaining £40, and then share with the other banks.[28]

2.20 A typical pro rata sharing clause might read as follows:

1.1 Payments to Finance Parties

If a Finance Party (a "**Recovering Finance Party**") receives or recovers any amount from the Borrower other than in accordance with Clause [ ] (*Payment mechanics*) and applies that amount to a payment due under the Finance Documents then:

(a)   the Recovering Finance Party shall, within three Business Days, notify details of the receipt or recovery to the Agent;

(b)   the Agent shall determine whether the receipt or recovery is in excess of the amount the Recovering Finance Party would have been paid had the receipt or recovery been received or made by the Agent and distributed in accordance with Clause [ ] (*Payment mechanics*), without taking account of any Tax which would be imposed on the Agent in relation to the receipt, recovery or distribution; and

(c)   the Recovering Finance Party shall, within three Business Days of demand by the Agent, pay to the Agent an amount (the "**Sharing Payment**") equal to such receipt or recovery less any amount which the Agent determines may be retained by the Recovering Finance Party as its share of any payment to be made, in accordance with Clause [ ] (*Partial payments*).

1.2 Redistribution of payments

The Agent shall treat the Sharing Payment as if it had been paid by the Borrower and distribute it between the Finance Parties (other than the Recovering Finance Party) in accordance with Clause [ ] (*Partial payments*).

---

28   On pro rata sharing clauses, see further Gabriel, *Legal Aspects of Syndicated Loans* (1986), pp 181–190; *Encyclopaedia of Banking Law*, para F(3503).

1.3   Recovering Finance Party's rights

(a)   On a distribution by the Agent under Clause 1.2 (*Redistribution of payments*), the Recovering Finance Party will be subrogated to the rights of the Finance Parties which have shared in the redistribution.

(b)   If and to the extent that the Recovering Finance Party is not able to rely on its rights under paragraph (a) above, the Borrower shall be liable to the Recovering Finance Party for a debt equal to the Sharing Payment which is immediately due and payable.

1.4   Reversal of redistribution

If any part of the Sharing Payment received or recovered by a Recovering Finance Party becomes repayable and is repaid by that Recovering Finance Party, then:

(a)   each Finance Party which has received a share of the relevant Sharing Payment pursuant to Clause 1.2 (*Redistribution of payments*) shall, upon request of the Agent, pay to the Agent for the account of that Recovering Finance Party an amount equal to the appropriate part of its share of the Sharing Payment (together with an amount as is necessary to reimburse that Recovering Finance Party for its proportion of any interest on the Sharing Payment which that Recovering Finance Party is required to pay); and

(b)   that Recovering Finance Party's rights of subrogation in respect of any reimbursement shall be cancelled and the Borrower will be liable to the reimbursing Finance Party for the amount so reimbursed.

1.5   Exceptions

(a)   This Clause shall not apply to the extent that the Recovering Finance Party would not, after making any payment pursuant to this Clause, have a valid and enforceable claim against the Borrower.

(b)   A Recovering Finance Party is not obliged to share with any other Finance Party any amount which the Recovering Finance Party has received or recovered as a result of taking legal or arbitration proceedings, if:

(i)   it notified that other Finance Party of the legal or arbitration proceedings; and

(ii)   that other Finance Party had an opportunity to participate in those legal or arbitration proceedings but did not do so as soon as reasonably practicable having received notice and did not take separate legal or arbitration proceedings.

Assignment and novation

2.21   It is also common to provide that the banks may transfer their interests, either by assignment (in the case of rights only) or by novation (where both rights and obligations are to be transferred). Novation can usually be effected with minimum effort, by virtue of a 'substitution certificate' or 'transfer certificate'. A similar commercial effect can also be achieved by sub-participation. All these methods are considered in **Chapter 15**.

Chapter Three

TYPES OF BORROWING (2): DEBT SECURITIES

GENERALLY

3.1 The term 'security' has no precise legal meaning, but is traditionally used to describe 'something which makes the enjoyment or enforcement of a right more secure or certain'.[1] Consequently, the term 'debt security' traditionally describes an instrument, given by the debtor in addition to the original debt, and either containing an additional promise or constituting evidence of the debt, designed to make the creditor's burden easier to discharge.[2] One major example of such an instrument is obviously one which creates security, but the creation of security is not essential. It appears to be enough that the instrument acknowledges a liability in a form which makes its enforcement easier or more convenient. Thus promissory notes and certificates for unsecured loan stock are 'securities',[3] and the term is now commonly used to describe virtually any form of financial instrument issued in connection with a loan.[4]

---

[1] Jowitt's *Dictionary of English Law* (2nd edn, 1977). Cf *Singer v Williams* [1921] 1 AC 41 at 49 (per Viscount Cave LC), 57 (per Lord Shaw), 59 (per Lord Wrenbury) and 63 (per Lord Phillimore): the comments are probably distinguishable as being primarily concerned with distinguishing securities from possessions (for income tax purposes).

[2] See *The British Oil and Cake Mills Ltd v IRC* [1903] 1 KB 689 at 697 to 698 per Stirling LJ; *Jones v IRC* [1895] 1 QB 484 at 494 per Collins J; *Brown, Shipley & Co v IRC* [1895] 2 QB 598.

[3] See *Speyer Brothers v IRC* [1908] AC 92; *Rowell v IRC* [1897] 2 QB 194.

[4] The term 'security', and variations of it, are also specifically defined for certain statutory and regulatory purposes: see, eg, Criminal Justice Act 1993, s 54 and Sch 2; Taxation of Chargeable Gains Act 1992, s 132(3)(b); Financial Services and Markets Act 2000, s 102A(2); Financial Services and Markets Act 2000 (Regulated Activities) Order 2001, SI 2001/544 (as amended), arts 3(1), 76–82, 89; Uncertificated Securities Regulations 2001, SI 2001/3755, reg 3(1); Stock Transfer Act 1963, s 4(1); Taxes Management Act 1970, s 21(7); Finance Act 1996, s 186(2); *Listing Rules* (UK Listing Authority), Appendix 1; Companies Act 1989, s 207(1); Trustee Act 1925, s 68(1), para (13); Income and Corporation Taxes Act 1988, s 710; Insolvency Act 1986, s 248. See also *Bristol Airport plc v Powdrill* [1990] Ch 744; *Tarmac Roadstone Holdings Ltd v Williams* [1996] STC (SCD) 409; *Taylor Clark International Ltd v Lewis* [1997] STC 499; *Re Douglas' Will Trusts* [1959] 1 WLR 744 at 749; *Brown, Shipley & Co v IRC* [1895] 2 QB 598; *Re Rayner* [1904] 1 Ch 176; *Re Gent and Eason's Contract* [1905] 1 Ch 386; *Re United Law Clerks Society* [1947] Ch 150 at 152 to 153; *IRC v Henry Ansbacher & Co* [1963] AC 191 at 207 per Lord Morris. For definitions of 'transferable securities', see Financial Services and Markets Act 2000, s 102A(3); Directive 93/22/EEC on investment services in the securities field, Art 1(4); Directive 2004/39/EC on markets in financial instruments, Art 4(18); *Prospectus Rules* (UK Listing Authority), Appendix 1; *Listing Rules* (UK Listing Authority), Appendix 1.

TYPES OF DEBT SECURITY

3.2   Debt securities can broadly be divided into two types: those issued domestically in the form of 'stock', and those issued internationally in the form of 'eurobonds'. In practice, the distinction is disappearing as issues in the UK domestic market are now usually documented in the form of eurobonds. That said, there still remains a relatively small UK market in domestic stock.

3.3   The two principal differences between stock and eurobonds are as follows:

(a)   A domestic stock issue is, traditionally, one made by a UK issuer, denominated in sterling, and targeted principally at UK investors (commonly pension funds and insurance companies). One exception, though, in the 1980s was the so-called 'bulldog' issue (which was sterling-denominated and targeted at UK investors, but made by a foreign issuer).[5] In contrast, an issue of eurobonds is one in which the securities are, or in theory could be, sold internationally to investors across the world and are usually, but not always, denominated in a currency other than that of the country in which the issue takes place.[6] The term 'eurobond' originates from the fact that what is generally agreed to be the first eurobond issue[7] was designed to raise money from the pool of 'eurodollars' that had grown up in Europe since the Second World War. A 'eurodollar' is merely a US dollar on deposit with a bank outside the USA.[8] Nowadays, eurobonds are denominated in all the major currencies, which, so long as they are held outside their country of origin, are known as 'eurocurrencies'.

As mentioned above, this distinction is becoming blurred, as many issues by UK issuers to UK investors in the domestic market are now documented in the form of eurobonds.

---

[5]   A variety of terms has grown up to describe domestic issues by foreign issuers: eg, 'matador' in the case of the Spanish domestic market, 'yankee' in the case of the US domestic market and 'samurai' in the case of the Japanese domestic market.

[6]   Inevitably, there are exceptions: in particular, an issue of eurobonds by an English company on the international markets is still regarded as an international issue even if denominated in sterling (ie 'eurosterling').

[7]   By Autostrade, the concessionaire and operator of toll motorways in Italy, in 1963. See, eg, the article by Roberts in *The Times*, 16 January 1993, p 37; Kerr, *A History of the Eurobond Market – The First 21 Years* (1984), pp 11–16; Kynaston, *The City of London, Vol IV: A Club No More 1945–2000* (2002), pp 275–280; Roberts, *Take Your Partners* (2001), pp 8–9.

[8]   See, eg, *Libyan Arab Foreign Bank v Bankers Trust Co* [1988] 1 Lloyd's Rep 259 at 263 per Staughton J ('a credit in dollars outside the United States, whether in Europe or elsewhere'); *Hazell v Hammersmith and Fulham LBC* [1992] 2 AC 1 at 24 per Lord Templeman ('Eurodollars are United States dollars held outside the United States'). On the growth of the eurodollar and the eurobond generally, see Fisher, *Eurosecurities and their Related Derivatives* (1997), Chapter 1; Tennekoon, *The Law and Regulation of International Finance* (1991), Chapter 1; Kerr, *A History of the Eurobond Market – The First 21 Years* (1984); Kynaston, *The City of London, Vol IV: A Club No More 1945–2000* (2002), passim; Roberts, *Take Your Partners* (2001); Shearlock and Ellington, *The Eurobond Diaries* (1994); Dosoo, *The Eurobond Market* (2nd edn, 1992); Gallant, *The Eurobond Market* (1988).

(b) Domestic stock issues are usually in registered form, with a holder's title to stock being determined by the entries in the register of holders maintained by the issuer's registrar. Stock is often held through CREST[9] (in which case, transfers are effected merely by electronic instructions to CREST). Where it is not held through CREST, each holder is issued with a stock certificate evidencing his holding of the stock and a transfer is effected by execution of a stock transfer form and delivery of the transfer form and certificate to the issuer's registrar for registration in the register.[10] Eurobond issues, however, are usually in bearer form (though some are issued in registered form[11]). It is rare, though, for definitive bonds (or certificates, in the case of a registered issue) to be issued to the investors. Instead, the usual practice is for the bonds to be represented by a 'global bond' (ie a single bond representing the entire issue) and held by or on behalf of Euroclear and Clearstream, the European clearing systems.[12] The investors hold the bonds either directly in accounts at the clearing systems or indirectly through custodians who have accounts at the clearing systems. Transfers between accounts are effected by electronic instructions to the clearing systems.[13]

3.4   There used to be a third major distinction, ie withholding tax on interest payments. Prior to 1 April 2001, interest under domestic stock issues would usually be paid subject to deduction of lower rate income tax, whereas eurobond issues would normally be structured so that interest could be paid gross, ie free of any deduction for tax arising in the company's home tax jurisdiction.[14] That distinction has now disappeared and interest may now be paid gross on both domestic stock issues and eurobonds that are quoted on a recognised stock exchange.[15] However, a legacy of the distinction is that, unlike domestic stock issues, eurobond issues normally contain a gross-up provision (requiring the company to pay an increased amount if tax is

---

[9]   As to which, see further **15.22ff**.

[10]   See **15.13ff**.

[11]   Particularly if a private placement in the USA is envisaged in compliance with Section 4(2) of, or Rule 144A under, the US Securities Act of 1933 (thereby avoiding the need for a registration of the securities with the US Securities and Exchange Commission): see further **14.14–14.21**.

[12]   Or The Depository Trust Company of New York ('DTC'), in the case of an issue, or part of an issue, placed with investors in the US.

[13]   The traditional approach to global bonds involves the deposit of the global bond with a 'common depositary' on behalf of the clearing systems, and physical annotations on the schedule(s) to the global bond to reflect changes in the outstanding amount of the issue. From the summer of 2006, an alternative structure (known as the 'New Global Note', or 'NGN', structure) is being introduced, which will be mandatory where an issuer wishes its international debt securities to be recognised as eligible collateral for Eurosystem monetary policy and intra-day credit operations. The NGN structure involves the global bond being safekept by a Common Safekeeper and serviced by a Common Service Provider, and the clearing systems' records, rather than physical annotations on the global bond itself, being used to determine the outstanding amount of the issue.

[14]   See further **18.15**. In contrast, a grossing-up provision in a loan facility relates sometimes to any tax and sometimes to taxes arising in the borrower's home jurisdiction or the jurisdiction through which payments are made (see further **2.11**).

[15]   See further **18.15(e)**.

required to be deducted by its home tax jurisdiction) and a prepayment
option for the company (in the event that the requirement to deduct results
from a change in law or regulation).[16]

3.5   A number of other differences are also common:

(c) Domestic stock issues are often long term, with maturities ranging from
     15 to 30 years. One exception, though, is loan stock issued on a
     takeover as an alternative to cash consideration, which usually has a
     maturity in the region of three to five years.[17] Eurobond issues,
     however, have maturities ranging from as little as two or three years to
     as much as 25 to 30 years, though the majority range from five to 10
     years[18] with short-term issues (ie with maturities of less than one year)
     usually being made pursuant to ECP programmes[19] rather than in the
     form of eurobonds.

(d) Domestic stock issues usually bear interest at a fixed rate, whereas
     eurobond issues usually bear interest either at a fixed rate or at a
     floating rate (ie fixed periodically by reference to market rates) and
     sometimes bear no interest at all ('zero coupon issues').

(e) The procedures for attracting the lenders and fixing the issue price and
     interest rate differ: these are considered at **13.3 to 13.12**.

(f) Where, as is common, the issue is to be underwritten, it may, in the case
     of a eurobond issue, often be underwritten (on a joint and several basis)
     by a group of financial institutions appointed as the 'managers',
     whereas, in the case of a domestic stock issue, it will usually be
     underwritten by only one, or sometimes two, underwriters:[20] see further
     13.3 to 13.12.

(g) Domestic stock issues are often (though by no means always) secured,
     either by floating charges over all the chargors'[21] undertakings and
     assets and/or by fixed charges over specific properties, whereas
     eurobond issues (with the exception of securitisations and other
     structured finance issues)[22] are usually unsecured.

(h) Domestic stock issues often incorporate borrowing limits and
     restrictions on disposals of assets and on changes in the nature of the

---

[16]   For an example gross-up provision, see **18.18**. For an example prepayment provision, see **5.13**.

[17]   The 'loan stock alternative' is common where there are a number of individual shareholders in the
       target company who could be liable to capital gains tax. The stock is usually redeemable in
       instalments. By virtue of the Taxation of Chargeable Gains Act 1992, s 135, a capital gains tax
       liability will not arise until redemption of the stock (whereas it would arise immediately if the cash
       consideration was accepted) and the stockholders can thus stagger redemption to utilise their annual
       exemptions from capital gains tax.

[18]   Some issues are 'perpetual', ie have no fixed maturity: this is more common in the international than
       the domestic market; see further **5.1–5.2**.

[19]   See **Chapter 4**.

[20]   Usually the company's financial adviser(s).

[21]   As to why security might be given by more than one chargor, see para (j) below.

[22]   Considered in **Chapter 7**.

company's business,[23] whereas the only major covenant usually contained in a eurobond issue is a negative pledge.[24]

(i) Domestic stock issues almost invariably involve the appointment of a trustee for the holders, whereas eurobond issues sometimes involve a trustee, sometimes not.[25]

(j) It is common in domestic stock issues for guarantees and/or security to be given by a number of subsidiaries of the company (known as 'guaranteeing subsidiaries' or 'charging subsidiaries', respectively). The purpose of having guaranteeing subsidiaries is to enhance the credit underpinning the stock (in order to achieve a lower interest rate for the company) and/or to give the company and its group some relaxation from the 'inner borrowing limit' (see **9.23 to 9.25**). The presence of charging subsidiaries, in the case of an issue secured by floating charges, is also intended to increase the attractiveness of the issue to investors whereas, in the case of an issue secured by fixed charges over specific properties, it is merely the result of the properties selected to be charged being held by those subsidiaries rather than by the issuer. In eurobond issues, a guarantee will be given by the issuer's parent if the issuer is merely a finance subsidiary,[26] but guaranteeing and charging subsidiaries are uncommon.

STOCK

3.6 In the context of loan capital,[27] stock is:[28]

'merely borrowed capital consolidated into one mass for the sake of convenience. Instead of each lender having a separate bond or mortgage, he has a certificate entitling him to a certain sum, being a portion of one large loan.'

---

[23] See further **9.23ff**. In the case of first mortgage debenture stock, capital cover and income cover covenants are usually incorporated.

[24] Considered at **9.28–9.32**. This is not the case, however, in relation to 'high yield' eurobond issues, which contain extremely detailed financial covenants. A restriction sometimes also seen in eurobond issues is an 'event risk' provision, under which the holders have a put option (ie a right to require the company to redeem the eurobonds early) if a specified event occurs (eg, a change of control or, most commonly in the case of utility companies, an adverse change to the regulatory regime affecting the company) which results in a sufficiently great downgrading of the ratings assigned to its securities by rating agencies such as Standard & Poor's or Moodys. Another provision giving greater protection to holders that is sometimes seen in eurobond issues is a 'coupon ratchet' provision. This is a provision that adjusts the interest rate in line with changes to the credit rating of the securities. Sometimes, event risk and coupon ratchet provisions are combined so that, if the specified corporate event occurs and results in a rating downgrade, this triggers an adjustment to the interest rate rather than a holder put right.

[25] On the role of trustees, see **Chapter 12**.

[26] Issues are usually structured in this way if the parent would otherwise have to deduct tax from payments of interest.

[27] As opposed to share capital, where stock is 'simply a set of shares put together in a bundle' (*Morrice v Aylmer* (1875) LR 7 HL 717 at 725 per Lord Hatherley). In effect, it is the holding expressed in pounds instead of in a number of shares. The power of a company to convert its paid-up shares into stock is contained in s 121 of the Companies Act 1985.

[28] *Lindley on Companies* (6th edn, 1902), p 346. See also *Re Herring* [1908] 2 Ch 493 at 497.

3.7   The essence, therefore, is that the whole stock constitutes one single debt, and that the holders do not have fixed indivisible entitlements but rather can transfer their stock in any amount (though usually only integral multiples of £1, in order to avoid complications), with the possibility of consolidating several holdings into one larger holding, with a single certificate being issued for the aggregate amount. In order to achieve this effect of one single debt, the covenant to repay and to pay interest, and any accompanying covenants and security, are usually given only to the trustee in the trust deed constituting the stock, rather than to the holders themselves. The trustee holds the benefit of these covenants (and any accompanying security) on trust for the stockholders (with a proviso that the company's payment obligations to the trustee will be satisfied pro tanto by payments to the stockholders). The stockholders are merely beneficiaries under a trust, possessing only equitable interests. The consequences of this are that:

(a)   the trustee, and not any of the stockholders, is the creditor of the company for the purposes of a winding up, administration or scheme of arrangement: *Re Dunderland Iron Ore Co Ltd*;[29]

(b)   the trustee is responsible for enforcing the obligations of the company, though if the trustee defaults in doing so the stockholders have a residual equitable right to do so by joining the trustee as co-defendant;[30]

(c)   transfer of a stockholder's interest can only be effected in writing[31] (hence stock being in registered form, at least where there is a trustee); and

(d)   transfer of a stockholder's interest cannot, in principle, give the transferee any better title than the transferor had (*nemo dat quod non habet*),[32] and thus differs from transfer of a bearer negotiable instrument, which can give the transferee a better title.[33] In practice, this does not matter, as trust deeds invariably provide that a person entered in the register of holders shall be treated as the absolute owner of the

---

29   [1909] 1 Ch 446. See also *Re Uruguay Central and Hygueritas Railway Co of Monte Video* (1879) 11 ChD 372; *Tomkinson v First Pennsylvania Banking and Trust Co* [1961] AC 1007 at 1039 (per Viscount Simonds) and 1076 (per Lord Morris). See, however, *Palmer's Company Law*, para 14.302, fn 4; *Palmer's Company Precedents*, vol 3 (16th edn, 1952), pp 10–11 and 412; Austin and Vann, *The Law of Public Company Finance* (1986), pp 266–267.

30   *Franklin v Franklin* [1915] WN 342; *Les Affréteurs Réunis SA v Leopold Walford (London) Ltd* [1919] AC 801; *Lloyd's v Harper* (1880) 16 ChD 290; *Vandepitte v Preferred Accident Insurance Corporation of New York* [1933] AC 70 at 79; *Harmer v Armstrong* [1934] 1 Ch 65.

31   Law of Property Act 1925, s 53(1)(c). The section applies to equitable interests in personalty as well as equitable interests in land: *Grey v IRC* [1960] AC 1; *Oughtred v IRC* [1960] AC 206; *Vandervell v IRC* [1967] 2 AC 291. See also Green [1984] MLR 385.

32   See, eg, *Mangles v Dixon* (1852) 3 HLC 702; *The Official Manager of the Athenaeum Life Assurance Society v Pooley* (1858) 3 De G&J 294; *Hilger Analytical Ltd v Rank Precision Industries Ltd* [1984] BCLC 301.

33   See **15.3ff**.

relevant amount of stock free of all set-offs between the company and the existing or any prior holder.[34]

3.8   If, however, there is no trustee, the concept of one single debt is achieved by the company's obligations being contained in a deed poll[35] (often known as an 'instrument') for the benefit of the stockholders for the time being. A deed poll is a document executed as a deed, expressed to be made only by the person(s) undertaking the obligations, but for the benefit of others (who are not, technically, parties). Prior to the Contracts (Rights of Third Parties) Act 1999, a deed poll represented an important exception to the privity of contract rules, in that it could be enforced by any person for whose benefit the deed poll purported to be made, even though not a party and not even named, provided he was sufficiently designated. As a result of the Contracts (Rights of Third Parties) Act 1999, a person who is not a party to a contract may enforce a term of the contract if the contract expressly provides that he may do so or the term purports to confer a benefit on him (unless it is clear from the contract that the parties did not intend that the third party be able to enforce rights under the contract). However, the rights envisaged by the Act arise where a contract is entered into between two or more parties that is intended to confer a benefit on a third person. Where the intention is for one person (the issuer) to confer rights unilaterally on a fluctuating group of other persons who are not parties (the stockholders), a deed poll remains the most efficient means of achieving this.

3.9   Current commercial practice is to refer to the stock as 'loan stock', 'unsecured loan stock' or 'ULS' where it is unsecured,[36] as 'first mortgage debenture stock' or 'FMDS' where it is secured by first-ranking fixed mortgages or charges, and as 'debenture stock' where it is secured only by floating charges.

EUROBONDS

Generally

3.10   A eurobond,[37] unlike stock, represents an entitlement to a fixed and indivisible sum. However, a number of the characteristics of stock are retained if a trustee for the holders is appointed. If there is a trustee, the covenant by the company to repay and to pay interest is given to the trustee in the trust deed, and, as with stock, the trustee holds the benefit of this covenant on trust for the holders. However, in the case of bearer eurobonds, it is normally considered important that the bonds constitute negotiable instruments[38] in order to provide certainty to purchasers of the bonds. As will be seen below,[39] the bond must contain an obligation owed to the holder for it to be negotiable, and thus contains on its face a covenant by the company to pay the holder. In order to preserve the advantages of having a trustee,[40] the terms of the eurobond provide that the holder may not sue the company to enforce that covenant unless the trustee has been directed by the holders to sue the company to enforce the covenant in the trust deed and has failed to do so.[41] Thus eurobonds are similar to stock in that the trustee, rather than the holders, is primarily responsible for enforcement. Whether, like stock, the trustee, rather than the holders, is the creditor for the purposes of a winding up, administration or scheme of arrangement is not clear. In the *Dunderland* case,[42] the court placed reliance on the fact that, in the context of stock, there was no contractual link between the company and the holders. Such a contractual link is, however, present in eurobonds, but clearly it would be odd for both the trustee and the holders to be regarded as creditors, and common sense suggests that the trustee should be regarded as the creditor.[43] In other respects, though, eurobonds, even where there is a trustee, differ from stock: since the holder has a negotiable instrument and not

---

[37]   On eurobonds generally, see Wood, *International Loans, Bonds and Securities Regulation* (1995), Chapters 8 and 9; Tennekoon, *The Law and Regulation of International Finance* (1991), Part III; Fisher, *Eurosecurities and their Related Derivatives* (1997); Carmichael and Wells (1996) VII (7) PLC, 41.

[38]   As to which, see **15.3ff**.

[39]   At **15.8**.

[40]   Considered at **12.3ff**.

[41]   For the form of wording, see **12.8(a)**.

[42]   See **3.7**.

[43]   Cf *Re Olathe Silver Mining Co* (1884) 27 ChD 278, where a bearer was entitled to petition for winding up. The decision may be distinguishable if the securities in question did not limit the bearer's rights to take action to the situation where the trustee had become obliged to take action and had failed to do so, as described above; but whether they contained such a limitation or not is unclear. It could be argued that the holders should be regarded as contingent creditors (ie, that their rights are contingent on the trustee having been directed by the holders to sue the company and having failed to do so). However, the normal principles relating to double-proof would presumably have the result that, as the trustee clearly has the better claim, the holders cannot prove unless the trustee fails, or agrees not, to do so.

merely an equitable interest, transfers need not be effected in writing, and a transferee can acquire a better title than the transferor had.[44]

3.11 Where there is no trustee, though, each eurobond constitutes a separate contract between the company and the holder. Consequently, each holder can decide whether or not to accelerate the repayment obligation of his own eurobonds if an event of default occurs (with the result that part of the issue may be accelerated and part not) and is responsible for taking his own enforcement action.

3.12 The term 'eurobond' is a generic one and is in fact used collectively to describe a variety of internationally issued securities which may themselves individually be called, amongst other things, either notes or bonds. Current commercial practice is, broadly speaking, to refer to the securities as 'notes' if they have a maturity of less than five years, and 'bonds' if they have a longer maturity. However, securities which bear interest at a floating rate (ie fixed periodically by reference to market rates) are invariably called 'floating rate notes' or 'FRNs' regardless of their maturity.

EMTN programmes

3.13 An important development in the eurobond market since the mid 1980s has been the emergence of 'euro medium-term note programmes' (or 'EMTN programmes'),[45] designed to standardise the terms on which the company issues securities and consequently to minimise the documentation and cost of each issue. This is done by setting out in the documents constituting the programme all the provisions which it is envisaged may be applicable to the company's issues, with the documentation for a particular issue (usually called a 'final terms' document or a 'pricing supplement')[46] needing only to set out the commercial terms (such as maturity date, interest rate, issue price, etc) and to apply or disapply provisions of the programme documentation as appropriate.[47] Like conventional eurobonds, the programme can be established either with or without a trustee. Issues are made to financial institutions who have been appointed in advance as 'dealers' under the programme, though provision is usually made for other institutions to be appointed as dealers, either permanently or for the purposes of a single issue. Most programmes also allow for issues to be sold by means of a syndicate of financial institutions, equivalent to a management group in

---

[44] See **15.3ff**.

[45] The term is, technically, a misnomer, since most programmes allow for securities to be issued with maturities from one month to 30 years, and the securities issued may themselves be called either notes or bonds. As regards the rapid growth of the EMTN market, see, eg, Bank of England *Quarterly Bulletin*, August 1992 (p 282) and February 1993 (p 74). The International Capital Market Association and the International Capital Market Services Association have both published a number of recommendations as to the provisions of, and procedures applicable to, EMTN programmes.

[46] Usual practice is to call the document 'final terms' where the programme is listed on a regulated market (as to which, see **Chapter 13**) and a 'pricing supplement' otherwise.

[47] If the issue is to be syndicated, a syndication agreement will also be required.

a conventional eurobond issue. One important difference from a loan facility is that, whereas at least some of the banks under a loan facility are usually committed to lend, EMTN programmes are uncommitted, in that the dealers are not under any prior obligation to purchase the securities, and it is a matter for agreement between the company and a dealer at the time of each proposed issue.[48]

---

48   On the issuance process under EMTN programmes, see further **13.9–13.12**.

Chapter Four

TYPES OF BORROWING (3):
ECP PROGRAMMES[1]

NOTE ISSUANCE AND REVOLVING UNDERWRITING FACILITIES

4.1   The distinction between bank lending and debt securities has been somewhat blurred by the growth in popularity of loan facilities under which the borrower's payment obligations are contained in debt securities issued pursuant to the facility. The practice of financial institutions making available facilities for the acceptance of bills of exchange[2] has been common for many years, but one of the significant developments of the early 1980s was the growth in note issuance facilities ('NIFs') and revolving underwriting facilities ('RUFs') enabling borrowers to raise their funds by issuing short-term bearer notes (known as 'euronotes') on a roll-over basis, usually for maturities of one, three or six months. Many acronyms developed, such as SNIF (a syndicated NIF), PUF (a prime underwriting facility) and TRUF (a transferable RUF, ie one in which the underwriters could 'transfer' their underwriting obligations to other financial institutions). The basic difference between NIFs and RUFs appears to have been that the former were uncommitted facilities, whereas the latter were committed facilities.[3] Various methods were used for the distribution of the notes,[4] but the most common was the tender panel structure, under which the members of the panel bid in competition with each other for the notes.

ECP PROGRAMMES

4.2   NIFs and RUFs became unpopular due to the relatively cumbersome nature of the tender panel process and an increasing view on the part of

---

[1]   On euronotes and ECP generally, see Wood, *International Loans, Bonds and Securities Regulation* (1995), pp 159–161; Graaf, *Euromarket Finance* (1991), pp 139–149; Choudhry, *Corporate Bond Markets* (2006), Chapter 6; Tennekoon, *The Law and Regulation of International Finance* (1991), Part VI; Bankson and Lee, *Euro Notes* (1985); Penn, Shea and Arora, *The Law and Practice of International Banking* (1987), Chapter 10; Bullock, *Euronotes and Euro-commercial paper* (1987); Bank of England *Quarterly Bulletin*, May 1988, p 203; Heller, *Eurocommercial Paper* (1988).

[2]   Described in **2.5**.

[3]   See, eg, Beaumont, IFLR, June 1985, p 31; Bankson and Lee, *Euro Notes* (1985), Chapter 7; Tennekoon, *The Law and Regulation of International Finance* (1991), Chapter 25.

[4]   See Bullock, *Euronotes and Euro-commercial paper* (1987), Chapter 3.

borrowers that the continuing commitments were not worth the commissions (largely because the commitments were conditional on satisfaction of no material adverse change conditions precedent which might not be satisfied when the facility was actually required). From the late 1980s onwards, they have been replaced by eurocommercial paper (or 'ECP') programmes.[5] These differ from NIFs and RUFs in three major respects: first, they are not underwritten, secondly, instead of a tender panel, the borrower uses a small group of appointed financial institutions as placing agents, with the ability either to solicit competitive bids (ie a mini tender panel, but with more flexible procedures) or to agree terms directly with the individual financial institutions, and, thirdly, they are targeted at different markets. Whereas NIFs and RUFs were generally entered into only by banks, ECP programmes are in practice entered into both by banks and by financial intermediaries, who solicit investors in the euro-markets (in a similar way to the marketing of eurobonds by managers).[6]

4.3 ECP is short-term, with no trustee, always in bearer form,[7] and with maturities which can range from seven days to one year but, in practice, are usually in the region of 45 to 60 days.[8] It usually does not bear interest, but is instead issued at a discount to its repayment amount. It is not usually listed on any stock exchange. Since the investors' credit risk is short-term, there is no real need for special credit protection, and so ECP does not contain events of default or a negative pledge provision. It does, however, contain a tax gross-up in the normal eurobond form.

4.4 As with an EMTN programme,[9] to which an ECP programme is in legal substance very similar,[10] all the provisions which may be applicable to the borrower's issues are agreed in advance between the borrower and the group of financial institutions (who are known as 'dealers') and set out in the programme documentation, with the commercial terms being agreed at the time of the relevant issue.

---

5   See Woolley, *Butterworths' JIBFL*, June 1986, p 13; Pigott, *Butterworths' JIBFL*, June 1986, p 16.

6   As to which, see further **13.4ff**.

7   Although, like eurobonds, usually represented by one global note rather than individual definitive notes being issued, with trading being effected by electronic book entry in the records of Euroclear and Clearstream, the European clearing systems.

8   'Commercial paper' is specifically defined in the Financial Services and Markets Act 2000 (Regulated Activities) Order 2001, SI 2001/544, art 9(3): see **10.12**.

9   Described in **Chapter 3**.

10   The principal difference being that securities issued under an ECP programme have a maximum maturity of one year, whereas those issued under an EMTN programme usually have possible maturities from one month to 30 years (the majority, though, being in the 2 to 5 year region).

Chapter Five

KEY COMMERCIAL TERMS

REPAYMENT

Clogs on the equity of redemption

5.1   It was seen earlier[1] that an obligation to repay is an essential characteristic of a loan, and various aspects of the repayment obligation have already been considered.[2] In particular, it was seen[3] that securities which are expressed to be perpetual or irredeemable are still loans if, on their true construction, they nevertheless become repayable on the winding up of the company. However, where they are secured, the postponement, or absence, of the right of redemption will be void if it amounts to a clog or fetter on the equity of redemption.[4]

5.2   A provision that the debt is truly irredeemable (ie not repayable in any circumstances) will clearly be a clog, but a provision that the debt is redeemable only in the company's winding up or at the company's option will probably not be, in the light of the Court of Appeal's decision in *Knightsbridge Estates Trust Ltd v Byrne*.[5] The court held in that case that the date for redemption of the security, provided that it is no later than the date for repayment of the loan, may be postponed for any period which the parties agree upon, so long as the right of redemption does not thereby become 'illusory'[6] and there are no circumstances of oppression or undue influence. In any event, in the case of debentures,[7] an exception to the prohibition on clogs and fetters is given by s 193 of the Companies Act 1985, which provides that a condition contained in any debentures, or in a

---

1   In **Chapter 1**.
2   In **Chapter 1 and 2.2ff**.
3   In **Chapter 1**.
4   As to what constitutes a clog or fetter, see, eg, *Noakes & Co Ltd v Rice* [1902] AC 24; *Reeve v Lisle* [1902] AC 461; *Bradley and Bradley v Carritt* [1903] AC 253; *Biggs v Hoddinott* [1898] 2 Ch 307; *Kreglinger v New Patagonia Meat and Cold Storage Co Ltd* [1914] AC 25; *De Beers Consolidated Mines Ltd v British South Africa Co* [1912] AC 52; *Re Cuban Land and Development Co (1911) Ltd* [1921] 2 Ch 147; *Multiservice Bookbinding Ltd v Marden* [1979] Ch 84; *Knightsbridge Estates Trust Ltd v Byrne* [1939] Ch 441, affd on other grounds [1940] AC 613; *Lewis v Frank Love Ltd* [1961] 1 All ER 446; *Jones v Morgan* [2001] Lloyd's Rep Bank 323; *Warnborough Ltd v Garmite Ltd* [2003] NPC 134; *Snell's Equity* (31st edn, 2005), pp 811–815.
5   [1939] Ch 441, affd on other grounds [1940] AC 613.
6   As in *Fairclough v Swan Brewery Co Ltd* [1912] AC 565, where, in a mortgage of a lease of 20 years, the right to redeem was postponed until six weeks before the expiration of the lease.
7   As to what constitutes a debenture for this purpose, see **Chapter 17**.

deed for securing debentures, is not invalid by reason only that the debentures are thereby made irredeemable, or redeemable only on the happening of a contingency (however remote) or on the expiration of a period (however long), any rule of equity to the contrary notwithstanding.

Time for repayment

5.3   Unless the debt is perpetual or irredeemable, the obligation to repay is usually expressed to be either on a fixed date[8] or on demand. However, a debt[9] expressed to be payable on demand rather than on a specific date (and, a fortiori, one expressed to be payable with no provision as to time) is in fact payable immediately without demand.[10] However, a guarantee expressed to be payable on demand does not become payable until demand is made,[11] and a debt that is to be transformed by a demand from a debt payable in instalments to one payable immediately does not become so payable until demand is made.[12] The question of whether demand is necessary is relevant for two reasons: whether demand must be made before proceedings are brought to recover the debt,[13] and when the limitation period commences.[14] The distinctions may seem difficult to follow, but the reason given by Scrutton LJ[15] is that demand is not necessary in the case of a present debt (ie one that presently exists but is expressed not to be payable until demand),

---

8   A loan expressed to be repayable 'on or after' a fixed date confers on the borrower an option to repay on that date and an obligation to repay after that date if and when demand is made by the lender: *Re Tewkesbury Gas Co* [1911] 2 Ch 279, affd [1912] 1 Ch 1. A covenant to pay 'on or before' a named date creates an obligation to pay on that date, with an option for the borrower of earlier payment: *Re Tewkesbury Gas Co* [1911] 2 Ch 279 at 284.

9   Other than an overdraft, where (in the absence of contrary agreement) demand is always necessary: see **2.3**.

10   *Norton v Ellam* (1837) 2 M & W 461; *Walton v Mascall* (1844) 13 M&W 452 at 457–458; *Atterbury v Jarvie* (1857) 2 H&N 114 at 120 per Martin B; *Re George* (1890) 44 ChD 627; *Rowe v Young* (1820) 2 Bligh 391 at 465 per Bayley J; *Re J Brown's Estate* [1893] 2 Ch 300 at 304–305; *High Street Services Ltd v Bank of Credit and Commerce International SA* [1993] BCC 360 at 364. This principle, however, does not apply in the case of a bank's liability to its customer to repay a current account: though the relationship between the parties is merely that of ordinary debtor and creditor, the bank is not obliged to repay until demand is made by the customer (*Foley v Hill* (1848) 2 HLC 28; *Joachimson v Swiss Bank Corporation* [1921] 2 KB 110).

11   *Bradford Old Bank Ltd v Sutcliffe* [1918] 2 KB 833. The position is different, though, where the 'guarantee' is in fact an indemnity (ie the 'guarantor' is liable as a principal debtor and not merely as a surety: see further **Chapter 11**). In that case, the indemnifier is immediately liable without demand: *High Street Services Ltd v Bank of Credit and Commerce International SA* [1993] BCC 360 at 364.

12   *Esso Petroleum Co Ltd v Alstonbridge Properties Ltd* [1975] 3 All ER 358. Demand is also necessary where the amount payable is uncertain: *Brown v The Great Eastern Railway Co* (1877) 2 QBD 406.

13   Service of proceedings does not constitute 'demand' for these purposes: *Esso Petroleum Co Ltd v Alstonbridge Properties Ltd* [1975] 3 All ER 358.

14   The position regarding limitation of actions has been modified in relation to debts expressed to be payable on demand (ie the first of Scrutton LJ's three categories described below), by the Limitation Act 1980. While the Act preserves the common law position, described above, that the debt is in fact payable immediately without demand (and therefore that no demand need be made before proceedings are brought to recover the debt), s 6(2) mitigates the potential hardship of this rule by providing that the limitation period does not commence until demand has been made. See, eg, *Boot v Boot* (1996) 72 P&CR D30; *Bank of Baroda v Mahomed* [1999] Lloyd's Rep Bank 14.

15   In *Bradford Old Bank Ltd v Sutcliffe* [1918] 2 KB 833 at 848, approved by Walton J in *Esso Petroleum Co Ltd v Alstonbridge Properties Ltd* [1975] 3 All ER 358 at 367.

but is in the case of a debt that is 'not present but to accrue' (eg one that is payable a specified period of time after demand) or a collateral promise (eg a guarantee). Where a loan is to be repayable early upon demand after an event of default, it falls within the second of Scrutton LJ's three categories, and thus is not payable until demand is made.[16]

5.4 Where, as is commonly the case with bearer securities, payment is to be made on presentation of the security at a specified place (usually either to the company or to one of its paying agents), the security is not payable until presentation is made at that place;[17] accordingly, so that the company is not in danger of being indefinitely liable, it is common in bearer debt securities to provide that claims will become void if presentation is not made within a specified period[18] of the payment being available at the paying agents. A typical provision to this effect would read as follows:

> Bonds and Coupons will become void unless presented for payment within periods of 10 years (in the case of principal) and five years (in the case of interest) from the Relevant Date in respect of the Bonds or, as the case may be, the Coupons, subject to the provisions of Condition [ ] (*Payments*).

> '**Relevant Date**' means the date on which the payment first becomes due but, if the full amount of the money payable has not been received in [principal financial centre of relevant currency] by the Principal Paying Agent or the Trustee on or before the due date, it means the date on which, the full amount of the money having been so received, notice to that effect shall have been duly given to the Bondholders by the Issuer in accordance with Condition [ ] (*Notices*).

Prepayment

(a) Generally

5.5 Borrowers are frequently given rights to repay early, either because withholding taxes are imposed on interest payments, resulting in the borrower being obliged under the terms of the borrowing to gross up, or simply at the borrower's option. Prepayment is not permissible unless

---

[16] *Esso Petroleum Co Ltd v Alstonbridge Properties Ltd* [1975] 3 All ER 358.
[17] *Thorn v City Rice Mills* (1889) 40 ChD 357; *Re Escalera Silver Lead Mining Co (Ltd)* (1908) 25 TLR 87; *Re Compania de Electricidad de la Provincia de Buenos Aires Ltd* [1980] Ch 146. If no place for presentation is specified, it is the duty of the company to seek out the holder once the due date has occurred, and (if interest is expressed to be payable until the date of actual repayment) the holder can recover interest down to that date: *Fowler v Midland Electric Corporation for Power Distribution Ltd* [1917] 1 Ch 656.
[18] Normally 10 or 12 years (in the case of principal) and five or six years (in the case of interest).

allowed by the contract[19] (except that, if the contract is regulated under the Consumer Credit Act 1974, the borrower has a right to make payment at any time).[20]

5.6   The existence of an option to repay early does not oblige the borrower to repay early,[21] but where the loan has become repayable (whether pursuant to exercise of an option by the borrower or for some other reason, eg by means of automatic acceleration on an event of default), the lender is bound to accept payment and must release any security that has been given for the loan.[22] An option to repay early may be expressed as a right to repay either all the money lent or only a part thereof: in the case of repayment of part, it is usual to provide that the amount to be repaid will (in the case of syndicated bank loans) be shared pro rata among the lending banks or (in the case of debt securities) be allocated among the securities by redeeming each security in part or by selecting the securities to be redeemed by ballot.[23]

---

[19]   *Hooper v Western Counties and South Wales Telephone Co Ltd* (1892) 68 LT 78 (in relation to debt securities). The Australian courts have held to the same effect in relation to a loan agreement (*Hyde Management Services (Pty) Ltd v FAI Insurances* (1979–80) 144 CLR 541). Where an early repayment right is included, the notice of repayment will be subject to the same rules of construction as contracts, and thus minor errors will be ignored so long as the notice is sufficiently clear and unambiguous to leave a reasonable recipient in no doubt as to how it is intended to operate (see eg *Mannai Investment Co Ltd v Eagle Star Life Assurance Co Ltd* [1997] AC 749 at 768–772 per Lord Steyn, 778–780 per Lord Hoffmann and 781–782 per Lord Clyde). Any specific requirements or preconditions that are expressed to be applicable nevertheless need to be satisfied (see eg *Nuova Safim SpA v Sakura Bank Ltd* [1999] 2 All ER (Comm) 526 (a notice of termination of a swap agreement (for illegality) that was given six months after the occurrence of the illegality was not valid as it did not satisfy a condition precedent that notice be given 'promptly')).

[20]   Section 94. As to the applicability of the Consumer Credit Act, see **9.38**.

[21]   See, eg, *Edinburgh Corporation v British Linen Bank* [1913] AC 133. The prima facie meaning of the word 'redeemable' is that the borrower has an option, but not an obligation, to repay early: *Re Chicago and North West Granaries Co Ltd* [1898] 1 Ch 263; *Re Joseph Stocks & Co Ltd* [1912] 2 Ch 134 at 140.

[22]   *Consolidated Goldfields of South Africa v Simmer and Jack East Ltd* (1913) 82 LJ Ch 214.

[23]   Certain circumstances could be envisaged (eg if partial early redemption was mandatory and the result of the drawings was that some holders received a significantly higher return than others) that would create a risk of the arrangements constituting an unlawful lottery for the purposes of the Lotteries and Amusements Act 1976 (see eg *Sykes v Beadon* (1879) LR 11 ChD 170 at 190 per Jessel MR: the case was overruled by *Smith v Anderson* (1880) LR 15 ChD 247, but without mention being made of the lottery point). However, in ordinary circumstances the mere selection by lot of securities pursuant to the exercise by an issuer of a discretionary right to redeem securities early in part is unlikely to constitute a lottery (see eg *Wallingford v Mutual Society* (1880) LR 5 App Cas 685, where a scheme that had as its object the carrying on of a legitimate business was not vitiated merely because it provided for the distribution of profits in certain events by lot). When the relevant provisions of the Gambling Act 2005 are brought into force, the Lotteries and Amusements Act 1976 will be repealed (Gambling Act 2005, s 356(3)(i), (4), Sch 17), and it will be expressly provided that the fact that a contract relates to gambling (defined as including participation in a lottery (ibid, ss 3, 14)) will not prevent its enforcement, although this will not override any other rule of law that prevents enforcement on the grounds of unlawfulness (ibid, s 335). At the time of writing (May 2006), these provisions were not yet in force.

(b) Typical provisions

(i) Loan facilities

5.7 It is normal in loan facilities for the borrower to have a general right of optional prepayment. However, this can usually only be exercised at the end of an interest period. This is because the banks fund themselves, notionally at least, on a revolving basis for periods equal to the interest periods, and thus could incur significant losses (known as 'broken funding' costs) if repayment is made by the borrower otherwise than at the end of an interest period. Furthermore, the right can only be exercised pro rata in relation to all banks, not just some.

5.8 As seen earlier,[24] it is also normal in loan facilities for the borrower to have an additional right of prepayment in relation to any affected bank in the event that the borrower is obliged to gross-up for tax or to pay increased costs. This would normally enable the borrower to terminate the relevant portion of the loan agreement more quickly (eg after five business days), so long as it indemnifies the banks in question against their 'broken funding' costs.

5.9 A typical prepayment clause for tax or increased costs, and the related 'broken funding' costs indemnity, are set out at **2.14**. A typical general optional prepayment clause in a syndicated loan facility (based on the Loan Markets Association's recommended form) reads as follows:

1.1 Voluntary cancellation

> The Borrower may, if it gives the Agent not less than [   ] Business Days' (or such shorter period as the Majority Lenders may agree) prior notice, cancel the whole or any part (being a minimum amount of [   ]) of the Facility. Any cancellation under this Clause shall reduce the Commitments of the Lenders rateably under the Facility.

1.2 Voluntary prepayment

> (a)   The Borrower may, if it gives the Agent not less than [   ] Business Days' (or such shorter period as the Majority Lenders may agree) prior notice, prepay the whole or any part of any Loan (but, if in part, being an amount that reduces the Base Currency Amount of the Loan by a minimum amount of [   ]).
>
> (b)   A Loan may only be prepaid after the last day of the Availability Period (or, if earlier, the day on which the applicable Available Facility is zero).

1.3 Restrictions

> (a)   Any notice of cancellation or prepayment given by the Borrower under this Clause shall be irrevocable and, unless a contrary indication appears in this Agreement, shall specify the date or dates upon which the relevant cancellation or prepayment is to be made and the amount of that cancellation or prepayment.

---

[24]   At **2.12**.

(b)   Any prepayment under this Agreement shall be made together with accrued interest on the amount prepaid and, subject to any Break Costs, without premium or penalty.

(c)   The Borrower may not reborrow any part of the Facility which is prepaid.

(d)   The Borrower shall not repay or prepay all or any part of the Loans or cancel all or any part of the Commitments except at the times and in the manner expressly provided for in this Agreement.

(e)   No amount of the Total Commitments cancelled under this Agreement may be subsequently reinstated.

(f)   If the Agent receives a notice from the Borrower under this Clause it shall promptly forward a copy of that notice to the Lenders.

(*For defined terms, see earlier examples*)

(ii)   Eurobonds

5.10   Whether the issuer will have a general right of optional redemption, and if so whether at par, or at a premium and whether of part of the issue on several occasions, or only of all of the issue at the same time, will vary from issue to issue. The option can usually be exercised at any time where the interest is payable at a fixed rate, but only at the end of an interest period where interest is payable at a floating rate.

5.11   Irrespective of whether a general right of optional redemption is included, it would be normal, as seen earlier,[25] for the issuer to have a redemption option in the event that it becomes obliged to gross-up for tax. Unlike the case in a loan facility, this would only permit redemption of all the issue, not merely the affected part of it, and the option will normally only be exercisable if the obligation to deduct arises from a change in law or regulation (ie not if it merely results from the issuer readjusting its tax affairs). Furthermore, the option will, like the general right of optional redemption, be exercisable at any time if interest is payable at a fixed rate, but only at the end of an interest period if interest is payable at a floating rate (thus differing from the equivalent provision in a loan facility, which is normally exercisable at any time during an interest period, subject to the 'broken funding' costs indemnity).

5.12   A typical general optional redemption provision in a eurobond issue (in this example, a fixed rate issue with a trustee, where redemption is to be at par and can be partial), would read as follows:

(1)   The Issuer may, having given not less than 15 nor more than 30 days' notice to the Bondholders in accordance with Condition [   ] (*Notices*) (which notice shall be irrevocable), redeem all the Bonds, or from time to time some only (being US$[   ] in principal amount or an integral multiple of US$[   ]), on or at any time after [   ] at their principal amount together in each case with interest accrued to the date of redemption.

---

25   At **3.4**.

(2) In the case of a partial redemption of Bonds, Bonds to be redeemed will be selected, in such place as the Trustee may approve and in such manner as the Trustee shall deem to be appropriate and fair, not more than 30 days before the date fixed for redemption. Each notice of redemption will specify the date fixed for redemption and, in the case of a partial redemption, the aggregate principal amount, and the serial numbers, of the Bonds to be redeemed, and serial numbers of Bonds previously called for redemption and not presented for payment and the aggregate principal amount of the Bonds which will be outstanding after the partial redemption.

(3) Upon the expiry of any notice as is referred to in paragraph (1) above the Issuer shall be bound to redeem the Bonds to which the notice refers at their principal amount together with interest accrued to but excluding the redemption date.

5.13 A typical tax redemption provision in a eurobond issue (in this example, a fixed rate issue with a trustee) would read as follows:[26]

(1) If the Issuer satisfies the Trustee immediately before the giving of the notice referred to below that (a) as a result of any change in, or amendment to, the laws or regulations of [   ] or any political-division of, or any authority in, or of, [   ] having power to tax, or any change in the application or official interpretation of such laws or regulations, which change or amendment becomes effective after [date of subscription agreement], on the occasion of the next payment due in respect of the Bonds the Issuer would be required to pay additional amounts as provided or referred to in Condition [   ] (*Taxation*), and (b) the requirement cannot be avoided by the Issuer taking reasonable measures available to it, the Issuer may at its option, having given not less than 30 nor more than 60 days' notice to the Bondholders in accordance with Condition [   ] (*Notices*) (which notice shall be irrevocable), redeem all (but not some only) of the Bonds at their principal amount together with interest accrued to but excluding the date of redemption, provided that no notice of redemption shall be given earlier than 90 days before the earliest date on which the Issuer would be required to pay the additional amounts were a payment in respect of the Bonds then due. Prior to the publication of any notice of redemption pursuant to this paragraph, the Issuer shall deliver to the Trustee a certificate signed by two Directors of the Issuer stating that the requirement referred to in (a) above will apply on the occasion of the next payment due in respect of the Bonds and cannot be avoided by the Issuer taking reasonable measures available to it and the Trustee shall be entitled to accept the certificate as sufficient evidence of the satisfaction of the conditions precedent set out above, in which event it shall be conclusive and binding on the Bondholders and the Couponholders.

---

[26] This follows a form recommended by ICMA (the International Capital Market Association). For an analysis of the effect of a clause that departed from the ICMA model form, see *Indofood International Finance Ltd v JP Morgan Chase Bank NA* [2005] EWHC 973 (as to construction of the clause) and [2006] STC 1195 (as to the factual determination of 'reasonable measures' in the light of that construction).

(2)   Upon the expiry of any notice as is referred to in paragraph (1) above the Issuer shall be bound to redeem the Bonds at their principal amount together with interest accrued to but excluding the redemption date.

(iii)   Domestic stock

5.14   Whether the issuer will have a general right of optional redemption, and if so whether of part of the issue on several occasions or only of all the issue at the same time, will vary from issue to issue. As most domestic stock issues carry interest at a fixed rate, such an option will usually be exercisable at any time during an interest period. The redemption price will normally be calculated by reference to the then current yield on a particular gilt-edged security (ie so that the redemption monies, if reinvested in that gilt-edged security, would continue to give the holder the same yield on the sum originally invested that he had hitherto received) – the so-called 'Spens' provision.[27]

5.15   A right of redemption for tax reasons has not, historically, normally been included since, as seen earlier,[28] interest under domestic stock issues used normally to be paid subject to deduction of income tax, with no obligation on the issuer to gross-up.

5.16   A typical general optional redemption provision in a domestic stock issue (in this example, where redemption may only be of all, and not merely part, of the issue) would read as follows:

> The Company shall be entitled at any time by giving to the holders of the Stock not less than 30 nor more than 45 days' notice in writing in a form approved by the Trustee to repay the whole (but not part only) of the Stock for the time being outstanding together with interest accrued up to and including the date of repayment at the Adjusted Redemption Price.
>
> On the expiration of the notice referred to above, the Company shall be bound to repay the Stock together with interest accrued up to and including the date of repayment.
>
> For the purpose of this provision:
>
> (i)   the **Adjusted Redemption Price** shall be par or, if higher, the price, as reported to the Company and the Trustee by the Financial Adviser, at which the Gross Redemption Yield on the Stock on the Calculation Date is equal to the Gross Redemption Yield (determined by reference to the middle market price) at 3.00 pm (London time) on that date of the Benchmark Gilt;
>
> (ii)   **Benchmark Gilt** means the [*title of gilt*] or (where the Financial Adviser advises the Trustee that, for reasons of illiquidity or

---

[27]   The Spens provision was originally a market price provision applicable only on a winding up, but the term tends now to be used for all forms of market price or yield basis redemption provisions, whether on an event of default or at the issuer's option. It is now also seen in eurobond issues.

[28]   At **3.4**.

otherwise, such stock is not appropriate for the purpose) such other UK government stock as the Financial Adviser may recommend;

    (iii)   **Calculation Date** means the date which is the third business day in London prior to the date of redemption;

    (iv)   **Financial Adviser** means a financial adviser selected by the Company and approved by the Trustee; and

    (v)   **Gross Redemption Yield** means a yield calculated on the basis set out by the United Kingdom Debt Management Office in the paper '*Formulae for calculating Gilt Prices from Yields*', Section One: Price/Yield Formulae 'Conventional Gilts; Double-dated and Undated Gilts with Assumed (or Actual) Redemption on a Quasi-Coupon Date' (3rd edition, 16/03/2005) (as supplemented, amended or replaced from time to time) or on such other basis as the Trustee may approve.[29]

Event of default

5.17   It is usual to provide that the borrower's repayment obligation can be accelerated by notice by the lender, upon the occurrence of an 'event of default'. The most common events of default that are specified are the borrower failing to pay interest or an instalment of principal, the borrower going into liquidation or other insolvency-related events occurring, or certain other debt obligations of the borrower either being accelerated (a 'cross-acceleration' clause) or becoming capable of being accelerated (a 'cross-default' clause).[30] The validity of such an acceleration provision will depend primarily upon whether the amount falling due constitutes a penalty or, in the case of secured loans, a clog on the equity of redemption.[31] Where the amount that becomes due is merely the balance of the principal, or such balance plus accrued interest, the provision is clearly not a penalty;[32] but

---

[29]   Prior to the introduction in 1998 by the UK Debt Management Office of its methodology for calculating gilt prices from yields, the calculation was carried out on a basis laid down by the Joint Index and Classification Committee of the Institute and Faculty of Actuaries.

[30]   In the eurobond market, the term cross-default is in practice used interchangeably for both types of clause. Care should be taken where the clause is expressed to relate only to borrowings, as it will not then cover many forms of indebtedness having the same commercial effect as borrowings: see **Chapter 1**.

[31]   As to which, see **5.1–5.2**. Other possible threats to the validity of such a provision (or, indeed, the transaction generally) are the court's powers to set aside extortionate credit transactions pursuant to s 244 of the Insolvency Act 1986 (exercisable if the company goes into administration or liquidation within three years of the relevant provision of credit) and the court's residual equitable jurisdiction to set aside transactions where one party has acted extortionately, oppressively or coercively towards the other (see *Alec Lobb (Garages) Ltd v Total Oil GB Ltd* [1985] 1 All ER 303).

[32]   See, eg, *The Protector Endowment Loan and Annuity Co v Grice* (1880) 5 QBD 592; *Wallingford v Mutual Society* (1880) 5 App Cas 685; *Latter v Colwill* [1937] 1 All ER 442; *The Angelic Star* [1988] 1 Lloyd's Rep 122.

where it includes future interest it may be, depending on the amount.[33] The amount would constitute a penalty if it did not represent a genuine pre-estimate of the probable loss arising from the default (and was not justified for some other reason).[34]

5.18   Consequently, a provision in debt securities requiring the payment of either a premium equal to the difference between the principal amount and the market price of the securities or designed to give the holder a price calculated by reference to the then current yield on a particular gilt-edged security[35] is unlikely to be a penalty. Similarly, a provision whereunder the amount payable on default is the same as that payable on exercise by the company of any prepayment option which it has is unlikely in most cases to be a penalty[36] (but may be if it is unjustifiably high[37]).

5.19   A typical event of default provision in a eurobond issue (in this example, one with a trustee) would read as follows:

> The Trustee at its discretion may, and if so requested in writing by the holders of at least one-fifth in principal amount of the Bonds then outstanding or if so directed by an Extraordinary Resolution of the Bondholders shall (subject in each case to being indemnified to its satisfaction), give notice to the Issuer that the Bonds are, and they shall accordingly forthwith become, immediately due and repayable at their principal amount, together with accrued interest as provided in the Trust Deed, in any of the following events ('**Events of Default**'):
>
> (a)   if default is made in the payment of any principal or interest due in respect of the Bonds or any of them and the default continues for a period of [   ] days in the case of principal or [   ] days in the case of interest; or
>
> (b)   if the Issuer fails to perform or observe any of its other obligations under these Conditions or the Trust Deed and (except in any case where the Trustee considers the failure to be incapable of remedy, when no continuation or notice as is hereinafter mentioned will be required) the failure continues for the period of 30 days (or such longer period as the Trustee may permit) following the service by the Trustee on the Issuer of notice requiring the same to be remedied; or

---

[33]   See, eg, *The Angelic Star* [1988] 1 Lloyd's Rep 122 (provision requiring payment of interest for the full term would be penal). One example, common in bank loan agreements, of a requirement to pay future interest that would be unlikely to be penal would be a requirement to pay the interest accruing up to the next interest payment date (on the basis that this is to prevent a funding mismatch for the banks).

[34]   *Dunlop Pneumatic Tyre Co Ltd v New Garage and Motor Co Ltd* [1915] AC 79; *Murray v Leisureplay plc* [2005] EWCA Civ 963. On penalties generally, see *Chitty on Contracts* (29th edn, 2004), paras 26-109–26-133.

[35]   See further **5.14–5.16**.

[36]   The aim of such a provision would normally be to prevent the issuer using the event of default provisions to effect a cheaper redemption. A premium payable on exercise by the issuer of an early redemption option cannot be a penalty, since it does not arise as a result of a breach by the issuer (see *Export Credits Guarantee Dept v Universal Oil Products Co* [1983] 1 WLR 399).

[37]   In other words, if the provision goes further than merely compensating holders for being redeemed early.

(c)   if any indebtedness for borrowed money of the Issuer or any of its Subsidiaries becomes due and repayable prematurely by reason of an event of default (however described), or the Issuer or any of its Subsidiaries fails to make any payment in respect of any indebtedness for borrowed money on the due date for payment, or any security given by the Issuer or any of its Subsidiaries for any indebtedness for borrowed money becomes enforceable, or default is made by the Issuer or any of its Subsidiaries in making any payment due under any guarantee and/or indemnity given by it in relation to any indebtedness for borrowed money of any other person; or

(d)   if any order is made by any competent court or resolution is passed for the winding up or dissolution of the Issuer or any of its Subsidiaries, save for the purposes of reorganisation on terms approved in writing by the Trustee or by an Extraordinary Resolution of the Bondholders; or

(e)   if the Issuer or any of its Subsidiaries ceases or threatens to cease to carry on the whole or a substantial part of its business, save for the purposes of reorganisation on terms approved in writing by the Trustee or by an Extraordinary Resolution of the Bondholders, or the Issuer or any of its Subsidiaries stops or threatens to stop payment of, or is unable to, or admits inability to, pay, its debts (or any class of its debts) as they fall due, or is deemed unable to pay its debts pursuant to or for the purposes of any applicable law, or is adjudicated or found bankrupt or insolvent; or

(f)   if (i) proceedings are initiated against the Issuer or any of its Subsidiaries under any applicable liquidation, insolvency, composition, reorganisation or other similar laws, or an application is made (or documents are filed with a court) for the appointment of an administrative or other receiver, manager, administrator or other similar official, or an administrative or other receiver, manager, administrator or other similar official is appointed, in relation to the Issuer or any of its Subsidiaries or, as the case may be, in relation to the whole or any part of the undertaking or assets of any of them, or an encumbrancer takes possession of the whole or any part of the undertaking or assets of any of them, or a distress, execution, attachment, sequestration or other process is levied, enforced upon, sued out or put in force against the whole or any part of the undertaking or assets of any of them, and (ii) in any case (other than the appointment of an administrator or an administrative receiver appointed following presentation of a petition for an administration order) unless initiated by the relevant company is not discharged within 14 days; or

(g)   if the Issuer or any of its Subsidiaries (or their respective directors or shareholders) initiates or consents to judicial proceedings relating to itself under any applicable liquidation, insolvency, composition, reorganisation or other similar laws (including the obtaining of a moratorium) or makes a conveyance or assignment for the benefit of, or enters into any composition or other arrangement with, its creditors generally (or any class of its creditors) or any meeting is convened to consider a proposal for an arrangement or composition with its creditors generally (or any class of its creditors),

PROVIDED, in the case of any Event of Default other than those described in sub-paragraphs (a) and (d) (in the case of a winding up or dissolution of the Issuer) above, the Trustee shall have certified in writing to the Issuer that the

Event of Default is, in its opinion, materially prejudicial to the interests of the Bondholders.[38]

Other acceleration

5.20   In certain cases, repayment of the loan may be accelerated, or treated as if it had been accelerated, even in the absence of contractual provision. In the case of secured loans, a failure to deliver the prescribed particulars to the Registrar of Companies in accordance with s 395 of the Companies Act 1985 renders the underlying debt immediately repayable.[39] And where a company which has borrowed money on the security of a floating charge (or, a fortiori, a fixed charge) goes into liquidation, the debt becomes immediately repayable and the security enforceable.[40]

Purchase

5.21   In the case of debt securities, the company is frequently permitted to purchase securities from the holders, which may then either be held, cancelled or reissued. Whether the company has a power of purchase in the absence of a contractual permission to do so is unclear, but where (as is normal) the securities are expressed to rank pari passu and without any preference among themselves, the view generally taken is that it does not. This is because the effect of such a pari passu provision is that no one holder should, in the absence of a contractual permission, be in a position in effect to get payment from the company before the other holders.[41] Whether or not a power of reissue or resale is reserved, debentures[42] that have been redeemed (which term is synonymous with repurchased)[43] may be reissued, either by the same debentures being reissued or by others being issued in their place.[44] On the reissue, the person entitled to the debenture has, and is deemed always to have had, the same priorities as if the debenture had never been redeemed.

---

[38]   This proviso is in practice one of the key distinctions between issues with trustees and those without. In an issue with no trustee, this proviso does not appear and thus each holder is entitled to accelerate his bonds immediately upon the occurrence of the event of default, irrespective of whether it is prejudicial to his interests or not. As to what constitute the 'interests' of the holders, see **12.8(c).**

[39]   Section 395(2).

[40]   *Wallace v Universal Automatic Machines Co* [1894] 2 Ch 547; *Hodson v Tea Co* (1880) 14 ChD 859; *Re Crompton & Co Ltd* [1914] 1 Ch 954.

[41]   On pari passu clauses generally, see the Financial Markets Law Committee paper 'Pari Passu Clauses' (March 2005). Relevant considerations for companies proposing to purchase their own securities, or to procure others to do so on their behalf, include listing requirements, the offences relating to misleading statements and practices under s 397 of the Financial Services and Markets Act 2000, the market abuse regime under s 118 (and related sections) of that Act, and the insider dealing regime under Part V of the Criminal Justice Act 1993.

[42]   As to what constitutes a debenture, see **Chapter 17**.

[43]   See, eg, *Edinburgh Corporation v British Linen Bank* [1913] AC 133 at 140–141 per Viscount Haldane LC.

[44]   Companies Act 1985, s 194. The power of reissue is not available if there is any provision to the contrary, whether express or implied, in the company's articles of association or in any contract entered into by the company, or if the company has, by passing a resolution to that effect or by some other act, manifested its intention that the debentures shall be cancelled.

5.22 A typical purchase provision in a eurobond issue would read as follows:

> (1) The Issuer or any of its Subsidiaries may at any time purchase Bonds (provided that all unmatured Coupons appertaining to the Bonds are purchased with the Bonds) in any manner and at any price.
>
> (2) All Bonds which are purchased by or on behalf of the Issuer or any of its Subsidiaries may, at the option of the Issuer, be held, resold or (together with all relative unmatured Coupons purchased with the Bonds) surrendered to the Principal Paying Agent for cancellation.

INTEREST

5.23 Interest is the 'payment by time for the use of money'.[45] The borrower's obligation to pay interest can be divided into three separate phases, to each of which different rules apply: interest up to the date on which repayment is due ('pre-default interest'), interest from the due date up to the date of judgment or, if earlier, payment ('default interest'), and interest from the date of judgment ('judgment interest').

Pre-default interest

5.24 Pre-default interest is not payable on a loan or a debt security except where statute provides[46] or by agreement.[47] Agreement may, however, be implied from a course of dealing between the parties[48] or from custom (as in the charging of interest on bank overdrafts).[49] In addition, interest is recoverable, in equity, in certain specific circumstances, even in the absence of any agreement or custom to that effect (though subject obviously to

---

[45] *Bennett v Ogston* (1930) 15 TC 374 at 379 per Rowlatt J. See also *Bond v Barrow Haematite Steel Company* [1902] 1 Ch 353 at 363 per Farwell J; *Schulze v Bensted* (1915) 7 TC 30 at 33 per Lord Strathclyde; *Riches v Westminster Bank Ltd* [1947] AC 390 at 396–397 per Viscount Simon and 400 per Lord Wright. For a statutory definition, see National Savings Bank Act 1971, s 27. Money paid in lieu of interest is not itself interest: *Tomkins v Tomkins* (1978) *The Times*, 24 May.

[46] Eg s 24(3) of the Partnership Act 1890 gives a partner a right to interest at the rate of 5% per annum on payments made by him for the purpose of the partnership beyond the amount of capital which he has agreed to subscribe.

[47] See, eg, *Calton v Bragg* (1812) 15 East 223; *Carr v Edwards* (1822) 3 Stark 132; *Higgins v Sargent* (1823) 2 B&C 348; *Page v Newman* (1829) 9 B&C 378; *Foster v Weston* (1830) 6 Bing 709; *Fruhling v Schroeder* (1835) 2 Bing NC 77; *Rhodes v Rhodes* (1860) Johns 653; *Hill v South Staffordshire Rly Co* (1874) LR 18 Eq 154; *Re Gosman* (1881) LR 17 ChD 771; *The London, Chatham and Dover Rly Co v The South Eastern Rly Co* [1893] AC 429; *President of India v La Pintada Compania Navigacion SA* [1985] AC 104; *Mathew v TM Sutton Ltd* [1994] 1 WLR 1455.

[48] See, eg, *Re Marquis of Anglesey* [1901] 2 Ch 548; *Re W W Duncan & Co* [1905] 1 Ch 307; *Great Western Insurance Co v Cunliffe* (1874) 9 Ch App 525; *Admiralty Commrs v Sir R Ropner & Co Ltd* (1917) 86 LJKB 1030.

[49] See **2.3**.

contrary agreement). For example, interest is payable on a mortgage debt,[50] as between principal and surety in respect of sums paid by the surety,[51] and where the obligor is in a fiduciary position towards the obligee.[52] It is normal, obviously, to make express provision for the payment of interest: both as to the frequency of payments[53] and as to the rate (which may be either fixed or floating, ie fixed periodically, usually by reference to a market rate such as LIBOR – the London interbank offered rate). Although the interest is usually expressed to be payable periodically, it nevertheless accrues from day to day.[54]

Default interest

5.25   Default interest may be payable on a debt (a) by agreement, (b) by way of special damages, (c) pursuant to statute, or (d) pursuant to the court's discretion.

(a)   Agreement

5.26   It is normal to provide that interest at the contractual rate (or, often, at a higher default rate – as to which, see below) shall continue to accrue not just until the due date but until actual payment. As with pre-default interest, though, an agreement that interest shall continue to accrue may also be implied from a course of dealing between the parties or from custom. The mere fact that the borrower has agreed to pay pre-default interest, though, will not be sufficient for an agreement to pay default interest to be implied.[55]

(b)   Special damages

5.27   Whereas general damages under the first part of the rule in *Hadley v Baxendale*[56] (ie damages arising in the ordinary course as a result of the

---

[50]   *Mendl v Smith* (1943) 112 LJ Ch 279; *Re Kerr's Policy* (1869) LR 8 Eq 331; *Lippard v Ricketts* (1872) LR 14 Eq 291; *Re King* (1881) LR 17 ChD 191 at 196; *Re Drax* [1903] 1 Ch 781; *Stoker v Elwell* [1942] Ch 243; *Cityland and Property (Holdings) Ltd v Dabrah* [1968] Ch 166 at 182; *Ezekiel v Orakpo* [1997] 1 WLR 340 at 347 per Millett LJ; *Al Wazir v Islamic Press Agency Inc* [2002] 1 Lloyd's Rep 410.

[51]   *Petre v Duncombe* (1851) 20 LJQB 242; *Re Fox, Walker & Co* (1880) 15 ChD 400; *Hitchman v Stewart* (1855) 3 Drew 271.

[52]   *Burdick v Garrick* (1870) LR 5 Ch App 233; *Harsant v Blaine MacDonald & Co* (1887) 56 LJQB 511; *Dominion Coal Co Ltd v Maskinonge Steamship Co Ltd* [1922] 2 KB 132; *Wallersteiner v Moir (No 2)* [1975] QB 373; *Mathew v TM Sutton Ltd* [1994] 1 WLR 1455; *Westdeutsche Landesbank Girozentrale v Islington LBC* [1996] AC 669.

[53]   In loan facilities, the borrower usually has the right to choose one, two, three or six month interest periods (or any other periods agreed to by the banks at the relevant time); in floating rate eurobond issues, interest is payable either quarterly or semi-annually; and in fixed rate eurobond issues and domestic stock issues, interest is usually payable either semi-annually or annually.

[54]   Apportionment Act 1870, ss 2 and 5; *Re Rogers' Trusts* (1863) 1 Dr&Sm 338.

[55]   *Cook v Fowler* (1874) 7 HL 27; *Re Roberts* (1880) 14 ChD 49.

[56]   (1854) 9 Ex 341.

breach) are not recoverable for the late payment of a debt,[57] special damages under the second part of the rule (ie damages flowing from the breach under special circumstances pertaining to the contract and which were known to the defendant or in the reasonable contemplation of the parties when the contract was entered into) are.[58] An example would be where the debtor knows that the creditor needs the funds in order to finance another transaction and that he will, as a consequence of the default, incur borrowing costs elsewhere in order to fund the separate transaction.[59]

(c) Statute

5.28   Examples of statutory provisions conferring a right to default interest include s 189 of the Insolvency Act 1986 (which provides that any debt proved in a winding up bears interest at the official rate, payable out of any surplus remaining after payment of the proved debts) and the Late Payment of Commercial Debts (Interest) Act 1998 (which confers a right to interest on the late payment of debts arising under commercial contracts for the supply of goods or services).[60]

(d) Discretion of the court

5.29   Such a discretion can arise either by statute or in equity.

(i) Statute

Section 35A of the Supreme Court Act 1981[61] confers a general discretion on the High Court, in proceedings for recovery of a debt or damages, to include in the judgment sum simple interest on all or any part of the debt or damages. The interest may be awarded for all or any part of the period from the date on which the cause of action arose to the date of the judgment or, if earlier, the date of payment. An important feature is that the court may award interest on sums paid prior to judgment being given, whereas previously[62] the court could only award interest on sums in respect of which judgment was given.[63] The discretion is not exercisable where interest is already payable for the period in question, whether by virtue of the terms of

---

[57] *The London, Chatham and Dover Railway Co v The South Eastern Railway Co* [1893] AC 429; *Wadsworth v Lydall* [1981] 2 All ER 401; *President of India v La Pintada Compania Navigacion SA* [1985] AC 104.

[58] *Wadsworth v Lydall* [1981] 2 All ER 401; *President of India v La Pintada Compania Navigacion SA* [1985] AC 104.

[59] As in *Wadsworth v Lydall* [1981] 2 All ER 401. However, special damages are, in practice, unlikely to be recoverable in relation to most loan agreements and debt securities, since they normally provide contractually that interest will continue to accrue following a default. This is likely to be construed as placing an agreed limitation on the extent of the borrower's liability (see *Chitty on Contracts* (29th edn, 2004), para 26–124).

[60] Other examples include Bills of Exchange Act 1882, s 57(1)(b) and Taxes Management Act 1970, ss 86–92.

[61] Inserted by the Administration of Justice Act 1982, s 15(1), Sch 1, Part I.

[62] Under s 3 of the Law Reform (Miscellaneous Provisions) Act 1934.

[63] *The Medina Princess* [1962] 2 Lloyd's Rep 17.

the contract or otherwise.[64] The rate of the interest is as the court thinks fit or as rules of court may provide.[65] No such rules have been made,[66] and the approach of the courts has been to award interest at the normal commercial rate at which a plaintiff would have had to borrow money to replace that withheld by a defendant, this being in most cases one per cent per annum above clearing bank base rate.[67] Provisions similar to s 35A are made for the county court by the County Courts Act 1984, s 69.

(ii)   Equity

The court has a general discretion to award interest in equity in a number of circumstances. One example is where a person in a fiduciary position has misapplied money or made use of it for his own benefit.[68] The court may, in its discretion, award simple interest,[69] compound interest[70] or interest at a rate equal to the actual return (whether simple or compound) earnt on the money by the defendant.[71] Another example is where a secured debt which is silent

---

64   Subsection (4).
65   Subsection (1).
66   Although rules have been made in relation to other aspects of s 35A: see CPR, rr 12.6, 14.14, 16.4 and 36.22.
67   *Jaura v Ahmed* [2002] EWCA 210 per Rix LJ; *Tate & Lyle Food and Distribution Ltd v Greater London Council* [1981] 3 All ER 716; *International Military Services Ltd v Capital and Counties plc* [1982] 3 All ER 20 at 30; *Buckingham v Francis* [1986] 2 All ER 738 at 743; *United Bank of Kuwait Ltd v Hammoud* [1988] 3 All ER 418 at 428 per Staughton LJ; *Shearson Lehman Hutton Inc v Maclaine Watson & Co Ltd* [1990] 3 All ER 723. The rate of 1% above base rate, though, is only a presumption and can be varied up or down to meet the plaintiff's particular circumstances (as in *Jaura v Ahmed*, ibid; *Brown v KMR Services* [1995] 2 Lloyd's Rep 513; *Deeny v Gooda Walker (No 4)* [1996] LRLR 168; *Jackson v Royal Bank of Scotland* (CA, 28 June 2000, unreported)). Where the judgment is given in a foreign currency, the court may look to interest rates in the country of the foreign currency (*Kinetics Technology International SpA v Cross Seas Shipping Corp* [2001] Lloyd's Rep 313). Where the plaintiff is a financial institution, the court will usually calculate the rate by reference to LIBOR rather than base rate (see eg *Banque Keyser Ullman SA v Skandia (UK) Insurance Co Ltd* (11 December 1987, unreported); *Birmingham Midshires Mortgage Services v Phillips* [1998] PNLR 468; *Nykredit Mortgage Bank plc v Edward Erdman Group (No 2)* [1997] 1 WLR 1627).
68   *Wallersteiner v Moir (No 2)* [1975] QB 373; *Mathew v TM Sutton Ltd* [1994] 1 WLR 1455. See also *Jones v Foxall* (1852) 15 Beav 388; *Attorney-General v Alford* (1855) 4 De GM&G 843; *Burdick v Garrick* (1870) 5 Ch App 233; *Johnson v The King* [1904] AC 817; *Dominion Coal Co Ltd v Maskinonge Steamship Co Ltd* [1922] 2 KB 132; *President of India v La Pintada Compania Navigacion SA* [1985] AC 104 at 116 per Lord Brandon; *Guardian Ocean v Banco do Brasil* [1994] 2 Lloyd's Rep 152 at 160 per Saville LJ; *Westdeutsche Landesbank Girozentrale v Islington LBC* [1996] AC 669.
69   As in *Bartlett v Barclays Trust Co Ltd (No 2)* [1980] Ch 515. See also *Attorney-General v Alford* (1855) De GM&G 843.
70   As in *Wallersteiner v Moir (No 2)* [1975] QB 373. See also *Jones v Foxall* (1852) 15 Beav 388 at 392; *Burdick v Garrick* (1870) LR 5 Ch App 233; *President of India v La Pintada Compania Navigacion SA* [1985] AC 104 at 116 per Lord Brandon; *Guardian Ocean Cargoes Ltd v Banco do Brasil SA* [1994] 2 Lloyd's Rep 152 at 160 per Saville LJ; *Westdeutsche Landesbank Girozentrale v Islington LBC* [1996] AC 669.
71   As in *Mathew v TM Sutton Ltd* [1994] 1 WLR 1455.

as to interest is paid late: the court may award interest from the date on which repayment was due if it is equitable to do so.[72]

Judgment interest

5.30 Pursuant to s 17 of the Judgments Act 1838, every High Court judgment debt carries interest at such rate as is from time to time prescribed by statutory instrument.[73] Similar provision is made in relation to county court judgment debts by s 74 of the County Courts Act 1984.[74]

5.31 However, the lender may still claim interest at the contractual rate (if that is higher) if the terms of the contract indicate (expressly or impliedly) that interest is intended to continue to accrue after judgment. If not, the contractual right to interest will merge in the judgment, which will carry interest only at the prescribed judgment rate.[75] Consequently, it is usual, in providing (as seen above) that interest at the contractual rate (or, often, at a higher default rate – as to which, see below) shall continue to accrue not just until the due date but until actual payment, to specify that the interest shall accrue 'after as well as before any judgment'.

Default rates

5.32 As mentioned above, where interest is expressed to accrue on overdue amounts, it is common to provide that the rate is to be higher, eg by one or two per cent per annum, than the normal contractual rate, or, sometimes, that the rate is to be the higher of the normal contractual rate and the statutory judgment debt rate. There are good reasons for this: not only has the borrower become a higher credit risk for which the lenders feel entitled to be compensated, but also greater time and expense on the part of the lenders are needed in attempting to resolve the situation. The primary concern regarding the validity of a default rate of interest is whether it is

---

[72] *Farquhar v Morris* (1797) 7 Term Rep 124; *Ex parte Hirtzel* (1858) 3 De G&J 464; *Re Kerr's Policy* (1869) LR 8 Eq 331; *Lippard v Rickets* (1872) LR 14 Eq 291; *Re Drax* [1903] 1 Ch 781; *Stoker v Elwell* [1942] Ch 243; *Mendl v Smith* (1943) 112 LJ Ch 279; *Cityland and Property (Holdings) Ltd v Dabrah* [1968] Ch 166; *Ezekiel v Orakpo* [1997] 1 WLR 340; *Al-Wazir v Islamic Press Agency Inc* [2001] TLR 559. It should be noted that the obligation to pay interest is imposed only on the secured property, not the chargor personally.

[73] The current rate is 8% per annum (Judgment Debts (Rate of Interest) Order 1993, SI 1993/564). However, where the judgment debt is expressed in a currency other than sterling, the court has a discretion to vary this rate (Administration of Justice Act 1970, s 44A). The interest runs from the date on which the judgment is given unless a rule in another Part of the Civil Procedure Rules or a practice direction makes different provision or the court orders otherwise (CPR, r 40.8(1)).

[74] The current rate is 8% per annum, but the section has only been applied to certain judgment debts: see County Courts (Interest on Judgment Debts) Order 1991, SI 1991/1184.

[75] *Re European Central Railway Co* (1876) 4 ChD 33; *Re Sneyd ex parte Fewings* (1883) 25 ChD 338; *Arbuthnot v Bunsilall* (1890) 62 LT 234; *Economic Life Assurance Society v Usborne* [1902] AC 147; *London Borough of Ealing v El Isaac* [1980] 2 All ER 548; *Director General of Fair Trading v First National Bank plc* [2002] 1 AC 481 (in particular at 487–488 per Lord Bingham and 505–506 per Lord Millett).

void as a penalty: as seen earlier,[76] this would be the case if the increase in the rate did not represent a genuine pre-estimate of the probable loss arising from the default (and was not justified for some other reason). An increase of one per cent per annum has been held not to be a penalty,[77] and it is thought unlikely, given the reasons for default rates described above, that an increase of two or three per cent per annum would be regarded as penal. It is also presumably unlikely that the statutory judgment debt rate would be regarded as penal.[78]

5.33   Other possible threats to the validity of a default rate (and, indeed, also to any pre-default rate) include the court's powers to set aside interest rates pursuant to the Consumer Credit Act 1974 or the Unfair Terms in Consumer Contract Regulations 1999[79] and to set aside extortionate credit transactions pursuant to s 244 of the Insolvency Act 1986,[80] and the court's residual equitable jurisdiction to set aside transactions where one party has acted extortionately, oppressively or coercively towards the other.[81]

Compound interest

5.34   An agreement to pay compound interest, ie interest on unpaid interest, is valid.[82] In the absence of such an agreement, interest on loans is simple rather than compound interest,[83] unless agreement to the contrary can

---

[76] At **5.17**.

[77] *Lordsvale Finance plc v Bank of Zambia* [1996] QB 752 (though, if the increase operated retrospectively, it might be a penalty: ibid). Contrast *Jeancharm Ltd v Barnet Football Club Ltd* [2003] EWCA Civ 58, applying *Lordsvale* and striking down as penal an interest rate equivalent to 260% per annum for late payments.

[78] See eg *All-In-One Design & Build Ltd v Motcomb Estates Ltd* (2000) *The Times*, 4 April, in which the enhanced rate of interest of up to 10% per annum above base rate awardable pursuant to CPR, r 36.21 was held not to be penal. In any event, it would appear that the doctrine of penalties can be circumvented by providing for a rate of interest that is higher than required and a reduction in the rate in the event of punctual payment: *Herbert v Salisbury and Yeovil Railway Co* (1866) 2 Eq 221 at 224; *Wallingford v Mutual Society* (1880) 5 App Cas 685; *Maclaine v Gatty* [1921] 1 AC 376; *Thompson v Hudson* (1869) 4 HL 1; *Lordsvale Finance plc v Bank of Zambia* [1996] QB 752 at 762 and 764.

[79] SI 1999/2083.

[80] The power is exercisable if the company goes into administration or liquidation within three years of the relevant provision of credit.

[81] See *Alec Lobb (Garages) Ltd v Total Oil GB Ltd* [1985] 1 All ER 303.

[82] *Fergusson v Fyffe* (1841) 8 Cl&Fin 121; *Ex parte Bevan* (1803) 9 Ves 223; *Morgan v Mather* (1792) 2 Ves Jun 15; *Clarkson v Henderson* (1880) LR 14 ChD 348; *Wrigley v Gill* [1906] 1 Ch 165.

[83] *Page v Broom* (1837) 4 Cl&Fin 436; *Fergusson v Fyffe* (1841) 8 Cl&Fin 121; *Williamson v Williamson* (1869) LR 7 Eq 542.

be implied from a previous course of dealing or from custom.[84] Default interest awarded by the court pursuant to s 35A of the Supreme Court Act 1981 can only be simple interest,[85] but, as seen earlier, default interest awarded by the court pursuant to its equitable jurisdiction can, at its discretion, be either simple or compound.[86] Judgment interest pursuant to s 17 of the Judgments Act 1838 is only simple interest.

Effect of liquidation

5.35 The foregoing description is subject to special rules applicable in the event that the company goes into liquidation, and which are contained in s 189 of the Insolvency Act 1986 and r 4.93 of the Insolvency Rules 1986.[87] Where a debt proved in the liquidation bears interest, that interest is provable as part of the debt insofar as it relates to the period up to the commencement of the liquidation.[88] Furthermore, in certain circumstances, interest up to the commencement of liquidation may be proved for even where the debt does not bear interest.[89] These circumstances are: (a) where the debt is due by virtue of a written instrument, and payable at a certain time, in which event interest may be claimed from that time to the commencement of liquidation,[90] and (b) where the debt is due otherwise, and before the commencement of liquidation the creditor had demanded in writing payment of the debt and given notice that interest would be payable from the date of demand to the date of payment,[91] in which event interest may be claimed from the date of demand to the commencement of liquidation.[92] In both (a) and (b), the rate of interest provable is the judgment debt rate under s 17 of the Judgments Act 1838.[93]

5.36 Whereas r 4.93 determines the extent to which interest accrued up to the commencement of liquidation may be proved for, s 189 determines the extent to which the amount proved for bears interest after the commencement of liquidation. The basic principle is that the whole amount

---

[84] For example, banking custom permits interest on a customer's indebtedness to be added periodically to the principal, thereby achieving compounding (see eg *Parr's Banking Co. Ltd. v Yates* [1898] 2 QB 460 at 467; *Yourell v Hibernian Bank Ltd* [1918] AC 372 at 385 per Lord Atkinson; *IRC v Holder* [1931] 2 KB 81 at 96 per Lord Hanworth MR and 98–100 per Romer LJ (affirmed on different grounds, *Holder v IRC* [1932] AC 624); *Paton v IRC* [1938] AC 341 at 357 and 364; *National Bank of Greece SA v Pinios Shipping Co (No 1)* [1990] 1 AC 637; *Kitchen v HSBC Bank plc* [2000] 1 All ER (Comm) 787). A different rule applies, however, to mortgage accounts where, in the absence of contrary agreement (either express or implied, eg from a course of dealings), simple interest only can be charged (*Daniell v Sinclair* (1881) LR 6 App Cas 181; *Kitchen v HSBC Bank plc* [2000] 1 All ER (Comm) 787 at 792 per Brooke LJ).
[85] See subs (1).
[86] See **5.29(ii)**.
[87] SI 1986/1925, as amended.
[88] Rule 4.93(1).
[89] Rule 4.93(2).
[90] Rule 4.93(3).
[91] Rule 4.93(4).
[92] Rule 4.93(5).
[93] Rule 4.93(6). See **5.30**.

(including the interest proved for) bears statutory interest at the official rate.[94] The official rate is the higher of the judgment debt rate under s 17 of the Judgments Act 1838[95] and the rate which would otherwise be applicable to the debt apart from the liquidation.[96] However, interest after the commencement of liquidation is only payable out of any surplus remaining after the payment of debts proved for in the liquidation (but before application of that surplus for any other purpose).[97] All interest under s 189 ranks equally, irrespective of whether the debt in respect of which it is payable is secured or subordinated.[98]

5.37 Where, however, the creditor goes into liquidation, the right to continue charging interest is unaffected (except to the extent that the contract provides otherwise).[99]

CONVERTIBLE SECURITIES[100]

Generally

(a) Conversion periods and adjustment events

5.38 Debt securities are sometimes issued on the basis that they are convertible at the option of the holders into fully paid shares of the company.[101] Loan stock is traditionally convertible only once a year for a one-month period after the company's annual report has been published, whereas eurobonds are normally convertible at any time from the start of the conversion period[102] until shortly before maturity.

---

[94] Subsection (1).

[95] See **5.30**.

[96] Subsection (4).

[97] Subsection (2).

[98] Subsection (3).

[99] *Bank of Credit and Commerce International SA v Malik* [1996] BCC 15.

[100] See generally Tennekoon, *The Law and Regulation of International Finance* (1991), pp 253–274; Aldred, *Convertibles and Warrants* (1987); Das, *Structured Products & Hybrid Securities* (2001), Chapter 9; Fisher, *Eurosecurities and Their Related Derivatives* (1997), pp 257–266; Choudhry, *Corporate Bond Markets* (2006), pp 295–331.

[101] On the reasons for issuing convertible debt securities, see Burgess, *Corporate Finance Law* (2nd edn, 1992), p 306; Tennekoon, *The Law and Regulation of International Finance* (1991), pp 254–256; Wood, *International Loans, Bonds and Securities Regulation* (1995), pp 146 and 147; Das, *Structured Products & Hybrid Securities* (2001), pp 371 373; Choudhry, *Corporate Bond Markets* (2006), pp 304–306.

[102] Which is usually at or shortly after the date of issue of the securities, but may sometimes be later (eg two or three years after issue).

5.39 As the debt is, in commercial terms, contingent equity, it is usual to provide that the conversion 'price'[103] is adjusted on the occurrence of certain specified events, so that the holder's contingent interest in the share capital of the company is not diluted. The practice in convertible eurobond issues is for the conversion price to be adjusted for any event which would otherwise reduce the bondholder's potential percentage interest in the company (thus, for example, an issue of shares at below market price to third parties would result in an adjustment, even though the existing shareholders receive no compensation),[104] whereas the practice in convertible loan stock issues is only to confer on the stockholder the equivalent of the benefits which he would have received had he been a shareholder. Thus, it is usual in convertible loan stock for the only adjustment events to be rights issues of ordinary shares and capitalisation issues, with a requirement that any offer to the shareholders be accompanied by a 'like offer' to the stockholders.

(b) Example adjustment provisions

5.40 In a domestic stock issue:

1.1 Capitalisation

Upon any allotment of Ordinary Share Capital pursuant to a capitalisation of profits or reserves (including, without limitation, share premium account and capital redemption reserve) to any Ordinary Shareholders on the register on a record date being a date on which any Stock remains capable of being converted, the nominal amount of Ordinary Share Capital to be allotted in respect of Stock converted on any Conversion Date following such record date shall be increased in due proportion.

1.2 Rights issue

If, whilst any Stock remains capable of being converted, the Issuer shall make any offer of Ordinary Shares ('New Shares') by way of rights to Ordinary Shareholders for which a listing on The Stock Exchange is obtained then the conversion rate shall be adjusted with effect on and from the record date for each such offer so that the nominal amount of Ordinary Share Capital thereafter allotted in respect of every £100 nominal of Stock converted shall be increased by an amount (expressed in pence) equal to:

$$\frac{A \times C}{B + C}$$

---

[103] Which can be expressed either as a rate (ie x shares per £100 nominal of debt) or as a price (ie £x per share). The issue price of convertible securities must not, when taken in conjunction with the conversion price, be such as to enable conversion to result in the shares being issued at a discount: *Mosely v Koffyfontein Mines Ltd* [1904] 2 Ch 108. The normal practice is to fix the conversion price at the time of issue of the securities at a premium to the then market price of the shares. It is generally regarded as attractive to the holders to convert when both the market price of the shares has risen above the conversion price and the dividend rate on the shares has risen above the interest rate on the convertible securities.

[104] Although, it is argued, they instead, unlike the bondholders, have control over the making of such an issue.

where:

A   equals the nominal amount (expressed in pence) of the New
           Shares which would have been offered to a holder of £100
           nominal of Stock had his Conversion Rights been
           exercisable and exercised in full with effect immediately
           before the record date for such offer at the conversion rate
           than applicable (such nominal amount to include any
           fraction of a New Share notwithstanding that under the offer
           fractional entitlements may not be offered or allotted or may
           be disregarded);

B   equals the price per share (expressed in pence) at which the
           New Shares are being offered to Ordinary Shareholders; and

C   equals the average (expressed in pence) of the middle
           market quotations on The Stock Exchange (calculated by
           reference to The Stock Exchange Daily Official List) for the
           rights to the New Shares nil paid for all dealing days during
           the period in which the rights to the New Shares are dealt in
           on The Stock Exchange nil paid.

5.41   In a eurobond issue (in this example, an issue with a trustee):[105]

The Conversion Price shall be adjusted as set out in the Trust Deed upon the
happening of any of the following events:

(i)   An alteration to the nominal value of the Ordinary Shares as a result
       of consolidation or subdivision.

(ii)   The issue by the Issuer wholly for cash of any Ordinary Shares
       (other than Ordinary Shares issued on exercise of the Conversion
       Rights or issued on the exercise of any other rights of conversion
       into or exchange or subscription for Ordinary Shares) at less than 95
       per cent of the Current Market Price (as defined in the Trust Deed)
       per Ordinary Share on the dealing day next preceding the date of the
       announcement of the terms of the issue of such Ordinary Shares.

(iii) The issue by or on behalf of the Issuer or any of its subsidiaries
       (other than pursuant to paragraph (x) below) wholly for cash of any
       securities (other than the Bonds) which by their terms of issue are
       convertible into or exchangeable or carry rights of subscription for
       Ordinary Shares ('Convertible Securities') at a consideration per
       Ordinary Share which is less than 95 per cent of the Current Market
       Price per Ordinary Share on the dealing day next preceding the date
       of the announcement of the terms of issue of such Convertible
       Securities.

(iv)   The grant by or on behalf of the Issuer or any of its subsidiaries in
       respect of any existing securities of rights of conversion into or
       exchange for Ordinary Shares or rights of subscription for Ordinary
       Shares so that the consideration per Ordinary Share receivable is
       less than 95 per cent of the Current Market Price per Ordinary Share

---

[105]   The normal practice is to describe the triggering events in the terms and conditions (endorsed on the
        bonds), and to set out the detailed formulae for calculating the adjustments in the trust deed. For
        brevity, only the former are reproduced here.

on the dealing day next preceding the date of the announcement of the terms of such grant.

(v) Any modification (other than pursuant to their terms) of the rights of conversion, exchange or subscription attaching to any Convertible Securities so that, following such modification, the consideration per Ordinary Share receivable is less than the Current Market Price per Ordinary Share on the dealing day next preceding the date of the announcement of the proposals for such modification.

(vi) The issue by the Issuer of any Ordinary Shares credited as fully paid to the Ordinary Shareholders by way of capitalisation of profits or reserves, other than a Scrip Dividend (as defined in the Trust Deed) where the Market Value (as defined in the Trust Deed) of the Ordinary Shares issued in respect of each existing Ordinary Share does not exceed the amount of the cash dividend (or the relevant part thereof where scrip is offered in place of part of the cash dividend) in respect of each existing Ordinary Share.

(vii) The payment or making by the Issuer of any Capital Distribution (as defined in the Trust Deed) to the Ordinary Shareholders (except where the Conversion Price falls to be adjusted under paragraph (vi) above).

(viii) The issue by or on behalf of the Issuer or any of its subsidiaries of any Ordinary Shares to the Ordinary Shareholders by way of rights, or there shall be so issued or so granted to Ordinary Shareholders any options, warrants or other rights to subscribe for or purchase Ordinary Shares, in each case at less than 95 per cent of the Current Market Price per Ordinary Share on the dealing day next preceding the date of the announcement of the terms of such issue or grant.

(ix) The offer by or on behalf of the Issuer or any of its subsidiaries or (at the direction or request of or pursuant to any arrangements with the Issuer or any of its subsidiaries) by any other company, person or entity of any securities in connection with which offer the holders of Ordinary Shares generally (meaning for these purposes the holders of at least 60 per cent of the Ordinary Shares outstanding at the time such offer is made) are entitled to participate by way of rights in arrangements whereby such securities may be acquired by them and the Conversion Price does not fall to be adjusted under paragraph (viii) above or paragraph (x) below.

(x) The issue by or on behalf of the Issuer or any of its subsidiaries of any securities (other than Ordinary Shares) by way of rights to Ordinary Shareholders or the grant of any options, warrants or other rights to Ordinary Shareholders entitling them to subscribe for or purchase any such securities by way of rights.

(xi) The determination by the Issuer (with the approval of the Trustee) that an adjustment should be made to the Conversion Price as a result of one or more events or circumstances not referred to in any of paragraphs (i) to (x) above (in which case the Issuer shall, at its own expense and acting reasonably, forthwith request the Auditors (in conjunction with an investment bank in London of international repute selected by the Issuer and approved by the Trustee) to determine as soon as practicable what adjustment (if any) to the Conversion Price is fair and reasonable to take account thereof)

provided that (A) the adjustment would result in a reduction in the
Conversion Price, and (B) the Auditors and such merchant or
investment bank are so requested to make such a determination not
more than 21 days after the occurrence of the relevant event or
circumstances.

Covenants

5.42 It is also usual for the company to give certain covenants for the
protection of the conversion rights, eg not to reduce share capital, not to
modify the rights attaching to the shares into which the holders can convert,
not to issue shares with more favourable rights, etc.[106] Certain of these
covenants may, however, be ineffective as a result of the decision of the
House of Lords in *Russell v Northern Bank Development Corporation Ltd
and Others*.[107] Their Lordships held that any provision in an agreement to
which the company is a party (and also, possibly, the whole agreement) is
void if it is inconsistent with a direct statutory power (eg the power under
s 135 of the Companies Act 1985 to reduce capital by special resolution if
authorised by the articles, or the power under s 9 of the Companies Act 1985
to alter the articles by special resolution).[108] As a result of the decision, the
practice has now developed in issues of convertible securities of: (a)
incorporating a severability clause, so that, if any covenant is void, it does
not taint the others or indeed the whole agreement; and (b) providing that
breaches of the covenants also take effect as events of default, so that, if they
are void as covenants, they nevertheless are still capable of triggering a
prepayment obligation.

5.43 A typical set of covenants (in this example, in a eurobond issue with
a trustee) would read as follows:

Whilst any Conversion Right remains exercisable, the Issuer will, save with the
approval of an Extraordinary Resolution (as defined in the Trust Deed) or with
the prior written approval of the Trustee where, in the Trustee's opinion, it is
not materially prejudicial to the interests of the Bondholders to give such
approval:

(a)   at all times keep available for issue free from pre-emptive rights out of its
authorised but unissued capital such number of Ordinary Shares as would

---

[106] Similar covenants are also often given in loan agreements, in order to protect the banks against
favourable treatment by the company of its shareholders.

[107] [1992] 3 All ER 161.

[108] The decision is contrary to previous authority to the effect that, whereas a company cannot preclude
itself from altering its articles, it can nevertheless be liable if the alteration is in breach of a
contractual obligation to a third party: see, eg, *Allen v Gold Reefs of West Africa Ltd* [1900] 1 Ch 656
at 673 per Lindley MR; *Baily v British Equitable Assurance Co* [1904] 1 Ch 374 at 385 (reversed on
other grounds [1906] AC 35); *British Murac Syndicate Ltd v Alperton Rubber Co Ltd* [1915] 2 Ch
186; *Southern Foundries (1926) Ltd v Shirlaw* [1940] AC 701 at 740–741 per Lord Porter; *Cumbrian
Newspapers Group Ltd v Cumberland & Westmorland Herald Newspaper & Printing Co Ltd* [1986]
BCLC 286 at 305–306. See also Davenport [1993] LQR 553 and [1993] *Butterworths' JIBFL*, p 469;
McGlynn [1994] Co Lawyer 301.

enable the Conversion Rights and all other rights of subscription and exchange for and conversion into Ordinary Shares to be satisfied in full;

(b)   not issue or pay up any securities, in either case by way of capitalisation of profits or reserves, other than (i) by the issue of fully paid Ordinary Shares to the Ordinary Shareholders and other persons entitled thereto or (ii) by the issue of Ordinary Shares paid up in full out of profits or reserves (in accordance with applicable law) and issued wholly, ignoring fractional entitlements, in lieu of a cash dividend or (iii) by the issue of fully paid equity share capital (other than Ordinary Shares) to the holders of equity share capital of the same class and other persons entitled thereto, unless in any such case the same gives rise (or would, but for the fact that the adjustment would be less than one per cent of the Conversion Price then in effect, give rise) to an adjustment of the Conversion Price;

(c)   not in any way modify the rights attaching to the Ordinary Shares with respect of voting, dividends or liquidation nor issue any other class of equity share capital carrying any rights which are more favourable than such rights but so that nothing in this paragraph (c) shall prevent (i) the issue of any equity share capital to employees (including directors holding executive office) whether of the Issuer or any of its subsidiary or associated companies by virtue of their office or employment pursuant to any scheme or plan approved by the Issuer in general meeting or which is established pursuant to such a scheme or plan which is or has been so approved, or (ii) any consolidation or subdivision of the Ordinary Shares or the conversion of any Ordinary Shares into stock or vice versa, or (iii) any modification of such rights which is not, in the opinion of an investment bank in London of international repute selected by the Issuer, approved in writing by the Trustee and acting as an expert, materially prejudicial to the interests of the holders of the Bonds, or (iv) without prejudice to any rule of law or legislation (including regulations made under section 207 of the Companies Act 1989 or any other provision of that or any other legislation), the conversion of Ordinary Shares into, or the issue of any Ordinary Shares in, uncertificated form (or the conversion of Ordinary Shares in uncertificated form into certificated form), or the amendment of the Articles of Association of the Issuer to enable title to securities of the Issuer (including Ordinary Shares) to be evidenced and transferred without a written instrument, or any other alteration to the Articles of Association of the Issuer made in connection with the matters described in this paragraph or which is supplemental or incidental to any of the foregoing (including any amendment made to enable or to facilitate procedures relating to such matters and any amendment dealing with the rights and obligations of holders of securities, including Ordinary Shares, dealt with under such procedures), or (v) any issue of equity share capital where the issue of such equity share capital results or would, but for the fact that the adjustment would be less than one per cent of the Conversion Price then in effect or that the consideration per Ordinary Share receivable therefor (as described in Condition [   ]) is at least 95 per cent of the Current Market Price (as defined in the Trust Deed) per Ordinary Share, result in an adjustment of the Conversion Price;

(d)   procure that no securities (whether issued by the Issuer or any of its Subsidiaries or procured by the Issuer or any of its Subsidiaries to be issued) issued without rights to convert into or exchange or subscribe for

Ordinary Shares shall subsequently include such rights exercisable at a consideration per Ordinary Share which is less than 95 per cent of the Current Market Price per Ordinary Share at the close of business on the last dealing day preceding the date of the announcement of the proposed inclusion of such rights unless the same gives rise (or would, but for the fact that the adjustment would be less than one per cent of the Conversion Price then in effect, give rise) to an adjustment of the Conversion Price and that at no time shall there be in issue Ordinary Shares of differing nominal values;

(e)   not make any issue, grant or distribution or take any other action if the effect thereof would be that, on the conversion of Bonds, Ordinary Shares would (but for the provisions of Condition [   ]) have to be issued at a discount or otherwise could not, under any applicable law then in effect, be legally issued as fully paid;

(f)   not reduce its issued share capital, share premium account or capital redemption reserve or any uncalled liability in respect thereof except (i) pursuant to the terms of issue of the relevant share capital, or (ii) by means of a purchase or redemption of share capital of the Issuer which would not constitute a Capital Distribution (as defined in the Trust Deed), or (iii) as permitted by section 130(2) of the Companies Act 1985, or (iv) where the reduction results (or would, but for the fact that the adjustment would be less than one per cent of the Conversion Price then in effect, result) in an adjustment of the Conversion Price;

(g)   if any offer is made to all (or as nearly as may be practicable all) Ordinary Shareholders (or all (or as nearly as may be practicable, all) Ordinary Shareholders other than the offeror and/or any associates of the offeror (as defined in section 430E(4) of the Companies Act 1985 or any modification or re-enactment thereof) to acquire all or a majority of the issued ordinary share capital of the Issuer, or if any person proposes a scheme with regard to such acquisition, give notice of such offer or scheme to the Bondholders at the same time as any notice thereof is sent to the Ordinary Shareholders (or as soon as practicable thereafter) stating that details concerning such offer or scheme may be obtained from the specified offices of the Paying and Conversion Agents and, where such an offer or scheme has been recommended by the Board of Directors of the Issuer or where such an offer has become or been declared unconditional in all respects, use all reasonable endeavours to procure that a like offer or scheme is extended to the holders of any Ordinary Shares issued during the period of the offer or scheme arising out of the exercise of the Conversion Rights and to the holders of the Bonds; and

(h)   use all reasonable endeavours to ensure that the Ordinary Shares issued upon conversion of any Bonds will be admitted to the Official List by the UK Listing Authority and to trading on the London Stock Exchange's market for listed securities and will be listed, quoted or dealt in on any other stock exchange or securities market on which the Ordinary Shares may then be listed or quoted or dealt in.

For the above purposes 'ordinary share capital' has the meaning ascribed to it in section 832 of the Income and Corporation Taxes Act 1988 and 'equity share capital' has the meaning ascribed to it in section 744 of the Companies Act 1985.

Companies Act 1985, ss 80 and 89

5.44 Convertible securities constitute 'relevant securities' for the purposes of s 80 of the Companies Act 1985,[109] and therefore the directors must be authorised pursuant to that section prior to allotting any convertible securities.[110] If the shares to be issued on conversion constitute 'relevant shares',[111] the convertible securities will constitute 'equity securities' for the purposes of s 89 of the Companies Act 1985[112] and therefore, if they are to be allotted fully for cash, they must be offered to the existing shareholders on a pre-emptive basis, unless that section has been disapplied pursuant to s 95.[113] In the context of takeover offers, convertible securities are treated as shares for the purposes of ss 428 to 430F of the Companies Act 1985.[114]

Put and call rights

5.45 Since the expectation of both the company and the investors is that the market price of the shares will increase during the life of the convertible securities to a level which exceeds the conversion price, a value is attributable to the conversion right. This enables the company to pay a lower rate of interest on the convertible securities than it would if it were issuing a 'straight' (or non-convertible) debt security.

5.46 As protection for the investors, it is common, in convertible eurobond issues, to include a 'put' option. This allows each investor to require the company to redeem its bonds at a specified future date (usually five years after the issue date). The amount payable includes a premium which, together with the interest already paid on the bonds, gives the investor a yield to the date of redemption similar to that which he would have expected on a comparable 'straight' bond. Investors are thus assured a reasonable commercial rate of return on their investment even if the company's share price fails to perform as expected.

---

[109] See subs (2).
[110] However, no further authority is required for the issue of the shares on conversion, as that does not constitute an allotment for the purposes of the section: see subs (2).
[111] As defined in s 94(5) of the Companies Act 1985.
[112] See s 94(1).
[113] However, s 89 does not apply to the issue of the shares on conversion: see s 94(2). Guidelines as to the maximum extent of disapplication that institutional shareholders should support have been drawn up by the 'Pre-emption Group', a working party consisting of representatives from the Association of British Insurers, the National Association of Pension Funds and certain UK public companies, and are available from the website of the Institutional Voting Information Service.
[114] See s 430F.

5.47   If the share price has performed, though, the company will be entitled to give notice of redemption of the bonds. As the redemption price would be either only par or at a small premium to par, it is thus more attractive to investors to convert, and the company thus 'forces' conversion by the investors. In order not to undermine the put right described above, this 'call' right should only be exercisable after the put date has passed.[115]

5.48   The put right thus protects the investors if the share price has not performed, and the call right enables the company to 'force' conversion if it has.

Comparison with warrants

5.49   As an alternative to issuing convertible debt securities, debt securities may be issued with warrants attached, giving the holder an option to subscribe a specified amount of cash for shares of the company (or its parent or subsidiary) at a specified 'exercise' price (which is subject to adjustment in a similar way to a conversion price). The key differences between convertible debt securities and warrants are:

(a)   Unlike conversion rights, warrants are usually detachable and can therefore be traded separately from the debt securities.

(b)   Once a warrant has been detached, the warrant holder is speculating solely on the performance of the share price, and does not receive income in the meantime; whereas the holder of a convertible debt security will be receiving interest.

(c)   On conversion of a convertible debt security, no consideration is payable by the investor (the subscription price of the shares being paid by set-off of the principal amount of the debt securities, which are surrendered to the company). Consequently, conversion results in a reduction of the company's loan capital and an increase in its equity capital. On exercise of a warrant, the subscription price is payable by

---

[115]   For an illustration of the difficulties that can be caused by a lack of precision, see *The Law Debenture Trust Corporation plc v Bell Resources Financial Services NV* (CA, 31 July 1992; *Butterworths JIBFL* (1991) Vol 6, p 630 and (1992) Vol 7, p 603). The holders had a put right, entitling them to redemption on 13 November 1991 at 117.70% (to compensate them if the share price did not perform and conversion was therefore unattractive). The issuer had a call right (at a lower percentage), subject to the proviso that the bonds could not be so redeemed *prior to* (as opposed to 'on or prior to') 13 November 1991 unless the share price over a specified period was at least 130% of the conversion price. The notice period for exercise of the call right commenced earlier than the notice period for exercise of the put right, and the put provisions stated that the put right could not be exercised for bonds in respect of which a call notice had already been given. The issuer gave notice to redeem the bonds on 13 November 1991 (at 103%), on the basis that the share price condition did not need to be satisfied, and that the call right (being exercised first) overrode any subsequent exercise by the holders of the put right. At first instance, Ferris J upheld the issuer's interpretation, but the decision was reversed by the Court of Appeal.

the holder. The company's equity capital will therefore be increased without any change in its loan capital (unless, of course, it applies the funds received on exercise of the warrants in redeeming or purchasing the original debt securities).

Chapter Six

SECURITY[1]

TYPES OF SECURITY INTEREST

6.1 It was seen earlier[2] that the term 'security' has traditionally been used to describe 'something which makes the enjoyment or enforcement of a right more secure or certain'. It therefore embraces (a) rights enabling the creditor to look to a third party for satisfaction[3] and (b) rights enabling the creditor to have recourse to particular property in priority to other creditors.[4] We are concerned here with the latter, ie rights giving the creditor a proprietary interest in property. There are four types of 'consensual' (ie granted by agreement, rather than by operation of law) security interests:[5] mortgage,[6] charge, pledge and contractual lien.

Mortgage

6.2 'The essential nature of a mortgage is that it is a conveyance of a legal or equitable interest in property, with a provision for redemption, ie that upon repayment of a loan or the performance of some other obligation the conveyance shall become void or the interest shall be reconveyed.'[7] This general principle has, however, to be read subject to ss 85, 86 and 87 of the Law of Property Act 1925 (dealt with below), which apply special rules to the creation of legal mortgages of land.

6.3 Mortgages can be either legal or equitable. A legal mortgage is one over a legal interest in property which complies with the formalities

---

[1] See generally *Fisher and Lightwood's Law of Mortgage* (11th edn, 2002); Gough, *Company Charges* (2nd edn, 1996); Goode, *Legal Problems of Credit and Security* (3rd edn, 2003); Wood, *Comparative Law of Security and Guarantees* (1995); Lingard, *Bank Security Documents* (3rd edn, 1993); *Paget's Law of Banking* (12th edn, 2002), Part VII; *Encylopaedia of Banking Law*, Div E; Ellinger, Lomnicka and Hooley, *Ellinger's Modern Banking Law* (4th edn, 2006), Chapters 18–21; Ferran, *Company Law and Corporate Finance* (1999), Chapter 15; Cranston, *Principles of Banking Law* (2nd edn, 2002), Chapter 15; Calnan, *Taking Security: Law and Practice* (2006).

[2] In **Chapter 3**.

[3] Such as guarantees and indemnities, considered in **Chapter 11**.

[4] See, eg, *Bristol Airport plc v Powdrill* [1990] Ch 744 at 760 per Browne-Wilkinson V-C.

[5] See *Re Cosslett (Contractors) Ltd* [1989] Ch 495 at 508 per Millett LJ.

[6] In certain cases (eg where the subject matter is a chose in action) referred to instead as an assignment.

[7] Megarry and Wade, *The Law of Real Property* (6th edn, 2000), p 1169. See also *Santley v Wilde* [1899] 2 Ch 474 per Lindley MR; *Noakes & Co Ltd v Rice* [1902] AC 24 at 28 per Lord Halsbury LC; *London County & Westminster Bank Ltd v Tompkins* [1918] 1 KB 515; *Re Bond Worth Ltd* [1980] Ch 228 at 250; *Swiss Bank Corporation v Lloyds Bank Ltd* [1982] AC 584 at 595 per Buckley LJ.

applicable to the type of property in question.[8] There are two types of equitable mortgage: first, a mortgage over an equitable interest in property (such as an interest under a trust);[9] and, secondly, a mortgage over a legal interest in property that fails to comply with the formal requirements of a legal mortgage but is recognised in equity as a mortgage.[10]

Charge

6.4   For practical purposes, there is today little difference between a mortgage and a charge.[11] In conceptual terms, though, 'a mortgage is a conveyance of property subject to a right of redemption, whereas a charge conveys nothing and merely gives the chargee certain rights over the property as security for the loan'.[12]

6.5   Charges (in the strict sense of the term) exist only in equity,[13] except for marine hypothecations (now largely obsolete) and in the case of land (the Law of Property Act 1925 providing[14] for a charge expressed to be by way of

---

8   See **6.12** to **6.32**.
9   Such a mortgage must be in writing to be valid: Law of Property Act 1925, s 53(1)(c) (which applies to equitable interests in personalty as well as realty; *Grey v IRC* [1960] AC 1; *Oughtred v IRC* [1960] AC 206; *Vandervell v IRC* [1967] 2 AC 291; see also Green [1984] MLR 385). Cf *Neville v Wilson* [1996] 3 WLR 460.
10   Where such a mortgage is of personalty, there is no requirement for writing (since Law of Property Act 1925, s 53(1)(c) only applies to mortgages of equitable interests, not equitable mortgages of legal interests; see also *Tibbits v George* (1836) 5 Ad&E 107; *Gurnell v Gardner* (1863) 4 Giff 626). Where such a mortgage is of an interest in land, however, the old law (that such a mortgage either had to be evidenced in writing (Law of Property Act 1925, s 40; *Mounsey v Rankin* (1885) Cab&El 496) or supported by some act of part performance, such as the deposit of title deeds (*Re Alton Corpn* [1985] BCLC 27)) has been amended by the Law of Property (Miscellaneous Provisions) Act 1989, s 2. That section requires any contract for the disposition of an interest in land (which includes a mortgage of such an interest) to be in writing and signed by or on behalf of each party to the contract. Thus mortgages by deposit of title deeds can no longer be created over an interest in land unless supported by a written memorandum of deposit signed by both mortgagor and mortgagee: *United Bank of Kuwait plc v Sahib* [1997] Ch 107.
11   See, eg, *London County and Westminster Bank Ltd v Tompkins* [1918] 1 KB 515 at 528–529 per Scrutton LJ; *Re Bond Worth Ltd* [1980] Ch 228 at 250; *Swiss Bank Corporation v Lloyds Bank Ltd* [1982] AC 584 at 594–595 per Buckley LJ; *Downsview Nominees Ltd v First City Corpn Ltd* [1993] AC 295 at 311; Jackson (1978) 94 LQR 571 at 574–576. Under the Law of Property Act 1925, mortgages include charges and liens (s 205(1)(xi)); under the Companies Act 1985, charges include mortgages (s 396(4)); under the Land Registration Act 2002, charges include mortgages and liens (s132(1)); and, in the construction of wills, mortgages include charges (but not a vendor's lien for unpaid purchase money) (*Re Beirnstein* [1925] Ch 12 at 18). See also *Brunton v Electrical Engineering Corporation* [1892] 1 Ch 434 ('mortgage or charge' does not include a solicitor's lien over client papers).
12   Megarry and Wade, *The Law of Real Property* (6th edn, 2000), p 1170; see also *Fisher and Lightwood's Law of Mortgage* (11th edn, 2002), pp 5–6; *National Provincial and Union Bank of England v Charnley* [1924] 1 KB 431 at 449–450 per Atkin LJ; *Carreras Rothmans Ltd v Freeman Mathews Treasure Ltd* [1985] Ch 207; *Re Bank of Credit and Commerce International SA (No 8)* [1998] AC 214 at 226 per Lord Hoffmann; *Re Cosslett (Contractors) Ltd* [1998] Ch 495 at 508 per Millett LJ; *Flightline Ltd v Edwards* [2003] 1 WLR 1200 at 1211–1212 per Jonathan Parker LJ; *Re TXU Europe Group plc* [2004] 1 P&CR DG20 at para 35; and the cases cited in the previous footnote.
13   See *Fisher and Lightwood's Law of Mortgage* (11th edn, 2002), p 25; Gough, *Company Charges* (2nd edn, 1996), pp 18–21.
14   In ss 85, 86 and 87; see further **6.13**.

legal mortgage to take effect as a legal mortgage). Charges may also be either fixed (in the sense that the chargee's rights attach immediately to the asset in question) or floating (in the sense that the chargee's rights attach at first only to a shifting pool of assets): floating charges are considered at **6.39ff**.

6.6 Hypothecation is sometimes spoken of as a separate form of security transaction, but it is in fact merely a form of equitable charge over goods created by a document (a 'letter of hypothecation') and used where it is impracticable to give possession of the goods or a document of title to them (eg because they are in the course of manufacture).

Pledge

6.7 The essence of a pledge is the delivery of possession of an asset to the creditor by way of security, but with ownership remaining with the pledgor.[15] In a mortgage, on the other hand, the creditor acquires ownership and the mortgagor usually retains possession.

6.8 Because of the necessity for delivery, land cannot be pledged, and movable assets can only be pledged if they are capable of being delivered. Thus, for example, bearer securities may be pledged by deposit,[16] but registered shares may not.[17] Delivery, however, may be either actual or constructive[18] (such as handing over the keys to the store where the pledged goods are kept, or instructing the custodian of the pledged goods, and the custodian acknowledging to the pledgee, that it will hold the goods to the pledgee's order ('attornment')).

Contractual lien

6.9 Like a pledge, a lien involves possession of the asset by the creditor. 'The difference between them is that in the case of a pledge the owner delivers possession to the creditor as security, whereas in the case of a lien

---

[15] See *Halliday v Holgate* (1868) LR 3 Exch 299 at 302; *Donald v Suckling* (1866) LR 1 QB 585; *Re Morritt* (1886) 18 QBD 222 at 232 per Cotton LJ; *Harrold v Plenty* [1901] 2 Ch 314 at 316 per Cozens-Hardy J; *Mathew v TM Sutton Ltd* [1994] 1 WLR 1455 at 1461 per Chadwick J; *Re Cosslett (Contractors) Ltd* [1998] Ch 495 at 508 per Millett LJ.

[16] *Gorgier v Mieville* (1824) 3 B&C 45; *Donald v Suckling* (1866) LR 1 QB 585; *Carter v Wake* (1877) 4 ChD 605.

[17] Although such a deposit, if accompanied by a blank transfer, may amount to an equitable mortgage: *London and Midland Bank v Mitchell* [1899] 2 Ch 161; *Stubbs v Slater* [1910] 1 Ch 632 at 639; *Harrold v Plenty* [1901] 2 Ch 314.

[18] *Martin v Reid* (1862) 11 CB (NS) 730; *Hilton v Tucker* (1888) 39 ChD 669; *Wrightson v McArthur and Hutchisons (1919) Ltd* [1921] 2 KB 807; *Dublin City Distillery Ltd v Doherty* [1914] AC 823; *Official Assignee of Madras v Mercantile Bank of India Ltd* [1935] AC 53.

the creditor retains possession of goods previously delivered to him for some other purpose.'[19]

6.10   In addition to liens created by contractual agreement, various types of lien can arise by operation of law. Such liens can arise at common law,[20] in equity[21] or under statute.[22]

Quasi-security

6.11   The above are the four categories of true consensual security interests. In addition, a number of other devices are often used to create the same commercial effects as security without in law creating a security interest. These include the reservation of title under a contract of sale,[23] contractual set-off,[24] title transfer[25] and a cash deposit expressed not to be

---

[19]   *Re Cosslett (Contractors) Ltd* [1998] Ch 495 at 508 per Millett LJ. The addition of a contractual power of sale does not convert a contractual lien into a charge (*Re Cosslett (Contractors) Ltd*, ibid; *Re Hamlet International plc* [1999] 2 BCLC 506): 'a true possessory lien depends entirely on possession and is lost with the loss of possession. A charge, on the other hand, exists independent of possession and confers an interest in the property which carries with it a right to resort to the property (as opposed to merely detaining it) to satisfy or discharge some obligation secured by the charge' (*Waitomo Wools (NZ) Ltd v Nelsons (NZ) Ltd* [1974] 1 NZLR 484 at 490 per Richmond J, cited in *Re Hamlet International plc* [1998] 2 BCLC 164 at 171–172 (affd CA [1999] 2 BCLC 506)).

[20]   An example is the garage proprietor's lien upon a car repaired by him (see eg *Green v All Motors Ltd* [1917] 1 KB 625).

[21]   An example is the unpaid vendor's lien: a vendor of land who has not received the full purchase price may (even though he no longer has possession) apply to the court for an order for sale of the land, with the money due being paid to him out of the proceeds.

[22]   An example is a master's maritime lien for liabilities and disbursements (Merchant Shipping Act 1995, s 41).

[23]   Known as a *Romalpa* clause, after the decision in *Aluminium Industrie Vaassen BV v Romalpa Aluminium Ltd* [1976] 2 All ER 552. If full legal title is not retained by the seller, the clause can be construed as a charge, and therefore void against a liquidator, administrator and creditors unless registered at the Companies Registry (*Re Bond Worth Ltd* [1980] Ch 228). See also *Re Curtain Dream plc* [1990] BCLC 925; *Clough Mill Ltd v Martin* [1985] 1 WLR 111; *Borden (UK) Ltd v Scottish Timber Products Ltd* [1981] Ch 25; *Re Weldtech Equipment Ltd* [1991] BCLC 393; *Re Andrabell Ltd* [1984] 3 All ER 407; *Armour v Thyssen Edelstahlwerke AG* [1991] 2 AC 339; *Re Peachdart Ltd* [1984] Ch 131; *Hendy Lennox (Industrial Engines) Ltd v Grahame Puttick Ltd* [1984] 1 WLR 485; *Specialist Plant Services Ltd v Braithwaite* [1987] BCLC 1; *E. Pfeiffer Weinkellerei-Weineinkauf GmbH & Co v Arbuthnot Factors Ltd* [1988] 1 WLR 150; *Tatung (UK) Ltd v Galex Telesure Ltd* [1989] 5 BCC 325; *Compaq Computer Ltd v Abercorn Group Ltd* [1993] BCLC 602; *Modelboard Ltd v Outer Box Ltd* [1993] BCLC 623; *Stroud Architectural Systems Ltd v John Laing Construction Ltd* [1994] 2 BCLC 276; *Ian Chisholm Textiles Ltd v Griffiths* [1994] 2 BCLC 291; McCormack, *Reservation of Title* (2nd edn, 1995); *Gore-Browne on Companies*, para 30[13A]; *Encyclopaedia of Banking Law*, paras E(1151)–E(1180); *Benjamin's Sale of Goods* (6th edn, 2002), paras 5-141–5-148.

[24]   See Wood, *English and International Set-Off* (1989), Chapter 5.

[25]   This is the method used by ISDA (the International Swaps and Derivatives Association, Inc) in its Credit Support Annex. It involves outright transfers of ownership of the relevant assets (and transfers back) upon periodic valuations of the transferor's obligations to the transferee. On a default, the value of the assets is converted into a monetary amount owing by the transferee to the transferor and netted off against the amount owing by the transferor to the transferee.

repayable until the debt 'secured' has been repaid (a 'flawed asset').[26] Trusts are also sometimes used as a form of security.[27] Where a trust is so used, it is in essence merely a form of equitable mortgage, subject to one exception. This is where goods which are already the subject of a pledge are released (so that they can be sold) with the debtor acknowledging that he holds the goods and the proceeds of sale on trust for the creditor. In such a situation, the declaration of trust has been held not to create a mortgage or charge (and therefore not to require registration with the Companies Registry), because the creditor's rights arise under the original pledge and not the declaration of trust.[28]

NATURE OF THE ASSET SECURED

6.12   The type of security interest available in any given case, and the formalities required in the case of legal security, will depend to a large extent upon the nature of the asset to be secured. The following are the principal categories of assets which can be secured and the main 'consensual' security interests that can arise in relation to them (ie excluding security interests arising by operation of law, and excluding also floating charges, which are considered separately at **6.39ff**).

Land

6.13   The methods available for creating legal security over a legal estate depend on whether the land is registered or unregistered. In the case of unregistered land, the security may be created either by a demise for a term of years absolute (ie a lease),[29] subject to a proviso that the term shall cease on redemption (ie repayment of the secured debt), or by a charge expressed

---

[26]   The 'flaw' in the 'asset' lies in the fact that the deposit is not repayable unless and until the contingency is satisfied. One question is whether a flawed asset constitutes a mortgage or charge (therefore possibly requiring registration in order to be valid). It is thought not (see, eg, *Re Bank of Credit and Commerce International SA (No 8)* [1998] AC 214 at 227 per Lord Hoffmann), the general practice being to register a flawed asset arrangement only if it is combined with a mortgage or charge. The effectiveness of flawed asset arrangements in insolvency has been recognised in *Re Bank of Credit and Commerce International SA (No 8)* by the Court of Appeal [1996] Ch 245 and in the House of Lords [1998] AC 214 at 227 per Lord Hoffmann. On flawed asset arrangements generally, see *Paget's Law of Banking* (12th edn, 2002), pp 631–633; Goode, *Legal Problems of Credit and Security* (3rd edn, 2003), pp 15–16; Ellinger, Lomnicka and Hooley, *Ellinger's Modern Banking Law* (4th edn, 2006), pp 827–830; *Encyclopaedia of Banking Law*, paras E(2481)–E(2484); Wood, *English and International Set-Off* (1989), pp 214–225.

[27]   Trusts can constitute security interests (see eg *Re Bond Worth Ltd* [1980] Ch 228 at 250; *Compaq Computer Ltd v Abercorn Group Ltd* [1993] BCLC 602 at 612). One of the key factors determining whether in any particular case a trust does constitute a security interest is whether the 'chargor' has a right to have his asset back if the debt is discharged (the equity of redemption) (see eg *Swiss Bank Corporation v Lloyds Bank Ltd* [1982] AC 584 at 595; *Re George Inglefield Ltd* [1933] Ch 1 at 27–28).

[28]   *Re David Allester Ltd* [1922] 2 Ch 211.

[29]   If the security is over a leasehold estate, the demise must take the form of a sub-demise for a term which is at least one day shorter than the unexpired residue of the lease: s 86.

to be by way of legal mortgage.[30] In the case of registered land, the security may be created either by the second of the above two methods (ie a charge expressed to be by way of legal mortgage)[31] or by charging the estate with the payment of money.[32] In each case, the security must be created by a deed.[33]

6.14   Equitable mortgages and charges over land can take a number of forms, ranging from a memorandum of deposit under seal containing a power of attorney and accompanied by registration of a notice[34] at the Land Registry (or, in the case of unregistered land, possession of the title deeds), to an informal deposit of the title deeds accompanied by a memorandum under hand. In each case, there must be a written charging document or memorandum of deposit signed by the chargor and the chargee and incorporating, either expressly or by reference, all the terms which they have expressly agreed.[35]

6.15   The requirements for registration under the Land Registration Act 2002 and the Land Charges Act 1972[36] are, very briefly, as follows:

(a)   A legal mortgage or charge of registered land is registrable as a registered charge.[37] Unless and until it is so registered, it takes effect in equity only and is capable of being overridden unless protected by registration of a notice at the Land Registry.[38] The priority of successive registered charges is determined by the order in which they are shown on the register (and not the order of creation).[39]

(b)   An equitable mortgage or charge (including a floating charge) of registered land, as with an unregistered legal mortgage or charge,[40] is

---

[30]   Law of Property Act 1925, ss 85, 86 and 87.

[31]   This is the combined effect of ss 85–87 of the Law of Property Act 1925 (which provides that legal mortgages of legal estates in land can only be created by the two methods described above) and s 23(1)(a) of the Land Registration Act 2002 (which provides that the owner of a registered estate may make a disposition of any kind permitted by the general law, other than a mortgage by demise or sub-demise).

[32]   Land Registration Act 2002, s 23(1)(b).

[33]   Law of Property Act 1925, ss 52, 85(1), 86(1) (in relation to unregistered land); Land Registration Act 2002, ss 25, 27 and Land Registration Rules 2003 (SI 2003/1417), r 206(3) and Sch 9 (in relation to registered land).

[34]   Under Land Registration Act 2002, ss 32–39.

[35]   Law of Property (Miscellaneous Provisions) Act 1989, s 2; *United Bank of Kuwait plc v Sahib* [1997] Ch 107: see also Hardcastle [1995] Sol Jo 246; Essien [1998] JIBL 80. Any variation of an equitable mortgage must also comply with s 2 in order to be valid: *McCausland v Duncan Lawrie Ltd* [1996] 4 All ER 995.

[36]   Which are additional to the Companies Act registration requirements considered in **6.54ff**.

[37]   Land Registration Act 2002, s 27(2), (3) and 132(1). This is in addition to the registration at the Companies Registry required under the Companies Act 1985 (as to which, see **6.54ff**).

[38]   Land Registration Act 2002, s 29(1), (2). The chargee's interest will, unless protected, be overridden by a registered disposition of the legal estate for valuable consideration, irrespective of notice on the part of the transferee (ibid, s 29(1)).

[39]   Land Registration Act 2003, s 48(1). However, a prospective lender who has 'priority protection' under s 72 whilst searching the register will take priority over a mortgage registered during the priority period (ibid, s 72(2)), unless the earlier entry is itself one that has priority protection (ibid, s 72(3)).

[40]   See (a) above.

capable of being overridden unless protected by registration of a notice at the Land Registry.[41]

(c) A mortgage or charge of unregistered land is registrable under the Land Charges Act 1972 as a 'land charge' if it falls within one of the six classes A to F defined in s 2 of the Act. The three most relevant are:

C(i)   a 'puisne mortgage', defined as a legal mortgage not protected by the deposit of title deeds. As a first mortgagee usually obtains the title deeds, puisne mortgages are almost always second or third mortgages.

C(iii) a 'general equitable charge', defined as any equitable charge not protected by the deposit of title deeds, not arising under a trust for sale or settlement, not given by way of indemnity against rents or covenants, and not included in any other category of land charge.

C(iv) an 'estate contract', defined as a contract, by an estate owner or a person entitled to call for a legal estate, to convey or create a legal estate.

6.16   The general approach of the legislation is that a mortgage or charge protected by deposit of the title deeds need not be registered (as possession of the title deeds should be sufficient protection) and that a mortgage or charge not so protected should be registered. However a difficulty arises in relation to an equitable mortgage of the legal estate. To the extent that it constitutes an agreement to create a legal mortgage, it is registrable as an estate contract, even if it is protected by deposit of the title deeds. If it is not so protected, the additional consequence is that the registrability as an estate contract takes it outside the definition of a general equitable charge.[42] Normal practice, though, is not to register equitable mortgages which are not protected by deposit of the title deeds, and to register those which are so protected as general equitable charges.

6.17   Where, however, the land charge is a floating charge, registration under the Companies Act 1985[43] is sufficient in place of registration under the Land Charges Act 1972.[44]

6.18   The effect of non-registration depends on the category. An unregistered puisne mortgage or general equitable charge is void against a

---

[41]   Land Registration Act 2003, s 29(1), (2). This is in addition to the registration at the Companies Registry required under the Companies Act 1985 (as to which, see **6.54ff**).

[42]   For arguments against this construction, see Megarry (1941) 7 CLJ 250 at 252; *Fisher and Lightwood's Law of Mortgage* (11th edn, 2002), p 113. See also *United Bank of Kuwait plc v Sahib* [1997] Ch 107; *Property Discount Corpn Ltd v Lyon Group Ltd* [1981] 1 WLR 300. The significance of which category the mortgage falls into lies in the consequences of non-registration, considered below.

[43]   See **6.54ff**.

[44]   Land Charges Act 1972, s 3(7). For other charges over unregistered land by companies, both sets of registration requirements must be complied with to the extent applicable.

purchaser[45] of any interest in the land,[46] whereas an unregistered estate contract is void against a purchaser for money or money's worth of a legal estate in the land.[47] In each case, the fact that the purchaser may have notice of the unregistered charge is irrelevant.[48]

6.19 Registered land charges (legal or equitable) rank in order of registration.[49] In other cases, priority is governed by the general rules described at **6.89ff** below, subject to the fact that registration under the Land Charges Act 1972 constitutes actual notice of the relevant instrument or matter to all persons and for all purposes connected with the land.[50] Land charges affecting registered land cannot be registered.[51]

6.20 In the case of both registered and unregistered land, special rules apply to the 'tacking' of further advances: these are considered in **6.89**.

Shares

6.21 As seen earlier,[52] registered shares cannot be pledged. The creation of legal security (ie a legal mortgage) over shares is effected by the mortgagee having the shares registered in his name or the name of his nominee, subject to an agreement that they will be transferred back when the debt is repaid. This will ensure that, during the life of the mortgage, the mortgagee will receive all documents sent to the shareholders and all dividends. However, if the shares are only partly paid, the mortgagee would become liable to meet calls and, if the mortgagee controls the exercise of voting rights in relation to the shares, he may become liable to contribute to the mortgagor company's pension deficit.[53]

---

45   Defined as 'any person (including a mortgagee or lessee) who, for valuable consideration, takes any interest in land or in a charge on land': Land Charges Act 1972, s 17(1).
46   Land Charges Act 1972, s 4(5).
47   Land Charges Act 1972, s 4(6).
48   Law of Property Act 1925, s 199(1).
49   Law of Property Act 1925, s 97.
50   Law of Property Act 1925, s 198(1). Consequently, a later legal land charge cannot, merely by virtue of the legal estate, prevail over an earlier registered equitable land charge (see eg *Williams v Burlington Investments Ltd* (1977) 121 Sol Jo 424).
51   Land Charges Act 1972, s 14(1).
52   At **6.8**.
53   Pensions Act 2004, ss 38–51. Whether the fact that the shares are registered in the name of the mortgagee, or his nominee, will result in the issuer of the shares being a subsidiary of the mortgagee or nominee will depend on the extent to which the mortgagee, or his nominee, can exercise the rights attached to the shares: see Companies Act 1985, s 736A(7) (rights attached to shares held by way of security shall be treated as held by the chargor where, apart from the right to exercise them for the purpose of preserving the value of, or realising, the security, the rights are exercisable only in accordance with the chargor's instructions or (in the case of loans granted as part of normal business activities) in the chargor's interests). Where the shares are in a public company, the mortgagee (whether legal or equitable) may be a person 'interested' in the shares and obliged to give information to the company under s 212 of the Companies Act 1985: certain security interests, however, are exempted (Companies Act 1985, s 209(1)(c), (2), (2A), (2B), (2C)). If the mortgagee is entitled to exercise one-third or more of the voting power at a general meeting of the issuer of the shares, the mortgagee will be 'connected with' the issuer of the shares for the purposes of the Insolvency Act 1986 (see ss 249 and 435(10) of that Act). In that case, transactions between the mortgagee and the issuer of the shares will be subject to increased avoidance provisions under ss 238 (transactions at an undervalue) and 239 (preferences).

6.22 In the case of shares held in uncertificated form in CREST,[54] a legal mortgage is effected by a transfer from the stock account of the mortgagor to the stock account of the mortgagee.

6.23 An equitable mortgage or charge of shares held in certificated form can be created merely by delivery of the share certificates and a share transfer form executed by the chargor in blank.[55] The chargee should also obtain appropriate authority for him to complete the blanks upon enforcement (though sometimes even blank transfer forms are dispensed with). Other methods of protection of the chargee's position include giving notice of the charge to the company, or serving a stop notice on the company (as described below).

6.24 Giving notice to the company is of little value, given s 360 of the Companies Act 1985 (a company cannot enter on its register notice of any trust, expressed, implied or constructive), except in one case. This is where, under the articles, the company has a lien on the shares for debts due to the company from the holder. In respect of money becoming due from the shareholder to the company after the giving of the notice, the company cannot claim priority over advances by the chargee after the giving of the notice.[56]

6.25 The procedure in relation to stop notices is regulated by rules 73.16 to 73.21 of the Civil Procedure Rules. A request for a stop notice may be made by any person claiming to be beneficially entitled to an interest in securities,[57] and must be supported by written evidence which (inter alia) identifies the securities and describes the applicant's interest in them.[58] Once a stop notice has been issued by the court and has been served on the company, the company must not register a transfer of the securities without first giving 14 days' notice to the person who obtained the stop notice[59] (thus giving him an opportunity to obtain a restraining order or injunction).[60]

6.26 Where shares are held in uncertificated form in CREST, an equitable mortgage is effected by the mortgagor transferring the shares from his

---

[54] As to which, see further **15.22ff**.

[55] *Stubbs v Slater* [1910] 1 Ch 632 at 639 per Cozens-Hardy V-C. An equitable mortgage is also the form of security created if the share certificates are delivered as security but without a transfer form: *Harrold v Plenty* [1901] 2 Ch 314. In all cases, though, a memorandum of deposit is also advisable, to avoid any implication that the chargee is merely holding the shares as custodian.

[56] *The Bradford Banking Co Ltd v Henry Briggs Son & Co Ltd* (1886) 12 App Cas 29; *Mackereth v Wigan Coal and Iron Co Ltd* [1916] 2 Ch 293; *Champagne Perrier-Jouet SA v H H Finch Ltd* [1982] 1 WLR 1359 at 1367.

[57] CPR, r 73.17(1).

[58] CPR, r 73.17(2).

[59] CPR, r 73.18(2).

[60] Notice to the company of the mortgage or charge may be required in any event by s 198 of the Companies Act 1985. The acquisition or disposal of any interest in shares comprising 3% or more of any class of voting shares must be notified to the company in writing. After that, notification is also required when the interest alters by at least 1% or falls below 3%. However, the obligation does not apply if, inter alia, the chargee is a bank and the interest in the shares is held by way of security only for the purposes of a transaction entered into in the ordinary course of its business as a bank: s 209(1)(c), (2), (2A).

'available balance' (used for general settlement purposes) to an 'escrow balance'. There is no transfer of legal title and the mortgagor's name remains entered on the issuer's register. However, once the shares are in the escrow balance, control over them passes to another CREST member, known as the 'escrow agent', specified by the mortgagor in his transfer instruction. The escrow agent is usually the mortgagee or his nominee. The escrow agent can transfer the shares back into the control of the mortgagor (eg upon repayment of the loan) or to himself (eg upon enforcement of the security).[61]

For the effect of the Financial Collateral Arrangements (No 2) Regulations 2003, see **6.33ff** below.

Contracts

6.27   Leaving aside life policies (to which special technicalities apply) and contracts embodied in bearer securities (considered below), a mortgage of the benefit of contractual rights takes the form of an assignment and, to be legal rather than equitable, must comply with the Law of Property Act 1925, s 136(1) (considered at **15.14ff**). A 'charge' over the benefit of such rights can only take effect in equity, due to the requirement in s 136(1) that the assignment must not purport 'to be by way of charge only'.[62] A pledge is not available in respect of such rights, due to the inability to transfer possession by delivery.

6.28   There used to be considerable controversy as to whether a chargor could charge the benefit of contractual rights to the other party to the contract. This particularly arose in the context of a charge over a deposit to the bank which holds it.[63] Such a charge has now been held by the House of Lords to constitute valid security.[64]

---

[61]   See further CREST Guidance Note, 'Equitable mortgages over CREST securities' (July 2001).

[62]   An assignment expressed to be by way of 'mortgage', or by way of 'security', or with a proviso for reassignment, does not offend this provision: *Tancred v Delagoa Bay and East Africa Rly Co* (1889) 23 QBD 239; *Durham Brothers v Robertson* [1898] 1 QB 765; *Hughes v Pump House Hotel Co Ltd* [1902] 2 KB 190.

[63]   As a result of *Re Charge Card Services Ltd* [1987] Ch 150, in which Millett J had held that such security was 'conceptually impossible'.

[64]   *Re Bank of Credit and Commerce International SA (No 8)* [1998] Ch 214. See also Calnan, *Butterworths' JIBFL*, April 1998, p 125; Yeowart, IFLR, January 1998, p 7; Goode (1998) 114 LQR 178; Randell-Khan and Graham [1998] PLC 21. The security would appear not to be valid, though, if it is in the form of an assignment rather than a charge. Buckley LJ held in *Re George Routledge & Sons Ltd* [1904] 2 Ch 474 (a case not referred to in Lord Hoffmann's judgment in *Re BCCI (No 8)*) that a person cannot be both mortgagor and mortgagee of the same property. Furthermore, in *Re BCCI (No 8)*, Lord Hoffmann was careful to restrict his analysis only to charges (see, eg, at 226), and indeed regarded it as an important factor in their validity that the chargor retained title (which he would not if the security were in the form of an assignment): see, eg, at 227B.

Goods and bearer securities

6.29   Were a security document over 'personal chattels'[65] (broadly, goods and other articles capable of transfer by delivery, but not securities in companies and other choses in action) to be executed by an individual, it would have to be in the statutory form laid down in the Bills of Sale Act (1878) Amendment Act 1882 and be registered as a bill of sale. However, the Bills of Sale Acts do not apply to limited companies.[66] Accordingly, security by a limited company over such chattels, as with security over other tangible movables (including bearer securities), can be created in the form of a legal mortgage (ie where the legal title is transferred to the mortgagee with a proviso express or implied for retransfer on redemption – in the case of bearer securities this will in reality be indistinguishable from a pledge), an equitable mortgage or charge (which may, but need not, take the form of a hypothecation)[67] or a pledge (ie where possession is actually or constructively delivered).[68] As well as the inherent weakness of all equitable mortgages and charges (in that the security can be overridden by a bona fide purchaser for value of the legal interest without notice – see **6.89(b)**)), all the above forms of security can, in the case of goods, be defeated in certain circumstances by provisions of the Factors Act 1889 and the Sale of Goods Act 1979.[69]

For the effect (in relation to bearer securities) of the Financial Collateral Arrangements (No 2) Regulations 2003, see **6.33ff** below.

Ships and aircraft

6.30   These are considered at **6.71**.

Goodwill and intellectual property

6.31   These are considered at **6.72ff**.

6.32   The above formalities are only those applying under English law. In the case of assets situated outside England and Wales, local law formalities will also need to be complied with.

---

[65]   See further **6.65**.
[66]   See **6.65**.
[67]   See **6.6**.
[68]   See **6.8**.
[69]   See Factors Act 1889, ss 2, 4, 8 and 9 (certain dispositions by mercantile agents in breach of authority treated as valid) and Sale of Goods Act 1979, ss 16 and 17 (property in unascertained goods does not pass to buyer until goods are ascertained) and 25 (repeating ss 8 and 9 of the Factors Act 1889); see also *Paget's Law of Banking* (12th edn, 2002), pp 644–647.

SECURITY OVER FINANCIAL COLLATERAL

Background

6.33   On 26 December 2003, the Financial Collateral Arrangements (No 2) Regulations 2003[70] (the 'Regulations') came into force in order to implement the EU Financial Collateral Directive[71] (the 'Directive'). The purpose of the Regulations, as with the Directive, is to strengthen the legal regime for the taking of 'financial collateral' by (i) making it easier to create, perfect (where necessary) and enforce financial collateral arrangements, (ii) protecting such arrangements from insolvency rules that might otherwise undermine them, and (iii) clarifying the conflict of laws rule applicable to transfers of securities as financial collateral through financial intermediaries.

When the Regulations apply

6.34   The Regulations apply to 'financial collateral arrangements', of which there are two types, 'security financial collateral arrangements' and 'title transfer financial collateral arrangements'.[72] A title transfer financial collateral arrangement involves outright transfer to the collateral-taker of legal and beneficial ownership in the financial collateral (on terms that when the relevant financial obligation has been discharged it must be transferred back to the collateral-provider),[73] whereas a security financial collateral arrangement involves the creation of a security interest in the financial collateral.

6.35   The practical impact of the Regulations in England and Wales is almost entirely in relation to security financial collateral arrangements. A security financial collateral arrangement is an agreement or arrangement, evidenced in writing, where:

(i)   the purpose of the agreement or arrangement is to secure the relevant financial obligations owed to the collateral-taker;

(ii)   the collateral-provider creates or there arises a security interest in financial collateral to secure those obligations;

(iii) the financial collateral is delivered, transferred, held, registered or otherwise designated so as to be in the possession or under the control of the collateral-taker or a person acting on its behalf; and

---

[70]   SI 2003/3226. The reason why these Regulations are the 'No 2' Regulations is that there was an error in the original Regulations, which were revoked before they came into effect.

[71]   Directive 2002/47/EC.

[72]   See the definitions of 'financial collateral arrangement', 'security financial collateral arrangement' and 'title transfer financial collateral arrangement' in reg 3.

[73]   As, for example, in the case of Eligible Credit Support under the ISDA Credit Support Annex.

(iv) the collateral-provider and the collateral-taker are both non-natural persons.[74]

6.36 For these purposes, 'financial collateral' means[75] cash and financial instruments. 'Cash' is defined broadly, and means (i) money credited to an account or a similar claim for repayment of money (including money market deposits)[76] and (ii) sums payable between parties in connection with the operation of a financial collateral arrangement or a close out netting provision.[77] 'Financial instruments' means shares in companies,[78] (ii) bonds and other debt instruments that are 'tradeable on the capital market',[79] and (iii) other securities which are 'normally dealt in' and which give the right to acquire shares, bonds and other securities by subscription, purchase or exchange or which give rise to a cash settlement (excluding instruments of payment).[80] The term thus covers most types of marketable securities.

6.37 It might be thought, given the above, that the Regulations apply to most forms of security over cash and marketable securities. However, one of the requirements that needs to be satisfied for the Regulations to apply is that the collateral must be 'in the possession or under the control of' the collateral-taker. The Regulations (and the Directive), however, are silent as to what constitutes possession or control in this context. A fully perfected legal mortgage of financial collateral will almost certainly meet the requirement, but a less formal equitable charge may not, and a floating charge is unlikely to. Until there has been case law on the point, it is unclear, for example, whether an arrangement that constitutes a fixed charge (in the light of the reasoning in the *Spectrum Plus* and *Brumark* decisions[81]) exhibits the necessary degree of 'control' for the purpose of the Regulations, or

---

[74] The definition of 'non-natural person' (reg 3) includes any company, any unincorporated firm (such as an English partnership, whether general or limited), a limited liability partnership and any other corporate body (such as a local authority or government department). It does not include an individual or the trustees (if individuals) of a trust – but does include a corporate trustee.

[75] See the definitions of 'financial collateral', 'cash' and 'financial instruments' in reg 3.

[76] In other words, cash collateral as commonly understood in the market.

[77] Thus including the benefit of close out amounts under a master agreement, which are not commonly considered cash collateral (but are commonly included within the scope of security arrangements, particularly in a structured financing).

[78] Note that there is no requirement that the shares be publicly listed or traded.

[79] This requirement may mean that some highly structured, closely held and/or illiquid securities may not fall within this definition.

[80] 'Financial instruments' also include units of a collective investment scheme, eligible debt securities, money market instruments, and 'claims or rights' relating to any of those financial instruments. The 'claims or rights' referred to are probably meant to be those, for example, arising against an intermediary in relation to securities credited to an account with that intermediary.

[81] See **6.48**.

indeed the extent to which the Regulations can apply to certain floating charges.[82]

Effect of the Regulations

6.38 The principal consequences in relation to a security financial collateral arrangement if the Regulations do apply are as follows:

(i) The registration requirement in s 395 of the Companies Act 1985 does not apply (if it would otherwise do so).[83] However, given the uncertainty described above in relation to the meaning of 'possession' and 'control', the prevailing practice is still to register as before, out of caution.

(ii) Certain provisions of the Insolvency Act 1986 are disapplied in respect of the arrangement. These include: the moratorium which arises on an administration of the chargor;[84] the obligation to set aside the 'prescribed part' under s 176A of the Insolvency Act 1986;[85] the provisions of s 245 of the Insolvency Act 1986 regarding the avoidance of floating charges;[86] and the provisions of s 196 of the Companies Act 1985, which require a floating charge holder taking possession of assets subject to the charge (other than in a winding-up) to pay preferential creditors first.[87]

(iii) Where the security is over book entry securities held through one or more intermediaries,[88] the Regulations clarify that the law applicable to determine the validity of the collateral arrangement (and related proprietary and perfection issues) is the law of the country in which the relevant account is situated[89] – the so-called PRIMA (Place of Relevant InterMediary Account) principle.

---

[82] Particularly as the definition of 'security financial collateral arrangement' (in reg 3) makes it clear that the right of a collateral-provider to substitute equivalent financial collateral or to remove excess financial collateral will not prevent the financial collateral being in the possession or under the control of the collateral-taker. In addition, certain provisions of the Regulations disapply provisions of the insolvency legislation that would otherwise be applicable to floating charges (eg regs 10(5), 10(6)) – indicating that in certain circumstances floating charges are envisaged as capable of constituting security financial collateral arrangements.

[83] Regulation 4(4).

[84] Regulation 8. The right of an administrator to dispose of charged property which is the subject of such an arrangement is also taken away.

[85] Regulation 10(3). On the 'prescribed part', see further **6.91**.

[86] Regulation 10(5). On s 245, see further **6.47**.

[87] Regulation 10(6). There may have been a technical mistake in the wording of the Regulations. If CA 1985, s 196 is disapplied it should follow that IA 1986, s 40 (requiring receivers appointed by floating charge holders, other than in a winding-up, to pay preferential creditors first) should also be disapplied, but it was not. Consequently, where the security is a floating charge (and the company is not in winding-up), preferential creditors need to be paid first if the charge holder appoints a receiver but not if it enforces by taking possession.

[88] Such as securities held in CREST, Euroclear or Clearstream, or through a custodian.

[89] Regulation 19.

FLOATING CHARGES[90]

The nature of a floating charge

6.39 As seen earlier,[91] a charge may be either 'fixed' or 'floating'. Where it is fixed, it attaches to the asset immediately and the chargor can only deal with the asset subject to the charge. But where the charge is floating, the chargor may deal with the assets covered by the charge in the ordinary course of its business without reference to the creditor.[92] The charge does not attach to any particular asset until an event occurs, or the creditor takes a step, which 'crystallises' the charge, in which event the charge becomes a fixed charge over the relevant assets.[93] A floating charge appears to be peculiar to companies.[94] It is a form of equitable charge, and accordingly the fixed charge resulting from crystallisation only takes effect in equity.[95]

---

[90] See generally Gough, *Company Charges* (2nd edn, 1996), Chapters 5–16; Goode, *Legal Problems of Credit and Security* (3rd edn, 2003), Chapter 4; Ferran, *Company Law and Corporate Finance* (1999), pp 506–533; *Gore-Browne on Companies*, Chapter 30; Ellinger, Lomnicka and Hooley, *Ellinger's Modern Banking Law* (4th edn, 2006), pp 781–794; *Encyclopaedia of Banking Law*, paras E(1051)–E(1100).

[91] At **6.5.**

[92] *Brunton v Electrical Engineering Corpn* [1892] 1 Ch 434; *Robson v Smith* [1895] 2 Ch 118. What is the 'ordinary course of business' will depend on the circumstances of each case: see, eg, *Ashborder BV v Green Gas Power Ltd* [2005] BCC 634; *Countrywide Banking Corpn Ltd v Dean* [1998] AC 338; *Cox Moore v Peruvian Corporation Ltd* [1908] 1 Ch 604; *Hubbuck v Helms* (1887) 56 LT 232; *Re H H Vivian & Co Ltd* [1900] 2 Ch 654; *Re Borax Co* [1901] 1 Ch 326; *Willmott v London Celluloid Co* (1886) 34 ChD 147; *Robson v Smith* [1895] 2 Ch 118; *Robinson v Burnell's Vienna Bakery Co* [1904] 2 KB 624; *Heaton & Dugard Ltd v Cutting Bros Ltd* [1925] 1 KB 655; *Brunton v Electrical Engineering Corpn* [1892] 1 Ch 434; *Re Hubbard & Co Ltd* (1898) 79 LT 665; *Davey & Co v Williamson & Sons* [1898] 2 QB 194; *Wallace v Evershed* [1899] 1 Ch 891; *Edward Nelson & Co v Faber & Co* [1903] 2 KB 367; *Re Standard Rotary Machine Co Ltd* (1906) 95 LT 829; *Re Ind, Coope & Co Ltd* [1911] 2 Ch 223; *Harmer v London City & Midland Bank Ltd* (1918) 118 LT 571; *Re Anglo-American Leather Cloth Co Ltd* (1880) 43 IT 43.

[93] See **6.49ff.**

[94] Though under general law individuals, partnerships and unincorporated associations have no inherent incapacity which precludes them from giving floating charges, the Bills of Sale Acts 1878–1882 make it effectively impossible for them to do so to the extent that the floating charge relates to 'personal chattels' (as the charge would not be in the form required by the Acts). Accordingly, an individual may be able to grant a floating charge on present and future book debts (because choses in action are excluded from the definition of 'personal chattels': see further **6.65**), so long as it is registered under the Bills of Sale Act 1878 as if it were an absolute bill of sale (as required by Insolvency Act 1986, s 344). See further Gough, *Company Charges* (2nd edn, 1996), pp 52–56; Ferran, *Company Law and Corporate Finance* (1999), p 508; Goode, *Legal Problems of Credit and Security* (3rd edn, 2003), pp 111–112. Companies are not subject to the Bills of Sale Acts (see further **6.65**). Building societies are prohibited by statute from granting floating charges (Building Societies Act 1986, s 9B(1)).

[95] A floating charge is an existing, and not a future, charge (see, eg, *Evans v Rival Granite Quarries Ltd* [1910] 2 KB 979 at 999 per Buckley LJ; *Cretanor Maritime Co Ltd v Irish Marine Management Ltd* [1978] 3 All ER 164 at 173 per Buckley LJ), and therefore crystallisation and enforcement of the charge does not constitute a disposition for the purpose of s 127 of the Insolvency Act 1986 and s 522 of the Companies Act 1985, the disposition taking place when the charge is created (*Re Margart Pty Ltd* [1985] BCLC 314 (NSW), approved in *Re French's (Wine Bar) Ltd* [1987] BCLC 499).

Protection of fixed security

6.40   Before the Insolvency Act 1986 was amended in 2003[96] by the
Enterprise Act 2002, it was common practice to supplement a grant of fixed
security with a floating charge over all the other assets of the company, in
order to enable the chargee to forestall the appointment of an administrator
to the company (for the reasons described below). The 2003 amendments
were intended to give primacy to the administration procedure as the
collective corporate rehabilitation procedure, and consequently they reduced
significantly the circumstances in which a floating charge holder can block
the appointment of an administrator. In the context of normal secured
corporate borrowing, the most relevant situation now in which a 'back-up'
floating charge is still effective to enable the appointment of an administrator
to be blocked is where the so-called 'capital market exception' applies
(described below).

6.41   The importance to a chargee of being able to block the appointment
of an administrator lies in the fact that, once an administrator has been
appointed, the chargee cannot enforce his security or take any legal
proceedings against the company except with the consent of the
administrator or the court.[97] In addition, though the administrator must apply
the proceeds of disposal of the property secured by the fixed charge towards
discharging the sums secured by that fixed charge,[98] the chargee nevertheless
has no say in whether, and, if so, when, disposal takes place.[99]

6.42   The method by which (assuming that a relevant exception applies, as
described below) a floating charge holder blocks the appointment of an
administrator is by appointing an 'administrative receiver'[100] before the
administrator can be appointed. An administrator may be appointed (inter
alia) either by: (i) an administration order of the court (the 'court route') in
response to an application filed by its directors, the company itself or one or
more creditors if the company is insolvent or likely to become so[101] or by the

---

96   The amendments took effect from 15 September 2003.
97   Insolvency Act 1986, Sch B1, para 43. This restriction is disapplied in relation to financial collateral
      arrangements: see further **6.38**. A similar effect applies if the chargor is a 'small company' that
      obtains a moratorium under the Insolvency Act 1986, Sch A1 (inserted by the Insolvency Act 2000).
      Under that Schedule, a small company (defined in Companies Act 1985, s 247) may obtain an
      optional moratorium for a period of 28 days with the option for the creditors to extend the
      moratorium for a further two months. Unlike administration, there is no requirement for prior notice
      to be given to any person entitled to appoint an administrative receiver (although, if the company is
      already in administrative receivership, no moratorium will be granted). A company is not eligible for
      a moratorium if it is party to certain types of capital markets arrangement or project or has incurred a
      liability under an agreement of £10 million or more.
98   Insolvency Act 1986, Sch B1, para 71(3).
99   The decision is the administrator's, subject in the case of fixed security to an order of the court: ibid,
      Sch B1, paras 70, 71. The administrator's power of disposal is disapplied in relation to assets subject
      to a financial collateral arrangement: see further **6.38**.
100   Pursuant to s 29 of the Insolvency Act 1986, an administrative receiver is a receiver of the whole (or
      substantially the whole) of a company's property appointed pursuant to a charge which, as created,
      was a floating charge, or pursuant to such a charge and one or more other securities.
101   Insolvency Act 1986, Sch B1, paras 11, 12.

holder of a 'qualifying floating charge' (as to the meaning of which, see below) if the security is enforceable;[102] or (ii) the filing of certain documents with the court (the 'out-of-court route') by its directors or the company itself[103] or by the holder of a qualifying floating charge (if the security is enforceable).[104] However, an administrator may not be appointed using the out-of-court route if an administrative receiver is in office;[105] and where an application is made to the court for an administration order and the court is satisfied that there is an administrative receiver of the company, the court will dismiss the application unless it is also satisfied that the person appointing the administrative receiver has consented to the administration or that, if the order were made, the security under which the administrative receiver was appointed would be liable to be set aside under ss 238–241 or s 245 of the Insolvency Act 1986.[106] In addition, any applicant for the appointment of an administrator using the court route must give notice of the application to (inter alia) any person who is or may be entitled to appoint an administrative receiver,[107] and a person seeking to appoint an administrator using the out-of-court route must give prior notice to, inter alia, (in the case of appointment by the directors or the company itself) any person who is or may be entitled to appoint an administrative receiver[108] and (in the case of appointment by a holder of a qualifying floating charge) any holder of a prior-ranking qualifying floating charge.[109] Consequently, so long as the chargee falls within the category of people entitled to receive notice and the taking of the relevant steps for the appointment of an administrator is expressed in the relevant borrowing to be an event of default entitling the chargee to appoint an administrative receiver, the chargee can thus forestall the appointment of the administrator by appointing its administrative receiver first.

6.43 However, as mentioned earlier, the Enterprise Act 2002 has significantly reduced the circumstances in which floating charge holders can block the appointment of an administrator. As seen above, where the application for the appointment of an administrator is being made by the holder of a qualifying floating charge, a chargee who might wish to block the appointment is only entitled to receive notice of the application if he is himself the holder of a prior-ranking qualifying floating charge. A floating charge is a qualifying floating charge if (inter alia) it is created by an instrument which states that para 14 of Sch B1 to the Insolvency Act 1986 applies to it[110], and a person is the holder of a qualifying floating charge in

---

102 Insolvency Act 1986, Sch B1, para 35.
103 Insolvency Act 1986, Sch B1, para 22.
104 Insolvency Act 1986, Sch B1, para 14.
105 Insolvency Act 1986, Sch B1, paras 17, 25.
106 Insolvency Act 1986, Sch B1, para 39.
107 Insolvency Act 1986, Sch B1, para 12(2).
108 Insolvency Act 1986, Sch B1, para 26.
109 Or, alternatively, obtain consent from such holder: Insolvency Act 1986, Sch B1, para 15(1).
110 Insolvency Act 1986, Sch B1, para 14(2).

respect of a company's property if (inter alia) he holds one or more debentures secured by charges and other forms of security which together relate to the whole (or substantially the whole) of the company's property and at least one of which is a qualifying floating charge.[111]

6.44   Accordingly, for a floating charge to be fully effective in enabling the chargee to block the appointment of an administrator, it needs to be a qualifying floating charge (and therefore should contain the statement that Sch B1, para 14 applies to it).[112] However, s 72A of the Insolvency Act 1986 prohibits the appointment of an administrative receiver by a holder of a qualifying floating charge unless the floating charge was created prior to 15 September 2003 or a specified exception applies. Of the exceptions specified, the most relevant in the context of corporate borrowing is the so-called 'capital market exception'.[113]

6.45   The capital market exception allows a holder of a qualifying floating charge to appoint an administrative receiver in pursuance of an agreement which is or forms part of a 'capital market arrangement' if: (i) a party incurs or, when the agreement is entered into, is expected to incur a debt of at least £50 million under the arrangement; and (ii) the arrangement involves the issue of a 'capital market investment'.[114] An arrangement is a 'capital market arrangement' if (inter alia): (i) it involves the grant of security to a trustee on behalf of the holder of a capital market investment issued by a party to the arrangement; or (ii) it involves a grant of security to a person who holds the security as trustee for a party to the arrangement in connection with the issue of a capital market investment.[115] A 'capital market investment' is defined to include (inter alia) an investment that is: (i) within art 77 of the Financial Services and Markets Act 2000 (Regulated Activities) Order 2001;[116] and (ii) rated,[117] listed[118] or traded[119] (or designed to be rated, listed or traded).[120] The list of instruments in art 77 of the Regulated Activities Order includes 'bond' and 'any other instrument creating or acknowledging indebtedness'.

---

[111]   Insolvency Act 1986, Sch B1, para 14(3).

[112]   In addition, as seen earlier, the chargee does not have the right to appoint an administrator using the out-of-court route unless he is the holder of a qualifying floating charge.

[113]   Contained in Insolvency Act 1986, s 72B. Other exceptions relate to: public-private partnership projects (s 72C); utility projects (s 72D); urban regeneration projects (s 72DA); financed projects (s 72E); charges to investment exchanges, clearing systems, etc in relation to settlement of financial markets transactions (s 72F); registered social landlords (s 72G); and certain water companies and transport companies (s 72GA). Note that the Secretary of State for Trade and Industry may by regulation modify the exceptions and/or provide for an exception to cease to have effect (s 72H). There is nothing in the Insolvency Act to prevent these powers being exercised with retrospective effect.

[114]   Insolvency Act 1986, s 72B(1).

[115]   Insolvency Act 1986, s 72B(2) and Sch 2A, para 1.

[116]   SI 2001/544.

[117]   Ie, rated for the purposes of investment by an internationally recognised rating agency (Insolvency Act 1986, Sch 2A, para 2(2)).

[118]   Ie, admitted to the official list (ibid).

[119]   Ie, admitted to trading on a market established under the rules of a recognised investment exchange or on a foreign market (ibid).

[120]   Insolvency Act 1986, s 72B(2) and Sch 2A, paras 2 and 3.

6.46 Accordingly, the capital market exception is available for bond and stock issues of at least £50 million that involve security granted to a trustee and that are designed to be rated, listed or traded (within the defined meanings). In such a case, a 'back-up' floating charge can still be effective to enable the chargee to block the appointment of an administrator.[121]

Distinction between fixed and floating charges

6.47 Whether a charge is fixed or floating depends, in essence, upon whether the chargor retains de facto power to deal with the charged assets, irrespective of the use of terms such as 'fixed' or 'specific'.[122] The distinction is important for a number of reasons: it may affect whether registration at the Companies Registry is required;[123] it will affect the chargee's priority;[124] it may affect the mechanics of enforcement;[125] it may affect whether the chargee can forestall the appointment by another creditor of an administrator to the chargor;[126] it will affect whether the charge is subject to avoidance under s 245 of the Insolvency Act 1986;[127] and it will affect whether the chargor can set off against the debt secured liabilities

---

[121] Though, for reasons mentioned earlier, there is no need to be able to do so where the grant of security constitutes a financial collateral arrangement. The validity of a floating charge created solely for the purpose of blocking an appointment of an administrator, with no substantive restrictions on the chargor, (known as a 'lightweight' or 'featherweight' floating charge) was upheld in *Re Croftbell Ltd* [1990] BCLC 844. The case was decided before the 2003 amendments to the Insolvency Act, but it is not thought that those amendments affect the point decided by the case.

[122] *Government Stock Investment Co Ltd v Manila Railway Co Ltd* [1897] AC 81; *Re Yorkshire Woolcombers' Association Ltd* [1903] 2 Ch 284, affd sub nom *Illingworth v Houldsworth* [1904] AC 355; *Evans v Rival Granite Quarries* [1910] 2 KB 979; *National Provincial Bank v United Electric Theatres Ltd* [1916] 1 Ch 132; *Mercantile Bank of India Ltd v Chartered Bank of India, Australia and China* [1937] 1 All ER 231; *Siebe Gorman & Co Ltd v Barclays Bank Ltd* [1979] 2 Lloyd's Rep 142; *Re Bond Worth Ltd* [1980] Ch 228; *Re Armagh Shoes Ltd* [1984] BCLC 405; *Re Keenan Bros Ltd* [1986] BCLC 242; *Re Brightlife Ltd* [1987] Ch 200; *Re A Company No 005009 of 1987* (1988) 4 BCC 424; *Re Atlantic Computer Systems plc* [1992] Ch 505; *Re Wogan's (Drogheda) Ltd* [1993] 1 IR 157; *Re CCG International Enterprises Ltd* [1993] BCLC 1428; *William Gaskell Group Ltd v Highley* [1993] BCC 200; *Re Atlantic Medical Ltd* [1993] BCLC 386; *Re New Bullas Trading Ltd* [1994] BCC 36; *Re G E Tunbridge Ltd* [1995] 1 BCLC 34; *Re Cimex Tissues Ltd* [1995] 1 BCLC 409; *Re Pearl Maintenance Services Ltd* [1995] 1 BCLC 449; *Royal Trust Bank v National Westminster Bank plc* [1996] 2 BCLC 682; *Re Cosslett (Contractors) Ltd* [1998] Ch 495; *Re Double S Printers Ltd* [1999] 1 BCLC 220; *Re Westmaze Ltd* [1999] BCC 441; *Re ASRS Establishment Ltd* [2000] 1 BCLC 727; *Re CIL Realisations Ltd* [2000] 2 BCLC 361; *Agnew v Commissioner of Inland Revenue* [2001] 2 AC 710; *Smith v Bridgend CBC* [2002] 1 AC 336; *Arthur D Little Ltd v Ableco Finance LLC* [2003] Ch 217; *Re TXU Europe Group plc* [2003] EWHC 3105; *Queens Moat Houses plc v Capita IRG Trustees Ltd* [2005] BCC 347; *Ashborder BV v Green Gas Power Ltd* [2005] BCC 634; *Re Spectrum Plus Ltd* [2005] UKHL 41.

[123] See **6.54ff**.

[124] See **6.89ff**.

[125] If a receiver is appointed of the whole (or substantially the whole) of the chargor's property by the holder of a charge that, as created, was a floating charge, the receiver will be an 'administrative receiver' and subject to special provisions under the Insolvency Act 1986. In addition, the holder of a 'qualifying floating charge' has, as an additional remedy that is not available to creditors who merely have fixed security, the right to appoint an administrator through the 'out-of-court' route: see further **6.42**.

[126] See **6.40ff**.

[127] The section applies to floating charges created within 12 months (or two years, if the charge is in favour of a 'connected person') of a petition for an administration order or the commencement of winding up.

owing to him from the chargee.[128] The three principal characteristics of a floating charge have been stated by the Court of Appeal to be: first, it is a charge upon all of a class of assets, present and future; secondly, the assets charged would in the ordinary course of business be changing from time to time; and, thirdly, the chargor, expressly or by necessary implication, has the power, until some step is taken by the chargee, of carrying on its business in the ordinary way so far as regards the assets charged.[129]

6.48   The difficulty in drawing the distinction has particularly arisen in the context of charges over book debts. Before a number of recent cases, it used to be possible in a number of situations for the chargor to be free to deal with the proceeds with the charge still being regarded as fixed. In the *Siebe Gorman* case,[130] for example, a charge under which the chargor was required to pay the proceeds into its account with the chargee bank, was prohibited from charging or assigning the book debts without the chargee's consent, but was otherwise free to withdraw the money unless the chargee stepped in to prevent it, had been held to be fixed. And in *Re New Bullas Trading Ltd*,[131] the Court of Appeal had held that the chargor's entitlement to deal with the proceeds without reference to the chargee could still be compatible with the charge being fixed if it was by agreement between the parties. Such arrangements, however, are not now sufficient; the House of Lords has overruled *Siebe Gorman* in *Re Spectrum Plus Ltd*,[132] and the Privy Council has expressed the view in *Agnew v Commissioner of Inland Revenue*[133] that *New Bullas* was wrongly decided. The decisions in *Spectrum Plus* and *Agnew*, and other recent decisions,[134] confirm that it is inconsistent with the existence of a fixed charge that the chargor is free to withdraw book debt proceeds at will without the consent of the chargee: there must be real, and not merely illusory, control provisions in respect of both the debts and their proceeds.

---

128 Prior to crystallisation, normal set-off rules apply as if there were no charge: *Biggerstaff v Rowatt's Wharf Ltd* [1896] 2 Ch 93; *Edward Nelson & Co Ltd v Faber & Co* [1903] 2 KB 367. See further Wood, *English and International Set-Off* (1989), pp 925–927.

129 *Re Yorkshire Woolcomber's Association Ltd* [1903] 2 Ch 284, affd sub nom *Illingworth v Houldsworth* [1904] AC 355, where it was held that a general charge on book debts, present and future, was a floating charge although not expressed to be so, and required registration at the Companies Registry. To be floating, the charge must embrace both present and future property (ibid, and see *Re Alfred Priestman & Co* [1936] 2 All ER 1340). See also *Cretanor Maritime Co Ltd v Irish Marine Management Ltd* [1978] 3 All ER 164 at 173 per Buckley LJ; *Re Atlantic Computer Systems plc* [1992] Ch 505; *Re Atlantic Medical Ltd* [1993] BCLC 386; *Re Cimex Tissues Ltd* [1995] 1 BCLC 409.

130 *Siebe Gorman & Co Ltd v Barclays Bank Ltd* [1979] 2 Lloyd's Rep 142.

131 [1994] BCC 36.

132 [2005] UKHL 41.

133 [2001] 2 AC 710.

134 Such as *Re Double S Printers Ltd* [1999] 1 BCLC 220; *Re Westmaze Ltd* [1999] BCC 441; *Re ASRS Establishment Ltd* [2000] 1 BCLC 727. See also (not specifically relating to book debts but emphasising the need for real control) *Re Cosslett (Contractors) Ltd* [1998] Ch 495; *Ashborder BV v Green Gas Power Ltd* [2005] BCC 634.

Crystallisation

6.49   Following Professor Goode's analysis,[135] the events on which a floating charge 'crystallises', or converts into a fixed charge,[136] fall broadly into three groups:[137] events denoting the cessation of trading by the chargor as a going concern; intervention by the chargee in accordance with the terms of the charge in a way which deprives the chargor of de jure control of the assets; and other acts or events specified in the charge. Crystallisation cannot occur during a moratorium under s1 of the Insolvency Act 2000.[138]

(1)   Events denoting cessation of trading as a going concern

6.50   The commencement of liquidation (whether by resolution of the members or by order of the court) will cause a floating charge to crystallise,[139] as will the cessation of trading[140] and the disposal of the whole or substantially the whole of the chargor's undertaking or assets with a view to the cessation of trading.[141] The charge will not be crystallised, however, by crystallisation of a prior floating charge,[142] nor, a fortiori, by the crystallisation of a subsequent floating charge (unless these are specified as crystallisation events in the charge).

(2)   Intervention by the chargee to take control of the assets

6.51   An act of intervention by the chargee, in accordance with the terms of the charge, will crystallise a floating charge if it is done with the intention of converting the charge into a fixed charge[143] and it deprives the chargor of

---

135 *Legal Problems of Credit and Security* (3rd edn, 2003), p 135.

136 The charge attaches to the assets of the chargor as they exist at the date of crystallisation (*Re Colonial Trusts Corpn* (1879) 15 ChD 465; *Hodson v Tea Co* (1880) 14 ChD 859; *Biggerstaff v Rowatt's Wharf Ltd* [1896] 2 Ch 93) and also to after-acquired assets: *N W Robbie & Co Ltd v Witney Warehouse Co Ltd* [1963] 3 All ER 613. Re-registration at the Companies Registry is not required, as no new security interest is created.

137 Goode actually lists four groups, but the fourth (events listed in the Agricultural Credits Act 1928 in relation to agricultural charges granted by a farmer) is disregarded here.

138 Insolvency Act 2000, s 1 and Sch 1, para 13.

139 *Re Panama, New Zealand and Australian Royal Mail Co* (1870) 5 Ch App 318; *Re Colonial Trusts Corp* (1879) 15 Ch D 465; *Wheatley v Silkstone and Haigh Moor Coal Co* (1885) 29 Ch D 715; *Wallace v Universal Automatic Machines Co* [1894] 2 Ch 547; *Re Roundwood Colliery Co* [1897] 1 Ch 373; *Evans v Rival Granite Quarries Ltd* [1910] 2 KB 979 at 1000 per Buckley LJ; *Re Crompton & Co Ltd* [1914] 1 Ch 954; *Hodson v Tea Co* (1880) 14 ChD 859; *Robson v Smith* [1895] 2 Ch 118 at 124; *Edward Nelson & Co Ltd v Faber & Co* [1903] 2 KB 367 at 376.

140 *Edward Nelson & Co Ltd v Faber & Co* [1903] 2 KB 367 at 376; *Re Woodroffes (Musical Instruments) Ltd* [1985] 2 All ER 908; *Re The Real Meat Co Ltd* [1996] BCC 254; *Robson v Smith* [1895] 2 Ch 118 at 124.

141 *Hubbuck v Helms* (1887) 56 LJ Ch 536; *Re The Real Meat Co Ltd* [1996] BCC 254. The charge will not crystallise, however, if, after the disposal, the company continues to be a going concern (*Re Borax Co* [1901] 1 Ch 326) or if the disposal is of only one of several businesses carried on by the company (*Re H H Vivian & Co Ltd* [1900] 2 Ch 654).

142 *Re Woodroffes (Musical Instruments) Ltd* [1985] 2 All ER 908. However, the charge will crystallise upon the appointment of a receiver by the prior chargee, if that results in a cessation of trading: *Re Woodroffe's (Musical Instruments) Ltd*, ibid.

143 *Evans v Rival Granite Quarries Ltd* [1910] 2 KB 979 at 997 per Fletcher Moulton LJ.

de jure control. Accordingly, appointing a receiver over the charged assets, or otherwise taking possession of them, with the requisite intention, will crystallise the floating charge.[144] Conversely, the mere institution of an action for the appointment of a receiver,[145] the mere fact of default by the chargor,[146] and a demand for payment by the chargee,[147] do not (unless specified as crystallisation events in the charge).

(3)   Other acts or events specified in the charge

6.52   Since crystallisation events are a matter of contract between chargor and chargee, it is open to the chargee to specify other acts or events in addition to the above[148] (or, a fortiori, to exclude or limit any of the above).[149] Two particular devices have been used: crystallisation on notice from the chargee (either at will or on the occurrence of specified events); and automatic crystallisation on the occurrence of specified events.

6.53   The first device (sometimes called 'semi-automatic' crystallisation) is valid.[150] The second, though, is more controversial. Certain dicta[151] have been interpreted as suggesting that active intervention by the chargee is required, but the decision of Hoffmann J in *Re Brightlife Ltd*[152] is nevertheless authority for the validity of automatic crystallisation.[153] The usefulness to a chargee, however, of an automatic crystallisation clause has

---

[144]   *Re Hamilton's Windsor Ironworks* (1879) 12 ChD 707; *Biggerstaff v Rowatt's Wharf Ltd* [1896] 2 Ch 93; *Mercantile Bank of India Ltd v Chartered Bank of India, Australia and China* [1937] 1 All ER 231; *Re Florence Land and Public Works Co* (1878) 10 ChD 530 at 541 per Jessel MR: *Re Colonial Trusts Corpn* (1879) 15 ChD 465; *Taunton v Sheriff of Warwickshire* [1895] 2 Ch 319; *Re Carshalton Park Estate Ltd* [1908] 2 Ch 62 at 66; *Evans v Rival Granite Quarries Ltd* [1910] 2 KB 979 at 1000 per Buckley LJ; *Rother Iron Works Ltd v Canterbury Precision Engineers Ltd* [1973] 1 All ER 394; *Edward Nelson & Co Ltd v Faber & Co* [1903] 2 KB 367 at 376; *Robson v Smith* [1895] 2 Ch 118 at 124; *Re Roundwood Colliery Co* [1897] 1 Ch 373.

[145]   *Re Hubbard & Co Ltd* (1898) 68 LJ Ch 54; *Re Roundwood Colliery Co* [1897] 1 Ch 373. Cf *Evans v Rival Granite Quarries Ltd* [1910] 2 KB 979 at 986 per Vaughan Williams LJ.

[146]   *Governments Stock and Other Securities Investment Co Ltd v Manila Railway Co Ltd* [1897] AC 81; *Evans v Rival Granite Quarries Ltd* [1910] 2 KB 979 at 993 per Fletcher Moulton LJ.

[147]   *Re Hubbard & Co Ltd* (1898) 68 LJ Ch 54; *Evans v Rival Granite Quarries Ltd* [1910] 2 KB 979. Obviously, the position is different if the charge provides otherwise: see (3) below.

[148]   *Re Brightlife Ltd* [1987] Ch 200; *Governments Stock and Other Securities Investment Co Ltd v Manila Rly Co Ltd* [1897] AC 81 at 85 per Lord Halsbury LC.

[149]   *Governments Stock and Other Securities Investment Co Ltd v Manila Railway Co Ltd* [1897] AC 81 at 86 per Lord MacNaghten; *Re Brightlife Ltd* [1987] Ch 200. Very clear words, however, are required: *Re The Real Meat Co Ltd* [1996] BCC 254 at 261.

[150]   *Re Brightlife Ltd* [1987] Ch 200. See also *Re Woodroffes (Musical Instruments) Ltd* [1985] 2 All ER 908.

[151]   Eg *Governments Stock and Other Securities Investment Co Ltd v Manila Rly Co Ltd* [1897] AC 81 at 86 per Lord Macnaghten; *Re Yorkshire Woolcombers' Association Ltd* [1903] 2 Ch 284 at 295 per Romer LJ; *Edward Nelson & Co Ltd v Faber & Co* [1903] 2 KB 367 at 376–377; *Evans v Rival Granite Quarries Ltd* [1910] 2 KB 979 per Vaughan Williams and Fletcher Moulton LJJ. See also the Canadian case of *R v Consolidated Churchill Copper Corporation Ltd* [1978] 5 WWR 652.

[152]   [1987] Ch 200.

[153]   On the basis of Hoffmann J's analysis that crystallisation events are purely a matter of contract. See also *Re Horne and Hellard* (1885) 29 ChD 736; *Davey & Co v Williamson & Sons Ltd* [1898] 2 QB 194; *Evans v Rival Granite Quarries Ltd* [1910] 2 KB 979 at 1000 per Buckley LJ; *Re Bond Worth Ltd* [1980] Ch 228 at 266; *Re Permanent Houses (Holdings) Ltd* [1988] BCLC 563; *Re The Real Meat Co Ltd* [1996] BCC 254 at 260.

been considerably reduced by the Insolvency Act 1986, which gives priority to preferential creditors[154] if the charge was a floating charge 'as created', ignoring any subsequent crystallisation.[155]

REGISTRATION OF CHARGES

Introduction

6.54 Every limited company must keep at its registered office a register of charges, and enter in it particulars of all charges specifically affecting property of the company and of all floating charges.[156] Every company must also keep at its registered office a copy of every instrument creating a charge requiring registration at the Companies Registry.[157] Under s 408 of the Companies Act 1985, that register of charges and those copies must be open during business hours[158] to the inspection of any creditor or member of the company without fee, and the register of charges must be open to inspection by any other person on payment of a fee not exceeding five pence.[159] The right to inspect involves a right to take copies without charge,[160] and a right to appoint a solicitor, accountant or other agent to inspect,[161] but the sections do not give a right to have copies supplied.[162]

6.55 In addition, ss 395–399 require particulars of charges created by English companies to be delivered to the Registrar of Companies within 21 days of the date of their creation if they fall within any of the following categories:[163]

(a)   a charge for the purpose of securing any issue of debentures;

---

[154]   Defined in Insolvency Act 1986, s 386 and Sch 6.

[155]   Sections 40, 175 and 251. See also Companies Act 1985, s 196. Note that s 196 of the Companies Act 1985 (but not ss 40 and 175 of the Insolvency Act 1986) have been disapplied in relation to financial collateral arrangements: see further **6.38**. The somewhat curious result is that, where a floating charge that constitutes a financial collateral arrangement is being enforced (other than in a winding-up), preferential creditors have priority if the chargee appoints a receiver but not if he enforces by taking possession.

[156]   Companies Act 1985, s 407. Note that this obligation extends to all charges, whether or not they are registrable at the Companies Registry under s 396.

[157]   Companies Act 1985, s 406.

[158]   Subject to such reasonable restrictions as the company in general meeting may impose, so that not less than two hours in each day be allowed for inspection.

[159]   Refusal of inspection renders every officer of the company who is in default (but not the company itself) liable to a fine: subs (3).

[160]   *Nelson v Anglo-American Land, etc, Co* [1897] 1 Ch 130. The position is different, though, in relation to the register of members (and, by analogy, the register of debenture-holders). The ability of the company in those cases to charge a fee for supplying copies (see **fn 162** below) negates the right to take copies without charge: *Re The Balaghât Gold Mining Company Ltd* [1901] 2 KB 665.

[161]   *Re Credit Company* (1879) 11 ChD 256; *Bevan v Webb* [1901] 2 Ch 59; *Norey v Keep* [1909] 1 Ch 561; *Dodd v Amalgamated Marine Worker's Union* [1924] 1 Ch 116.

[162]   Thus differing from the position regarding the register of members and the register of debenture-holders, where copies must be supplied on payment of the appropriate fee: see ss 356 and 191 respectively. As to the register of debenture-holders, see further **17.1**.

[163]   Listed in s 396(1).

(b) a charge on uncalled share capital of the company;

(c) a charge created or evidenced by an instrument which, if executed by an individual, would require registration as a bill of sale;

(d) a charge on land (wherever situate) or any interest in it, but not including a charge for any rent or other periodical sum issuing out of the land;

(e) a charge on book debts of the company;

(f) a floating charge on the undertaking or property of the company;

(g) a charge on calls made but not paid;

(h) a charge on a ship or aircraft or any share in a ship; and

(i) a charge on goodwill or on any intellectual property.[164]

6.56   However, the obligation to register does not apply in relation to a security financial collateral arrangement[165] or any charge created or otherwise arising under a security financial collateral arrangement.[166]

6.57   Although the above categories cover most charges given by companies, there are a number of notable exceptions, which do not fall within any of the categories and therefore are not registrable at all. These include fixed charges (where they are not securing an issue of debentures) over receivables which do not constitute 'book debts', shareholdings in other companies and insurance policies. The registration requirements under ss 395–399 also extend to foreign companies in certain situations: see **6.86ff**.

6.58   Registrations or filings may need to be made in another country in the case of assets situated abroad. Registrations may also be needed if the security covers particular types of property, eg land (see **6.15**), a ship (Merchant Shipping Act 1995, Sch 1), an aircraft (Civil Aviation Act 1982 and Mortgaging of Aircraft Order 1972),[167] a patent (Patents Act 1977) or a registered trade mark (Trade Marks Act 1994). This chapter, however, is concerned only with the registration of charges under the Companies Act 1985.

---

[164] Defined in s 396(3A) as any patent, trade mark, registered design, copyright or design right, or any licence under or in respect of any such right.

[165] As to the meaning of which, see **6.35**.

[166] Financial Collateral Arrangements (No 2) Regulations 2003 (SI 2003/3226), reg 4(4). However, given the uncertainty (described at **6.37**) in relation to the meaning of 'possession' and 'control', the prevailing practice is still to register, out of caution.

[167] SI 1972/1268, as amended.

What constitutes a registrable charge

6.59 For the purposes of ss 395–399, 'charge' is defined as including a mortgage.[168] The governing law of the charge is irrelevant: what matters is whether it falls within one of the categories in s 396(1). A charge is still registrable even if it is not created or evidenced in writing.[169] However, a security interest which is not 'created' by the company but which arises by operation of law, eg an unpaid vendor's lien over land, need not be registered.[170] An agreement creating a present obligation to give a charge in the future is registrable,[171] but an agreement merely entitling one of the parties to a charge upon satisfaction of a contingency is not registrable until the occurrence of the contingency.[172]

6.60 Whether a charge of substituted property is registrable depends on the circumstances. The general principle is that a charge of substituted property that falls within one of the categories in s 396(1) should be registered,[173] unless the chargee has, pursuant to a power in the charge, effected the substitution without the chargor being made a party.[174] It has been held, however, that, where the charge secures an issue of debentures (including debenture stock) and particulars of the charge have been registered, a charge of substituted property thereunder need not be registered.[175]

[168] Section 396(4). The nature of charges and mortgages is considered at **6.2ff**. 'Charge' here can in certain circumstances include a pledge (see *Dublin City Distillery Ltd v Doherty* [1914] AC 823; *Re South Durham Iron Co* (1879) 11 ChD 579), but would not normally do so (see eg Gough, *Company Charges* (2nd edn, 1996), p 465; Calnan, *Taking Security: Law and Practice* (2006), pp 30–31). 'Charge' does not include a contractual lien (*Re Hamlet International plc* [1999] 2 BCLC 506). As to the position regarding title retention clauses, see **6.11**.

[169] *Sun Tai Cheung Credits Ltd v Attorney-General of Hong Kong* [1987] 1 WLR 948; *Re FLE Holdings Ltd* [1967] 1 WLR 1409. The position is obviously different if the particular head of registration refers to a document, as with s 396(1)(c) (see **6.65**).

[170] *London and Cheshire Insurance Co Ltd v Laplagrene Property Co Ltd* [1971] Ch 499. In fact, no lien (whether created by the company or arising by operation of law) need be registered: *Re Hamlet International plc* [1999] 2 BCLC 506. See also *Brunton v Electrical Engineering Corporation* [1892] 1 Ch 434; *Burston Finance Ltd v Speirway Ltd* [1974] 3 All ER 735.

[171] On the basis that equity looks on that as done which ought to be done: see *Eyre v McDowell* (1861) 9 HLC 619; *Levy v Abercorris Slate and Slab Co* (1887) 37 ChD 260 at 265; *Re Jackson & Bassford Ltd* [1906] 2 Ch 467 at 477; *Re Columbian Fireproofing Co Ltd* [1910] 2 Ch 120; *Re Shoe Lace Ltd* [1993] BCC 609 at 619 per Sir Christopher Slade.

[172] *Re Gregory Love & Co* [1916] 1 Ch 203; *Re C L Nye Ltd* [1971] Ch 442 at 465 per Harman LJ. See also *Williams v Burlington Investments Ltd* (1977) 121 SJ 424; *Levy v Abercorris Slate and Slab Co* (1887) 37 ChD 260. Cf *Alan Estates Ltd v W G Stores Ltd* [1982] Ch 511 (effect of a deed executed in escrow 'relates back' to the date of execution): see further **19.83**.

[173] *Cornbrook, etc, Co Ltd v Law Debenture Corporation Ltd* [1904] 1 Ch 103.

[174] *Bristol United Breweries Ltd v Abbott* [1908] 1 Ch 279.

[175] *Cunard Steamship Co Ltd v Hopwood* [1908] 2 Ch 564. How far the case may still be relied on is unclear, since the section in question (s 14(4) of the Companies Act 1900) required 'a general description of the property charged'. Swinfen Eady J held (at 579) that a 'particular description, sufficient to identify each item or particular property charged, is not required'. Under the Companies Act 1985, however, 'brief particulars' of the property charged are required (Companies (Forms) Regulations 1985, SI 1985/854).

Categories of registrable charge

6.61   As mentioned above, these are listed in s 396(1). Note that, even though a charge may fall within one of these categories, it will not require to be registered to the extent it constitutes a security financial collateral arrangement (ie, where the collateral is cash or financial instruments in the possession or under the control of the chargee, where both chargor and chargee are non-natural persons):[176] this is most likely to be relevant for categories (1) (charge for securing an issue of debentures) and (5) (charge on book debts).

(1)   A charge for the purpose of securing any issue of debentures

6.62   The question of what constitutes a 'debenture' is considered in **Chapter 17**. This is an unusual category, in that it is the only one where registrability depends on the nature of the debt for which the security is given rather than on the nature of the security interest itself. It is not clear whether the category covers a charge securing a single debenture: the better view is that it does not,[177] and this is the view taken by the courts in both New Zealand[178] and Australia,[179] which have held that the category only refers in a collective sense to a group of debentures.

6.63   Where the charge secures 'a series of debentures'[180] of a company, s 397 prescribes an alternative set of registration requirements, compliance with which is sufficient for the purposes of s 395.[181]

(2)   A charge on uncalled share capital of the company

6.64   This form of security is rare. The category does not cover a fixed charge over shares in another company[182] (which, as mentioned earlier, is not registrable at all unless it is securing an issue of debentures).

---

[176]   See further **6.33ff**. As mentioned earlier, given the uncertainty in relation to the meaning of 'possession' and 'control', the prevailing practice is still to register, out of caution. It should also be noted that, where a charge extends to other assets as well as financial collateral, the charge may still need to be registered because of the other assets.

[177]   See, eg, Gough, *Company Charges* (2nd edn, 1996), pp 655–657.

[178]   *Automatic Association (Canterbury) Inc v Australasian Secured Deposits Ltd* [1973] 1 NZLR 417.

[179]   *Nuhan Ltd v Jewel Superannuation Fund Pty Ltd* (1980) 5 ACLR 199. The requirement in Australia to register a charge for the purpose of securing an issue of debentures has since been repealed.

[180]   Which includes an issue of debenture stock: *Cunard Steamship Co Ltd v Hopwood* [1908] 2 Ch 564.

[181]   The purpose of s 397 is to avoid the potential need for separate registration in respect of each debenture. The Companies Registry takes the view that, where s 397 applies, registration must be made under that section and not s 395.

[182]   *Arthur D Little Ltd v Ableco Finance LLC* [2003] Ch 217. However, a fixed charge on dividends and/or the proceeds of sale of shares may be registrable as a charge on book debts (see **6.67–6.68**), and a floating charge over shares will be registrable (see **6.69**).

(3)   A charge created or evidenced by an instrument which, if executed by an individual, would require registration as a bill of sale

6.65   Mortgages and charges by companies are not registrable under the Bills of Sale Acts.[183] Whether a security created by an individual is registrable under the Acts depends both on the nature of the asset secured and on the form of the security. For it to be registrable, the asset secured must be a 'personal chattel', as defined in s 4 of the Bills of Sale Act 1878. These are, broadly, goods and other articles capable of complete transfer by delivery, but excluding shares and other securities in companies and other choses in action.[184] The security must be such that it is created by a document:[185] accordingly, the Acts do not apply to pledges (even where the terms of the pledge are recorded in a separate document or where the goods are returned to the pledgor against a trust receipt),[186] liens,[187] or oral agreements giving security where possession follows later.[188] In addition, to fall within this category, the instrument must not only require registration as a bill of sale if executed by an individual but must also create or evidence a charge.[189]

(4)   A charge on land (wherever situate) or any interest in it, but not including a charge for any rent or other periodical sum issuing out of the land

6.66   For this purpose, the holding of debentures charging land is deemed not to be an interest in land,[190] and accordingly a charge over such debentures does not require registration.

---

[183]   *Re Standard Manufacturing Co* [1891] 1 Ch 627. In that case, the exemption from registration under the Bills of Sale Acts is only expressed to apply to mortgages and charges for which there are separate registration provisions under the companies legislation. However, the existence of this category in s 396(1)(c) means in practice that all mortgages and charges by companies are exempt from registration under the Bills of Sale Acts. See also *Richards v Overseers of Kidderminister* [1896] 2 Ch 212; *Clark v Balm, Hill & Co* [1908] 1 KB 667; *NV Slavenburg's Bank v Intercontinental Natural Resources Ltd* [1980] 1 All ER 955; Gough, *Company Charges* (2nd edn, 1996), pp 863–867.

[184]   See also *Re Sugar Properties (Derisley Wood) Ltd* (1987) 3 BCC 88. A general assignment of book debts, however, is void against a trustee in bankruptcy unless registered under the Bills of Sale Act 1878: Insolvency Act 1986, s 344. An exemption is also provided in certain circumstances by the Bills of Sale Act 1890 (as amended by the Bills of Sale Act 1891) for goods to be imported.

[185]   By virtue of the definition of 'bill of sale' in s 4 of the Bills of Sale Act 1878; and see *North Central Wagon Co v Manchester, Sheffield and Lincolnshire Rly Co* (1887) 35 ChD 191 (affd (1888) 13 App Cas 554); *Newlove v Shrewsbury* (1888) 21 QBD 41.

[186]   *Ex parte Hubbard* (1886) 17 QBD 690; *Charlesworth v Mills* [1892] AC 231; *Wilkinson v Girard Frères* (1891) 7 TLR 266; *Re Cunningham & Co Ltd* (1884) 28 ChD 682; *Re Hall* (1884) 14 QBD 386; *Wrightson v McArthur and Hutchisons (1919) Ltd* [1921] 2 KB 807; *Re David Allester Ltd* [1923] 2 Ch 211. As to trust receipts, see further **6.11**.

[187]   *Re The Vulcan Ironworks (Limited)* (1888) 4 TLR 312; *Re Webber* (1891) 64 LT 426; *Lord's Trustee v Great Eastern Rly Co* [1908] 2 KB 54 at 60 per Cozens-Hardy MR.

[188]   *Charlesworth v Mills* [1892] AC 231; *Ramsay v Margrett* [1894] 2 QB 18.

[189]   *Stoneleigh Finance Ltd v Phillips* [1965] 2 QB 537.

[190]   Section 396(3).

(5) A charge on book debts of the company

6.67 For this purpose, the deposit of a negotiable instrument as security for the payment of a book debt of the depositor is not a charge on book debts.[191]

6.68 The term 'book debts' is not defined in the Companies Act, but has been defined by Lord Esher MR as 'debts arising in a business in which it is the proper and usual course to keep books, and which ought to be entered in such books'.[192] A charge over such a debt is registrable, whether or not the debt is in fact entered in such company's books.[193] A charge over future book debts is also registrable.[194] A letter of hypothecation[195] will be registrable as a charge on book debts if (as it usually does) it extends to the proceeds of sale of the goods in question.[196] However, an insurance policy does not constitute a book debt,[197] nor, it has been held, does a credit balance in the company's bank account.[198]

---

[191] Section 396(2). Note that the exception only extends to the deposit (ie pledge) of the instrument. If the instrument is instead charged (eg by a letter of hypothecation), that charge remains registrable: see, eg, *Chase Manhattan Asia Ltd v Official Receiver and Liquidator of First Bangkok City Finance Ltd* [1990] 1 WLR 1181.

[192] *Official Receiver v Tailby* (1886) 18 QBD 25 at 29, revd on other grounds sub nom *Tailby v Official Receiver* (1888) 13 App Cas 523. See also *Shipley v Marshall* (1863) 14 CB (NS) 566; *Dawson v Isle* [1906] 1 Ch 633; *Re Law Car, etc, Corporation Ltd* [1911] WN 91, affd [1911] WN 101; *Independent Automatic Sales Ltd v Knowles & Foster* [1962] 1 WLR 974; *Paul & Frank Ltd v Discount Bank (Overseas) Ltd* [1967] Ch 348; *Ladenburg & Co v Goodwin, Ferreira & Co Ltd* [1912] 3 KB 275; *Re Brush Aggregates Ltd* [1983] BCLC 320; *Re Welsh Irish Ferries Ltd* [1986] Ch 471; *Re Kent & Sussex Sawmills Ltd* [1947] Ch 177; *Re Buildlead Ltd (No 2)* [2005] BCC 138 at 159; *Re SSSL Realisations (2002) Ltd* [2005] 1 BCLC 1 at 18–19 per Lloyd J (affd CA [2006] 2 WLR 1369 at 1423).

[193] *Independent Automatic Sales Ltd v Knowles & Foster* [1962] 1 WLR 974; *Official Receiver v Tailby* (1886) 18 QBD 25 at 29–30 per Lord Esher MR, rvsd on other grounds sub nom *Tailby v Official Receiver* (1888) 13 App Cas 523; *Siebe Gorman & Co Ltd v Barclays Bank Ltd* [1979] 2 Lloyd's Rep 142.

[194] *Independent Automatic Sales Ltd v Knowles & Foster* [1962] 1 WLR 974; *Re Brush Aggregates Ltd* [1983] BCLC 320.

[195] See **6.6**.

[196] *Ladenburg & Co v Goodwin, Ferreira & Co Ltd* [1912] 3 KB 275.

[197] *Paul & Frank Ltd v Discount Bank (Overseas) Ltd* [1967] Ch 348.

[198] *Re Stevens* [1888] WN 110; *Re Brightlife Ltd* [1987] Ch 200; *Northern Bank Ltd v Ross* [1991] BCLC 504; *Re Buildlead Ltd (No 2)* [2005] BCC 138 at 159. Cf *Re Permanent Houses (Holdings) Ltd* [1988] BCLC 563 at 566–567 (where Hoffmann J pointed out that his judgment in *Re Brightlife Ltd* had been concerned with the construction of the term 'book debts' in a charging document, and expressly left open the construction of the term for the purposes of s 395). See also *Re Bank of Credit and Commerce International SA (No 8)* [1998] AC 214 at 227 (where Lord Hoffmann, while expressing no view as to whether a deposit with a bank is a book debt for registration purposes, noted the view of Lord Hutton in *Northern Bank Ltd v Ross* that an obligation to register is unlikely to arise). See also **6.48**.

(6) A floating charge on the undertaking or property of the company

6.69 Floating charges have already been considered at **6.39ff**. A floating charge is registrable under this category even though it is over part only of the undertaking or property.[199]

(7) A charge on calls made but not paid

6.70 Charges on uncalled capital have been considered above.[200] This category applies where calls have been made but not yet paid. Such calls are a form of debt, but are not regarded as book debts.

(8) A charge on a ship or aircraft or any share in a ship

6.71 A legal mortgage[201] of a registered British ship must be made in the form prescribed under the Merchant Shipping Act 1995, and is registrable under that Act.[202] The mortgaging of aircraft is governed by s 86 of the Civil Aviation Act 1982 and the Mortgaging of Aircraft Order 1972,[203] which provide for the registration of such mortgages in a register to be maintained by the Civil Aviation Authority.[204]

(9) A charge on goodwill or on any intellectual property

6.72 Goodwill has been defined as 'the benefit and advantage of the good name, reputation, and connection of a business. It is the attractive force which brings in custom. It is the one thing which distinguishes an old-fashioned business from a new business at its first start'.[205] It accordingly follows that goodwill cannot be assigned or charged except together with the business to which it attaches.

6.73 Intellectual property is defined in s 396(3A) of the Companies Act 1985 as any patent, trade mark, registered design, copyright or design right, or any licence under or in respect of any such right. Taking these in turn:

---

[199] *Re Yorkshire Woolcombers Association Ltd* [1903] 2 Ch 284 at 298 per Cozens-Hardy LJ, affd sub nom *Illingworth v Houldsworth* [1904] AC 355.

[200] At **6.64**.

[201] The formalities under the Merchant Shipping Act 1995 do not apply to equitable mortgages and charges. A duly registered legal mortgage of a ship has priority over an equitable charge previously created, even where the legal mortgagee has notice of the equitable charge: *Black v Williams* [1895] 1 Ch 408; *Barclay & Co Ltd v Poole* [1907] 2 Ch 284.

[202] Merchant Shipping Act 1995, Sch 1, para 7. Where two or more mortgages are registered in respect of the same ship, the priority of the mortgagees between themselves shall be determined by the order of registration: ibid, Sch 1, para 8(1).

[203] SI 1972/1268, as amended.

[204] A duly registered mortgage has priority over any other mortgage or charge of the relevant aircraft, other than a prior registered mortgage: Mortgaging of Aircraft Order 1972, art 14(1).

[205] *IRC v Muller & Co's Margarine Ltd* [1901] AC 217 at 223–224 per Lord MacNaghten. See also *Churton v Douglas* (1859) Johns 174 at 188 per Page Wood V-C.

(a) Patents

6.74 A mortgage[206] of a patent or application or right in a patent or application is void unless it is in writing and signed by or on behalf of the mortgagor.[207] Registration of the mortgage in the register of patents is not essential for validity, but a duly registered mortgage has priority over an earlier unregistered mortgage, so long as the later mortgagee did not know of the earlier mortgage.[208]

(b) Registered trade marks

6.75 Registered trade marks can be either UK registered trade marks[209] or Community trade marks[210] (which are applied for in respect of, and have effect throughout, the territory of the European Community). However, the registration requirement under s 395 only applies where the security is over a UK registered trade mark.[211] A UK registered trade mark[212] may be either assigned[213] or charged.[214] An assignment[215] of a UK registered trade mark is not effective unless it is in writing signed by or on behalf of the assignor.[216] The granting of any security interest (fixed or floating) over a UK registered trade mark or any right in or under it is registrable in the register of trade marks;[217] registration is not essential for validity, but, until an application has been made for registration, the security interest is ineffective as against a person acquiring a conflicting interest in or under the registered trade mark in ignorance of it.[218]

(c) Unregistered trade marks

6.76 Since the only legal right which arises from an unregistered trade mark is the right to sue for passing off, an unregistered trade mark, like goodwill, cannot be assigned or charged except together with the business to which it attaches.

---

[206] Defined as including a charge for securing money or money's worth: Patents Act 1977, s 130(1).

[207] Patents Act 1977, s 30(6). In the case of a mortgage by a body corporate, references to being signed by or on behalf of the mortgagor include references to its being under the seal of the body corporate: ibid, s 30(6A).

[208] Patents Act 1977, s 33(1).

[209] Under the Trade Marks Act 1994.

[210] Under EC Council Regulation 40/94 (which is directly applicable in all member states).

[211] By the Trade Marks Act 1994, s 106(1) and Sch 4, para 1, the reference in s 396(3A) to a trade mark is to be construed as a reference to a trade mark within the meaning of the 1994 Act. Security may be granted over Community trade marks (EC Council Regulation 40/94, art 19(1)). At the request of one of the parties, the rights of the chargee must be entered in the register of Community trade marks (art 19(2)): if they are not so entered, a third party who acquires rights in the trade mark is not bound by the security unless he knows of it (art 23(1)).

[212] Defined as any sign capable of being represented graphically which is capable of distinguishing goods or services of one undertaking from those of other undertakings: Trade Marks Act 1994, s 1(1).

[213] Trade Marks Act 1994, s 24(1).

[214] Trade Marks Act 1994, s 24(5).

[215] Including an assignment by way of security: Trade Marks Act 1994, s 24(4).

[216] Trade Marks Act 1994, s 24(3). Where the assignor is a body corporate, this requirement may be satisfied by affixing the seal of the body corporate: ibid, s 24(3).

[217] Trade Marks Act 1994, s 25(2).

[218] Trade Marks Act 1994, s 25(3).

(d)   Registered designs

6.77   Where a person becomes entitled as mortgagee or otherwise to any interest in a registered design, he is under a duty[219] to apply to the registrar of designs for registration of notice of his interest in the register of designs.[220] A document not referred to in the register is not admissible in court as evidence of the relevant security interest unless the court otherwise directs.[221]

(e)   Copyright

6.78   Copyright exists solely by virtue of the Copyright, Designs and Patents Act 1988. It arises automatically, and there is no provision under that Act for registration, whether of creation, assignment or grant of security. However, an assignment, to be effective, must be in writing signed by or on behalf of the assignor[222] (or, in the case of a body corporate, executed under its seal[223]).

6.79   The reference in s 396(3A) to copyright includes also publication right[224] (a property right equivalent to copyright given in certain circumstances to a person who, after the expiry of copyright protection, publishes for the first time a previously unpublished work).[225]

(f)   Design rights

6.80   Design rights, a form of property rights in original designs, arise by virtue of the Copyright, Designs and Patents Act 1988. As with copyright, there is no provision for registration, and an assignment, to be effective, must be in writing signed by or on behalf of the assignor[226] (or, in the case of a body corporate, executed under its seal[227]).

Effects of registration and failure to register

6.81   Failure to deliver to the Registrar of Companies[228] within 21 days of the creation of the charge the prescribed particulars,[229] together with the

---

[219]   Although there is no criminal penalty for failure to comply.

[220]   Registered Designs Act 1949, s 19(1).

[221]   Registered Designs Act 1949, s 19(5).

[222]   Copyright, Designs and Patents Act 1988, s 90(3).

[223]   Copyright, Designs and Patents Act 1988, s 176(1).

[224]   Copyright and Related Rights Regulations 1996 (SI 1996/2967), reg 17(5).

[225]   Publication right exists by virtue of the Copyright and Related Rights Regulations 1996 (SI 1996/2967).

[226]   Copyright, Designs and Patents Act 1988, s 222(3).

[227]   Copyright, Designs and Patents Act 1988, s 261.

[228]   It is the delivery to the Registrar of Companies that matters, not the entry in the register: *NV Slavenburg's Bank v Intercontinental Natural Resources Ltd* [1980] 1 All ER 955; *National Provincial and Union Bank of England v Charnley* [1924] 1 KB 431 at 447 per Scrutton LJ. However, the issue of a certificate of registration, even where the particulars have been presented out of time, will prevent the charge becoming void for want of registration: see further below.

[229]   Although the details required by Form 395, which sets out the prescribed particulars (Companies (Forms) Regulations 1985 (SI 1985/854), para 4(2)), include the company's registered number, the number is not a 'prescribed particular', because it is a particular of the mortgagor rather than a particular of the charge: *Grove v Advantage Healthcare (T10) Ltd* [2000] BCC 985.

instrument, if any, by which the charge is created or evidenced, makes the charge[230] void against the liquidator or administrator and any creditor of the company[231] (even if the creditor is a second mortgagee with notice of the prior unregistered charge),[232] and renders the company and every officer who is in default liable to a fine.[233] When the charge becomes void, the money secured becomes immediately payable.[234] There are provisions in s 404, however, for the extension of the 21-day limit[235] and for the rectification of mistakes.[236]

6.82   Registration, besides giving actual notice of the charge to those who search the register, also gives constructive notice to all those who ought reasonably to have searched.[237] The notice does not extend to the contents of the charge,[238] merely to 'any matter which would have come to [the relevant person's] knowledge if such inquiries and inspections had been made as ought reasonably to have been made by [him]'.[239] These inquiries include

---

[230] But not the underlying debt: s 395(2). 'The failure to register the charge renders the security ... void as against the administrator, but does not affect any other right ... which is not a security and which does not require registration' (*Re Cosslett (Contractors) Ltd* [1989] Ch 495 at 511 per Millett LJ). See also *Re Monolithic Building Co* [1915] 1 Ch 643 at 667 per Phillimore LJ; *Smith v Bridgend CBC* [2002] 1 AC 336 at 348 per Lord Hoffmann and 359 per Lord Scott.

[231] Section 395(1). The charge remains valid against third parties who are not creditors (*Stroud Architectural Systems Ltd v John Laing Construction Ltd* [1994] BCC 18) and against the company so long as it is not in liquidation or administration (see *Re Monolithic Building Co* [1915] 1 Ch 643 at 667 per Lord Cozens-Hardy MR and Phillimore LJ; *Independent Automatic Sales Ltd v Knowles & Foster* [1962] 1 WLR 974; *Smith v Bridgend CBC* [2002] 1 AC 336 at 348 per Lord Hoffmann and 359 per Lord Scott). The rationale behind the requirement to register and the consequences of failure to register was explained by Lord Hoffmann in *Smith v Bridgend CBC* [2002] 1 AC 336 at 347–348: 'Section 395, which can be traced back to the Companies Act 1900, was intended for the protection of the creditors of an insolvent company. It was intended to give persons dealing with a company the opportunity to discover, by consulting the register, whether its assets were burdened by floating and certain fixed charges which would reduce the amount available for unsecured creditors in a liquidation. Whether this was a realistic form of protection and whether the choice of registrable charges was entirely logical is not presently relevant. The plain intention of the legislature was that property subject to a registrable but unregistered charge should be available to the general body of creditors (or a secured creditor ranking after the unregistered charge) as if no such charge existed.'

[232] *Re Monolithic Building Co* [1915] 1 Ch 643. Cf *Eyre v McDowell* (1861) 9 HLC 619 at 646 per Lord Cranworth.

[233] Section 399(3).

[234] Section 395(2).

[235] If the court is satisfied that the omission to register or the omission or misstatement of any particular 'was accidental, or due to inadvertence or to some other sufficient cause, or is not of a nature to prejudice the position of creditors or shareholders of the company, or that on other grounds it is just and equitable to grant relief' (Companies Act 1985, s 404(1)). In *Re Braemar Investments Ltd* [1988] BCLC 556 at 561 (cited with approval in *Confiance Ltd v Timespan Images Ltd* [2005] 2 BCLC 693 at 699–701), Hoffmann J said that 'the underlying guide to the exercise of the discretion is whether for any reason, whether specified in the section or not, it would be just and equitable to grant relief'.

[236] In *igroup Ltd v Ocwen* [2004] 1 WLR 451, it was held that the power of rectification is limited to correcting mistakes in the particulars that the registrar is required to enter on the register or in the memorandum of satisfaction that he is permitted to enter on the register. If therefore does not extend to details in other documents, such as a prescribed form, even if referred to in an entry on the register.

[237] *Siebe Gorman & Co Ltd v Barclays Bank Ltd* [1979] 2 Lloyd's Rep 142 at 160. See also *Channel Airways Ltd v Manchester Corpn* [1974] 1 Lloyd's Rep 456 at 459.

[238] *Wilson v Kelland* [1910] 2 Ch 306; *Re Standard Rotary Machine Co Ltd* (1906) 95 LT 829; *The English and Scottish Mercantile Investment Co Ltd v Brunton* [1892] 2 QB 700, *G and T Earle Ltd v Hemsworth RDC* (1928) 44 TLR 605.

[239] *Siebe Gorman & Co Ltd v Barclays Bank Ltd* [1979] 2 Lloyd's Rep 142 at 160.

searching the register but not, ordinarily, inspecting the charging document.[240] Consequently, it is usual to include in the registered particulars a note of any restriction on the creation of other security, in an attempt to give potential subsequent purchasers and chargees constructive notice of the restriction.[241]

6.83 The Registrar must give a certificate of the registration, stating the amount secured, and the certificate will be conclusive evidence that the requirements of the Companies Act as to registration have been complied with.[242] The charge therefore cannot subsequently be set aside for non-registration,[243] even if the particulars omitted the date of the authorising resolution[244] or part of the charged property[245] or incorrectly stated the amount secured[246] or the date of the charge,[247] or were delivered more than 21 days after the creation of the charge. However, the issue of the Registrar's certificate does not confer validity on a charge which is invalid for reasons other than lack of due registration.[248]

6.84 The Companies Registry's practice regarding the type of particulars that will be acceptable for registration is set out in Guidance Booklet A8.[249] In particular, it should be noted that the form must be completed in full, and

---

240 Ibid.
241 As to the extent to which this does give rise to constructive notice, see Goode, *Legal Problems of Credit and Security* (3rd edn, 2003), pp 81–82.
242 Section 401(2). The company must cause a copy of every certificate issued under s 401 to be endorsed on every debenture (as to the meaning of which, see **Chapter 17**) or certificate of debenture stock issued by it, the payment of which is secured by the charge so registered: s 402(1). It is not entirely clear from this wording whether it includes debentures issued by third parties (eg stock secured by charges from charging subsidiaries – see **3.5(j)**), although the usual practice is for the relevant certificates to be endorsed. There is no need for endorsement, however, where debentures or certificates for debenture stock have already been issued and further charges are created: s 402(2).
243 *Re Yolland, Husson & Birkett Ltd* [1908] 1 Ch 152; *Re Mechanisations (Eaglescliffe) Ltd* [1966] Ch 20; *Re CL Nye Ltd* [1971] Ch 442; *National Provincial and Union Bank of England v Charnley* [1924] 1 KB 431; *Cunard Steamship Co Ltd v Hopwood* [1908] 2 Ch 564; *Re Eric Holmes (Property) Ltd* [1965] Ch 1052; *R v Registrar of Companies ex parte Central Bank of India* [1986] 1 All ER 105; *Exeter Trust Ltd v Screenways Ltd* [1991] BCC 477. However, where the certificate contains an error that renders it meaningless (eg referring to the wrong company name and number), it is worthless and therefore s 401(2) cannot apply to it: *Grove v Advantage Healthcare (T10) Ltd* [2000] BCC 985. It has also been suggested that the charge could be set aside, or the chargee prevented from taking advantage of it, on the application of the Attorney-General or if the certificate was obtained by fraud or discloses some other error on its face (*R v Registrar of Companies ex parte Central Bank of India* [1986] 1 All ER 105 at 123 per Slade LJ; see also *Sun Tai Cheung Credits Ltd v Attorney-General of Hong Kong* [1987] 1 WLR 948 at 953). In any event, if the certificate is obtained by fraud, the fraudulent party may be estopped from relying on the conclusiveness of the certificate or proceedings for damages against the fraudulent party may be possible: *National Provincial Bank v Charnley* [1924] 1 KB 431 at 454 per Atkin LJ; *Re CL Nye Ltd* [1971] Ch 442 at 474 per Russell LJ; *R v Registrar of Companies ex parte Central Bank of India* [1986] 1 All ER 105 at 123 per Slade LJ.
244 *Cunard Steamship Co Ltd v Hopwood* [1908] 2 Ch 564.
245 *National Provincial and Union Bank of England v Charnley* [1924] 1 KB 431.
246 *Re Mechanisations (Eaglescliffe) Ltd* [1966] Ch 20.
247 *Re Eric Holmes (Property) Ltd* [1965] Ch 1052; *Re CL Nye Ltd* [1971] 1 Ch 442; *R v Registrar of Companies ex parte Central Bank of India* [1986] 1 All ER 105.
248 See, eg, *R v Registrar of Companies ex parte Central Bank of India* [1986] QB 1114 at 1177 per Slade LJ.
249 February 2005.

that it is not sufficient merely to cross-refer to the charging document. Substantive errors will need to be corrected and the form re-submitted within the 21-day period.[250] The original charging document must be sent,[251] unless a charge already exists on the property[252] or the charge is on property outside the UK,[253] in which event an appropriately certified or verified copy will suffice.

Property acquired subject to a charge

6.85　　If a company acquires property subject to one of the charges listed in s 396(1), it must register the charge within 21 days of the completion of the acquisition.[254] Failure to register exposes the company and every officer who is in default to a fine,[255] but does not invalidate the charge.[256]

'Slavenburg' filings

6.86　　A particular problem arises in relation to security granted by a foreign company. The registration requirements described above apply if the foreign company has 'an established place of business' in England and Wales, and the security is over property in England and Wales.[257] Whether the company has an established place of business[258] is a question of fact, to be determined as at the date of creation of the charge,[259] irrespective of the state of affairs at any other time.[260]

6.87　　Part XXIII of the Companies Act 1985 requires a company incorporated outside Great Britain to deliver prescribed documents and details to the Registrar of Companies if it establishes a place of business in

---

[250]　The previous practice of accepting a re-submitted form even if the 21-day period had expired is no longer followed, as a result of the criticisms in *R v Registrar of Companies ex parte Esal (Commodities) Ltd* [1985] 2 WLR 447, rvsd sub nom *R v Registrar of Companies ex parte Central Bank of India* [1986] 1 All ER 105.

[251]　Companies Act 1985, s 395(1).

[252]　Companies Act 1985, s 400(2).

[253]　Companies Act 1985, s 398(1).

[254]　Companies Act 1985, s 400.

[255]　Companies Act 1985, s 400(4).

[256]　*Capital Finance Co Ltd v Stokes* [1969] 1 Ch 261.

[257]　Companies Act 1985, s 409. The section applies not only to charges created by the company over property in England and Wales but also to charges on property in England and Wales which is acquired by the company (ie extending s 400 (described at **6.85**) to such acquisitions).

[258]　'Some more or less permanent location, not necessarily owned or even leased by the company, but at least associated with the company and from which habitually or with some degree of regularity business is conducted': *Re Oriel Ltd* [1985] 3 All ER 216 at 220 per Oliver LJ.

[259]　Or the date of acquisition, in the case of secured property in England and Wales acquired by the company.

[260]　*Re Oriel Ltd* [1985] 3 All ER 216 at 219 per Oliver LJ; *Re Alton Corporation* [1985] BCLC 27 at 30. Consequently, it is irrelevant if the company no longer has an established place of business at the time of enforcement, or if the company establishes a place of business only after the creation of the security (or acquisition of the property).

England.[261] Prior to the decision in *NV Slavenburg's Bank v Intercontinental Natural Resources Ltd*,[262] it had been assumed that, where a foreign company had not complied with Part XXIII,[263] the charge registration requirements did not apply,[264] and indeed the Registrar of Companies would not accept particulars for registration unless the company had been registered under Part XXIII. In *Slavenburg*, however, Lloyd J held that the correct test was whether the foreign company had, as a factual matter, an established place of business in England and Wales, and not whether it had been registered under Part XXIII. Moreover, registration was required not only for property in England and Wales at the time of creation of the charge, but also for property outside England and Wales at the time of creation, but which was subsequently brought in.[265] Despite the Registrar's practice, Lloyd J held that the requirements could be complied with, since what matters is the delivery to the Registrar, not the entry in the register.[266]

6.88   As a result of the decision the normal practice now in relation to security created by foreign companies is to file the prescribed particulars and charging instrument in accordance with s 395 whenever there is a concern that the company might be deemed to have an established place of business in England and Wales, and that the secured property might be regarded as being in England and Wales, or might subsequently be brought in. This is known as a 'Slavenburg' filing. The Registrar will make a note of the documents sent and then return them to the sender with a standard form letter as proof of delivery to the Registrar.[267]

---

[261] Companies Act 1985, s 691. Since 1 January 1993, however, different documents and details are required in the case of a limited company incorporated outside the UK and Gibraltar with a branch in Great Britain: Companies Act 1985, s 690A and Sch 21A, giving effect to the Eleventh Company Law Directive (89/666/EEC).

[262] [1980] 1 All ER 955. See also *Re Oriel Ltd* [1985] 3 All ER 216; *Re Alton Corporation* [1985] BCLC 27.

[263] Or its then equivalent.

[264] See, eg, *Re Alton Corporation* [1985] BCLC 27 at 34.

[265] *Slavenburg*, ibid, at 966.

[266] *Slavenburg*, ibid. at 963; *National Provincial and Union Bank of England v Charnley* [1924] 1 KB 431 at 447 per Scrutton LJ. See further **2.81**.

[267] 'A curious state of affairs': *Re Alton Corporation* [1985] BCLC 27 at 34 per Sir Robert Megarry V-C.

PRIORITY[268]

Priority between competing fixed security interests

6.89   The general rule is that security interests rank in order of creation (*'qui prior est tempore, potior est jure'*),[269] subject to a number of exceptions, of which the following are the most important:

(a) A charge requiring registration at the Companies Registry and not registered will be void against the liquidator or administrator and any creditor of the company.[270] Consequently, a registered charge will take priority over an unregistered charge, whether created previously or subsequently, unless the unregistered charge has been created within the 21 days (or longer, if an extension of time for registration is granted)[271] before the creation of the registered charge and is subsequently duly registered. In that case, the subsequently registered charge will achieve priority in accordance with the general rule above, unless one of the other exceptions below applies.

(b) A legal interest will override a prior equitable interest, provided it has been purchased for value and without notice of the equitable interest.[272] Notice can be either actual or constructive. Registration of a charge at the Companies Registry constitutes constructive notice to all those who ought reasonably to search,[273] and registration under the Land Charges Act 1972 constitutes actual notice.[274] Where a holder of equitable security exercises his right to call for legal title (the *tabula in naufragio*),[275] the fact that he has in the meantime acquired notice of a

---

268 See further Gough, *Company Charges* (2nd edn, 1996), Chapters 37–42; *Fisher and Lightwood's Law of Mortgage* (11th edn, 2002), Chapter 24; Goode, *Legal Problems of Credit and Security* (3rd edn, 2003), Chapter 5; *MacMillan Inc v Bishopsgate Investment Trust plc (No 3)* [1995] 1 WLR 978 at 999–1005 per Millett J (affd CA, [1996] 1 WLR 387).

269 See, eg, *Beckett v Cordley* (1784) 1 Bro CC 353; *Jones v Jones* (1838) 8 Sim 633; *Wilmot v Pike* (1845) 5 Hare 14; *Re Samuel Allen & Sons Ltd* [1907] 1 Ch 575; *Barclays Bank Ltd v Bird* [1954] 1 Ch 274.

270 See **6.81**.

271 Although the usual practice is for the order to be expressed to be without prejudice to the rights of parties acquired prior to the time when the hitherto unregistered charge is actually registered. Cf *Watson v Duff Morgan & Vermont (Holdings) Ltd* [1974] 1 WLR 450.

272 See, eg, *Pilcher v Rawlins* (1872) LR 7 Ch App 259; *Sheffield v London Joint Stock Bank Ltd* (1888) 13 App Cas 333; *Coleman v London County and Westminster Bank Ltd* [1916] 2 Ch 353.

273 See **6.82**.

274 See **6.19**.

275 The 'plank in the shipwreck': 'the insufficiency of the security was the "shipwreck", and the legal estate was the "plank" which any equitable mortgagee might seize without concern for the others. The metaphor implies a disaster where someone must lose, and each party may save himself as best he can' (Megarry & Wade, *The Law of Real Property* (6th edn, 2000), pp 1280–1281). In relation to mortgages of land, the right to obtain priority through a *tabula in naufragio* (except in relation to the tacking of further advances, considered at (f) below) was abolished by s 94(3) of the Law of Property Act 1925.

prior equitable right does not lose him priority: what matters is whether he had notice when he took the initial security.[276]

(c) Special rules apply to land: these are considered at **6.13ff**.

(d) Priority may be lost by misconduct, eg fraud or negligence, by estoppel, by imputed consent or (in the case of equitable security) by inequitable conduct.[277]

(e) The priority of successive assignments of a debt or other thing in action is governed by the rule in *Dearle v Hall*,[278] as extended by the Law of Property Act 1925, ss 136 and 137,[279] under which an assignee who takes without notice of an earlier assignment and is the first to give notice of the assignment to the obligor gains priority.[280] The rule, however, is inapplicable to shares,[281] to negotiable instruments,[282] or to uncertificated securities held electronically through CREST.[283]

(f) In general, a mortgagee can tack further advances ranking in priority to a subsequent mortgagee until he has notice of the subsequent mortgage, but not thereafter.[284] However, in the case of unregistered land, a mortgagee is not deemed to have notice of a subsequent mortgage merely because it has been registered as a land charge, if it was not registered when the original mortgage was created or when the mortgagee last searched.[285] He may also continue to tack, whether or not he has notice, if the mortgage imposes an obligation on him to make further advances.[286] Furthermore, in the case of registered land, the first mortgagee may tack if: he has not received from the subsequent mortgagee[287] notice of the creation of the subsequent mortgage[288]; or the further advance is made pursuant to an obligation which was entered in

---

[276] *Taylor v Russell* [1892] AC 244; *Bailey v Barnes* [1894] 1 Ch 25; *Macmillan Inc v Bishopsgate Investment Trust (No 3)* [1995] 1 WLR 978 at 1002–1005 per Millett J (affd CA [1996] 1 WLR 387). It seems that this principle only applies to the promotion of a fixed equitable interest and not to the crystallisation of a floating charge. Nor does the principle apply to competing assignments of a debt, the priority of which is determined in accordance with exception (e) below (see, eg, *Harding Carpets Ltd v Royal Bank of Canada* [1980] 4 WWR 149).

[277] See, eg, *Dixon v Muckleston* (1872) LR 8 Ch App 155; *Oliver v Hinton* [1899] 2 Ch 264; *Clarke v Palmer* (1882) 21 ChD 124; *Bristol & West Building Society v Henning* [1985] 2 All ER 606; *Northern Counties of England Fire Insurance Co v Whipp* (1884) 26 ChD 482; *Shropshire Union Railways and Canal Co v The Queen* (1875) LR 7 HL 496; *Equity and Law Home Loans Ltd v Prestidge* [1992] 1 All ER 909.

[278] (1828) 3 Russ 1.

[279] The most important extension is to equitable interests in land (s 137(1)).

[280] See further **15.18**.

[281] *Société Générale de Paris v Walker* (1885) 11 App Cas 20.

[282] See further **15.3ff**.

[283] Uncertificated Securities Regulations 2001 (SI 2001/3755), reg 23(3), which prohibits CREST from entering on the CREST register notice of any trust, express, implied or constructive. As regards mortgages of securities held in CREST, see **6.22**.

[284] See further Goode, *Legal Problems of Credit and Security* (3rd edn, 2003), pp 163–167.

[285] Law of Property Act 1925, s 94(2). However, the mortgagee may still have constructive notice of the subsequent mortgage if it has been registered at the Companies Registry.

[286] Law of Property Act 1925, s 94(1).

[287] Accordingly, notice from another source does not prevent the ability to tack.

[288] Land Registration Act 2002, s 49(1).

the register at the time of creation of the subsequent mortgage[289]; or the parties to the prior mortgage have agreed a maximum amount for which the mortgage is security and such agreement was entered in the register at the time of creation of the subsequent mortgage.[290]

(g) Special rules apply to judgment creditors[291] and to mortgages of ships,[292] aircraft[293] and intellectual property.[294]

(h) A charge over after-acquired property will usually be postponed to the interest of a person who provides the purchase money for the property and contracts for security over it.[295]

(i) In the absence of a provision to the contrary, priority may be varied by agreement between the chargees without the consent of the chargor,[296] and in any event may always be varied by agreement between the chargees and the chargor.[297] In the case of registered land, though, the variation is not effective until an entry is made in the register.[298]

Priority of floating charges

6.90 The general rule is that a duly registered floating charge[299] will rank after all prior and subsequent charges and other interests (legal or equitable) arising before crystallisation, unless the other charge or interest:

(a) is a registrable charge which is void for non-registration;

(b) is a subsequently created floating charge;[300]

---

[289] Land Registration Act 2002, s 49(3).

[290] Land Registration Act 2002, s 49(4). This limb is an important change to the previous position, in that it allows the first mortgagee to tack even if the further advance is made after notice of the subsequent mortgage and is made entirely voluntarily. It thus allows a mortgage to be drawn down in tranches (up to a maximum) in priority to subsequent mortgages.

[291] See *Fisher and Lightwood's Law of Mortgage* (11th edn, 2002), pp 741–742.

[292] See **6.71**.

[293] See **6.71**.

[294] See **6.72ff**.

[295] *Abbey National Building Society v Cann* [1991] 1 AC 56. See also *Chohan v Saggar* [1993] BCLC 661 at 667.

[296] *Cheah Theam Swee v Equiticorp Finance Group Ltd* [1992] 1 AC 472. Special rules apply, however, in relation to land: see below.

[297] *Re Portbase Clothing Ltd* [1993] Ch 388.

[298] Land Registration Act 2002, s 48 and Land Registration Rules 2003 (SI 2003/1417), regs 101 and 102. The application to alter the register must be made by or with the consent of the chargee whose priority is being adversely affected, but no such consent is required if the chargee has executed the instrument altering the priority: Land Registration Rules 2003 (SI 2003/1417), reg 102(1). In the case of unregistered land, it would appear, however, from the wording of Law of Property Act 1925, s 97 (C(i) and C(iii) charges registered under the Land Charges Act 1972 affecting a legal estate rank in order or registration) that priority in relation to such charges cannot be varied.

[299] If it is not duly registered, it is void against a liquidator or administrator and any creditor of the company: see **6.81**.

[300] *Re Benjamin Cope & Sons Ltd* [1914] 1 Ch 800; *Smith v English and Scottish Mercantile Investment Trust* [1896] WN 86. This rule applies even though the later charge is the first to crystallise (*Re Household Products Co Ltd* (1981) 124 DLR (3d) 325; but cf *Griffiths v Yorkshire Bank plc* [1994] 1 WLR 1427 at 1435, which is inconsistent with the previous authorities) but not where the first chargee has agreed to the subsequent charge ranking in priority (*Re Automatic Bottle Makers Ltd* [1926] Ch 412).

(c) is a previously created floating charge in which the chargee has agreed to the subsequent charge ranking in priority;[301]

(d) is a subsequently created charge (fixed or floating) or other interest which breaches a restrictive clause in the first charge of which the subsequent chargee has notice;[302]

(e) arises subsequently and derives from a transaction outside the ordinary course of the chargor's business;[303] or

(f) ranks behind the floating charge by virtue of an agreement between the relevant chargees varying priority, whether with the chargor's agreement[304] or without.[305]

6.91 Certain unsecured creditors also have priority over a floating charge. An execution creditor has priority if the execution is completed, or payment is made to avoid execution, before crystallisation, but not otherwise.[306] A landlord levying distress for rent[307] has priority[308] except, possibly, where there is fraud or unfair dealing.[309] Preferential creditors[310] have priority if, when the chargor company is not in winding up, the chargee takes possession of the charged property[311] or appoints a receiver,[312] or if the

---

[301] *Re Automatic Bottle Makers Ltd* [1926] Ch 412.

[302] *Wilson v Kelland* [1910] 2 Ch 306; *English and Scottish Mercantile Investment Co Ltd v Brunton* [1892] 2 QB 700 at 707 per Lord Esher MR; *G and T Earle Ltd v Hemsworth RDC* (1928) 44 TLR 605 at 608; *Re Portbase Clothing Ltd* [1993] Ch 399. Cf *Griffiths v Yorkshire Bank plc* [1994] 1 WLR 1427 at 1435, which is inconsistent with the previous authorities. Notice of the charge, though, is not by itself notice of the restrictive clause (*Wilson v Kelland* [1910] 2 Ch 306; *English & Scottish Mercantile Investment Co Ltd v Brunton* [1892] 2 QB 700; *G and T Earle Ltd v Hemsworth RDC* (1928) 44 TLR 605; *Re Standard Rotary Machine Co Ltd* (1906) 95 LT 829; *Siebe Gorman & Co Ltd v Barclays Bank Ltd* [1979] 2 Lloyd's Rep 142), hence the practice, mentioned earlier, of including a note of restrictive clauses in the particulars filed at the Companies Registry. As to the extent to which this gives rise to constructive notice, see Goode, *Legal Problems of Credit and Security* (3rd edn, 2003), pp 81–82.

[303] On the basis that the transaction is outside the range of transactions permitted by the floating charge, and therefore is of the same effect as a breach of a restrictive clause of which the subsequent buyer or incumbrancer had notice.

[304] *Re Portbase Clothing Ltd* [1993] Ch 388.

[305] *Cheah Theam Swee v Equiticorp Finance Group Ltd* [1992] 1 AC 472; *Re Portbase Clothing Ltd* [1993] Ch 388 at 398.

[306] *Re Opera Ltd* [1891] 3 Ch 260; *Robson v Smith* [1895] 2 Ch 118; *Norton v Yates* [1906] 1 KB 112; *Cairney v Back* [1906] 2 KB 746; *Robinson v Burnell's Vienna Bakery Co Ltd* [1904] 2 KB 624; *Evans v Rival Granite Quarries Ltd* [1910] 2 KB 979; *Heaton and Dugard Ltd v Cutting Brothers Ltd* [1925] 1 KB 655.

[307] It is irrelevant whether the levying is before or after crystallisation: see below.

[308] *Re Roundwood Colliery Co* [1897] 1 Ch 373.

[309] *Herbert Berry Associates Ltd v IRC* [1978] 1 All ER 161 at 168 per Lord Simon.

[310] For this purpose, 'preferential debts' means the categories of debts listed in Sch 6 to the Insolvency Act 1986 (as amended by the Enterprise Act 2002): Insolvency Act 1986, s 386. Preferential creditors do not have preference in administration.

[311] Companies Act 1985, s 196. The priority does not apply if the floating charge is created or otherwise arises under a financial collateral arrangement (Financial Collateral Arrangements (No 2) Regulations 2003 (SI 2003/3226), reg 10(6). On financial collateral arrangements, see **6.33ff**. As mentioned earlier (at **6.38**), it is curious that s 196 (relating to the chargee taking possession) is disapplied but s 40 of the Insolvency Act 1986 (relating to the chargee appointing a receiver – referred to in the next footnote) is not.

chargor company goes into winding up.[313] And any receiver,[314] liquidator or administrator of a company is required to make a 'prescribed part'[315] of the floating charge realisations available for the satisfaction of unsecured debts in priority to the claims of the floating charge-holder.[316]

6.92   Once the charge crystallises, so as to become fixed, priority in relation to charges and other interests arising after crystallisation will be determined in the manner set out at **6.89**, subject to two exceptions:

(a) a landlord levying distress for rent, even after crystallisation, will, it appears, still have priority;[317] and

(b) crystallisation does not alter the relationship with preferential creditors, who remain in priority.[318]

---

[312] Insolvency Act 1986, s 40. The priority is over all floating chargees, not just the chargee appointing the receiver: *Re H&K (Medway) Ltd* [1997] 2 All ER 321. Cf *Griffiths v Yorkshire Bank plc* [1994] 1 WLR 1427.

[313] Insolvency Act 1986, s 175. Although s 175(2)(a) refers to preferential debts ranking 'equally among themselves after the expenses of the winding up', the House of Lords held in *Buchler v Talbot (Re Leyland Daf Ltd)* [2004] 2 AC 298 that the general costs and expenses of a liquidation are not payable out of floating charge assets in priority to the claims of the floating charge-holder. However, a clause has been included in the Companies Bill (introduced in Parliament in November 2005) which, if brought into force in its current form, would reverse this decision.

[314] Including an administrative receiver.

[315] Defined in the Insolvency Act 1986 (Prescribed Part) Order 2003 (SI 2003/2097) to be an amount equal to 50% of the first £10,000 of floating charge realisations plus 20% of the floating charge realisations thereafter, subject to a maximum of £600,000: reg 3.

[316] Insolvency Act 1986, s 176A. The obligation does not apply (inter alia) if the floating charge realisations are less than a prescribed minimum and the relevant officeholder is of the view that the cost of making a distribution to unsecured creditors would be disproportionate to the benefits (s 176A(3)) or if the officeholder applies to court for an order that the obligation shall not apply on the ground that the cost of making a distribution to unsecured creditors would be disproportionate to the benefits and the court so orders (s 176A(5)). The obligation is also disapplied if the floating charge is created or otherwise arises under a financial collateral arrangement (Financial Collateral Arrangements (No 2) Regulations 2003 (SI 2003/3226), reg 10(3)). On financial collateral arrangements, see **6.33ff**.

[317] *Rhodes v Allied Dunbar Pension Services Ltd* [1989] 1 All ER 1161; Goode, *Legal Problems of Credit and Security* (2nd edn, 1988), p 90. Cf *Re Roundwood Colliery Co* [1897] 1 Ch 373 at 393 per Lindley LJ. The position is different for a local authority levying distress for rates: *Re ELS Ltd* [1995] Ch 11.

[318] Since the relevant statutory provisions (Insolvency Act 1986, ss 40, 175 and 251 and Companies Act 1985, s 196(2)) refer to a charge which 'as created' was a floating charge.

Chapter Seven

STRUCTURED FINANCE

7.1   A notable feature of the international securities markets in recent years has been the growth of structured financing techniques, and in particular the issuance of asset-backed securities. The purpose of this chapter is to give a brief description of four of the main types of asset-backed securities: repackagings; securitisations; CDOs (collateralised debt obligations); and SIVs (structured investment vehicles).

OVERVIEW

Structured finance generally

7.2   All four of these types of structured finance transactions are essentially variations of one basic theme, namely the use of a single or special purpose entity, company or vehicle (SPE, SPC or SPV – the term used in this chapter is SPV) to convert cashflows arising from underlying assets or debts ('receivables'[1]) into a smoothed payment stream on bonds or notes issued by the SPV to investors ('asset-backed securities', or 'ABS'). The purpose can be: to raise finance for the originator (the entity which created the receivables) on cheaper terms than would apply to a conventional borrowing by the originator; to remove the receivables from the balance sheet of the originator, thereby (in the case of a financial institution) reducing the amount of regulatory capital needed by the institution; or to exploit an arbitrage or mismatch between the yield derived from the receivables and that payable by the SPV on the ABS, in order to create a profit. The differences in the various structures derive principally from: which of these purposes is applicable; the nature of the underlying assets; how the profit is generated; and who is intended to receive the profit.

7.3   There is a tendency in some quarters (particularly in the light of recent major insolvencies such as Enron and Parmalat, and the questionable use that they appear to have made of structured finance transactions) to regard structured finance and the use of SPVs with suspicion. But that is to misunderstand the nature of structured finance and the role of SPVs. In themselves, they are merely neutral techniques to generate either a profit or a cost-saving for originators, intermediaries and/or investors. The mere fact

---

[1]   The term 'receivable' has no specific legal definition, but is used as a general description of amounts owed to a business by its debtors.

that a car, for example, can be driven dangerously by someone so minded does not make cars per se dangerous machines.

Transaction structures and history

(i)　Repackagings

7.4　Repackagings are usually the most straightforward of the various types of ABS. They had their origins in 'asset swaps'. A typical asset swap consists of a bank selling bonds (which the bank either currently holds on its books or acquires in the market) to an investor and simultaneously entering into a swap agreement with the investor under which the investor pays the cashflows received by it under the bonds to the bank in return for a different set of cashflows (eg a different currency, or a floating rate instead of a fixed rate). The technique, developed in the early 1980s, was designed to make unattractive or illiquid bonds more saleable. However, it had a number of disadvantages, principally due to the fact that the two elements of the transaction (the bonds and the swap) are in fact separate transactions and not interdependent. Thus, even if the bonds were in default, the investor would still have to make payment under the swap. In addition, if the investor wished to sell, he would have to transfer the bonds and assign his rights under the swap in two separate transactions.

7.5　It was to overcome these problems that repackagings were developed in the mid-1980s.[2] Instead of the investor holding the bonds and entering into the swap, an SPV does so, and issues ABS to the investor. The arranging bank sells the underlying bonds to the SPV, in return for the issue proceeds of the ABS, and acts as the counterparty under the swap. The ABS have a cashflow profile matching the SPV's receipts under the swap, and are secured on the underlying bonds and the swap. If the investor wishes to sell, he can merely transfer his ABS through the clearing systems in the normal way.

7.6　Transactions have since become considerably more complex, with portfolios of underlying assets and linkage with credit default swaps, for example, now common features.

7.7　The primary purpose of a traditional repackaging is to facilitate an investment in particular tradeable securities where the investor is prepared to take the credit risk associated with those securities but prefers a different interest rate or currency profile. The motivation for the bank in arranging the deal is to make a profit through (sometimes) the price at which it sells the underlying bonds to the SPV or (more usually) through the pricing of the swap.

2　　The first two repackagings appeared in September 1985, one arranged by Hill Samuel and the other ('MECS' or Marketable Eurodollar Collateralised Securities Limited) by Merrill Lynch (Das, *Structured Products and Hybrid Securities* (2001), p 17).

(ii)   Securitisations

7.8   Securitisations have a number of similarities to repackagings, in particular an SPV issuing ABS secured over underlying assets. But whereas in a repackaging the underlying assets are a pool of bonds and a swap agreement, in a securitisation they can be a wide range of assets, so long as they produce regular cashflows. Whereas the usual purpose of a repackaging is to create an end product that is more attractive to investors than the already existing underlying bonds, the usual purpose of a securitisation is to raise finance for the originator on the security of those cashflows and (often) to remove those cashflows from the originator's balance sheet for regulatory capital purposes.[3] Examples of the assets that can be used include mortgage portfolios, credit card receivables, utility receivables, student loans and even ferry ticket receivables. Compared with a pool of bonds backing a repackaging, the receivables backing a securitisation are usually a more disparate group, with a range of payment and credit profiles. Consequently, securitisations usually involve greater structural complexity, to deal with the greater risks involved.

7.9   Though securitisation is often spoken of as having originated in the US in the 1970s, the original securitisation transactions were made in late eighteenth century Prussia. To enable landowners to raise funds in the aftermath of the Seven Years War (1756–63),[4] the Prussian government organised landowners into land companies (*Landschaften*). These companies issued bonds secured by mortgages over the estates of the *Landschaft* members, the interest payments on the bonds being funded by the interest payments by the landowners on their mortgages. The first of these bonds, known as *Pfandbriefe*, were issued in about 1770.[5]

7.10   An important feature of modern securitisations, though, is the removal of the assets that are being securitised from the originator's balance sheet. This was achieved in the US domestic market in the 1970s, the first US mortgage-backed securities being an issue by the Government National Mortgage Association ('Ginnie Mae') in 1970 of 'pass-through' certificates

---

[3]   These differences are also reflected in the names of the transactions: 'securitisation' refers to the fact that the structure is based on underlying assets that are not securities but the end product is; and 'repackaging' reflects the fact that the underlying assets are securities and the end product is merely another security with different characteristics.

[4]   Between Prussia, Britain and Hanover on one side and Austria, France, Russia, Sweden and Spain on the other.

[5]   Kindleberger, *A Financial History of Western Europe* (2nd edn, 1993), p 130; Homer and Sylla, *A History of Interest Rates* (3rd edn, 1996), p 256; Deacon, *Global Securitisation and CDOs* (2004), p 119; Fabozzi and Choudhry (ed), *The Handbook of European Structured Financial Products* (2004), pp 525–526; Morrissey, *International Securitisation* (1992), p 6. *Pfandbriefe* are today still widely used in Germany, and are considered further at **7.52(c)**.

in respect of a pool of mortgages.[6] Investors in a pass-through security own undivided interests in the pool of underlying mortgages, and receive pro rata shares of the cashflows. However, these cashflows would include early, unscheduled, repayments of the underlying mortgages by the borrowers, which would lead to early partial repayments of the pass-through securities. The consequent lack of certainty about the length of the investment detracts from the appeal of pass-throughs. The need to deal with this 'prepayment risk' led to the introduction of Collateralised Mortgage Obligations ('CMOs') in 1983.[7] CMOs consist of several tranches of securities, with differing priorities over the underlying cashflows, each appealing to a different category of investor. In the event of early repayment of the underlying mortgages, the lower-ranking tranches get repaid first. The higher-ranking tranches thus carry greater certainty of cashflow, the lower-ranking tranches greater risk of prepayment, with each tranche being priced accordingly.[8]

7.11　　The first securitisation of UK mortgages was by Bank of America in 1985.[9] The first that attracted widespread attention, though, was by National Home Loans in 1987.[10] During the 1990s, securitisation techniques began to be applied to a wider range of assets than just mortgages. In relation to UK assets, for example, the first securitisation backed by car loans appeared in 1990;[11] the first backed by personal loans appeared in 1993;[12] and the first backed by credit card receivables appeared in 1995.[13] In 1997 an important new category of securitisation appeared[14] – the 'whole business'

6　　Morrissey, ibid, p 8; Stone, Zissu and Lederman (ed), *Asset Securitisation: Theory & Practice in Europe* (1991), p 2; Fisher, *Eurosecurities and Their Related Derivatives* (1997), p 300; Moore, *Autostrade to the Superhighway* (2001), p 78; Henderson, *Asset Securitization: Current Techniques and Emerging Market Applications* (1997), p 3. The first non-mortgage asset-backed securities in the US market appeared in 1985, with an issue originated by Sperry Lease Corporation and backed by computer lease receivables (Henderson, ibid, p 3).

7　　Morrissey, ibid, p 10; Stone, Zissu and Lederman, ibid, p 2; Fisher, ibid, p 300.

8　　For other techniques that have been developed subsequently to deal with prepayment risk, see **7.51(d)**. Tranching is considered in more detail at **7.28ff**.

9　　Ferran, *Mortgage Securitisation – Legal Aspects* (1992), p 2; *Bank of England Quarterly Bulletin*, May 1989 p 260, May 1994 p 134 and May 1996 p 156. The issuer was Mortgage Intermediary Note Issuer (No 1) Amsterdam BV (known as 'MINI').

10　　Ferran, ibid p 2; Stone, Zissu and Lederman, ibid, p 6; Morrissey, ibid, p 538; Moore, ibid, p 78. The issuer was NHL First Funding Corporation plc, and the issue was rated by Standard & Poor's (whereas the 1985 MINI deal had not been rated).

11　　Stone, Zissu and Lederman, ibid, pp 6–7; Fisher, ibid, p 29. The loans had been made by Standard Chartered, and the issuer was Cardiff Automated Receivables Securitisation (UK) plc (known as 'CARS UK').

12　　Moore, ibid, p 79. The loans had been made by Barclays Bank, and the issuer was Gracechurch Personal Loan Finance (No 1) PLC.

13　　*Bank of England Quarterly Bulletin* (May 1996), p 157. The credit card accounts were with MBNA International, and issuer was Chester Asset Receivables Dealings No 1 Limited (known as 'CARDS No 1').

14　　The first whole business securitisation was done that year by Welcome Break, a securitisation of 21 motorway service stations (Deacon, *Global Securitisation and CDOs* (2004), p 188). On the development of the whole business securitisation market, see further Fabozzi and Choudhry (ed), *The Handbook of European Structured Finance Products* (2004), pp 330–331.

securitisation, in which the cashflows derive not from specific assets but from the entire range of operating revenues generated by a business.

(iii)   CDOs

7.12   CDOs started appearing in the 1990s. The term 'CDO' is in fact a broad category name for a number of different products. Originally, CDOs could be split into two main types, CBOs (or Collateralised Bond Obligations) and CLOs (or Collateralised Loan Obligations). In CBOs, the underlying assets consisted of a portfolio of bonds that was actively managed by a portfolio manager, and the primary purpose of the transaction was to make a profit out of the differences between the returns on the portfolio and the SPV's funding costs, and to share this profit between the portfolio manager and the subordinated noteholders (ie the holders of the lowest tranche of ABS issued by the SPV; tranching is described below). In CLOs, though, the underlying portfolio consisted of loans, and the primary purpose (as with a traditional securitisation) was to raise finance for the originator (which was usually a bank) whilst at the same time removing the loans from its balance sheet (in order to improve its capital adequacy ratios). The first CLO in the international securities market appeared in 1996, with NatWest's 'ROSE Funding' CLO.[15]

7.13   The CBO/CLO distinction has since become blurred, as CDOs increasingly cater for underlying portfolios which are a mixture of bonds, loans and swaps. Current terminology focuses instead on the purpose for which the CDO is set up: a CDO the primary purpose of which is to make a profit out of the difference between the portfolio returns and the funding costs is an 'arbitrage CDO', whereas one the primary purpose of which is to remove the underlying assets from the originator's balance sheet is a 'balance sheet CDO'.

7.14   CDOs combine features of both repackagings and securitisations. The underlying assets are often bonds or notes (as in a repackaging), but are also often a diverse pool that is actively managed. Consequently, securitisation techniques are incorporated, to deal with the greater risks involved.

(iv)   SIVs

7.15   SIVs are, in effect, highly structured investment funds. Investors purchase equity or subordinated notes issued by the SPV; the SPV sets up secured debt issuance programmes (usually EMTN, ECP, USMTN and USCP programmes) which are rated AAA; and the moneys borrowed under these programmes are invested in a portfolio of bonds, which is managed by an investment manager. Risks associated with the portfolio are hedged

---

[15]   The full name of the issuer was Repeat Offering Securitisation Entity Funding No 1 Limited.

through swap agreements, and detailed composition criteria and sensitivity tests have to be satisfied to ensure that the funding programmes retain their AAA ratings. Whereas with a CDO the funding for the structure is usually raised through a series of bond issues at the establishment of the CDO, the funding for a SIV is continuously rolled over and refinanced under the funding programmes throughout the life of the SIV (which, in theory, could be perpetual). The vehicle's profit is made from the difference between the returns generated by the portfolio and the lower rates of interest payable on the AAA debt raised under the funding programmes. The profit is shared between the investment manager and the investors (by way of return on their equity or subordinated notes).

7.16　　Although the first SIV was established in 1988,[16] there are relatively few SIVs currently in existence (19 as at December 2005[17]), due principally to the complexity, large start-up costs and long lead-in time. They have a significant influence, however, on the structured finance and capital markets, with senior debt issuance during 2005 of over US$185 billion and assets under management at December 2005 of over US$200 billion.[18]

Overview of common themes

7.17　　Many of these deals involve a transfer of the receivables from the originator or the arranger to the SPV, in a way that separates the receivables from the insolvency risk of the originator or arranger. This is referred to as a 'true sale' structure. The SPV then issues the ABS (which are secured over the receivables) and transfers the issue proceeds to the originator or arranger by way of purchase price for the receivables. The income stream from the receivables funds the SPV's payment obligations under the ABS. Other structures that can be used involve the SPV making a loan to the originator or a company in its group (with the receivables being charged to the SPV, rather than sold to it), or the SPV gaining exposure to the receivables 'synthetically' through a credit default swap or total return swap.

7.18　　The ABS usually have the benefit of security over the relevant assets of the SPV backing the deal.[19] and are 'limited recourse', in the sense that the SPV is only obliged to pay on the ABS to the extent that it receives funds in respect of the assets backing the deal. In addition, the SPV is usually structured as 'insolvency-remote' (ie reducing as much as possible the risk of it becoming insolvent) and is often established in a tax-free or low-tax jurisdiction. This is so that, having isolated the receivables from the insolvency risk of the originator or arranger, there is no additional credit

---

[16]　Alpha Finance Corporation Ltd, established by Citibank.

[17]　Source: Standard & Poor's.

[18]　Source: Standard & Poor's.

[19]　Being, principally, the receivables themselves (in the case of a true sale deal), the SPV's rights under the loan and the benefit of the security over the receivables (in the case of a secured loan deal), or the credit default swap or total return swap (in the case of a synthetic deal).

risk, and no additional drain on the cashflows from the receivables, as a result of the insertion of the SPV into the structure.

7.19   The ABS will often be issued in tranches, ie a series of layers with different levels of priority and risk profiles. Risk (and potential return) increase the more subordinated in the capital structure a tranche is, with the most subordinated tranche (known as the 'first-loss' piece) being the first to bear any shortfall on the cashflow from the underlying assets, followed in ascending order by the intermediate or mezzanine tranches. The ABS are usually rated by one or more of the main credit rating agencies (Standard & Poor's, Moody's and Fitch), with the highest tranche(s) having the highest rating and the first-loss tranche having either a very low rating or not rated at all. The ratings address for investors the likelihood of their being paid the amounts due on the ABS, and consequently much of the structuring process for these deals is driven by the rating agencies' criteria for assigning particular levels of rating to the various tranches of the ABS.

7.20   These common themes are described in more detail below, and then the four main transaction types are described in more detail.

7.21   Terminology in relation to structured finance is often imprecise. In particular, the term 'securitisation' is sometimes used in a wide sense to cover all these forms of structured finance (ie meaning, essentially, the issue of ABS that convert the cashflows from a set of receivables into another set of cashflows). In this chapter, however, 'securitisation' is used in its narrower (and original) sense, to mean the second of the four main transaction types referred to above (the main distinguishing feature of which is the issue of ABS backed by receivables that are not themselves securities).

COMMON THEMES

The SPV and insolvency-remoteness

7.22   As mentioned earlier, the issuer of the ABS is usually referred to as a special purpose vehicle (SPV), special purpose company (SPC) or special purpose entity (SPE). The SPV may be intended to be used for only the one transaction (a 'single-issuance vehicle') or for a succession of similar transactions (a 'multi-issuance vehicle'). The SPV will ordinarily be structured so as to be insolvency-remote (ie reducing as much as possible the risk of it being declared bankrupt or insolvent), and so as to eliminate any unnecessary drain on the cashflows of the structure.

7.23   The latter objective (eliminating unnecessary drains on cashflows) is usually achieved by:

(a) Establishing the SPV, so far as possible, in a zero or low-tax jurisdiction – this is considered further below.

(b) Restricting the SPV from engaging in activities other than the transaction(s) in question, and in particular restricting it from having employees and subsidiaries.

(c) Structuring the SPV's arrangements with its various service providers (the roles of which are considered further below) so as to reduce or eliminate any VAT charges.

(d) Providing in the 'waterfalls' (ie the priorities of payment) that the amounts payable to service providers, etc, in priority to payments on the rated tranches of the ABS are capped at specified levels, with any residual amounts only being payable after the rated ABS tranches have been paid in full.

7.24   The former objective (insolvency-remoteness) is achieved by a combination of elements, including:

(a) Establishing the SPV, so far as possible, in a zero or low-tax jurisdiction, or, if this is not possible, in a jurisdiction where the amount of tax can be agreed with the tax authorities in advance (so that a cash reserve can be maintained in the structure for that amount). This is in order to reduce the risk of the tax authorities being able to wind up the SPV for non-payment of tax.

(b) Prohibiting the SPV from engaging in activities or incurring indebtedness other than under the transaction(s) in question. This is usually done through both contractual limitations in the transaction documents and constitutional limitations under the objects clause in the SPV's memorandum of association.

(c) Prohibiting the SPV from having any employees, and from merging or consolidating with any other entity (since, if that other entity had liabilities, that would increase the risk of insolvency of the resultant merged entity).

(d) Requiring all creditors of the SPV to agree that their claims are limited in recourse solely to the cash derived from the underlying assets backing their ABS (and only in accordance with the priorities of payment in the relevant waterfall), and that any residual shortfall will be extinguished.[20] Whilst these limited recourse provisions are most obviously relevant in the case of a multi-issuance vehicle (in order to

---

[20] Such limited recourse provisions are in effect a form of subordination (the validity of which, under English law, is now beyond doubt: see further **Chapter 8**). Limited recourse provisions are not usually possible, however, in the case of a UK SPV, as HM Revenue & Customs take the view that these provisions make the interest payable by the SPV dependent on the results of a business (as to which, see further **18.14**), with the result that the payments are treated as distributions rather than interest and are thus not deductible for the SPV. At the time of writing (July 2006), HM Revenue & Customs had published (on 13 June 2006) the draft Taxation of Securitisation Companies Regulations which, if enacted, would remove this concern, and instead allow UK securitisation SPVs to pay a pre-determined amount of corporation tax (or in some cases no tax at all), irrespective of deductibility. At present, a different mechanism, involving deferral of the interest if there are insufficient proceeds, is used in the case of UK SPVs instead of limited recourse provisions.

prevent the creditors under one transaction obtaining recourse to the underlying assets backing another of the SPV's transactions[21]), they are also relevant in the case of a single-issuance vehicle. By ensuring that the SPV's liabilities cannot exceed the amount of its assets, the provisions reduce the risk of the SPV's directors feeling obliged to file for winding up or administration as a result of wrongful trading concerns.

(e) The limited recourse provisions are supported by 'non-petition' provisions, ie undertakings from the SPV's creditors not to take any action to seek the winding up of the SPV as a result of any shortfall in amounts payable to them.[22]

(f) Ensuring that the SPV's creditors in relation to the transaction have the benefit of first-ranking security over the underlying assets – so as to act as a disincentive to any third parties who might otherwise seek to wind up the SPV.

(g) Requiring independent directors for the SPV.

(h) The SPV is usually structured as an 'orphan company', whose shares are held by a trustee on trust for a charity. If the SPV is not an orphan company, the rating agencies will wish to satisfy themselves that there is no risk of 'substantive consolidation' of the SPV with the group of which it forms part (ie that it cannot be liable for the debts of other members of the group and that it does not become subject to, eg, tax or pension liabilities as a result of being part of a group).

7.25 Since the SPV cannot have any employees, it has to sub-contract all its functions to third-party service providers. The most significant of these functions is usually the servicing of the portfolio of receivables (ie collecting the cash, monitoring the performance of the receivables and, if necessary, taking appropriate enforcement action), and cash management (ie the correct application of the cash in accordance with the relevant waterfalls). In the case of a securitisation, this is generally undertaken by the originator (sometimes with a separate cash manager for the cash management), whereas in a repackaging, CDO or SIV these roles are usually performed by the investment/portfolio manager and/or an independent financial institution acting as custodian, collateral administrator and/or cash manager. A corporate services provider is normally appointed to provide independent directors for the SPV and the share trustee. A trustee is appointed to hold the security on trust for the various transaction parties (in accordance with their

---

21 This is also addressed by requiring that the transaction documents for each transaction do not contain cross-default provisions (so that one transaction cannot go into default as a result of a default under another of the SPV's transactions).

22 In principle, if the limited recourse provisions are effective, the non-petition provisions should be as well (since there will be no unpaid debt on which to base the petition). However, a concern is recognised that a court might in reality allow a winding up petition despite contractual agreement to the contrary (on the basis, eg, that the contractual agreement is an attempt to oust the jurisdiction of the court and therefore contrary to public policy).

priorities under the waterfalls), and (as is usual in bond issues) paying agents are appointed to make the payments to the ABS holders.

7.26　　The choice of jurisdiction for the SPV is influenced primarily by local regulatory requirements and tax considerations. Local regulatory requirements generally relate to the transfer or true sale of assets, and may mean that an onshore SPV (ie located in the same jurisdiction as the assets) may need to be used, despite the more complex tax treatment that may result.[23] Tax considerations relating to the assets may also mean that the SPV has to be located either in the same jurisdiction as the assets,[24] or in a jurisdiction where it can obtain double tax treaty relief in respect of the cashflow from the assets. This would rule out most tax-free jurisdictions (as tax havens do not generally have the benefit of double tax treaties), and so a suitable jurisdiction with as low a tax rate as possible will be chosen.[25] Alternatively, where treaty relief is not required, and assuming that it is acceptable to the relevant investors,[26] a tax-free jurisdiction is the most cost-efficient choice.[27]

7.27　　As with other corporate entities, the directors of the SPV usually need to satisfy themselves that entering into the transaction has corporate benefit for the SPV. Since, as seen below, the residual profit in the transaction is designed to go to either the originator or the subordinated noteholders, it might seem that the SPV does not derive a corporate benefit from the transaction. However, this is not so, the requirement of corporate benefit normally being satisfied by a combination of the limited recourse provisions (ie demonstrating that there is no 'downside' for the SPV, since it cannot become insolvent as a result of the transaction) and a transaction fee payable to the SPV out of the proceeds of the issue (ie its 'upside').

Tranching

7.28　　As mentioned earlier, a key feature of many ABS issues is the tranching of the liabilities of the SPV under the ABS. The risk on the underlying assets is effectively sliced by the SPV issuing various classes of ABS, each with a different level of priority in terms of rights to the cashflows received by the SPV.

---

[23]　Eg, Law 130 in Italy provides for simpler transfer requirements for receivables if the transferee is a Law 130 company (an Italian SPV).

[24]　Eg, where the underlying assets are loans to a UK corporate, the SPV usually needs to be subject to UK corporation tax in order to receive the interest free of withholding tax (see further **18.15(a)**).

[25]　The most popular EU jurisdictions with low tax rates for an SPV are Ireland, Luxembourg and The Netherlands. For a discussion of the principles applicable to SPVs seeking to rely on double tax treaty relief, see *Indofood International Finance Ltd v JP Morgan Chase Bank NA* [2006] STC 1195.

[26]　Some investors, for example, have constitutional and/or regulatory restrictions that permit them to invest only in securities issued by EU and/or OECD issuers.

[27]　The most popular tax-free jurisdictions for SPVs are the Cayman Islands and Jersey.

7.29   Investors in the senior ranking tranches, for example, will be paid in priority to other investors (after payment of certain priority expenses, such as fees payable to the SPV's service providers, up to a capped amount), as well as being paid first in priority where there has been a default and enforcement (after payment of priority expenses and enforcement expenses – usually on an uncapped basis). Investors in the lower ranking tranches, often referred to as the 'mezzanine notes', are paid a fixed rate of return but are subordinated in right of payment to the senior investors.

7.30   To the extent that there is a residual profit in the SPV after payments to the senior and mezzanine noteholders and the other transaction parties, this profit may (depending on the type of transaction) be paid either to the originator or to the holders of a further tranche of ABS ranking below the senior and mezzanine notes (the 'subordinated notes'). In securitisations, the profit is usually payable to the originator, with the exact characterisation of the payments depending on the originator's preferred tax treatment. Thus the payments may be structured as: payments of deferred purchase consideration for the acquisition of the receivables by the SPV; payments of interest and principal on a subordinated loan provided to the SPV by the originator; payments of interest and principal on subordinated notes held by the originator; fee payments to the originator for the provision of services to the SPV (eg acting as servicer in relation to the receivables); payment of dividends (if the SPV is in the same group as the originator, rather than being an orphan); or payments under a receivables trust (usually regarded as the most tax-efficient method of all).[28] In the case of CDOs and SIVs, however, the residual profit is usually payable to third-party investors, as holders of subordinated notes.[29]

7.31   Investors in the subordinated notes are subordinated in right of payment to all other investors and are only entitled to any excess proceeds, both in respect of periodic cashflows in respect of the underlying assets and on enforcement. Although commonly structured as a debt instrument, the subordinated notes are economically more akin to a share, in that the investor has no guaranteed rate of return but rather shares in any excess profits, representing a leveraged exposure (and increased potential return) in respect of the portfolio. For this reason the subordinated notes are commonly referred to as the 'equity'.

7.32   Tranching therefore provide a means for investors to obtain exposure to a certain 'slice' of the risk on the underlying assets depending on their appetite for risk, each slice representing a different risk/reward trade-

---

[28] A receivables trust involves the originator selling the receivables to a trust (rather than to the SPV issuing the ABS), with beneficial ownership split between the originator and the SPV. Proceeds from the receivables are held on trust for the SPV to the extent that it needs funds to service the ABS, with the surplus being held on trust for the originator. By structuring the receivables trust as a bare trust, it is fiscally transparent and therefore prevents the originator's share being taxed twice.

[29] Repackagings normally involve the issue of only one tranche of ABS, with the residual profit usually being taken by the swap counterparty through the pricing of the swap.

off. It is also used as a form of credit enhancement for the senior tranches (on the basis that the lower tranches absorb losses first, thereby reducing the risk of a shortfall in the amounts required to service the senior tranches).

7.33   Payments are normally made 'sequentially', ie in sequential order from the senior investors downwards – though in certain cases 'pro rata' payment (ie paying several tranches pro rata notwithstanding the levels of seniority) is seen. The rationale for pro rata payment is that the lower tranches (because of their greater risk of loss in the event that there is a shortfall in the amounts received from the assets) carry a higher funding cost for the SPV, and therefore repayment of the senior tranches while the lower tranches remain outstanding could lead to a disproportionately higher funding cost for the SPV relative to the level of its outstanding debt. Where pro rata payment is permitted, it is usual for the occurrence of specified trigger events (often referred to as 'early amortisation events'), indicating eg a deterioration in the quality of the receivables, a reduction in the yield they generate or an insolvency-related event in relation to the originator, to lead to the order of payments switching to a sequential basis.

Cash v synthetic structures

7.34   One of the key structural objectives is to separate the credit risk of the receivables from the credit risk of the entity that created them and/or transfers them to the SPV for the purposes of the transaction. The traditional way of achieving this in many cases is to effect a 'true sale' of the receivables to the SPV. In such a transaction, the proceeds of issue of the ABS are used by the SPV to purchase the underlying assets, 'true sale' legal opinions are required by the rating agencies (confirming that the acquisition cannot be either set aside on a subsequent insolvency of the transferor or recharacterised as a disguised security interest – which would be void for non-registration), the SPV grants security over the assets in favour of the transaction parties in accordance with their priorities of payment, and the cashflows generated by the assets are used to fund the payments on the ABS.

7.35   An alternative true sale structure is the 'master trust' or 'undivided interest' structure. Instead of the assets being acquired by the SPV that issues the ABS, they are acquired by another SPV, acting as trustee. The trust property is held by the trustee on trust for the originator and the issuing SPV, who each have a joint and undivided interest in each asset in the trust property. The size of the percentage shares that they each have in the trust property is recalculated periodically, and their entitlement to proceeds from the trust property is in proportion to their respective shares in the trust property. The proceeds of issue of the ABS are paid by the issuing SPV to the originator in return for an increase in the issuing SPV's share of the trust property (ie increasing the issuing SPV's share and decreasing the originator's share). The structure is used where the size of the receivables varies significantly from one period to the next (and is designed to avoid the need for the issuing SPV to have a fluctuating level of funding in order to match fluctuations in the size of its assets). The master trust structure allows amounts to be redrawn by the obligors under the receivables (by means of the originator funding the redraws and then adjusting its share of the trust property when the shares are next recalculated), without the issuing SPV having to fund the redrawn amounts by issuing fresh ABS. The structure is most often seen in credit card securitisations, commercial mortgage-backed securitisation (CMBS) deals, and residential mortgage-backed securitisation (RMBS) deals involving flexible mortgages.

7.36   As an alternative to a true sale structure, the SPV may use the proceeds of issue of the ABS to make a loan to the originator or another member of its group.[30] The cashflows generated by the underlying assets are used to fund the payments on the loan, which in turn funds the payments on the ABS. Instead of the SPV having title to the underlying assets, the ABS holders rely on rights of control over the underlying assets through grants of security by the originator's group to a security trustee on behalf of the transaction parties. This approach is sometimes referred to as 'true control', and is seen, for example, in certain CMBS deals and in whole business securitisations. The aim is to ensure that the ABS holders can control the manner and timing of enforcement proceedings and can obtain the benefit of the underlying assets in priority to other creditors.

7.37   True sale and secured loan structures are collectively referred to as 'cashflow' or 'cash' deals (as the relevant receivables generate the cashflow for the ABS).

7.38   By contrast, synthetic structures use credit derivatives to effect a synthetic transfer of risk, without effecting a true sale of, or grants of security over, the receivables. Instead of the SPV taking actual title to, or security over, the relevant receivables, it usually obtains the credit exposure to them by entering into a credit default swap (CDS) or total return swap (TRS) with one or more counterparties. This results in the credit risk of the receivables being effectively transferred to the SPV.

7.39   In a synthetic securitisation or CDO,[31] as the SPV does not need to acquire (and therefore pay for) the receivables, or to make a loan to the originator, the proceeds of issue of the ABS are invested in high quality investments, being either highly rated securities (usually referred to as 'eligible investments'), a GIC (guaranteed investment contract) or a deposit account with a highly rated bank. The SPV 'sells' credit protection (in the case of a securitisation) to the originator or (in the case of a CDO) to either a panel of counterparties or (more commonly) a single counterparty that in turn hedges its exposure with market counterparties. The relevant

---

[30]   Some master trust structures may combine elements of true sale and secured loan structures, with the issuing SPV making a secured loan to an intermediate SPV that then uses the proceeds to acquire the undivided interest in the trust property.

[31]   Synthetic repackagings usually involve a simpler structure (which is described at **7.46**).

receivables are specified as 'reference obligations' (or, alternatively, the obligor in respect of them may be specified as a 'reference entity') under the CDS or TRS. By 'selling' protection, the SPV agrees to reimburse the counterparty for losses on that reference portfolio, in return for receipt of (in the case of a CDS) a periodic premium or (in the case of a TRS) amounts equal to the interest actually paid on the assets in the reference portfolio.[32] The interest on the ABS is funded by a combination of the interest on the eligible investments/GIC/deposit account and the amounts received from the counterparty under the swap. The SPV may sell the protection through either a series of swaps (a separate one for each reference entity or reference obligation) or a portfolio swap (with reference entities or reference obligations being added or removed by addition or removal notices). If a reference entity or reference obligation experiences a credit event, the SPV must either pay the counterparty the decline in value (if the swap is cash settled) or purchase the relevant receivable from the counterparty at its par amount (if the swap is physically settled). In each case, the payment is funded out of the eligible investments/GIC/deposit account, reducing the amount available to repay the ABS holders at maturity. The investors thereby assume the default risk in respect of the receivables.

7.40 Synthetic structures are currently seen in three main transaction types: CDOs, RMBS, and CMBS. They have a number of advantages over cash structures, and the general move towards synthetics has been associated with the acceleration of the credit derivatives market in recent years. As at July 2006, for example, synthetic CDOs accounted for over 85% of CDO transactions (by number of transactions) rated in Europe.[33] The advantages of synthetic structures over cash structures include:

(a) *No asset transfer/security* – unlike cash structures, in a synthetic transaction there is no legal or beneficial transfer of title in, or grant of security over, the receivables to the SPV. In certain asset classes, particularly loans, this can result in a significant cost and resource saving, given that it avoids both the need to conduct due diligence on the loans to determine their transferability and, in the case of some loans, the need to obtain consent from the underlying borrower. Synthetic structures also allow the transfer of credit risk in respect of assets which may not otherwise be capable of being transferred or being made subject to security due, for instance, to contractual restrictions.

(b) *Economic arbitrage* – synthetic structures facilitate obtaining a higher average credit rating (and therefore increase the potential arbitrage opportunity) as a result of it being possible to have a smaller equity tranche and therefore a higher level of leverage in the transaction.

---

[32] In the case of a TRS, the SPV would also pay the counterparty a floating reference rate (usually LIBOR or EURIBOR plus a margin), funded out of the interest on the eligible investments/GIC/deposit account.

[33] Source: Standard & Poor's.

(c) *Portfolio ramp-up* – in the case of CDOs where there is an undersupply of collateral, using synthetic technology may assist in the SPV 'ramping-up' (or building up) the portfolio of underlying assets by allowing it to obtain exposure to assets before it is able to source and obtain legal title to those assets.

7.41 The principal disadvantage, though, of a synthetic structure is that the investors are exposed not just to the credit risk of the relevant receivables but also to that of the counterparty. In order to minimise the extent to which the counterparty's credit risk could adversely affect the transaction, the counterparty would normally be obliged either to collateralise its obligations or to novate its obligations to a new counterparty if its rating is downgraded below a specified level.

Ratings

7.42 The ABS issued by the SPV are usually rated by one or more of the main credit rating agencies (Standard & Poor's, Moody's and Fitch). These ratings address the likelihood of full payment of interest (on a timely basis) and principal (on either a timely or ultimate basis) on the relevant tranche of ABS. Ratings may be obtained to increase the marketability of the ABS (either because certain investors can only invest in rated securities, or by giving investors an additional means of evaluating the transaction), or as an integral part of the pricing of the transaction. By obtaining (as a result of the structure) a rating higher than that on the underlying assets (therefore leading to a cheaper cost of funding for the SPV), a profit is obtained through the arbitrage that is created between the cashflow receivable on the underlying assets and the cost of funding in respect of the rated ABS.

7.43 The criteria used by the rating agencies in awarding their ratings are therefore at the heart of the structuring of these transactions. Each rating agency has its own set of criteria, but the common features are: eligibility criteria and portfolio profile tests in relation to the underlying assets; first-ranking security; limited recourse and non-petition provisions; insolvency-remoteness of the SPV; to the extent relevant, structural features to address credit risk, liquidity risk, currency/basis risk and prepayment/reinvestment risk (described in more detail below); provision for extraordinary expenses; sufficient provision for unavoidable third party liabilities (eg tax); rating agency consultation before modifications may be made; and legal opinions covering relevant legal matters (such as enforceability of security, effectiveness of the limited recourse provisions and, where relevant, the 'true sale' nature of the acquisition of the receivables).

REPACKAGINGS[34]

7.44   As seen earlier, the most basic form of repackaging involves the SPV issuing ABS, using the proceeds to purchase the underlying assets (which are usually tradeable debt securities) from the arranging bank, and entering into a swap agreement with the arranging bank as counterparty. The underlying assets have a different cashflow profile from the ABS issued by the SPV: the payments received by the SPV on the underlying assets are paid to the counterparty, and in return the counterparty pays the SPV amounts equal to the principal and/or interest due under the ABS. The underlying assets are thus said to have been 'repackaged' into the ABS. The ABS holders have the benefit of security over the underlying assets and the swap agreement (and the counterparty has the benefit of security over the underlying assets), and (by virtue of the limited recourse provisions) the ABS holders rely solely on the underlying assets and the swap agreement and do not have any other claim against the SPV.

7.45   The primary purpose of a traditional repackaging is to facilitate an investment in particular securities where the investor is prepared to take the credit risk associated with those securities but prefers a different interest rate or currency profile. Consequently, the counterparty is typically a bank with a high credit rating, in order to minimise the impact of the counterparty's credit risk on the structure. As seen earlier, a traditional repackaging achieves the same commercial effect as an asset swap, but in a more easily tradeable form. As techniques have become sophisticated, however, repackagings are now also used for a wide range of other purposes. These include: allowing international investors access to domestic bond markets; exploiting inconsistent tax treatments;[35] making bonds or notes with a high credit risk more marketable; separating out the risk and return profiles of the interest element and the equity option in convertible bonds; enabling the counterparty to 'buy' credit protection in relation to specified reference obligations or reference entities from the investor; and allowing investors access to otherwise illiquid assets (such as hedge funds or private equity).

7.46   Whereas traditional repackagings are in the form of 'true sale' transactions (ie the SPV buys the underlying securities from the arranger with the proceeds of issue of the ABS), many now are synthetic transactions (though somewhat simpler in structure than the synthetic securitisation and CDO structures described earlier[36]). Instead of the SPV acquiring the underlying securities, the SPV (and thereby the ABS holders) obtain their

---

[34]   See further Das, *Structured Products and Hybrid Securities* (2001), pp 15–28, 613–627; Das, *Credit Derivatives, CDOs and Structured Credit Products* (3rd edn, 2005), pp 275–298; Deacon, *Global Securitisation and CDOs* (2004), pp 131–133; Carmichael, *IFLR*, Dec 1985, p 17; Lewis, *IFLR*, Nov 1996, p 23.

[35]   For a cautionary tale of how repackaging Italian postal bonds to exploit inconsistent tax treatment became an international political issue, see the articles in the *Economist* ('Why didn't I think of that?'), 16 Dec 2004 and *Euromoney* ('The Temptation of St David'), Jan 1997.

[36]   At **7.39**.

exposure to the credit risk of the underlying securities (the 'reference obligations') synthetically through a CDS or TRS with the counterparty. The proceeds of issue of the ABS are either (i) paid to the counterparty under the swap or (ii) used to acquire other 'safe' securities with a high credit rating. In the case of (ii), the ABS are secured over the 'safe' securities and the swap (with the 'safe' securities being used either to pay the counterparty if a credit event occurs in respect of the reference obligations or otherwise to repay the ABS holders). In the case of (i), the ABS are secured over merely the swap (with the amounts payable by the counterparty being reduced or cancelled if a credit event occurs in respect of the reference obligations but otherwise the counterparty being obliged to pay the SPV the amounts due from the SPV under the ABS). Where the swap relates to a single reference obligation, the ABS will usually redeem early (at the reduced amount), and the transaction will be unwound, as soon as a credit event occurs. Where the swap relates to a portfolio of reference obligations, however, various permutations are seen (eg pro rata reduction for each credit event, early redemption as soon as a credit event occurs in respect of any of the reference obligations ('first to default'), or early redemption once a specified number of reference obligations have experienced credit events (eg 'first five to default')).

7.47   In both cash and synthetic transactions, the swap counterparty usually ranks ahead of the ABS holders (including where there is an early redemption as a result of a default or credit event in respect of the underlying assets or reference obligations). If, however, the ABS are rated, the rating agencies would normally expect the counterparty to rank after the ABS holders where the early redemption is as a result of a counterparty default under the swap.

7.48   Though single-issuance vehicles are sometimes seen, the vast majority of repackaging SPVs are multi-issuance vehicles issuing under a programme. This is in order to reduce the individual transaction costs and the length of time required to document and close a transaction.[37] Each transaction is 'ring-fenced' or 'fire-walled' from the SPV's other transactions through the combination of first-ranking security, limited recourse and non-petition provisions and the absence of cross-default provisions (as described earlier).[38] In addition, to reduce costs and delay further, most repackaging programmes use an 'umbrella' or 'coathanger' structure, allowing an unlimited number of SPVs to issue under the programme, with new SPVs being added to the programme by executing a simple deed of adherence to the programme documents.

---

[37]   It also allows the arranging bank to brand its repackaging products more easily.

[38]   It is therefore crucial to know that these provisions will be upheld under the insolvency regime in the jurisdiction of incorporation of the SPV. If there is doubt about the effectiveness of these provisions, the rating agencies' usual approach is to make the rating dependent on the SPV only issuing ABS that are all rated at the same level (with the result that under the programme, for example, one SPV would be used for AAA rated ABS and another for AA rated ABS).

7.49   As mentioned earlier, most repackaging transactions only involve the issuance of one tranche of ABS. Although in some cases a collateral manager is appointed with the obligation to manage the portfolio of assets, most repackagings involve static portfolios (though, sometimes, with limited substitution rights exercisable by the counterparty).

SECURITISATION[39]

7.50   As with a repackaging, a securitisation involves the SPV issuing ABS and using the proceeds either to acquire the receivables from the originator or to make a loan to the originator secured on the receivables (or, in the case of a synthetic securitisation, investing the proceeds in high quality collateral and entering into a CDS or TRS with the originator). A fundamental distinction, though, is the nature of the underlying assets: whereas they are usually bonds or notes in the case of a repackaging, they are usually some other form of receivable in the case of a securitisation (hence the terminology: 'securitisation' refers to the production of a debt security out of an asset that is not a debt security, whereas repackagings are so called because they involve merely a change of profile of something that is already a debt security). This usually means that the underlying assets in a securitisation (mortgages, credit cards, property rents, car rentals, etc) are a more disparate group, with varying payment and credit profiles. Consequently, securitisations usually involve greater structural complexity, to deal with the greater risks involved.

7.51   The principal risks can be divided into four main categories:

(a)   *Credit risk*. This is, essentially, the risk that the receivables will go into default. In a repackaging, the credit risk of the obligors under the underlying bonds or notes can usually be easily assessed, and is usually borne by the investor. In a securitisation, credit risk is usually greater and more difficult to evaluate, and various techniques are used to protect the investors: these can include over-collateralisation (ie receivables of a greater principal amount than that of the ABS issued by the SPV), the use of tranching (with junior tranches of ABS that absorb losses before the senior tranches), trapping surplus returns on the receivables ('excess spread') to build up a cash reserve, and insurance.

---

[39]   See further Fabozzi and Choudhry (ed), *The Handbook of European Structured Financial Products* (2004); Jeffrey (ed), *A Practitioner's Guide to Securitisation* (2006); Watson and Carter (ed), *Asset Securitisation and Synthetic Structures* (2006); Deacon, *Securitisation: Principles, Markets and Terms* (2nd edn, 2000); Borrows (ed), *Current Issues in Securitisation* (2002); Deacon, *Global Securitisation and CDOs* (2004); Cranston, *Principles of Banking Law* (2nd edn, 2002), Chapter 13; Ferran, *Mortgage Securitisation – Legal Aspects* (1992); Bonsall, *Securitisation* (1990); Morrissey, *International Securitisation* (1992); Stone, Zissu and Lederman (ed), *Asset Securitisation: Theory & Practice in Europe* (1991); Henderson, *Asset Securitization: Current Techniques and Emerging Market Applications* (1997); Lambie, *PLC* (Dec 2000), p 41; *Paragon Finance plc v Pender* [2005] 1 WLR 3412 at 3416 per Jonathan Parker LJ.

(b) *Liquidity risk.* This is the risk that the obligors under the receivables pay late, leaving the SPV temporarily unable to make payments in full on the ABS issued by it. In a repackaging, the risk is usually borne by the investor (since the counterparty would not be obliged to pay the SPV under the swap until the missing amounts had been received), and, if the delay continued beyond the relevant grace period under the underlying securities, it would constitute an event of default leading to an early redemption of the ABS and an unwinding of the transaction. In a securitisation, however, where the risk is less predictable and the point at which it becomes a credit issue rather than merely a liquidity issue is less clear-cut, the techniques used to protect the ABS holders include liquidity facilities (which can be drawn by the SPV in the event of a liquidity shortfall but are repaid out of future receipts on the receivables), a reserve fund, and deferral of interest on the junior tranche of ABS. Another form of liquidity risk arises in conduit structures. 'Conduit' (or 'ABCP conduit') is the term given to an SPV that funds itself through commercial paper (CP, often referred to as ABCP, ie asset-backed commercial paper).[40] Given the short-term nature of CP, rollover of the CP (ie refinancing through a fresh issue) must take place on a regular basis. The rating agencies usually expect ABCP conduits to have in place liquidity cover for the full amount of their CP, in case market conditions prevent a rollover when the CP matures.

(c) *Currency/basis risk.* This is the risk of shortfalls arising as a result of a mismatch, due to market movements, between the currency of, or the basis of calculation of interest on, the receivables and the ABS.[41] In both repackagings and securitisations, this risk is usually absorbed by a swap counterparty through an appropriate currency and/or interest rate swap agreement.

(d) *Prepayment/reinvestment risk.* This is the risk that the underlying assets repay early, leaving the SPV with surplus funds. In a repackaging, this would usually lead to the early redemption of the ABS (but is sometimes instead absorbed in the swap). In a securitisation, there are a number of possible options. The repayment amounts could be used to fund partial early redemptions ('amortisation') of the ABS – this is referred to as a 'pass-through' structure. However, to the extent that repayments are received faster than expected, this could be unattractive to investors, who have to reinvest their money in a new security and are therefore exposed to the risk that the yields or spreads that can be earned on the reinvestment have fallen since their original investment. This can in many cases be minimised by an analysis of historic

---

[40] Conduits are described further at **7.52(e)**.

[41] For example, interest on mortgages is usually calculated by reference to the originator's base rate, whereas interest on ABS is usually calculated by reference to LIBOR or EURIBOR.

prepayment rates and trends and structuring the portfolio accordingly so that it has the relevant expected 'weighted average life'. However, that approach obviously offers less protection where the data is less available or less reliable (eg new asset classes or assets in new jurisdictions) or where the asset portfolio is not 'granular' (ie it consists of only a few large assets – as is often the case in CMBS deals), and in addition is not appropriate where the assets are shorter-term than the ABS or are by their nature revolving (such as credit card receivables or trade receivables). In those cases, it would be normal to use a 'revolving' structure, in which principal receipts are, for a specified period (the 'revolving period'), or until a specified trigger/early amortisation event occurs, reinvested in new receivables. Once the end of the revolving period has been reached, the options for applying principal include: depositing the principal in a reserve account or GIC (guaranteed investment contract) until the maturity date (referred to as a 'principal accumulation period'), and then repaying principal in a 'bullet' (ie single) payment on the maturity date; or paying the principal out to ABS holders in regular instalments (referred to as a 'controlled amortisation period').

Another mechanism that can be used to give greater certainty for investors as to when they will be repaid is to repay different tranches of the ABS on a fast-pay, slow-pay basis (with principal receipts being applied first to the fast-pay tranche).[42]

A related form of reinvestment risk is that arising from payments being received on the underlying assets part way through an interest period on the ABS. If this is a payment of principal, interest on that principal will be likely to have ceased accruing from the repayment date, whereas interest on the equivalent principal amount of the ABS will continue accruing until the next interest payment date. This risk of a potential shortfall is usually addressed by providing that the payments be invested in either a GIC or a deposit account with a suitably rated entity that pays a pre-agreed rate of interest.

7.52　　Securitisations are usually categorised by reference to the classes of underlying assets. The following are some of the main asset classes:

(a) *Consumer ABS*. This category mainly includes auto loans (including auto leases and hire purchase agreements), consumer loans (typically unsecured personal loans) and credit cards. These asset types usually have a significantly shorter repayment profile than that of the ABS (in the case of auto loans and consumer loans) or are revolving in nature (in the case of credit cards). Consequently, many securitisations of consumer assets use a revolving structure, in order to give the ABS a

---

[42]　Sometimes referred to as a 'turbo' tranche.

longer average life than if the securitisation were structured as a straight pass-through.

(b) *CMBS (Commercial mortgage-backed securitisations).* CMBS deals cover a range of transaction types. These include: commercial mortgage transactions (where the originator is a mortgagee lender, and the receivables funding the ABS are the mortgages – these deals usually use a true sale or a synthetic structure); commercial and residential real estate transactions (where the originator is an owner of property leased to tenants, and the receivables funding the ABS are the leases – these deals usually use a secured loan structure); and sale and leaseback transactions (where the originator sells the property to the SPV and then leases it back, with the lease payments servicing the ABS). Many CMBS deals are not 'self-liquidating' (ie the receivables themselves do not generate sufficient proceeds to repay the ABS), with repayment of the ABS being therefore dependent on a disposal of the properties or a refinancing by the originator.

(c) *Covered bonds.* Covered bonds had their origins in the German *Pfandbriefe* first issued in the late eighteenth century.[43] Most other European jurisdictions have in recent years enacted legislation to provide for similar instruments to *Pfandbriefe*, and the term 'covered bonds' is now used generally to describe these various forms of instrument. They are, in essence, bonds issued by an originator that are backed by a dynamically changing pool of assets of the originator recorded in a 'cover register', which is maintained by the originator under the supervision of the relevant regulatory authority. By statute, the bondholders have a priority claim (equivalent to security, but arising automatically by statute) over this 'cover pool' in addition to their contractual debt claim against the originator under the bonds. The assets in the cover pool remain on the originator's balance sheet, but the bondholders are insulated from the effect of the originator's insolvency: in the event of the originator's insolvency, the bondholders would continue to receive their scheduled interest and principal payments from the cover pool, and an early redemption would only be triggered if the assets cease to satisfy the relevant regulatory requirements. For the originator, the advantages are cheaper funding (as a result of the statutory priority claim given to the bondholders) and greater flexibility than a securitisation structure involving a SPV (since assets in the cover pool can be easily substituted, without grants and releases of security being necessary). In the UK, there is no legislation on covered bonds, but a similar effect has been achieved contractually (using a structure developed by HBOS in 2003).

(d) *RMBS (Residential mortgage-backed securitisations).* Unlike certain types of CMBS, RMBS deals are usually self-liquidating, ie the

---

[43] See **7.9**.

receivables themselves fund the repayment of the ABS. Most RMBS deals use either a 'true sale' structure (sometimes involving a master trust,[44] particularly where the portfolio includes flexible mortgages) or a synthetic structure.

(e) *Trade receivables.* These are payments by businesses for goods or services on trade credit. They are short-term in nature, can fluctuate significantly in amount, and do not bear interest. The most suitable form of funding for the SPV is therefore commercial paper (CP) issued at a discount, with the amount of funding being quickly and easily adjustable as the CP rolls over. The deals are revolving in nature, in that, as the receivables mature, proceeds are used to purchase fresh receivables unless a specified trigger/early amortisation event has occurred. The SPV is therefore usually structured as an ABCP conduit (ie funding itself on a revolving basis through the issuance of asset-backed commercial paper). In the context of trade receivables, the conduit is usually a 'multi-seller conduit' (ie designed to fund a range of transactions for different originators). Such a conduit is usually established and managed by a financial institution as its sponsor, to enable the institution's clients to raise finance by selling receivables to the conduit.[45]

(f) *Whole business securitisations.* These are in fact hybrid transactions, combining elements of both securitisation and secured corporate debt. The cashflows backing the deal do not derive from specific ring-fenced assets but from the whole range of operating revenues generated by a business. The investors are thus exposed to the operating risk of the originator (ie how well run its business is) as opposed to merely the risks attached to specific assets. Whole business securitisations are therefore used where businesses have stable and predictable cashflows and more value can be obtained by securitising the entire range of the cashflows rather than individual categories of receivables. Most transactions so far are UK deals, in sectors such as motorway service stations, pubs, transport and healthcare. The structure usually involves the SPV making a loan to one of the companies in the operating structure, with the benefit of security from all the members of the group that own the relevant assets.

---

[44]   Described at **7.35**.

[45]   As well as being used to securitise trade receivables, ABCP conduits are also used for securities arbitrage (ie securitising a managed pool of tradeable securities in order to generate profit through the funding cost being lower than the return on the pool). When used in this way, ABCP conduits have certain similarities to SIVs (see further **7.62ff**).

CDOS[46]

7.53 As mentioned earlier, CDOs, when they were first developed, were referred to as either CBOs or CLOs, depending on whether the portfolio consisted of bonds or loans.

7.54 CBOs were primarily driven by arbitrage opportunities, with a collateral manager being appointed to trade the portfolio so as to maximise excess spread payable to the holders of the subordinated notes. CLOs, on the other hand, were traditionally balance sheet and funding driven.

7.55 In terms of the underlying assets and the commercial rationale, the CBO/CLO distinction has blurred, as CDOs increasingly cater for underlying portfolios which are a mixture of bonds, loans and derivative instruments. Current terminology to describe the type of transaction focuses instead on a number of features, including the purpose for which the CDO is set up, how the SPV's liabilities are funded, and the nature of the assets. Several more recent terms used to describe different forms of CDOs include:

(a) Collateralised swap obligation ('CSO') – a synthetic CDO where the portfolio is made up of various credit default swaps, each referencing the risk on a particular reference obligation or reference entity.

(b) CDO of asset-backed securities ('CDO of ABS') – a CDO with an underlying portfolio consisting of ABS, such as CMBS or RMBS.

(c) Collateralised fund obligation ('CFO') – a CDO involving a portfolio of interest in funds.

(d) Collateralised equity obligation ('CEO') – a CDO with a portfolio of equity default swaps, thereby exposing investors to a portfolio of equity rather than debt risk. Although not common, there have been several examples of this structure.

(e) Hybrid CDOs – a CDO that gives the manager the ability to shift between cash and synthetic assets.[47]

(f) CDO-squared/CDO-cubed – CDO-squared transactions contain portfolios which consist of tranches of other CDOs. This have been a particular growth area in the recent past, and has led to increasingly complex synthetic CDO structures utilising cutting-edge credit derivative techniques. CDO-cubed transactions add an additional layer, consisting of a portfolio of CDO-squared transactions.

---

[46] See further Tavakoli, *Collateralized Debt Obligations & Structured Finance* (2003); Fuller and Ranero, *Butterworth's JIBFL* (Oct 2005), pp 343–351; Das, *Credit Derivatives, CDOs and Structured Credit Products* (2005), Chapter 4; Lucas, Goodman and Fabozzi, *Collateralized Debt Obligations: Structures & Analysis* (2nd edn, 2006); Deacon, *Global Securitisation and CDOs* (2004); Fabozzi and Choudhry (ed), *The Handbook of European Structured Financial Products* (2004), Chapters 30–34; Watson and Carter (ed), *Asset Securitisation and Synthetic Structures* (2006), Chapters 14–15; Joannas and Choudhry, *A Primer on Synthetic Collateralised Debt Obligations* (2003); Borrows (ed), *Current Issues in Securitisation* (2002), Chapter 5.

[47] This flexibility also exists in traditional cash CDOs, but within much tighter limits.

7.56 CDOs are also described as either 'static' or 'managed'. In a static CDO the portfolio is selected at the outset and remains fixed for the life of the transaction, though sometimes with assets being removed in very limited circumstances (such as upon a default or the assets becoming 'credit-impaired').

7.57 In a managed CDO, the assets may be added to and removed from the portfolio during a specified reinvestment period, subject to certain eligibility criteria and portfolio diversity and quality tests being satisfied. In a typical managed CDO, a collateral manager (in synthetic transactions more commonly referred to as a portfolio manager) is appointed by the SPV to select the initial portfolio and to manage it during the life of the transaction. The collateral manager would ordinarily receive a 'base management fee', payable pari passu with the senior and/or mezzanine noteholders, and in addition one or more 'incentive management fees' if the transaction performs well (the most junior incentive fee being, effectively, a sharing of the excess spread with the holders of the subordinated notes). Frequently, the collateral manager is required to hold and to retain a proportion of the subordinated notes in order to show an alignment of interest between the collateral manager and the investors in the subordinated notes (who ultimately bear the risk and receive the benefit of the collateral manager's performance).

7.58 Although a static CDO provides investors with greater certainty, and they do not need to share any excess spread with the collateral manager, the reason for appointing a collateral manager is so that the transaction can benefit from the collateral manager's expertise to produce a lower level of defaults or credit events or to benefit from trading profits, hence achieving a better rate of return for the investors.

7.59 A further distinction is between 'cashflow CDOs' and 'market value CDOs'. In a cashflow CDO (as with other cashflow structures), interest received in respect of the portfolio is used to pay interest on the ABS and the expenses of the transaction, and principal received in respect of the portfolio is either reinvested in additional collateral or used to make principal payments on the ABS. As a result, the market value of the portfolio is generally unimportant because the assets are either held to maturity or sold to provide funds to purchase new assets.

7.60 In market value CDOs, which are less common in the European market, the money to fund payments of principal and interest on the ABS is primarily obtained through trading the portfolio. The market value of the portfolio is monitored by the rating agencies and assets are sold to repay investors if the market value falls below a specified percentage level.

7.61 As already mentioned, a key feature of CDOs is the slicing of the risk in the portfolio and the tranching of the ABS issued by the SPV. CDOS have traditionally been full capital structure transactions, involving the issuance of various classes of ABS which, together, represent the whole risk in respect of the portfolio. A more recent and fast developing structure in the synthetic CDO market, however, is the single-tranche CDO, which involves a specific slice of the portfolio credit risk being transferred rather than the risk in respect of the whole portfolio. The remaining risk in respect of the portfolio is dynamically hedged by the portfolio manager through credit trading techniques referred to as 'delta hedging' or 'correlation trading'. Single-tranche transactions are simpler to execute, and are generally bespoke transactions, tailored and sold to particular investors rather than being marketed and distributed widely.

SIVs[48]

7.62 A SIV is, in effect, a highly structured investment fund. The SPV sets up secured debt issuance programmes (usually EMTN, ECP, USMTN and USCP, in order to tap as many markets as possible), which are usually rated AAA and which permit the SPV to borrow up to (usually) 20 times the amount of the 'equity'. The equity is usually issued in the form of subordinated notes under a separate programme. Unlike securitisations and CDOs, where the tranching of the ABS issued by the SPV can involve a large number of layers, the ABS issued by the SPV are usually only of two tranches (the equity and the senior, AAA, notes) – though structures with more layers are beginning to develop.

7.63 The equity and the moneys borrowed under the senior notes are invested in a portfolio of investment grade bonds, which is managed by an investment manager. Risks associated with the portfolio are hedged through swap agreements. In addition to the management of the assets, the SPV's liabilities are also managed on an active basis, by a funding manager. Consequently, on a daily basis, assets in the portfolio mature or are sold, debt matures, fresh debt is borrowed, and fresh assets are purchased.

7.64 The aim of the structure is to make a profit, to be shared between the investment manager and the equity investors. This profit is made from the difference between the yield on the portfolio and the lower rates of interest payable on the AAA rated senior debt raised under the programmes. This is achieved partly because the AAA rating enables the SPV to borrow at a cheaper funding cost than the yield on the portfolio, and partly though differences between the maturity profiles of the portfolio and the AAA debt. The SPV typically borrows on a shorter-term basis than the average life of the portfolio, which therefore also reduces its funding cost.

---

[48] See further Watson and Carter (ed), *Asset Securitisation and Synthetic Structures* (2006), pp 116–120; Hamilton and Anderson, *IFLR, The 2005 Guide to Structured Finance*, pp 72–75; Tavakoli, *Collateralized Debt Obligations & Structured Finance* (2003), pp 302–303.

7.65   In this respect, SIVs bear similarities to ABCP conduits.[49] These, however, fund themselves solely through commercial paper, and typically have to have liquidity facilities in place to cover the full amount of their CP (in case market conditions make it difficult for them to refinance when the CP matures), whereas SIVs have a wider range of maturities (funding themselves through MTNs as well), and typically only need liquidity cover for approximately 7–9% of their liabilities.

7.66   The principal differences between a SIV and a CDO are: the ongoing management on the funding side of the balance sheet of a SIV; the (usually) more complex capital structure of a CDO; SIVs have an unlimited life; SIVs have more rigorous monitoring and risk management; and the ongoing tests and limits are different in each structure.[50]

7.67   The maintenance of the AAA ratings for the senior debt programmes is key to the continued viability of the SIV. This is achieved through the detailed composition criteria and sensitivity tests, and a highly complex software model that is reviewed by the rating agencies.

---

[49]   Which, as seen earlier, are used not only for securitising trade receivables but also as a means of securities arbitrage, in a similar way to SIVs.

[50]   For example, a typical cashflow CDO would have weighted average life, weighted average spread, overcollateralisation and interest coverage tests. The tests and limits to which a SIV is typically subject include portfolio concentration and diversification, capital loss, leverage, interest rate sensitivity and FX sensitivity limits.

Chapter Eight

SUBORDINATION[1]

INTRODUCTION

8.1 It is common for companies to borrow on a subordinated basis, ie for the lender (the subordinated, or junior, creditor) to agree not to be repaid by the company until one or more other creditors (the senior creditors) have been paid in full. The effectiveness of the subordination is clearly most relevant where the company is insolvent (since if the company is solvent all creditors, both senior and junior, can be paid in full), and hence the primary objective is always to ensure that the subordination is effective in insolvency.

8.2 There are many ways in which one creditor of an English company can rank junior to another in an insolvent winding up: unsecured creditors rank junior to secured and preferential creditors; floating chargees rank junior to fixed chargees and preferential creditors; preferential creditors rank junior to fixed chargees; and one fixed chargee may rank junior to another.[2] However, a major development in recent years has been the use of methods to achieve an order of ranking as between *unsecured* creditors, with the junior creditor being intended to rank junior to a particular senior creditor, a class of senior creditors or sometimes to all other creditors of the company. It is this ranking between unsecured creditors that is described by the term 'subordination'.

8.3 A similar commercial effect can be achieved by 'structural subordination'. Structural subordination arises where the main assets of a group are owned by one or more subsidiaries, but the borrowing is undertaken by the parent company. The money lent to the parent is advanced to the subsidiaries by way of either a capital contribution or a loan which is agreed contractually to be subordinate to the subsidiaries' debts to other

---

1 See generally Wood, *The Law of Subordinated Debt* (1990) and *Project Finance, Subordinated Debt and State Loans* (1995), Chapters 6–9; Lingard, *Bank Security Documents* (3rd edn, 1993), pp 332–337; Goode, *Legal Problems of Credit and Security* (3rd edn, 2003), pp 55–57, 185–197; Ferran, *Company Law and Corporate Finance* (1999) pp 545–564; Gough, *Company Charges* (2nd end, 1996), Chapter 40; Cranston, *Principles of Banking Law* (2nd edn, 2002), pp 329–331; Nolan [1995] JIBL 485; Oditah (1992) 108 LQR 459; Powell [1993] LMCLQ 357; Johnston [1991] JBL 225; Johnston [1987] ABLR 80; Nicolaides [1989] *Butterworths' JIBFL*, p 247; Capper (1995) 14 Insolv L 3.

2 See further **6.89ff**.

creditors (as described below). Consequently, in a liquidation of the group (and assuming no guarantee from the subsidiaries), the lenders will have no direct claim on the subsidiaries' assets, but only on the parent company's assets. The parent can only recover from the subsidiaries after the subsidiaries' other creditors have been paid. De facto, therefore, the lenders are subordinated to the creditors of the subsidiaries.

8.4 However, it is with 'true' subordination, rather than with structural subordination, that this chapter is concerned.

REASONS FOR SUBORDINATION

8.5 There are a number of reasons why companies borrow on a subordinated basis:[3]

(a) In the case of banks, to increase their capital base for regulatory purposes. As the acceptance of deposits is a regulated activity under the Financial Services and Markets Act 2000,[4] permission is required under the Act from the Financial Services Authority (the 'Authority'). One of the conditions that must be satisfied before permission can be granted is that the resources of the person concerned must, in the opinion of the Authority, be adequate.[5]

The rules on the adequacy of resources (or 'capital adequacy' as it is more commonly known) are set out in the European Banking Consolidation Directive[6] and the European Capital Adequacy Directive,[7] which are implemented in the UK by the Interim Prudential Sourcebook for Banks of the Authority.[8]

Under the Sourcebook, a bank is required to meet, on a continuing basis, the capital ratio set for it by the Authority, which must not be less than eight per cent of the bank's weighted assets.[9] For this purpose, capital is divided into three tiers:[10] Tier 1, such as equity, disclosed reserves and perpetual non-cumulative preference shares;[11] supplementary capital (or Tier 2), which can include certain categories of subordinated debt; and ancillary capital (or Tier 3), which can

---

3   See Wood, *The Law of Subordinated Debt* (1990), pp 2–3.
4   See **Chapter 10**.
5   Financial Services and Markets Act 2000, s 41(2) and Sch 6, para 4(1).
6   Directive 2000/12/EC.
7   Directive 93/6/EC, as amended by Directive 98/31/EC.
8   The Authority took over from the Bank of England on 1 June 1998 as the competent authority for banking supervision, and accordingly its Interim Prudential Sourcebook ('IPRU (Banks)') replaces the Bank of England's previous Notices on capital adequacy.
9   IPRU (Banks), Chapter CO, para 4.1.1.
10 Chapter CA, Section 4.
11 Chapter CA, para 4.2 and Section 5.

include certain other categories of subordinated debt.[12] Tier 1 is divided into Core Tier 1 (the highest quality capital) and Innovative Tier 1 (instruments with features which marginally weaken the quality of the capital).[13] Tier 2 is divided into Lower Tier 2 (which can include subordinated debt with a minimum original maturity of five years and one day)[14] and Upper Tier 2 (which can include 'perpetual'[15] subordinated debt).[16]

(b) So that lenders on a senior basis will be more likely to lend greater amounts. The subordinated debt acts as a cushion in the event of insolvency, with the subordinated lenders generally taking a higher interest rate to compensate them for their larger risk. So long as the subordinated lenders' interest rate is not too high, this is attractive to the company, as the unsubordinated lenders will be more likely to lend greater amounts and thus the total amount of money available to the company will be increased. This is particularly relevant both where the company is in financial trouble (the parent company agreeing to subordinate inter-company indebtedness to it to allow the company to borrow fresh amounts without the directors incurring liability for wrongful trading) and also where the loans are to finance a take-over or a management buy-out on highly leveraged terms.[17]

(c) So that external lenders can be sure that the proceeds of their loans are not used to repay debts to 'insiders', such as a parent company or a major shareholder. This is particularly relevant in relation to project finance where the external lenders commonly wish insiders' debt to be treated as 'proprietorial' capital and therefore subordinated so that it remains locked in until the external lenders have been repaid.

DIFFICULTIES IN ACHIEVING SUBORDINATION

8.6   The difficulties in achieving effective subordination in the case of English companies are presented by s 107 of the Insolvency Act 1986 and r 4.181 of the Insolvency Rules 1986.[18] Section 107 provides that, subject to the priority of preferential debts, 'the company's property in a voluntary

---

[12] In essence, debt with a minimum original maturity of two years and containing a requirement for principal and interest payments to be deferred if capital falls below the target ratio (Chapter CA, para 4.4 and Section 9). Tier 3 capital (unlike Tiers 1 and 2) may only be used to support the bank's 'trading' book and not its 'banking' book, and accordingly is only applicable for banks whose trading book is above a certain size and therefore subject to capital requirements (see Chapter CB of the Sourcebook).

[13] Chapter CA, para 4.2 and Section 5.

[14] Chapter CA, para 4.3 and Sections 7 and 8.

[15] See **Chapter 1 and 5.1**.

[16] Chapter CA, para 4.3 and Sections 6 and 8.

[17] Although in practice it is more common in the latter two cases for all the lenders to be secured at different levels of ranking. The junior secured debt is usually known as 'mezzanine' debt.

[18] SI 1986/1925, as amended.

winding up shall on the winding up be applied in satisfaction of the company's liabilities pari passu . . .'. Rule 4.181 provides that, in a compulsory winding up, 'debts other than preferential debts rank equally between themselves in the winding up'.

8.7   Prior to the decision of Vinelott J in *Re Maxwell Communications Corporation plc (No 2)*,[19] concern was felt that the effect of s 107 and r 4.181 is that all unsecured creditors *must* be paid equally and thus that no arrangements for subordination can be effective in a winding up.[20] This concern arose out of two House of Lords' decisions, *National Westminster Bank Ltd v Halesowen Presswork & Assemblies Ltd*[21] and *British Eagle International Airlines Ltd v Compagnie Nationale Air France.*[22] In *Halesowen*, the House of Lords held that, on the construction of the agreement in question, the parties had not purported to contract out of the set-off provisions of s 31 of the Bankruptcy Act 1914.[23] However, some of their Lordships[24] also stated[25] that, had the agreement purported to contract out of s 31, this would have been invalid since s 31 stated that there 'shall' be a set-off, and therefore this was mandatory as a matter of statutory construction. Concern was felt in the light of these comments that the same construction of the word 'shall' should logically apply in s 107: in other words, if set-off is mandatory, pari passu treatment of unsecured creditors should be as well.

8.8   In *British Eagle*, the House of Lords held, by a majority, that the clearing arrangements in question between airlines, which would have had the effect of preferring one class of unsecured creditors (ie the airlines), were unenforceable in the winding up of British Eagle as being contrary to the pari passu principle. Dicta,[26] however, suggested that the requirement of pari passu payment could not be contracted out of. This was accepted as the correct interpretation of the principle by, for example, the Cork Committee on Insolvency Law and Practice[27] and by Peter Gibson J in *Carreras Rothmans Ltd v Freeman Mathews Treasure Ltd.*[28]

---

[19]   [1994] 1 All ER 737. See Ferran, *Company Law News*, 28 June 1993, p 8; Nolan [1995] JIBL 485.

[20]   The alternative view, that the pari passu rule does not prevent subordination arrangements being effective, has been taken in South Africa (*Re Carbon Developments (Pty) Ltd (in liq)* [1993] 1 SA 493) and has received statutory recognition in Australia (Corporations Act 2001, s 563C) and in New Zealand (Companies Act 1993, s 313(3), and Companies Amendment Act 1993, s 287(3)).

[21]   [1972] AC 785.

[22]   [1975] 2 All ER 390.

[23]   As applied to companies by s 317 of the Companies Act 1948: in relation to companies, the provisions are now contained in r 4.90 of the Insolvency Rules 1986, SI 1986/1925.

[24]   Namely, Viscount Dilhorne and Lords Simon and Kilbrandon.

[25]   At pp 805, 808 to 809 and 824 respectively. Lord Cross, at pp 813 and 818, was of the view that contracting out is permissible.

[26]   [1975] 2 All ER 390 at 403 per Lord Simon and 411 per Lord Cross.

[27]   Cmnd 8558 (1982), para 1148.

[28]   [1985] Ch 207 at 226.

8.9 However, Vinelott J held in *Re Maxwell Communications Corporation plc (No 2)*[29] that a clause providing that 'creditors of unsubordinated indebtedness of [the company] should be entitled to be paid in full before any payment shall be made on account of payments under [the junior debt]' is valid. Vinelott J held that he was not bound by the comments in the *Halesowen* and *British Eagle* cases as they were only dicta, and that, in any event, whereas there were good public policy reasons for set-off to be mandatory in a winding up, there were no good public policy reasons for the pari passu rule to be mandatory.

8.10 Similarly, in *Re SSSL Realisations (2002) Ltd*,[30] the Court of Appeal affirmed the decision of Lloyd J[31] that an undertaking not to 'claim rank prove or vote as a creditor' and not to 'receive, claim or have the benefit of any payment distribution' until a third party had been paid created a valid subordination arrangement and did not infringe the pari passu rule.

8.11 Accordingly, in the light of the *Maxwell* and *SSSL* decisions, it is clear that subordination can be effected by simple contractual agreement[32]. However, for various reasons,[33] it is still the norm for subordination to be effected by one of the methods developed prior to the *Maxwell* decision.

EXISTING METHODS OF SUBORDINATION

8.12 Prior to *Maxwell*, two methods were in use for effecting subordination without infringing the principle of pari passu treatment:

(1) Trust subordination

8.13 The junior creditor agrees that any payments received in respect of his debt in a winding up of the company will be held on trust for the senior creditors to the extent that their debts remain unpaid. Section 107 and r 4.181 are not infringed since the junior creditor still proves for his debt and is paid pari passu with the other unsecured creditors; once paid, however, he holds the money on trust for the senior creditors. In practice, most liquidators will give effect to such an agreement on the junior creditor's behalf by paying the money direct to the senior creditors. This method was

---

[29]   [1994] 1 All ER 737.

[30]   [2006] 2 WLR 1369.

[31]   [2005] 1 BCLC 1.

[32]   See also *Re Pinecord Ltd* [1995] 2 BCLC 57 (a clause purporting to convert loan rights into share rights in a winding up did not achieve this effect, but was nevertheless successful as a subordination clause).

[33]   Including habit and (as discussed at **8.26**) a lack of certainty about the correct procedural treatment in a liquidation.

accepted as effective in *Re British & Commonwealth Holdings plc (No 3)*[34] and in *Maxwell* and *SSSL*.

8.14   A typical clause to this effect (in this example, in a eurobond trust deed) would read as follows:

(1) In the event of the winding-up of the Issuer, all amounts paid to the Trustee by the liquidator of the Issuer in the winding-up of the Issuer shall be held by the Trustee upon trust:

   (i)   FIRST in payment or satisfaction of all remuneration, costs, charges, expenses and liabilities then due and unpaid under Clauses [ ] (*Remuneration*) and [ ] (*Indemnity*) to the Trustee;

   (ii) SECONDLY in or towards payment pari passu and rateably of claims of all Senior Creditors of the Issuer in the winding-up of the Issuer to the extent that such claims are admitted to proof in the winding up (not having been satisfied out of the other resources of the Issuer) excluding interest accruing after commencement of the winding up; and

   (iii) THIRDLY as to the balance (if any) in or towards payment to the Bondholders and Couponholders in accordance with Clause [ ] (*Application of monies*).

(2) The trust secondly mentioned in sub-clause (1) above may be performed by the Trustee paying over to the liquidator for the time being in the winding-up of the Issuer the amounts received by the Trustee as aforesaid (less any amounts thereof applied in the implementation of the trust first mentioned in sub-clause (1) above) on terms that such liquidator shall distribute the same accordingly and the receipt of such liquidator for the same shall be a good discharge to the Trustee for the performance by it of the trust secondly mentioned in sub-clause (1) above.

(3) The Trustee shall be entitled to call for and to accept as conclusive evidence thereof a certificate from the liquidator for the time being of the Issuer as to:

   (i)   the amount of the claims of the Senior Creditors of the Issuer referred to in sub-clause (1) above (other than as therein mentioned); and

   (ii) the persons entitled thereto and their respective entitlements.

(4) For the purposes of the above provisions, '**Senior Creditors of the Issuer**' means all secured creditors of the Issuer and all other creditors of the Issuer except those whose claims are or are expressed to be subordinated, in the event of the winding-up of the Issuer, to the right to payment of all unsubordinated creditors of the Issuer.

(2) Contingent debt subordination

8.15   The junior creditor agrees that his debt shall only become due and payable if and to the extent that the company will have sufficient assets left

---

34   [1992] 1 WLR 672.

to pay the senior creditors in full. Sometimes, this is achieved by the junior creditor agreeing that, in a winding up of the company, he is only entitled to what he would have received had he been the holder of a first-ranking preference share; on other occasions, it is achieved by reference to a definition of 'solvency' that takes into account the senior debt but excludes the junior debt, with the junior debt only becoming due and payable to the extent that the company can remain 'solvent' thereafter. Section 107 and r 4.181 are not infringed since, to the extent that the contingency is not satisfied, the junior creditor's claim in the winding up is valued at nil; to the extent that the contingency is satisfied, his claim is valued at the relevant amount available to pay him, and he is paid that amount pari passu with the other unsecured creditors.[35]

8.16   A typical provision to this effect (in this example, in a eurobond issue with a trustee) would read as follows:

> The rights of the Bondholders and Couponholders against the Issuer are subordinated in right of payment to the claims of all Senior Creditors (as defined below). Accordingly payments of principal and interest by the Issuer are conditional upon the Issuer being solvent at the time of such payment and no principal or interest shall be payable by the Issuer in respect of the Bonds except to the extent that the Issuer could make such payment and still be solvent immediately thereafter. For this purpose the Issuer shall be solvent if (i) it is able to pay its debts as they fall due and (ii) its Assets exceed its Liabilities (each as defined below) (other than its Liabilities to persons who are not Senior Creditors). A report as to the solvency of the Issuer by two Directors of the Issuer or, in certain circumstances as provided in the Trust Deed, the Auditors (as defined in the Trust Deed) of the Issuer or, if the Issuer is dissolved or being wound up, its liquidator shall, in the absence of proven error, be treated and accepted by the Issuer, the Trustee and the Bondholders and Couponholders as correct and sufficient evidence thereof.

> For the purposes of the above provisions:

> '**Senior Creditors**' means creditors of the Issuer (i) who are unsubordinated creditors of the Issuer or (ii) whose claims are, or are expressed to be, subordinated (whether only in the event that the Issuer is dissolved or an order is made or an effective resolution is passed for the winding-up of the Issuer or otherwise) to the claims of unsubordinated creditors of the Issuer but not further or otherwise or (iii) who are subordinated creditors of the Issuer other than those with whose claims the claims of the Bondholders and Couponholders are expressed to rank pari passu and those whose claims rank, or are expressed to rank, pari passu with, or junior to, the claims of the Bondholders and Couponholders; and

> '**Assets**' means the unconsolidated gross assets of the Issuer and '**Liabilities**' means the unconsolidated gross liabilities of the Issuer, all as shown by the latest published audited balance sheet of the Issuer, but adjusted for

---

[35] Contingent debts are provable: Insolvency Rules 1986, SI 1986/1925, as amended, r 12.3(1).

contingencies and for subsequent events, all in such manner as two Directors of the Issuer, its Auditors or its liquidator (as the case may be) may determine.

8.17   Various considerations might influence which of these two methods is chosen. First, the economic effect for both the senior and the junior creditor in terms of recoveries is always no worse, and sometimes better, under trust subordination than under contingent debt subordination.[36] Secondly, where the junior creditor is a trustee under an issue of debt securities, it will prefer trust subordination to be used, since the terms of trust subordinations commonly allow the trustee to deduct, or 'top-slice', its unpaid remuneration and expenses (which are not subordinated) before paying the monies over to the senior creditors. In a contingent debt subordination, there is no money for it to 'top-slice' unless there are sufficient assets to pay the senior creditors in full. Thirdly, trust subordination is subject to the rule against perpetuities, whereby trust property must vest in the beneficiary within the perpetuity period.[37] Under normal trust subordination arrangements, the trust property will not vest until the winding up of the company. The perpetuity period which is most likely to apply is 21 years.[38] Alternatively, a perpetuity period of up to 80 years can be specified in the subordination agreement.[39] If it is possible that the junior creditor's claim might fall due only after the expiry of the perpetuity period, it is clearly preferable to use contingent debt subordination instead.[40]

LEGAL ISSUES ARISING FROM SUBORDINATION

8.18   There are three important legal issues arising from subordination:

Whether the arrangements can be modified without the consent of the senior creditors

8.19   In the case of trust subordination, this would seem to depend upon whether the trust is expressed to be of the junior debt itself or only of the payments to be received thereunder in the winding up. Where (as is usually the case) it is the latter, the trust is of future property, and therefore incompletely constituted. Accordingly, the senior creditor will not be able to prevent the terms of the trust being modified without his consent unless he has given consideration for his interest thereunder, as volunteers cannot

---

[36]   See the examples given by Wood, *The Law of Subordinated Debt* (1990), pp 13–16.

[37]   See Megarry and Wade, *The Law of Real Property* (6th edn, 2000), pp 300–356.

[38]   See s 3(4) of the Perpetuities and Accumulations Act 1964.

[39]   Section 1(1) of the 1964 Act.

[40]   Contingent debt subordination in fact first became common specifically as a way of overcoming the perpetuity problem in relation to perpetual subordinated bonds: see *IFLR*, June 1985, pp 24–25.

enforce an incompletely constituted trust.[41] If it is thought desirable that the senior creditor should be able to prevent the terms of the trust being modified without his consent, possible solutions include the entry by the company and/or the junior creditor into an agreement with the senior creditor not to modify (ie an 'intercreditor agreement'),[42] or the junior creditor contracting with the company either to return the payment or not to modify, and the company holding the benefit of that contract on trust for the senior creditors. Being a trust of a present chose in action, it is completely constituted and therefore enforceable by the senior creditors even though they are volunteers.[43]

8.20 In the case of contingent debt subordination and subordination effected by simple contractual agreement (as in *Maxwell* and *SSSL*), the rules on privity of contract mean that the subordination arrangements are capable of modification without the consent of the senior creditor, except to the extent that the senior creditor is a party to the subordination agreement, a beneficiary under a deed poll executed in his favour by the company and/or the junior creditor covenanting not to modify, a third party beneficiary under the Contracts (Rights of Third Parties) Act 1999 who has assented to or relied on the subordination arrangement,[44] or a beneficiary under a trust of a present chose in action as described above.

Whether the arrangements constitute a grant of security by the junior creditor in favour of the senior creditor

8.21 If they do, then, where the junior creditor is an English company, the arrangements will be void as against the liquidator, administrator and creditors of the junior creditor unless the prescribed particulars are lodged with the Registrar of Companies within 21 days of creation.[45] There may also be consequences for a negative pledge[46] to which the junior creditor is subject. The question does not arise in relation to contingent debt subordination or subordination by simple contractual agreement, since the senior creditors are not given any proprietary interest in the junior creditor's claim against the company or its proceeds. However, the question is relevant for trust subordination, since in that case the senior creditors are potentially given such an interest.

---

[41] See *Snell's Equity* (31st edn, 2005) pp 494–499; Underhill and Hayton, *Law Relating to Trusts and Trustees* (16th edn, 2003), pp 144–182.

[42] Which, if the senior creditors are a large and changing class, is (despite the Contracts (Rights of Third Parties) Act 1999) best achieved by means of a deed poll: see further **19.7**.

[43] *Ellison v Ellison* (1802) 6 Ves Jun 656.

[44] In circumstances entitling him to rely on the restrictions on variation in s 2 of the Act.

[45] Companies Act 1985, s 395: see **6.81**.

[46] As to which, see **9.28ff**.

8.22   Trusts can constitute security interests.[47] One of the key elements, though, is the right of the 'chargor' to have his asset back if the debt is discharged (the equity of redemption).[48] If there is no equity of redemption, the arrangement will not constitute a grant of security. Where (as is normal) the trust is drafted as applying only to the proceeds received by the junior creditor up to the amount necessary to pay the senior creditors in full, there is no equity of redemption, as there is never a surplus to be transferred back to the junior creditor, merely an outright transfer of part of the beneficial ownership of the proceeds. The position would be different, however, if the trust was expressed to be over the debt itself, or over all the proceeds on the basis that any surplus was to be handed back. In either case, the junior creditor has an equity of redemption, as he has a right to receive back any surplus from the senior creditors.[49]

8.23   If the arrangement is construed as a grant of security, the possible categories of registrable charge that could be applicable include: a charge on book debts;[50] a floating charge (if the senior creditors have no rights to block variations of the subordinated debt);[51] and (if the senior debt is in the form of debt securities) a charge for the purposes of securing an issue of debtentures.[52]

Whether the effectiveness of subordination arrangements can be defeated by set-off rights between the company and the junior creditor

8.24   If the junior creditor is able to set off the subordinated debt against a debt owed by him to the company, this will clearly negate the effect of the subordination, since, in effect, the junior creditor will get paid – by means of his set-off right – on an unsubordinated basis.

8.25   It is clear that the set-off in liquidation in respect of 'mutual dealings' provided for in r 4.90 of the Insolvency Rules 1986[53] is

---

47   *Re Bond Worth Ltd* [1980] Ch 228 at 250; *Compaq Computer Ltd v Abercorn Group Ltd* [1993] BCLC 602 at 612.

48   *Swiss Bank Corporation v Lloyds Bank Ltd* [1982] AC 584 at 595; *Re George Inglefield Ltd* [1933] Ch 1 at 27–28.

49   *Re SSSL Realisations (2002) Ltd* [2006] 2 WLR 1369 at 1423.

50   Companies Act 1985, s 396(1)(e). Whether the junior debt constitutes a book debt in any particular case will depend on the nature of the junior creditor's business. In *Re SSSL Realisations (2002) Ltd* [2006] 2 WLR 1369 (at 1423), the Court of Appeal held that a subordination trust arrangement, even if it had created a charge, would not have been a charge on book debts.

51   Companies Act 1985, s 396(1)(f).

52   Companies Act 1985, s 396(1)(a).

53   SI 1986/1925.

mandatory.[54] However, it is thought that neither trust nor contingent debt subordination is defeated by the mandatory set-off. In the case of trust subordination, the fact that the ultimate beneficial owner of the junior claim is the senior creditor is thought sufficient to destroy the mutuality required for a set-off to arise between the company and the junior creditor.[55] In the case of contingent debt subordination, the amount of the junior debt available for set-off purposes will only be the amount at which it would be valued for the purposes of proof.[56] As seen earlier, the junior debt will be valued at nil or such other amount as reflects the surplus of assets available after the senior creditors have been paid in full. To the extent that the junior debt is given a substantive value and that amount is then set off against debts due from the junior creditor, no harm is done since the junior creditor is recovering no more than he would otherwise have done.

8.26 Where, however, as in *Maxwell* and *SSSL*, subordination is effected merely by contractual agreement, the impact of the mandatory set-off is not clear, and depends upon how the subordinated debt is to be treated in a liquidation of the company. The liquidator, as seen earlier, must pay all ordinary creditors on a pari passu basis. If he is to give effect to the subordination (as he is required to do, in the light of *Maxwell* and *SSSL*) without breaching the pari passu rule, he will have to treat the subordinated debt as either: (i) not provable until the senior creditors have been paid in full; or (ii) provable but only at a reduced or nominal amount. The better view is that the latter is the correct approach,[57] in which event the subordinated debt is admitted to proof, at a reduced or nil value, in the same way as with contingent debt subordination, and therefore the junior creditor should only be able to set off an amount equal to what he would have received anyway.[58]

---

[54] There are unequivocal statements to this effect by three of their Lordships in *Halesowen* which, though obiter, were not suggested by Vinelott J in *Maxwell* to be wrong, merely not applicable in the *Maxwell* case. Indeed, as mentioned above, Vinelott J adduced strong public policy reasons for the set-off to be mandatory. See also *High Street Services Ltd v Bank of Credit and Commerce International SA* [1993] BCC 360 at 363 per Dillon LJ.

[55] See Wood, *The Law of Subordinated Debt* (1990), pp 45–46; Ferran, *Company Law and Corporate Finance* (1999), p 563.

[56] See Derham, *The Law of Set-Off* (3rd edn, 2003), pp 344–359: Wood, *English and International Set-Off* (1989), pp 301–303, 573–594; *Stein v Blake* [1996] AC 243 at 252–253 per Lord Hoffmann.

[57] On the basis that, under r 12.3(1) of the Insolvency Rules 1986, SI 1986/1925, all claims are provable unless they fall within one of the specified categories of non-provable debts. These include claims under certain specific statutory provisions (none of which are relevant here) and any claim which is to be postponed by virtue of the Insolvency Act 'or any other enactment'. Subordination by simple contractual agreement would not fall into this category, because it is achieved by contract rather than by a statutory enactment.

[58] See also Ferran, *Company Law and Corporate Finance* (1999), p 561.

Chapter Nine

THE POWER TO BORROW, TO GUARANTEE AND TO GIVE SECURITY

INTRODUCTION

9.1 Three questions present themselves in relation to a company's capacity: first, whether the company has power to enter into the transaction; secondly, whether that power can be exercised by the directors or another agent of the company without a resolution of the company or, as is sometimes required, the consent of a class of shareholders; and, thirdly, whether there is any limit or restriction on the exercise of that power.

CORPORATE POWER

9.2 Prior to the insertion of the new s 35 of the Companies Act 1985,[1] the validity of a transaction could be affected where that transaction was outside the scope of the company's objects and powers (ie ultra vires). Notwithstanding s 35, the 'old' ultra vires law, which is outside the scope of this book, is still relevant in respect of:

(a) acts done by a company prior to 4 February 1991;[2]
(b) shareholders' remedies (such as the power to restrain an ultra vires act)[3] and directors' duties;[4] and
(c) certain acts of charitable companies.[5]

9.3 Section 35(1) provides that: 'The validity of an act done by a company shall not be called into question on the ground of lack of capacity by reason of anything in the company's memorandum'. Consequently, a

---

[1] Inserted by s 108 of the Companies Act 1989.
[2] Article 7(1) of the 1990 Order.
[3] See s 35(2). A member of the company may bring proceedings to restrain the doing of an act which, but for s 35(1), would be ultra vires; but not if the act is done in fulfilment of a legal obligation arising from a previous act of the company. The subsection only permits the restraining of 'the doing' of an act: accordingly, no action may be taken by the member to invalidate the act on the grounds of it being ultra vires once the act has been done (though proceedings would still be available against the directors for breach of duty – see the next footnote).
[4] See s 35(3). The directors remain under a duty to observe limitations on their powers flowing from the memorandum, and breaches may only be ratified by special resolution.
[5] See ss 111 and 112 of the Companies Act 1989.

transaction entered into by a company can no longer be invalid merely on the grounds of lack of corporate power.

9.4 However, in practice, it is still important to check the memorandum and articles for corporate power to enter into the transaction. This is because:

(a) even though the creditor may have the protection of s 35, the directors who approve an ultra vires guarantee may be liable to the company;[6]

(b) a lack of corporate capacity limits the actual authority of the company's agents, and therefore the creditor is not fully protected unless the requirements in relation to authority (described at **9.6ff**) are also satisfied; and

(c) there is the risk that the creditor (depending on his level of knowledge of, or failure to enquire into, the directors' breach of duty) may be required to hold any proceeds received under a transaction that is beyond the company's capacity as constructive trustee for the company.[7]

9.5 Consequently, where the power to borrow/guarantee/charge is, or could be construed as, an ancillary power rather than a substantive object, the creditor should ensure that the board minutes record that the transaction is in the interests of the company and in furtherance of its objects, and the reasons (and the creditor should satisfy himself that these are reasonable); and, if there is any doubt about whether this is the case or about whether the company has power to enter into the transaction at all, the transaction should be approved by a shareholders' resolution. The resolution should, at the very least, be a special resolution (in order to effect the requisite amendment to the objects clause[8]), but (if practicable) should be a unanimous resolution (in order to prevent any claim by minority shareholders of fraud on the minority or unfairly prejudicial conduct[9]).

---

[6] Companies Act 1985, s 35(3) expressly preserves the directors' obligations to observe limitations on their powers flowing from the company's memorandum.

[7] On the basis of either 'knowing receipt' of misapplied assets or being an 'accessory' to the breach of a fiduciary duty (formerly referred to as 'knowing assistance'). Section 35(3) retains the liability not just of directors but also of third parties, unless they are specifically relieved from liability by a special resolution: and in *International Sales and Agencies Ltd v Marcus* ([1982] 3 All ER 551) Lawson LJ held that the 'old' s 35 (ie prior to amendment in 1989) did not affect the application of the principles of constructive trust, and the current s 35 does not appear to be sufficiently different to alter this position.

[8] Pursuant to Companies Act 1985, s 4.

[9] Within Companies Act 1985, s 459.

AUTHORITY

9.6   Before the introduction of ss 35A and 35B of the Companies Act 1985,[10] the position was that: acts done by a person purporting to contract on behalf of a company bound the company if that person had actual or ostensible authority to bind the company in that way, unless the other party had actual or constructive notice that the person was acting in excess of his actual authority; but (under the so-called '*Turquand* rule')[11] the third party, even though he had actual or constructive notice of the contents of the company's memorandum and articles, was not required to satisfy himself that internal procedures referred to in the articles had been complied with unless he was actually aware of an internal irregularity or there were circumstances putting him on enquiry.

9.7   However, greater protection for third parties in their dealings with companies is now provided by ss 35A and 35B. So far as persons dealing with[12] a company in 'good faith' are concerned, the power of the board of directors to bind the company, or to authorise others to do so, is deemed to be free of any limitation under the company's constitution.[13] A person shall not be regarded as acting in bad faith by reason only of knowledge that an act is beyond the powers of the directors under the company's constitution.[14] In addition, a third party is not bound to inquire whether the transaction is permitted by the company's memorandum or whether there is any limitation on the powers of the board of directors to bind the company or to authorise others to do so.[15]

9.8   On the face of it, these provisions would seem to provide comprehensive protection for creditors against the risk of an internal lack of authority on the part of the company. However, some difficulties do remain:

(a)   The exact effect of the requirement that the creditor be acting 'in good faith' is unclear. Section 35A(2) provides that a person shall be presumed to have acted in good faith unless the contrary is proved, and (as described above) that a person will not be regarded as acting in bad faith merely because he knows of a lack of authority. However, it does not follow that the lack of such knowledge automatically equates to good faith, merely that some other factor over and above (or instead of) knowledge is necessary for bad faith.[16] Consequently, where the

---

10   By s 108 of the Companies Act 1989.
11   After *Royal British Bank v Turquand* (1856) 6 E&B 327.
12   A person deals with a company for this purpose if he is a party to a transaction or other act to which the company is a party: Companies Act 1985, s 35A(2)(a).
13   Companies Act 1985, s 35A(1).
14   Companies Act 1985, s 35A(2).
15   Companies Act 1985, s 35B.
16   See eg *Barclays Bank Ltd v TOSG Trust Fund Ltd* [1984] BCLC 1 at 18 (rvsd [1984] AC 626 without affecting this point), where Nourse J held that good faith is different from mere absence of notice and requires that the relevant person acts 'genuinely and honestly'.

creditor has a close commercial relationship with the company and consequently knows of, or deliberately shuts its eyes to, restrictions on the directors' authority, the protections of ss 35A and 35B may not necessarily be available.

(b) Section 35A refers to the power of the board to bind the company, or to authorise others to do so, being free of limitations. It does **not** say that the board shall be deemed to have exercised the power to authorise others to bind the company. Consequently, the protections of ss 35A and 35B would not appear to be available where the transaction is entered into by an officer (such as the corporate treasurer) who has not in fact been authorised by the board: in that case, validity will be tested by reference to the actual or ostensible authority of the officer and the *Turquand* rule described earlier.

(c) The limitations which are overridden are those arising under the company's constitution (defined as including shareholder resolutions and shareholder agreements).[17] However, it has been held at first instance that these do not include quorum requirements,[18] and so a board decision purportedly taken at an inquorate board meeting would appear not to be 'cured' by s 35A.

(d) As with a transaction beyond the company's capacity, the directors remain liable to the company for their breach of duty.[19] It is also theoretically possible that, even though the transaction has been preserved under ss 35A and 35B, the creditor may still be required to hold any proceeds as constructive trustee for the company.[20]

(e) Under Companies Act 1985, s 322A, the protections of ss 35 and 35A do not apply where the transaction exceeds a limitation on the powers of the board of directors under the company's constitution and the other parties include a director of the company or its holding company, or a person connected with[21] such a director, or a company with which such a director is associated.[22] In those circumstances, the transaction is voidable at the instance of the company[23] and, whether or not it is avoided, such parties and any director who authorised the transaction,

---

17 Companies Act 1985, s 35A(3).

18 On the basis that a quorum requirement is not a limitation on the power of the board to bind the company but rather a limitation on what constitutes a decision of the board: *Smith v Henniker-Major & Co* [2002] BCC 544. The decision was upheld by the Court of Appeal ([2002] BCC 768), but only one judge (Carnwath LJ) supported the first instance reasoning on this point.

19 Companies Act 1985, s 35A(5).

20 On the basis of either knowing receipt or being an accessory to a breach of fiduciary duty. This is because s 35A(5) preserves the liability not just of directors but also of any other person, and the tests of liability are different: whereas the requirement for validity under s 35A(1) is good faith, and good faith is presumed unless the contrary is proved, a third party's knowledge needs to be 'unconscionable' for knowing receipt or 'objectively dishonest' for accessory liability, without a similar presumption to the contrary being applicable (*BCCI (Overseas) Ltd v Akindele* [2001] Ch 437 at 455 per Nourse LJ; *Royal Brunei Airlines Sdn Bhd v Tan* [1995] 2 AC 378 at 390).

21 As defined in Companies Act 1985, s 346(2).

22 As defined in Companies Act 1985, s 346(4).

23 Companies Act 1985, s 322A(1) and (2).

knowing that it exceeded the board's powers, are liable to account to the company for any gains they make and to indemnify the company against any loss it suffers.[24] The transaction ceases to be voidable if, inter alia, it is ratified by the company in general meeting.[25] Though the section does not affect the ability of any other party to the transaction to rely on s 35A, the court may make an order affirming, severing or setting aside the transaction, in each case on such terms as appear to the court to be just.[26] An application for that order may be made by either the unconnected party or by the company itself. It is obviously preferable, from the point of view of the relevant creditors, not to have to seek a court order to affirm the transaction (and indeed it will not always be certain that the court will affirm the transaction). Consequently, if there is any suggestion that the relevant creditors include a director of the company or its holding company, or a connected or associated person,[27] then it would be advisable to have the transaction approved by a shareholders' resolution in order to remove any argument that the board of directors is exceeding a limitation on its powers.[28]

9.9 It should also be borne in mind, as indicated at **9.4**, that a lack of corporate capacity limits the actual authority of the company's agents. Therefore, where the proposed transaction is beyond the company's capacity, the creditor is not protected by relying on s 35 unless the requirements described above in relation to authority are also satisfied.

9.10 Consequently, it is always important (for the protection of the directors as well as of the relevant creditors) to check the constitutional documents of the company for limits on the directors' authority.[29] Where there are no relevant limits that would be breached, the transaction should be approved by a properly minuted and quorate board meeting[30] or by a shareholder resolution. Alternatively, if the transaction is being authorised by an officer rather than the board, evidence of his actual or ostensible

---

24 Companies Act 1985, s 322A(3) and (6).
25 Companies Act 1985, s 322A(5). The other circumstances where the transaction ceases to be voidable are where: restitution is no longer possible; the company has been indemnified for any loss resulting from the transaction; or avoidance would affect rights acquired, bona fide for value and without actual notice of the directors exceeding their powers, by a person who was not a party to the transaction.
26 Companies Act 1985, s 322A(7).
27 An example would be (in a case where a trustee is appointed for the holders) if a director of the company were also a director of the trustee.
28 As to what type of resolution would be appropriate, see below. Where, however, the decision is taken not to obtain a shareholders' resolution and to rely instead on authorisation by a board resolution, the articles of association should nevertheless be checked for the position regarding directors' interests in contracts, in particular the voting and quorum implications.
29 In addition to checking for corporate capacity as described at **9.4**.
30 Which, for the reasons discussed below, should also reference the commercial benefit to be received by the company.

authority should be provided, together with a memorandum or other evidence of his approval.[31]. Where, however, the approval of the transaction would exceed a limit on the authority of the directors, a shareholder resolution will be required. This should be at the very least a special resolution (in order to effect the relevant amendment to the articles),[32] but a unanimous resolution is the safest option (because it prevents challenge by minority shareholders).

COMMERCIAL BENEFIT

9.11   The directors of a company have a fiduciary duty to the company to exercise their powers *bona fide* in the best interests of the company.[33] As Bowen LJ put it:[34] 'The law does not say that there are to be no cakes and ale, but there are to be no cakes and ale except such as are required for the benefit of the company.' Where the directors breach this duty in entering into a transaction, the transaction will be voidable at the option of the company if the creditor knows of the breach.[35] Section 35A applies only where the directors exceed their powers (or authority) and not where the directors are 'abusing' their powers, eg acting in breach of their fiduciary duties: consequently, a person dealing with the company who knows that the directors are acting in breach of their fiduciary duties will not be protected by s 35A.[36]

9.12   The duty to act in good faith in the best interests of the company is a subjective one: directors must act '*bona fide* in what they consider – not

---

[31]   Which, likewise, should also reference the commercial benefit.

[32]   Whereas acts in breach of the directors' powers under the articles can be ratified after the event by an ordinary resolution, an authorisation of such acts in advance is in effect an alteration of the articles and can therefore only be effected by a special resolution (see *Irvine v Union Bank of Australia* (1877) LR 2 App Cas 366; *Grant v United Kingdom Switchback Railways Co* (1889) LR 40 ChD 135).

[33]   See eg *Re Smith and Fawcett Ltd* [1942] Ch 304 at 306 per Lord Greene MR; *Alexander v Automatic Telephone Co* [1900] 2 Ch 56 at 66–67 per Lindley MR and 72–73 per Rigby LJ; *Charterbridge Corporation Ltd v Lloyd's Bank Ltd* [1970] Ch 62 at 74; *Gething v Kilner* [1972] 1 All ER 1166 at 1169; *Clemens v Clemens Bros Ltd* [1976] 2 All ER 268 at 279; *Regentcrest plc v Cohen* [2001] 2 BCLC 80; *Piercy v S Mills & Co Ltd* [1920] Ch 77; *Lee Panavision Ltd v Lee Lighting Ltd* [1992] BCLC 22 at 29–30 per Dillon LJ.

[34]   In *Hutton v West Cork Railway* (1883) LR 23 ChD 654 at 673 (adapting a line by Sir Toby Belch in Shakespeare's *Twelfth Night*, Act 2, Scene 3).

[35]   *Charterbridge Corporation Ltd v Lloyd's Bank Ltd* [1970] Ch 62 at 69, 75; *Lindgren v L&P Estates Ltd* [1968] Ch 572; *Rolled Steel Products v British Steel Corporation* [1984] BCLC 466. In addition, as seen earlier, the directors may be personally liable to the company to make good any losses caused by their breach of duty, and the creditor (depending on his level of knowledge of, or failure to enquire into, the breach of duty) may be required to hold any proceeds as constructive trustee for the company.

[36]   *Cooperatieve Rabobank v Minderhoud* [1998] 2 BCLC 507. The case, technically, only dealt with a situation where the directors had a conflict of interest, but the principle laid down must, logically, be equally applicable to other breaches of fiduciary duty.

what a court may consider – is in the interests of the company …'.[37]
However, the directors may breach the duty by failing to direct their minds
to the question of whether the transaction is in the best interests of the
company.[38]

9.13   The question of commercial benefit is of particular importance in
relation to the giving of guarantees or the grant of security in respect of
debts of another member of the group. Where the guarantee or security is a
'downstream' guarantee or charge (ie given by a parent company in respect
of its subsidiary's debt), it is generally relatively easy to find some benefit to
the parent flowing from the increased financial strength of the subsidiary
and the consequential increase in the value of the parent's shares in it
(assuming that the subsidiary is not in financial difficulties). The position is
more difficult in the case of 'upstream' or 'cross-stream' guarantees or
security (ie given by a subsidiary in respect of debt of the parent or of a
sister subsidiary), where commercial benefit for the guarantor/chargor may
be harder to find: the benefit must be to the individual company giving the
guarantee or security rather than to the group as a whole.

9.14   Consequently, it is important for the authorising board resolution to
set out the reasons why the directors consider that the giving of the
guarantee or the security is in the company's interests (in order to
demonstrate that they have addressed their minds to the issue).[39] Where an
upstream or cross-stream guarantee or charge is being given by a subsidiary
(or where there are any other grounds for believing that there may not be
sufficient corporate benefit), the giving of the guarantee should be
authorised by an appropriate shareholders' resolution.[40]

9.15   Where, however, the company is insolvent or on the verge of
insolvency, corporate benefit must be assessed by reference to the interests
of the company's creditors (rather than its shareholders),[41] and thus a
shareholder resolution may not be sufficient to cure a lack of corporate

---

[37]   *Re Smith and Fawcett Ltd* [1942] Ch 304 at 306 per Lord Greene MR. See also *Regentcrest plc v
Cohen* [2001] 2 BCLC 80; *Lee Panavision Ltd v Lee Lighting Ltd* [1992] BCLC 22 at 29 per Dillon
LJ.

[38]   *Re W&M Roith Ltd* [1967] 1 All ER 427; *Re Lee, Behrens & Co Ltd* [1932] 2 Ch 46 at 52–53;
Alexander v Automatic Telephone Co [1900] 2 Ch 56.

[39]   For reasons described below, the minutes should also record that the guarantor/chargor is and will
remain solvent.

[40]   So that the approval is an act of the company rather than of the directors. As with a shareholder
resolution to override a limitation in the articles, a unanimous resolution is preferable, in order to
avoid the risk of challenge by minority shareholders.

[41]   *Lonhro Ltd v Shell Petroleum Co Ltd* [1980] 1 WLR 627 at 634 per Lord Diplock; *West Mercia
Safetywear Ltd v Dodd* [1988] BCLC 250 at 252–253 per Dillon LJ; *Brady v Brady* [1988] BCLC
20 at 40–41 per Nourse LJ (rvsd on other grounds [1989] AC 755); *Facia Footwear Ltd v
Hinchcliffe* [1998] 1 BCLC 218; *Colin Gwyer & Associates Ltd v London Wharf (Limehouse) Ltd*
[2003] 2 BCLC 153. The directors may also be liable for wrongful trading under Insolvency Act
1986, s 214.

- Consequently, in the case of an upstream or cross-stream guarantee charge (or any other guarantee or security where there are grounds for believing that there may not be sufficient corporate benefit), it is important, in addition to obtaining shareholder approval, either for the board resolution to record that the company is fully solvent or for a directors' certificate as to solvency to be provided. Although these steps will not eliminate the risk of the guarantee or security being set aside if the company is actually insolvent or approaching insolvency, they are nevertheless helpful comfort from the point of view of the creditors. In general, if solvency cannot be demonstrated, the guarantee or security should not be given.

9.16 In addition to the duty to act in the best interests of the company, the directors owe other fiduciary duties to the company. As seen earlier, a person dealing with a company who knows that the directors are acting in breach of their fiduciary duties will not be protected by s 35A.[43] Consequently, in addition to the above steps in relation to corporate benefit, care should also be taken to ensure that there are no circumstances suggesting that the directors may be breaching their fiduciary duties, for example that:

(a) they are acting for an improper purpose (eg to promote the interests of someone other than the company); or

(b) they are acting in a way which would enable themselves or another party to obtain a secret or unauthorised profit; or

(c) they have a conflict of interest or conflict of duty.

RESTRICTIONS (1): CONTRACTS

Introduction

9.17 Restrictions on the amount of a company's borrowings outstanding at a given time, or on the grant of security, may be contained in the terms of a loan agreement or trust deed. Such restrictions usually relate to borrowings and security not just of the company but also of its subsidiaries. The definition of 'moneys borrowed' is usually lengthy and wide-ranging, in order to catch other forms of financing that have the same economic effect as a borrowing or would otherwise have priority over the parent's shareholding in the subsidiaries (such as preferred shares of subsidiaries held outside the group, acceptance credits, deferred purchase price, etc).

---

42 *Rolled Steel Products (Holdings) Ltd v British Steel Corporation* [1986] Ch 246 at 296 per Slade LJ; *West Mercia Safetywear Ltd v Dodd* [1988] BCLC 250 at 251–252 per Dillon LJ.
43 *Cooperatieve Rabobank v Minderhoud* [1998] 2 BCLC 507.

9.18 Leaving aside 'high yield' eurobond issues (which contain very detailed financial covenants), restrictions on borrowings and security commonly take three main forms – the so-called 'outer', 'inner' and 'secured' limits.

Outer borrowing limit

9.19 The outer limit (sometimes referred to instead as an 'overall' borrowing limit) is intended simply to prevent over-gearing of the group, so that it does not take on financial commitments which it is unable to service. It therefore restricts all borrowings of the group, whether secured or unsecured, and limits them by reference to a multiple of the group's 'adjusted capital and reserves' (or 'ACR'), the case of stock and bond issues, or its 'tangible net worth' (or 'TNW'), in the case of loan facilities.

9.20 The definitions of ACR and TNW are relatively standard but nevertheless lengthy and involved. The areas of negotiation (apart from the multiple itself) tend to centre around the manner in which goodwill, deferred tax, revaluations and post-balance sheet movements are treated.

9.21 A typical outer borrowing limit in a domestic stock issue reads as follows:

> The Issuer will procure that so long as any of the Stock remains outstanding the aggregate principal amount (including any fixed or minimum premium payable on final redemption) for the time being outstanding of all moneys borrowed (whether secured or not) by the Issuer and the Subsidiaries (excluding moneys borrowed by the Issuer from a Subsidiary or by a Subsidiary from the Issuer or from another Subsidiary) shall not exceed an amount equal to [ ] times the Adjusted Capital and Reserves.
>
> '**Adjusted Capital and Reserves**' means at any time the aggregate of:
>
> (1) the amount paid up or credited as paid up on the issued share capital of the Issuer; and
> (2) the amounts standing to the credit of the capital and revenue reserves (including any share premium account and capital redemption reserve and the amount standing to the credit of the profit and loss account) of the Issuer and the Subsidiaries,
>
> all as shown by a consolidation of the then latest audited balance sheets of the Issuer and the Subsidiaries (which shall be prepared on the basis of the historical cost convention modified, if applicable, by the revaluation of land and buildings) but:
>
> (a) adjusted in respect of any subsequent variation in interests in Subsidiaries and in the share capital of the Issuer paid up or credited as paid up and in the amounts of the said reserves (other than variations in profit and loss account arising from normal trading) since the dates of such balance sheets and taking account of the net subscription moneys (including any

premium) in respect of any share capital of the Issuer proposed to be issued for cash to the extent to which the subscription thereof has been unconditionally underwritten (provided such subscription moneys and any premium are payable not later than four months after the date of allotment) with effect from the date on which such issue became so underwritten;

(b)   excluding all sums set aside for taxation whether in respect of deferred taxation or otherwise;

(c)   excluding all amounts attributable to outside interests in Subsidiaries and any distributions to shareholders of the Issuer and (to the extent not attributable directly or indirectly to the Issuer) shareholders of Subsidiaries out of profits accrued prior to the dates of the relative audited balance sheets and not provided for therein;

(d)   excluding all amounts attributable to goodwill (other than goodwill arising only on consolidation), other intangible assets and any such securities as are described in paragraph (1)(i) of the definition of 'moneys borrowed';

(e)   deducting any debit balance on profit and loss account or any other reserve account;

(f)   excluding such part of the interests of the Issuer or a Subsidiary in an associated company (as defined in the Trust Deed), not being a Subsidiary, as is attributable to any post-acquisition undistributed profits and reserves, but including such interests at original cost or, if lower, book value;

(g)   excluding any share capital paid up by way of a capitalisation of, or reserves derived from, the whole or any part of the amount of any writing up after [*date of last financial year end*] (or in the case of a body corporate thereafter becoming a Subsidiary (an 'after-acquired Subsidiary') after the date of its becoming a Subsidiary) of the book value of any assets of the Issuer or any Subsidiary, except to the extent of:

(i)   any writing up of the book values of freehold and leasehold properties of the Issuer or of any Subsidiary arising from a revaluation of all the freehold and leasehold properties of the Issuer and the Subsidiaries or such part thereof as the Trustee may in its absolute discretion agree, such revaluation being made and such writing up being effected on bases respectively approved by the Trustee who may for this purpose require a valuation to be made by a professional valuer approved by the Trustee and to be not earlier than two years after the last previous such valuation (if any); and

(ii)   any writing up of the book values of any fixed assets of an after-acquired Subsidiary by an amount not exceeding the excess of the purchase consideration given by the Issuer or by another Subsidiary for its investment in such after-acquired Subsidiary over the amount of the net assets of such after-acquired Subsidiary attributable to the investment so acquired as appearing in its books at the date of acquisition, and so that a transfer of any asset by the Issuer to a Subsidiary, or by a Subsidiary to the Issuer or another Subsidiary, for a consideration in excess of the book value thereof, shall be deemed to be a writing up of the book value of such asset;

(h)　deducting (if not otherwise excluded) such amount as the Auditors (as defined in the Trust Deed) shall consider appropriate in respect of any contingent taxation liabilities on the net amount by which the fixed assets of the Issuer and the Subsidiaries shall have been written up as a result of any revaluation, and for this purpose a transfer of any asset by the Issuer to a Subsidiary, or by a Subsidiary to the Issuer or another Subsidiary, for a consideration in excess of the book value thereof shall be deemed to be a writing up of the book value of such asset as a result of a revaluation; and

(i)　after making such other adjustments (if any) as the Auditors may consider appropriate.

'**Moneys borrowed**' means amounts borrowed and for the time being outstanding and shall be deemed to include:

(1)　the principal amount for the time being owing in respect of any debenture (within the meaning of section 744 of the Companies Act 1985), whether issued for cash or in whole or in part for a consideration other than cash and so that (i) debentures shall be deemed to include any securities (whether or not repayable) of any person which carry rights of conversion into or exchange or similar substitution for other securities of that person or any other person; and (ii) the principal amount owing in respect of any debentures at any relevant time shall be deemed to be the highest amount which would be repayable in respect of such debentures were they to have become repayable at the relevant time pursuant to any provision whether for prepayment, acceleration or otherwise or, if greater, in the case of any securities first mentioned in (i) above, the highest amount which would be payable in respect of the securities secondly mentioned in (i) above (not being equity share capital) had they in lieu of the securities first-mentioned in (i) above been outstanding and become repayable at the relevant time pursuant to any provision whether for prepayment, acceleration or otherwise;

(2)　the principal amount for the time being owing of any moneys borrowed by or other indebtedness of and the nominal amount of any share capital of any person or body whether corporate or incorporate the repayment whereof or the payment of any premium, interest or dividends whereon is for the time being guaranteed or secured or the subject of an indemnity given by the Issuer or a Subsidiary and the beneficial interest in the right to such repayment or payment is not owned by the Issuer or a Subsidiary, which principal or nominal amount shall, except insofar as otherwise taken into account, be deemed to be moneys borrowed of the Issuer or by such first-mentioned Subsidiary, as the case may be;

(3)　the nominal amount of any issued share capital of any Subsidiary (not being equity share capital which as regards capital and dividends has rights no more favourable than those attached to its ordinary share capital) owned otherwise than by the Issuer or another Subsidiary, which is wholly owned, which nominal amount shall be deemed to be moneys borrowed of such first-mentioned Subsidiary;

(4) the principal amount raised by any person by acceptances or under any acceptance credit opened on its behalf by any bank or accepting house;

(5) the principal amount of any book debts of the Issuer or any Subsidiary which have been sold or agreed to be sold, to the extent that the Issuer or any Subsidiary is for the time being liable to indemnify or reimburse the purchaser in respect of any non-payment;

(6) any amount prospectively payable by the Issuer or any Subsidiary for the hire or lease of moveable or immoveable assets (excluding land and any buildings thereon but including fixtures and fittings affixed thereto or upon or within the same and being the subject of a separate hiring or leasing agreement), whether or not a capital amount in respect of such amount shall be included as a liability in its latest audited balance sheet; and

(7) any part of the purchase price of any moveable or immoveable assets acquired by the Issuer or a Subsidiary, the payment of which is deferred beyond the date of completion of the conveyance, assignment or transfer of the legal estate to such assets or, if no such conveyance, assignment or transfer is to take place within six months after the date on which the contract for such purchase is entered into or (if later) becomes unconditional, beyond that date;

but shall be deemed not to include:

(8) moneys borrowed otherwise falling to be taken into account pursuant to the limit set out above and intended to be applied within four months of being so borrowed in the repayment of moneys borrowed then outstanding which fall to be taken into account pursuant to such limit pending their application for such purpose or the expiry of such period whichever shall be the earlier;

(9) a proportion of the moneys borrowed of any partly-owned Subsidiary (but only to the extent that an amount equivalent to such proportion exceeds moneys borrowed (if any) from such partly-owned Subsidiary by the Issuer or another Subsidiary) such proportion being that which the issued ordinary share capital of such partly-owned Subsidiary which is not for the time being beneficially owned directly or indirectly by the Issuer bears to the whole of the issued ordinary share capital of such partly-owned Subsidiary; or

(10) moneys borrowed of a company which becomes a Subsidiary after [*date of offering circular*] and which are outstanding at the date when such company becomes a Subsidiary for the period of six months from the date of such event, to the extent that they exceed any increase in the limit set out above arising out of the adjustments to be made to the Adjusted Capital and Reserves on account of the transaction whereby such company becomes a Subsidiary and of any other transaction effected during such period of six months whereby the outside interest (if any) in such Subsidiary is reduced Provided that the foregoing shall not apply if such moneys borrowed were borrowed or raised in contemplation or as part of a transaction under which such company shall become a Subsidiary.

9.22   A typical outer borrowing limit in a loan facility, on the other hand, reads as follows:

1.1   Definitions

In this Clause:

Adjusted Consolidated EBITDA means, in relation to a Measurement Period, Consolidated EBITDA for the period adjusted by:

(a)   including the operating profit before interest, tax, depreciation, amortisation and impairment charges (EBITDA) of a member of the Group or attributable to a business or assets acquired during the Measurement Period for that part of the Measurement Period when it was not a member of the Group and/or the business or assets were not owned by a member of the Group; and

(b)   excluding the EBITDA attributable to any member of the Group or to any business or assets sold during that Measurement Period.

Consolidated EBIT means, in relation to a Measurement Period, the aggregate of:

(a)   the consolidated operating profits of the Group (including the results from discontinued operations) before finance costs and tax for that Measurement Period;

(b)   plus or minus the Group's share of the profits or losses of associates for that period (after finance costs and tax) and the Group's share of profits or losses of any joint ventures;

adjusted by:

(i)   taking no account of any material items which represent gains or losses arising on:

(A)   restructurings of the activities of an entity and reversals of any provisions for the costs of restructuring;

(B)   disposals of non-current assets;

(C)   the disposal of assets associated with discontinued operations; and

(D)   reversals of any provision;

(ii)   taking no account of any unrealised gain or losses on any derivative instrument (other than any derivative instrument which is accounted for on a hedge accounting basis) which is reported through the income statement; and

(iii)   taking no account of any income or charge attributable to a post-employment benefit scheme other than the current service costs and any past service costs and curtailments and settlements attributable to the scheme.

Consolidated EBITDA means, in relation to a Measurement Period, Consolidated EBIT for that Measurement Period after adding back any depreciation and amortisation and taking no account of any charge for impairment or any reversal of any previous impairment charge made in the period.

Consolidated Finance Costs means, in relation to a Measurement Period, all finance costs whether paid, payable or added to principal) incurred by the Group during that period calculated on a consolidated basis but adjusted as follows:

(a)   taking no account of any unrealised gains or losses on any derivative instrument (other than any derivative instrument which is accounted for on a hedge accounting basis) which is reported through the income statement; and

(b)   taking no account of any interest cost or expected return on plan assets in relation to any post-employment benefit scheme.

Consolidated Tangible Net Worth means at any time the aggregate of:

(a)   the amount paid up or credited as paid up on the issued share capital of the Company; and

(b)   the net amount standing to the credit (or debit) of the consolidated reserves of the Group;

based on the latest published audited consolidated balance sheet of the Company (the **latest balance sheet**) but adjusted by:

(i)   deducting any dividend or other distribution proposed, declared or made by the Company (except to the extent it has been taken into account in the latest balance sheet);

(ii)   deducting any amount attributable to goodwill or any other intangible asset;

(iii)   deducting any amount attributable to an upward revaluation of assets (other than financial instruments) after [   ] or, in the case of assets of a company which becomes a member of the Group after that date, the date on which that company becomes a member of the Group;

(iv)   reflecting any variation in the amount of the issued share capital of the Company after the date of the latest balance sheet (and any change in the consolidated reserves of the Group resulting from that variation);

(v)   reflecting any variation in the interest of the Company in any other member of the Group since the date of the latest balance sheet (to be calculated on the assumption that the variation had occurred immediately before the latest balance sheet date); and

(vi)   excluding any amounts debited or credited to deferred tax which relates to the revaluation of any item which is excluded from the calculation.

Consolidated Total Borrowings means, in respect of the Group, at any time, the aggregate of the following liabilities calculated at the nominal, principal or other amount at which the liabilities would be carried in a consolidated balance sheet of the Company drawn up at that time:

(a)   any moneys borrowed;

(b)   any redeemable preference shares;

(c)   any acceptance under any acceptance credit (including any dematerialised equivalent);

(d)   any bond, note, debenture, loan stock or other similar instrument;

(e)   any indebtedness under a finance or capital lease;

(f)   any moneys owing in connection with the sale or discounting of receivables (except to the extent that there is no recourse);

(g)   any indebtedness arising from any deferred payment agreements arranged primarily as a method of raising finance or financing the acquisition of an asset;

(h)   any indebtedness arising in connection with any other transaction (including any forward sale or purchase agreement) which has the commercial effect of a borrowing; and

(i)   any indebtedness of any person of a type referred to in the above paragraphs which is the subject of a guarantee, indemnity or similar assurance against financial loss given by a member of the Group.

Measurement Period means a financial year of the Company.

1.2 Interpretation

(a)   Except as provided to the contrary in this Agreement, an accounting term used in this Clause is to be construed in accordance with the principles applied in connection with the Original Financial Statements.

(b)   Any amount in a currency other than sterling is to be taken into account at its sterling equivalent calculated on the basis of:

      (i)   the Facility Agent's spot rate of exchange for the purchase of the relevant currency in the London foreign exchange market with sterling at or about 11.00 a.m. on the day the relevant amount falls to be calculated; or

      (ii)   if the amount is to be calculated on the last day of a financial period of the Company, the relevant rates of exchange used by the Company in, or in connection with, its financial statements for that period.

(c)   No item must be credited or deducted more than once in any calculation under this Clause.

1.3 Consolidated Tangible Net Worth

The Company must ensure that Consolidated Tangible Net Worth is not at any time less than £[   ].

1.4 Gearing

The Company must ensure that Consolidated Total Borrowings do not at any time exceed [   ] per cent. of Consolidated Tangible Net Worth at that time.

1.5 Leverage

The Company must ensure that Consolidated Total Borrowings do not, at the end of each Measurement Period, exceed [   ] times Adjusted Consolidated EBITDA for that Measurement Period.

1.6 Interest Cover

The Company must ensure that the ratio of Consolidated EBITDA to Consolidated Finance Costs is not, at the end of each Measurement Period, less than [   ] to 1.

Inner borrowing limit

9.23 The purpose of an inner (or 'priority') borrowing limit (which is usually seen only in unsecured stock issues and long-dated bond issues),[44] however, is to restrict prior-ranking borrowings of the group, ie borrowings in respect of which the right to repayment will, in a liquidation of the whole group, rank ahead of the right to repayment of the debt containing the covenant. This includes not only secured borrowings of the company but also secured and unsecured borrowings of each subsidiary.[45] Therefore, an inner borrowing limit restricts both the company's ability to borrow on a secured basis and the subsidiaries' ability to borrow on a secured or unsecured basis by reference to a multiple of the ACR of the group.

9.24 One method often used of easing the company's burden under an inner borrowing limit whilst at the same time preserving protection for the lender is a 'guaranteeing subsidiaries' provision. The effect of this is to permit the company to procure one or more of its subsidiaries to guarantee the loan in return for which all *unsecured* borrowings of the guaranteeing subsidiaries will no longer count towards the inner borrowing limit. The logic behind this is that by virtue of the guarantees the lender now has direct unsecured claims on the subsidiaries' assets, and thus the subsidiaries' other unsecured creditors no longer rank in priority to the lender. Their secured creditors still do, though, which is why their secured borrowings will still count towards the inner borrowing limit.

9.25 A typical inner borrowing covenant in a domestic stock issue (in this example, incorporating a 'guaranteeing subsidiaries' provision) reads as follows:

1. **Priority Borrowing Restriction**

    (A)   The Issuer will procure that so long as any of the Stock remains outstanding the aggregate principal amount (including any fixed or minimum premium payable on final redemption) for the time being outstanding of:

    (a)   all moneys borrowed[46] by the Issuer and the Guaranteeing Subsidiaries (excluding moneys borrowed by the Issuer from a Guaranteeing Subsidiary or by a Guaranteeing Subsidiary from the Issuer or from another Guaranteeing Subsidiary) and secured by

---

44   In first mortgage debenture stock issues, it is not necessary to restrict prior-ranking borrowings, as the holders have the benefit of first-ranking security over the relevant assets. In debenture stock issues (ie issues secured only by floating charges), both prior and pari passu borrowings are usually restricted by means of the 'secured' borrowing limit described at **9.26**.

45   The reason for this is that (in the absence of intra-group loan agreements) the only claim that a parent company has in relation to a subsidiary is via the shares that it holds in the subsidiary. Accordingly, it is only the value of those shares that will be available to creditors of the parent, and obviously the value of those shares depends on the assets of the subsidiary less all its liabilities whether secured or unsecured. This is the concept of 'structural subordination', which is described further at **8.3**.

46   The definition will be broadly similar to that in **9.21**.

any charge on all or any part of the undertaking, property and
assets of the Issuer or any Subsidiary; and

(b)   all moneys borrowed (whether secured or not) by Subsidiaries
which are not Guaranteeing Subsidiaries (excluding moneys
borrowed from the Issuer or from another Subsidiary),

shall not exceed an amount equal to [ ] per cent of the Adjusted Capital and
Reserves.[47]

(B)   '**Guaranteeing Subsidiary**' means any United Kingdom
Subsidiary which shall have given and shall have outstanding for the time
being a guarantee of the principal of, premium (if any) and interest on, the
Stock pursuant to the provisions of paragraph 2 below.

2.   **Guaranteeing Subsidiaries**

(A)   The principal of, premium (if any) and interest on, the Stock and
all other moneys payable under or pursuant to the Trust Deed has been
unconditionally and irrevocably guaranteed in the Trust Deed by the
following wholly-owned United Kingdom Subsidiaries:

[ ]

(B)   Power is reserved to the Issuer:

(1)   to procure (subject to the consent of the Trustee) any
other United Kingdom Subsidiary to give an
unconditional and irrevocable guarantee in favour of the
Trustee of the principal of, premium (if any) and interest
on, the Stock; and

(2)   to require the Trustee to release any Guaranteeing
Subsidiary from the guarantee given by it of the principal
of, premium (if any) and interest on, the Stock, such
release being for the purpose of either:

(a)   the sale or other disposal for full consideration
of the whole of the interest of the Issuer and the
Subsidiaries in such Guaranteeing Subsidiary (as
a result of which such Guaranteeing Subsidiary
ceases to be a Subsidiary) subject to the receipt
by one or more of the Issuer and the remaining
Guaranteeing Subsidiaries of the consideration
for such sale or disposal or such part thereof as
may be attributable to the Issuer and the
remaining Guaranteeing Subsidiaries; or

(b)   the members' voluntary winding up of such
Guaranteeing Subsidiary subject to the
distribution of such of its assets as may be
attributable to the Issuer and the remaining
Guaranteeing Subsidiaries to one or more of the
Issuer and the remaining Guaranteeing
Subsidiaries,

provided that in either such case the Auditors shall have
certified to the Trustee that immediately after such sale,

---

47   Again, the definition will be broadly similar to that in **9.21**.

disposal or winding up the limit set out in paragraph 1 above will not be exceeded.

(C)   The Trustee in addition has power, subject to its being satisfied that the interests of the Stockholders will not be materially prejudiced thereby, to release any Guaranteeing Subsidiary from the guarantee given by it of the principal of, premium (if any) and interest on, the Stock.

Secured borrowing limit

9.26   The purpose of a secured borrowing limit (which is usually only seen in debenture stock issues)[48] is to restrict prior and pari passu ranking security of the charging group (ie those members of the group which have given floating charges to secure the debenture stock). It is usually expressed as a prohibition on such security, with the exception that certain secured borrowings are permitted if the company's auditors certify at the time the security is granted that a specified limit (usually a fraction of the ACR of the charging group) is not exceeded. It is thus a 'snapshot' limit rather than a running limit (unlike the outer and inner limits).

9.27   A typical secured borrowing covenant in a debenture stock issue (in this example, where there is no charging group and the issuer is thus the only chargor) reads as follows:

1.   So long as any part of the Stock remains outstanding, the Company may not, except with the prior written consent of the Trustee, create or have outstanding or extend any mortgage, charge or other security on the whole or any part of its undertaking, property, assets or rights, both present and future, wherever situated, (including any uncalled capital) ranking in priority to or (except as permitted by Clause 2 below) pari passu with the floating charge created by it as security for the Stock.

2.   Pari passu charges:

2.1   The Company shall be entitled, subject to the following provisions of this Clause, to create or extend charges ranking pari passu with the floating charge created by it as security for the Stock.

2.2   No such charge may be created or extended unless, not more than 14 days prior to the date of such creation or extension, the Auditors shall have reported to the Trustee that, immediately thereafter, the limit set out in Clause [ ] (*Outer borrowing covenant*) will be complied with.

Negative pledge provision

9.28   The other main restriction on the grant of security is the so-called 'negative pledge' provision.[49] This commonly takes one of two forms. In a

---

[48]   As to which, see **Chapter 3**.

[49]   See Wood, *International Loans, Bonds and Securities Regulation* (1995), pp 34–41 and 137; Goode, *Legal Problems of Credit and Security* (3rd edn, 2003), pp 49–55; Ferran, *Company Law and Corporate Finance* (1999), pp 474–479; Cranston, *Principles of Banking Law* (2nd edn, 2002), pp 315–321.

loan agreement, it usually takes the form of a restriction either on any grant of security (subject to some usual exceptions) or merely on pari passu or prior-ranking security. However, in a eurobond issue, it usually takes the form of a covenant not to give security to similar debt securities without giving similar security to the eurobonds containing the negative pledge.

9.29 Whereas the purpose of the former type of negative pledge is to protect the lender's priority, the purpose of the latter type is essentially to protect the market price of the eurobonds.[50] This has two main consequences: the typical eurobond negative pledge is not an absolute prohibition but merely a prohibition on the company granting security without granting the same security to the eurobonds; and the types of other debt to which it relates are usually narrowly defined so as to include only debt securities which are similar to the eurobonds in question.

9.30 Since a restriction merely on the 'creation' of security does not restrict the acquisition of property subject to security,[51] it is usual for the negative pledge (in whichever form) also to restrict the company 'permitting or suffering to exist' security of the relevant type.

9.31 A typical example of a negative pledge in a loan facility (in this case, based on the Loan Market Association's recommended form) reads as follows:

(a) The Borrower shall not (and shall ensure that no other member of the Group will) create or permit to subsist any Security over any of its assets.

(b) The Borrower shall not (and shall ensure that no other member of the Group will):

(i) sell, transfer or otherwise dispose of any of its assets on terms whereby they are or may be leased to or re-acquired by the Borrower or any other member of the Group;

(ii) sell, transfer or otherwise dispose of any of its receivables on recourse terms;

(iii) enter into any arrangement under which money or the benefit of a bank or other account may be applied, set-off or made subject to a combination of accounts; or

(iv) enter into any other preferential arrangement having a similar effect,

in circumstances where the arrangement or transaction is entered into primarily as a method of raising Financial Indebtedness or of financing the acquisition of an asset.

(c) Paragraphs (a) and (b) above do not apply to:

---

[50] Since a further issue of bonds by the same issuer into the same market with the benefit of security would render the existing unsecured bonds less attractive to potential purchasers.

[51] By analogy from the reasoning in *Re Connolly Brothers Ltd (No 2)* [1912] 2 Ch 25 and *Security Trust Co v Royal Bank of Canada* [1976] AC 503.

(i)   any Security listed in Schedule [ ] (*Existing Security*) except to the extent the principal amount secured by that Security exceeds the amount stated in that Schedule;

(ii)   any netting or set-off arrangement entered into by any member of the Group in the ordinary course of its banking arrangements for the purpose of netting debit and credit balances;

(iii)   any lien arising by operation of law and in the ordinary course of trading;

(iv)   any Security over or affecting any asset acquired by a member of the Group after the date of this Agreement if:

    (A)   the Security was not created in contemplation of the acquisition of that asset by a member of the Group;

    (B)   the principal amount secured has not been increased in contemplation of or since the acquisition of that asset by a member of the Group; and

    (C)   the Security is removed or discharged within [   ] months of the date of acquisition of such asset;

(v)   any Security over or affecting any asset of any company which becomes a member of the Group after the date of this Agreement, where the Security is created prior to the date on which that company becomes a member of the Group, if:

    (A)   the Security was not created in contemplation of the acquisition of that company;

    (B)   the principal amount secured has not increased in contemplation of or since the acquisition of that company; and

    (C)   the Security is removed or discharged within [   ] months of that company becoming a member of the Group;

(vi)   any Security entered into pursuant to any Finance Document; or

(vii)   any Security securing indebtedness the principal amount of which (when aggregated with the principal amount of any other indebtedness which has the benefit of Security given by any member of the Group other than any permitted under paragraphs (i) to (vi) above) does not exceed [   ] (or its equivalent in another currency or currencies).

Related definitions:

Financial Indebtedness means any indebtedness for or in respect of:

(a)   moneys borrowed;

(b)   any amount raised by acceptance under any acceptance credit facility or dematerialised equivalent;

(c)   any amount raised pursuant to any note purchase facility or the issue of bonds, notes, debentures, loan stock or any similar instrument;

(d)   the amount of any liability in respect of any lease or hire purchase contract which would, in accordance with GAAP, be treated as a finance or capital lease;

(e)   receivables sold or discounted (other than any receivables to the extent they are sold on a non-recourse basis);

(f)   any amount raised under any other transaction (including any forward sale or purchase agreement) having the commercial effect of a borrowing;

(g)   any derivative transaction entered into in connection with protection against or benefit from fluctuation in any rate or price (and, when calculating the value of any derivative transaction, only the marked to market value shall be taken into account);

(h)   any counter-indemnity obligation in respect of a guarantee, indemnity, bond, standby or documentary letter of credit or any other instrument issued by a bank or financial institution; and

(i)   the amount of any liability in respect of any guarantee or indemnity for any of the items referred to in paragraphs (a) to (h) above.

GAAP means generally accepted accounting principles in the United Kingdom including IFRS.

IFRS means international accounting standards within the meaning of the IAS Regulation 1606/2002 to the extent applicable to the relevant financial statements.

Security means a mortgage, charge, pledge, lien or other security interest securing any obligation of any person or any other agreement or arrangement having a similar effect.

9.32   A typical example of a negative pledge in a eurobond issue (in this example, one with a trustee) reads as follows:

So long as any of the Bonds remains outstanding the Issuer will not create or have outstanding any mortgage, charge, lien, pledge or other security interest (each a **'Security Interest'**) upon, or with respect to, any of its present or future business, undertaking, assets or revenues (including any uncalled capital) to secure any Relevant Indebtedness (as defined below) of the Issuer or any of its Subsidiaries, unless the Issuer, in the case of the creation of a Security Interest, before or at the same time and, in any other case, promptly, takes any and all action necessary to ensure that:

(i)   all amounts payable by it under the Bonds, the Coupons and the Trust Deed are secured equally and rateably with the Relevant Indebtedness by the Security Interest to the satisfaction of the Trustee; or

(ii) such other Security Interest or other arrangement (whether or not it includes the giving of a Security Interest) is provided either (A) as the Trustee in its absolute discretion deems not materially less beneficial to the interests of the Bondholders or (B) as is approved by an Extraordinary Resolution of the Bondholders.

'**Relevant Indebtedness**' means (i) any present or future indebtedness (whether being principal, premium, interest or other amounts) for or in respect of any notes, bonds, debentures, debenture stock, loan stock or other securities which for the time being are, or are capable of being, quoted, listed or ordinarily dealt in on any stock exchange, over-the-counter or other securities market, and (ii) any guarantee or indemnity in respect of any such indebtedness.

Restriction on disposal of assets

9.33   The grant of security may also be restricted by a restriction on disposals of assets (often referred to loosely as a 'Tickler' clause).[52] The usual form of the provision restricts the group's ability to 'sell, transfer, lease or otherwise dispose of' assets (subject to some usual exceptions) either by reference to a stated percentage of gross assets or, more traditionally, by reference to a level which can be considered substantial in relation to the total assets of the group. The purpose of the provision is to preserve the quantity and, equally importantly, the quality of the group's assets.

9.34   Whether a grant of security is restricted will depend on the actual terms of the clause in question. A mortgage, for example, may constitute a 'transfer' or a 'lease' for this purpose,[53] and the term 'dispose' may, depending on the context, be construed as covering the grant of security.[54]

Borrowing etc in breach of contractual restrictions

9.35   If the company does borrow and/or give security in breach of contractual restrictions in a loan agreement or debt securities, the remedies of the lenders or holders are necessarily limited. The principal sanction is that the breach will (after the expiry of a specified period) constitute an event of default,[55] entitling the lenders or holders to accelerate the maturity of the loan or bonds and triggering cross-defaults in the obligor's other borrowings. The lenders or holders would also be entitled to claim damages for breach of contract if they suffered loss as a result of the breach, but this may well be a lengthy and costly process. There is also the weakness, in the

---

[52]   After the decision in *Commercial Union Assurance Co Ltd v TG Tickler Ltd* (unreported) 4 March 1959, in which Danckwerts J held that a sale by the defendant company of one of its four factories was not a sale of a part of the company's 'undertaking', and thus did not give rise to an event of default. As a result of the decision, specific restrictions on disposals of assets became common in the UK domestic capital market.

[53]   As to the methods of creating a mortgage over land, see **6.13ff**.

[54]   See, eg, Law of Property Act 1925, s 205(1)(ii) (disposal includes mortgage and charge); *Duke of Northumberland v A-G* [1905] AC 406 at 410–411 per Lord MacNaghten (disposition in the Succession Duty Act 1853 comprehends 'every conceivable mode by which property can pass'). The precise meaning of 'dispose' will always depend on the construction of the document as a whole (on the principle of *noscitur a sociis*), and therefore it may be, for example, that the presence elsewhere of a negative pledge would indicate that 'dispose', where it appears in the Tickler clause, does not cover the grant of security.

[55]   See further **5.17ff**.

case of a breach of a negative pledge, that, in an insolvency of the obligor, a claim for damages, like the claim for repayment on acceleration, is an unsecured claim and therefore ranks behind the claims of the third parties that were granted the security in breach of the restriction.

9.36   Possible remedies that might be sought to overcome this loss of priority include the following:

(a) If the lenders or holders discover in advance that the company is about to breach the restriction, they may seek an injunction to restrain the company from doing so. The normal rule is that, to obtain an injunction, the applicant must show that damages would not be an adequate remedy: however, under English law, there is authority that an injunction may be granted for breach of a negative stipulation regardless of the adequacy of damages.[56]

(b) In the case of a eurobond negative pledge, the holders may seek specific performance of the obligation to grant 'equal and rateable' security for the bonds. However, it is difficult to see how specific performance can be achieved, since it cannot operate retrospectively: consequently, any security interest granted for the bonds will, since it is granted later, have to rank lower in priority than the third party's security interest unless the third party agrees otherwise (which it is presumably unlikely to do).

(c) There may be a tort claim against the third party for inducing a breach of contract or wrongful interference with contractual rights. However, the claimant would have to show that the third party deliberately (or, possibly, recklessly) violated its contractual rights.[57]

(d) In the case of breach of a negative pledge or a restriction on disposals, another possible claim against the third party is under the *de Mattos v Gibson*[58] principle. This is the equitable principle that, where a person acquires property or an interest in property with knowledge of a previous contract affecting that property, he can be restrained by injunction from acting in a manner that is inconsistent with that contract. However, it is doubtful whether the de Mattos principle is applicable in the case of a negative pledge or a restriction on disposals. The principle applies where a person acquires property and thereafter seeks to deal with it in a manner inconsistent with the previous contract: but in the case of breach of a negative pledge or a restriction on disposals it is the very acquisition of the security interest or the

---

[56] It is not clear, however, whether a typical negative pledge in a bond issue should properly be regarded as a negative stipulation (ie a covenant not to grant security unless certain conditions are satisfied) or a positive stipulation (ie a covenant to grant security for the bonds in certain circumstances). There is some authority that in exceptional cases, the court may (instead of granting an injunction) appoint a receiver to take control of the assets: see further Ferran, *Company Law and Corporate Finance* (1999), p 475; Cranston, *Principles of Banking Law* (2nd edn, 2002), p 317.

[57] See eg *Torquay Hotels Co Ltd. v Cousins* [1969] 1 All ER 522.

[58] (1858) De G & J 276.

property, rather than any subsequent dealings, that infringes the restriction.[59]

9.37   The upshot is that the remedies for borrowing, security or disposals in breach of a contractual restriction, whether against the obligor or a third party, are limited. In practice, the threat of acceleration and cross-default is regarded as the real sanction.

RESTRICTIONS (2): STATUTE AND FINANCIAL REGULATION

Statutory restrictions

(1) Consumer protection legislation

9.38   The Consumer Credit Act 1974 (which provides for the licensing of those carrying on consumer credit and ancillary businesses and regulates credit and hire agreements) applies (inter alia) where credit[60] not exceeding £25,000[61] is supplied in the United Kingdom to an individual.[62] Consequently, borrowing by a company, whether secured or unsecured, is not regulated by the Act (even where repayment is guaranteed by an individual, eg a director[63]). However, if credit is provided to the company jointly with an individual (and does not exceed £25,000), then it becomes subject to the provisions of the Act: see s 185(5).

9.39   The Unfair Contract Terms Act 1977 may invalidate certain exemption clauses. Any provision excluding or restricting liability for death or personal injury resulting from negligence is ineffective,[64] and a provision excluding or restricting liability for other loss or damage resulting from

---

59 See further Ferran, *Company Law and Corporate Finance* (1999), pp 475–477 (and the literature there cited); Cranston, *Principles of Banking Law* (2nd edn, 2002), pp 319–320 (and the literature there cited); Sealy and Hooley, *Commercial Law – Text, Cases and Materials* (3rd edn, 2003), pp 70–71.

60 Which is stated to include 'a cash loan, and any form of financial accommodation' (Consumer Credit Act 1974, s 9(1)).

61 The limit was originally £5,000. It was raised to £15,000 in 1985 by SI 1983/1878 and to £25,000 in 1998 by SI 1998/996. The Consumer Credit Act 2006 (s 2) removes this financial limit, so that in future all consumer credit agreements will be regulated by the 1974 Act unless specifically exempted, regardless of the amount of the credit. At the time of writing (May 2006), the 2006 Act was not yet in force.

62 See the definitions of 'personal credit agreement' (ibid, s 8(1)) and 'consumer credit agreement' (ibid, s 8(2)). The term 'individual' is stated to include a partnership or other unincorporated body not consisting entirely of bodies corporate (ibid, s 189(1)). The Consumer Credit Act 2006 amends the definition to exclude partnerships with more than three members (Consumer Credit Act 2006, s 1). At the time of writing (May 2006), the 2006 Act was not yet in force.

63 Since no credit is being provided to the individual.

64 Unfair Contract Terms Act 1977, s 2(1).

negligence is effective only in so far as it satisfies the requirement of reasonableness.[65] Certain other provisions of the Act apply where one party is a 'consumer' or deals on the other's written standard terms of business. For a party to be a consumer, two conditions must be satisfied: first, he neither makes the contract in the course of a business nor hold himself out as doing so: and, secondly, the other party does make the contract in the course of a business.[66] These conditions are usually unlikely to be satisfied in the context of normal borrowing by commercial companies.[67] Where they are satisfied, however, any term of the contract which excludes or restricts the liability of the non-consumer for breach of contract, or allows it to render a contractual performance substantially different from that which was reasonably expected or to render no performance at all, will be effective only in so far as it satisfies the requirement of reasonableness.[68]

9.40   The Unfair Terms in Consumer Contracts Regulations 1999[69] regulate unfair terms in contracts between consumers and commercial sellers of goods or suppliers of goods or services.[70] The exact extent of the term 'services' is not clear, but the better view seems to be that it includes transactions in transferable securities and other finance-related transactions.[71] The term 'consumer', however, is defined narrowly and includes only a natural person acting outside his trade, business or profession.[72] Consequently, the Regulations are unlikely to apply to normal borrowing by commercial companies.[73]

(2) Control of Borrowing Order 1958

9.41   This Order[74] used to make it necessary for the approval of the Bank of England on behalf of the Treasury to be obtained for the issue of any sterling securities where the amount to be raised was £3m or more. Such consent is no longer necessary, as a result of the repeal of the Borrowing (Control and Guarantees) Act 1946.[75] However, the Bank of England has

---

[65]   Unfair Contract Terms Act 1977, s 2(2).

[66]   Unfair Contract Terms Act 1977, s 12(1).

[67]   Except, possibly, in relation to a retail offering of debt securities.

[68]   Unfair Contract Terms Act 1997, s 3(2).

[69]   SI 1999/2083.

[70]   An unfair term is one which has not been individually negotiated and which, contrary to the requirement of good faith, causes a significant imbalance in the parties' rights and obligations under the contract to the detriment of the consumer (reg 5(1)). Where a term is unfair, it will not bind the consumer, but the contract continues to bind the parties if it is capable of continuing in existence without the unfair term (reg 8). The Regulations also require written terms to be expressed in 'plain, intelligible language', and where there is any doubt about the meaning of a written term, the doubt will be resolved in favour of the consumer (reg 7).

[71]   See eg *Chitty on Contracts* (29th edn, 2004), para 15-019.

[72]   Regulation 3(1).

[73]   Except, possibly, to a retail offering of debt securities.

[74]   SI 1958/1208 (as amended), made under the Borrowing (Control and Guarantees) Act 1946.

[75]   By the Government Trading Act 1990, s 4, Sch 2, which came into effect on 11 February 1991.

requested that it be notified of the main details of any new issue in sterling with a maturity of one year and over for an amount of £50m or more.[76]

(3) Financial Services and Markets Act 2000 ('FSMA 2000')

9.42   Section 19 of the FSMA 2000 prohibits a person from carrying on a regulated activity in the UK unless that person is an authorised person or an exempt person under Part III of the FSMA 2000.

9.43   Persons are authorised for the purposes of the FSMA 2000 if they:

(i)   have permission (under Part IV of the FSMA 2000) to carry on a regulated activity;
(ii) are an EEA firm qualifying for authorisation under Sch 3 to the FSMA 2000;
(iii) are a Treaty firm qualifying for authorisation under Sch 4 to the FSMA 2000;
(iv) are otherwise authorised under the FSMA 2000.

9.44   Section 22 of and Sch 2 to the FSMA 2000 and the Financial Services and Markets Act 2000 (Regulated Activities) Order 2001 (the 'RA Order')[77] set out the meaning of 'regulated activities'. An activity is a 'regulated activity' (inter alia) if it is an activity of a specified kind carried on by way of business which relates to an investment of a specified kind.[78] The specified activities include buying, selling, subscribing for or underwriting securities or certain contractually based investments (whether as principal or agent), and making arrangements for another person to do so.[79] The specified activities also include accepting deposits[80] (as to which, see **Chapter 10**).

9.45   The specified investments are listed in Part II of Sch 2 to the FSMA 2000. In relation to borrowing by a company, the categories most likely to be relevant are 'instruments creating or acknowledging indebtedness' (defined as including debentures, debenture stock, loan stock, bonds, certificates of deposit and any other instruments creating or acknowledging a present or future indebtedness) and 'deposits' (as to which, see **10.5**).

9.46   Various exclusions are available, however. In relation to a borrowing by a company, the most likely to be relevant are contained in the RA Order, arts 18 (by which the regulated activity of dealing in investments as principal does not include the issue by a person of his own debentures),

---

76   The Bank of England's Notice dated 10 April 2002, which contains this requirement in relation to issues of £20m or more, has lapsed, and the Bank has let it be known informally that it expects a courtesy call in respect of issues of £50m or more.
77   SI 2001/544 (as amended).
78   FSMA 2000, s 22(1).
79   RA Order, arts 14–36.
80   RA Order, arts 5–9.

28 (by which the regulated activity of arranging deals in investments does not include the arrangement of transactions to which the arranger is a party) and 34 (by which the regulated activity of arranging deals in investments does not include arrangements by a person for the issue of his own debentures). Another exclusion (relevant to lenders but not the company) is contained in art 17 of the RA Order, which provides that the regulated activity of dealing in investments as principal does not include the acceptance by a person of an instrument creating or acknowledging indebtedness in respect of any loan, credit, guarantee or other similar financial accommodation or assurance which he has made, granted or provided. The exclusions relating to the acceptance of deposits are dealt with at **10.10ff**.

(4) Exchange control

9.47   Exchange control was abolished in the UK in 1979,[81] and the Exchange Control Act 1947 was formally repealed by the Finance Act 1987.[82]

(5) Companies Act 1985, ss 80 and 89

9.48   These sections are applicable to issues of convertible securities: see **5.44**.

(6) Income and Corporation Taxes Act 1988, s 765

9.49   This section makes it a criminal offence for any body corporate resident in the UK to cause or permit a body corporate not resident in the UK over which it has control to create or issue any shares or debentures,[83] unless the Treasury has consented to the transaction.[84] The issue of debentures by overseas finance vehicle subsidiaries[85] therefore falls within

---

[81]   By virtue of SI 1979/1339 and 1979/1662, consolidated into SI 1979/1660.
[82]   Section 68.
[83]   As to the meaning of which, see **Chapter 17**.
[84]   ICTA 1988, s 765(1)(c). The restriction, however, does not apply to the giving to the bankers of the non-UK body corporate of security for the payment of sums due or to become due from it to them by reason of transactions between them in the ordinary course of their business as bankers (s 765(2)) or the giving by the non-UK body corporate to an insurance company of security for the payment of sums due or to become due from the body corporate to the insurance company by reason of transactions between them in the ordinary course of the insurance company's business by way of investment of its funds (s 765(3)). Section 765(1)(d) also makes it a criminal offence for a body corporate resident in the UK to transfer, or cause to permit to be transferred, to any person any shares or debentures of a body corporate not resident in the UK over which it has control, being shares or debentures which it owns or in which it has an interest.
[85]   With the proceeds usually being on-lent to the parent. Structuring the loan in this way may be necessary to avoid the imposition of withholding tax.

this prohibition, but, if certain conditions are fulfilled, is nevertheless permitted by virtue of the Treasury General Consents 1988.[86]

(7) Companies Act 1985, ss 330 to 344

9.50 Subject to certain exceptions, these sections prohibit, inter alia, the giving of guarantees (including indemnities) and security by a company in connection with loans made by any person to any of its directors or the directors of its holding company. Breach of the prohibition renders the arrangement voidable[87] and can give rise to criminal offences.

(8) Companies Act 1985, s 151

9.51 This section prohibits a company or any of its subsidiaries, in certain circumstances, giving financial assistance for the purpose of the acquisition of shares in the company or for the purpose of reducing or discharging liability incurred by any person for the purpose of such acquisition. Thus, a guarantee or security given by a company to secure the obligation of a purchaser of its shares to pay the purchase price, or to repay a loan incurred for such purpose, is capable of constituting a breach of the section.

(9) Gaming Act 1845, s 18

9.52 This section provides that 'All contracts or agreements . . . by way of gaming or wagering shall be null and void; and . . . no suit shall be brought or maintained in any court of law or equity for recovering any sum of money or valuable thing alleged to be won upon any wager . . .'. Gaming for this purpose has been defined as the playing of any game for money or money's-worth.[88] Loans under which the repayment amount or rate of interest is linked to events beyond the control of the parties, such as movements in an index, could in certain circumstances be regarded as

---

[86] In addition, the restrictions in s 765 do not apply to a transaction which is a movement of capital between EU member states falling with the EU Movement of Capital Directive (88/361/EEC): s 765A(1). To take advantage of that exemption, the UK body corporate must give certain prescribed information about the transaction to HM Revenue & Customs within six months of the transaction (and such further information as HM Revenue & Customs may subsequently require): s 765A(2).

[87] See, eg, *Tait Consibee (Oxford) Ltd v Tait* [1997] 2 BCLC 349. A loan in breach of the sections does not, in the absence of special circumstances, give rise to a constructive trust: *Re Ciro Citterio Menswear plc* [2002] 2 All ER 717.

[88] *Ellesmere v Wallace* [1929] 2 Ch 1 at 55 per Russell LJ; *Ankers v Bartlett* [1936] 1 KB 147. A wagering contract is 'one by which two persons, professing to hold opposite views touching the issue of a future uncertain event, mutually agree that, dependent upon the determination of that event, one shall win from the other, and that other shall pay or hand over to him, a sum of money or other stake; neither of the contracting parties having any other interest in that contract than the sum or stake he will so win or lose, there being no other real consideration for the making of such contract by either of the parties': *Carlill v The Carbolic Smoke Ball Co* [1892] 2 QB 484 at 490 per Hawkins J, affd [1893] 1 QB 256. As to gaming and wagering generally, see *Chitty on Contracts*, (29th edn, 2004), Chapter 40.

gaming, and therefore might be void under s 18. Section 18 does not apply, however, if the loan is entered into by way of business and the entering into or performance of it by either party constitutes a regulated activity under the FSMA 2000 and the contract relates to a specified investment under the FSMA 2000 (as to which, see **9.45**).[89]

9.53   When the relevant provisions of the Gambling Act 2005 are brought into force, s 18 of the 1845 Act will be repealed,[90] and it will be expressly provided that the fact that a contract relates to gambling (defined as including gaming[91]) will not prevent its enforcement, although this will not override any other rule of law that prevents enforcement on the grounds of unlawfulness.[92] At the time of writing (May 2006), these provisions were not yet in force.

(10) Financial Services Authority

9.54   The Authority[93] requires that bank borrowers do not give floating charges over their assets as security for their borrowings. Any security given by a bank for its borrowings must be over specific assets or limited to a certain proportion of specified assets, such as hire purchase agreements, so as to ensure that there will always be sufficient unencumbered assets to meet the claims of depositors in a liquidation of the bank. The Authority expects to be informed in advance of any agreement which would create a floating charge on the bank's assets.[94]

(11) State aid

9.55   If repayment is guaranteed by an EU Member State or through 'state resources' of an EU Member State,[95] the guarantee may constitute 'state aid', in which event it must be notified to the European Commission before it is granted, so that the Commission can assess whether it is 'compatible with the common market'.[96]

---

[89]   FSMA 2000, s 412.
[90]   Gambling Act 2005, s 334.
[91]   Gambling Act 2005, ss 3, 6.
[92]   Gambling Act 2005, s 335.
[93]   Which took over from the Bank of England on 1 June 1998 as the competent authority for banking supervision; accordingly its Interim Prudential Sourcebook for Banks ('IPRU (Banks)' replaces the Bank of England's previous Notice on the giving of collateral.
[94]   IPRU (Banks), Chapter NE, para 4.6.
[95]   Eg guaranteed by a local authority or a state controlled enterprise.
[96]   Pursuant to Treaty of Rome, Arts 87 and 88 as amended (previously Arts 92 and 93), which are directly applicable as law in the UK as a Member State (*Costa v ENEL* Case 6/64 [1964] ECR 585). The procedure for notification and review is set out in Art 88 and Council Regulation (EC) 659/1999 of 22 March 1999 (1999 OJ L83/1): the Member State must notify the Commission 'in sufficient time'; the Commission then conducts a preliminary review; if it is satisfied that the aid is compatible with the common market or does not indicate objections within two months, the Member State may put the aid into effect; otherwise, the prescribed consultation procedure must then be followed.

9.56   Whilst state aid can take many forms, the most relevant in the context of corporate borrowing is guarantees (and other assurances against financial loss). A guarantee will constitute 'state aid' if all the following elements are present: aid or advantage; given by, or through 'state resources' of, an EU Member State; favouring certain undertakings or the production of certain goods; thereby distorting or threatening to distort competition; and affecting trade between EU Member States.[97] In particular, the European Commission has stated[98] that a state guarantee will not constitute 'state aid' if the borrower is not in financial difficulty, pays the market price for the guarantee, and would in principle be able to obtain a loan on market conditions from the financial markets without any intervention by the state, and certain limits on the extent of the guarantee are met. Generally speaking, therefore, a state guarantee will constitute 'state aid' if trade between EU Member States is affected and no market premium is paid.[99] The borrower receives aid to the extent that is able to obtain a loan more cheaply than it otherwise could. The aid is granted at the moment when the guarantee is given, and it is thus immaterial whether any payments ever actually have to be made under the guarantee.[100]

9.57   Where a guarantee is notified to the Commission and the Commission decides that the aid element is incompatible with the common market, then the arrangements will not be approved and granting the guarantee will be unlawful. Furthermore, if a guarantee which constitutes 'state aid' is not notified to the Commission, the aid element is automatically unlawful.[101]

(12) Competition law

9.58   It is possible that over-restrictive covenants might be void as being anti-competitive or an abuse of a dominant position by virtue of Articles 81 and 82, respectively, of the Treaty of Rome, as amended.[102] In practice, this is unlikely: it has been held, for example, that secured loan arrangements containing covenants by the borrower not to borrow, charge its assets, issue or redeem shares or sell the charged debts without the consent of the lender are neither anti-competitive nor an abuse of a dominant position.[103]

---

97   Treaty of Rome, Art 87(1) as amended. On state aid generally, see further the Financial Law Panel's papers of October 1998, February 1999, July 1999 and February 2000.

98   In its Notice of 24 November 1999, para 4.2.

99   See the European Commission's Notice of 24 November 1999, para 2.1.1.

100   European Commission's Notice of 24 November 1999, para 2.1.2.

101   Council Regulation (EC) 659/1999 of 22 March 1999 (OJ L83/1), art 1(f); European Commission's Notice of 24 November 1999, para 6.1. As to whether unlawful state aid is unenforceable under English law on the grounds of illegality, see the Financial Law Panel's discussion in their paper *'State Aid in the Form of Guarantees – Notes to Sponsors'* February 2000, pp 4–5.

102   (Previously Arts 85 and 86). These are directly applicable as law in the UK as a Member State.

103   *Oakdale (Richmond) Ltd v National Westminster Bank plc* [1996] BCC 919.

(13) Companies Act 1985, s 117

9.59 This section prohibits a public company, if it was originally incorporated as a public company, doing business or exercising any borrowing powers unless the Registrar of Companies has issued it with a certificate under s 117.[104] The Registrar may only issue such a certificate if[105] he is satisfied that the nominal value of the company's allotted share capital is not less than the authorised minimum[106] and a statutory declaration in prescribed form[107] is delivered to him. Contravention of the section is a criminal offence,[108] but transactions entered into in breach of the section are still valid.[109]

Listing restrictions

9.60 In the case of companies whose securities are listed, certain transactions may be restricted by listing requirements. Thus, in the case of a company whose shares are listed on the London Stock Exchange, a transaction between the company, or any of its subsidiary undertakings, and a substantial shareholder, a director, a shadow director or an associate thereof (subject to certain exceptions, including the grant of credit upon normal commercial terms in the ordinary course of business) will require the approval of the company's shareholders.[110]

---

[104] The position in relation to a public company that was originally incorporated as a private company and then re-registered is governed by s 43. No separate certificate from the Registrar is required, but re-registration can only occur if the Registrar is satisfied, inter alia, that the capital requirements are complied with and a statutory declaration in the prescribed form is delivered to him.

[105] Section 117(2).

[106] Currently £50,000: s 118(1). Any share allotted must be paid up as to at least one-quarter of its nominal value and the whole of any premium (Companies Act 1985, s 101(1)). The effect therefore is that at least £12,500 (plus any premium) must have been paid up.

[107] Covering the matters set out in s 117(3). Alternatively, an electronic statement containing the requisite information may be delivered to the Registrar of Companies instead (s 117(3A)).

[108] Section 117(7). The company and any officer who is in default become liable to a fine.

[109] Section 117(8). If, however, the company fails to comply with its obligations under such a transaction within 21 days of being called upon to do so (ie by the other party), the directors become jointly and severally liable to indemnify the other party in respect of any resultant loss or damage suffered by it: s 117(8).

[110] *Listing Rules*, Chapter 11.

Chapter Ten

ACCEPTING DEPOSITS

INTRODUCTION

10.1   The Banking Act 1987 and the Banking Act 1987 (Exempt Transactions) Regulations 1997 which regulated the accepting of deposits in the UK were repealed by the Financial Services and Markets Act 2000 (the 'FSMA 2000') which came into force on 1 December 2001. The FSMA 2000 now regulates the accepting of deposits in the UK.

10.2   Section 19 of the FSMA 2000 provides that a regulated activity can only be carried out in the UK by a person who is authorised under the FSMA 2000 to carry out such activity in the UK or who is exempt under the FSMA 2000.[1] Section 22 of the FSMA 2000 provides that an activity is a regulated activity if (inter alia) it is an activity of a specified kind carried on by way of business[2] and it relates to investments of a specified kind.[3]

10.3   The specified activities are listed in the Financial Services and Markets Act 2000 (Regulated Activities) Order 2001[4] (the 'RA Order'). Under art 5 of the RA Order, the accepting of deposits is a specified activity if certain conditions are met.

10.4   The potential problem for UK companies borrowing money prior to the FSMA 2000 was that the word 'deposit' was so widely defined that many forms of borrowing were potentially capable of breaching the restriction. However, a number of exclusions to the definition of 'deposit' are now provided in arts 6 to 9 of the RA Order. As will be seen below, most loan facilities and issues of debt securities will fall within one of these exclusions, and so in practice the restriction on accepting deposits is now much less relevant than it used to be in the context of companies raising loan capital.

---

[1]   See **9.42ff**.

[2]   As to which, in the context of accepting deposits, see FSMA 2000, s 419 and the Financial Services and Markets Act 2000 (Carrying on Regulated Activities by Way of Business) Order 2001, SI 2001/1177, art 2.

[3]   See **9.45**.

[4]   SI 2001/544.

DEPOSITS

10.5   'Deposit' is defined in art 5(2) of the RA Order as:

'. . . a sum of money . . . paid on terms –
(a) under which it will be repaid, with or without interest or premium, and
either on demand or at a time and in circumstances agreed by or on behalf of the
person making the payment and the person receiving it; and
(b) which are not referable to the provision of property (other than currency) or
services or the giving of security.'

10.6   The provisions of para (a) are clearly capable of encompassing all
forms of loans of money (including overdrafts), since, as has been seen,[5] the
essence of a loan is an initial advance coupled with an obligation to repay,
the same criteria as underlie para (a).[6]

10.7   Under art 5(3) of the RA Order, money is paid on terms which are
referable to the provision of property or services or the giving of security if
'and only if':

(a)   it is paid by way of advance or part-payment under a contract for the
      sale, hire or other provision of property or services, and is repayable
      only in the event that the property or services is or are not in fact sold,
      hired or otherwise provided. The Financial Service Authority (the
      'Authority') interprets this as referring to an advance or part payment
      for a specific item of property or a specific service;
(b)   it is paid by way of security for the performance of a contract or by way
      of security in respect of loss which may result from non-performance of
      a contract. An example is a deposit placed with a commodity or futures
      broker as security for margin exposures;[7] or
(c)   it is paid by way of security for the delivery up or return of any
      property, whether in a particular state of repair or otherwise. An
      example is a deposit required by a landlord of a furnished letting.

10.8   Clearly, all the various forms of loans described in **Chapters 2 to 4**
will fall outside art 5(3), and accordingly will fall within the meaning of
deposit in art 5(2). Under art 5(1) of the RA Order, the accepting of deposits
is a regulated activity if:

'(a)   money received by way of deposit is lent to others; or
(b)   any other activity of the person accepting the deposit is financed wholly,
       or to a material extent, out of the capital of or interest on money received
       by way of deposit.'

---

5   See **Chapter 1**.
6   See, eg, *SCF Finance Co Ltd v Masri (No 2)* [1986] 1 All ER 40 at 52 per Leggatt J (affd [1987] 1
      All ER 175).
7   *SCF Finance Co Ltd v Masri (No 2)* [1987] 1 All ER 175.

10.9 The conditions are alternative: satisfaction of either, therefore, will mean that the activity is prima facie a regulated activity. While para (a) clearly envisages traditional banking operations, para (b) is much wider and potentially encompasses all forms of borrowing undertaken to finance *any* activity of the business.

EXCLUSIONS

10.10 Certain sums of money, however, will not be treated as deposits if they fall within the exclusions in arts 6–9 of the RA Order. Article 6 provides that a sum of money is not a deposit if it is paid by certain institutions (including the Bank of England and the European Central Bank),[8] an authorised person with permission under the FSMA 2000 to accept deposits,[9] or a person carrying on a business consisting wholly or to a significant extent of lending money.[10] Consequently, most overdrafts and loans under loan facilities will not constitute deposits and will therefore not result in the company being deemed to carry on a regulated activity.

10.11 A further exclusion under art 6 is for money paid by one company to another when the two companies are members of the same group or have a common majority shareholder.[11]

10.12 In the context of issues of debt securities, the most relevant exclusion is that in art 9, for sums received in consideration for the issue of debt securities. For the exclusion to apply, the securities must fall within art 77 of the RA Order ('Instruments creating or acknowledging indebtedness')[12] or art 78 ('Government and public securities'). However, if the securities have a maturity of less than one year from the date of issue, they constitute 'commercial paper'.[13] In that case, the exclusion will only apply if the commercial paper is issued to persons:

(a) whose ordinary activities involve them in acquiring, holding, managing or disposing of investments (as principal or agent) for the purposes of their businesses; or

(b) who it is reasonable to expect will acquire, hold, manage or dispose of investments (as principal or agent) for the purposes of their businesses.[14]

---

[8] Article 6(1)(a)(i).

[9] Article 6(1)(a)(ii).

[10] Article 6(1)(b).

[11] Article 6(1)(c). The definition of majority shareholder is given in art 6(2).

[12] Defined as including debentures, debenture stock, loan stock, bonds, certificates of deposit and any other instrument creating or acknowledging indebtedness: art 77(1).

[13] Article 9(3) (as amended by the Financial Services and Markets Act 2000 (Regulated Activities) (Amendment) Order 2002, SI 2002/682).

[14] Article 9(2)(a).

10.13   In addition, the redemption value of the commercial paper must not be less than £100,000 (or equivalent if other than sterling) and no part of the commercial paper may be transferred unless the redemption value of that part is not less than £100,000 (or equivalent).[15]

CONCLUSION

10.14   Prior to the FSMA 2000, the restrictions on accepting deposits under the Banking Act 1987 were very widely drawn, with the result that they potentially applied, inadvertently, to the otherwise legitimate borrowing of money by companies that were not banks. However, the exclusions that are now provided in arts 6 to 9 of the RA Order mean that most loan facilities and issues of debt securities by UK companies will no longer be subject to the restrictions, other than in the case of commercial paper. Even then, it will not be subject to the restrictions so long as it has sufficiently large denominations and is only issued to 'professionals'.

---

[15]   Article 9(2)(b).

Chapter Eleven

GUARANTEES[1]

INTRODUCTION

11.1   Borrowings are frequently guaranteed, in order to provide a second debtor to pay in case the first defaults. In some cases, such as where the borrowing has been undertaken by a finance vehicle subsidiary to be on-lent within the group,[2] a guarantee by the parent company or the company which holds the bulk of the group's assets is commercially necessary, since the subsidiary has no credit-standing of its own. In other cases, guarantees by other members of the group with a suitable asset value are desirable in that, by increasing the lenders' chances of repayment, a lower interest rate might be possible for the borrower. This is particularly common in domestic issues of debt securities, where the companies giving guarantees are usually referred to as 'guaranteeing subsidiaries' or, if they give security,[3] 'charging subsidiaries'. In the case of debt securities, the form of the guarantee will depend on whether a trustee for the holders is appointed. If there is a trustee, the guarantee is usually included in the trust deed, with the trustee holding the benefit on trust for the holders. If there is no trustee, the guarantee is

---

[1]   On guarantees generally, see Andrews and Millett, *Law of Guarantees* (4th edn, 2005); *Rowlatt on Principal and Surety* (6th edn, 1999); O'Donovan and Phillips, *The Modern Contract of Guarantee* (2003); Wood, *Comparative Law of Security and Guarantees* (1995), Chapters 24 to 29; *Paget's Law of Banking* (12th edn, 2002), Chapter 33; Lingard, *Bank Security Documents* (3rd edn, 1993), Chapter 13; Goode, *Legal Problems of Credit and Security* (3rd edn, 2003), Chapter 8, and *Commercial Law* (3rd edn, 2004), Chapter 30; *Chitty on Contracts* (29th edn, 2004), Chapter 44; McGuinness, *The Law of Guarantee* (1996); *Encyclopaedia of Banking Law*, paras E (2001)– E(2190); Sealey and Hooley, *Commercial Law* (3rd edn, 2003), Chapter 27; *Halsbury's Laws of England* (4th edn reissue, 1993), Vol 20, paras 101–400; Calnan, *Taking Security: Law and Practice* (2006), Chapter 11.

[2]   It may be necessary to structure the borrowing in this way to avoid the imposition of withholding tax.

[3]   Sometimes the security is merely for the underlying debt itself, ie collateral security, but it is generally more common for the subsidiary to give a guarantee and for the security to be for its liability under the guarantee. In this way, the lender retains an unsecured right against the guarantor if the value of the security should prove to be inadequate. In the context of domestic debt securities, the former structure is more common in first mortgage debenture stock (where, commercially, the lenders are relying on the quality of the assets charged rather than the general credit-standing of the chargors), and the latter more common in debenture stock (ie stock secured only by floating charges), where the general credit-standing of the chargors is commercially more important.

usually either contained in a separate deed poll for the benefit of the holders[4] or, in the case of bearer securities, endorsed on the securities themselves, so that the benefit of the guarantee passes by negotiation of the securities.[5]

TYPES OF GUARANTEE

11.2 The term 'guarantee' is used loosely and is often used to refer to what is strictly an indemnity rather than a guarantee (or, possibly, a mixture of the two). Under a guarantee, the guarantor agrees that, if the borrower does not meet a legally binding obligation, the guarantor will be liable for the borrower's debt or default. The guarantor's liability is secondary, or 'collateral': it is dependent on the borrower's default, and, in the absence of agreement to the contrary by the guarantor, will be extinguished if the borrower is not itself liable[6] or if there is a material variation of the borrower's liability, such as an extension of time to pay,[7] an amendment to the terms of the underlying debt that could prejudice the guarantor,[8] a release of the borrower[9] or a set-off, counterclaim or defence available to the

---

4   As to deeds poll, see **19.7**. As a result of the Contracts (Rights of Third Parties) Act 1999, third party beneficiaries now have direct rights of action under contracts to which they are not party. However, the rights envisaged by the Act arise where a contract is entered into between A and B that is intended to confer a benefit on C. Where (as here) the intention is for A (the guarantor) to confer rights unilaterally on C (the holder) without C needing to execute an assignment of his rights to a subsequent holder of his bonds, the deed poll remains the most efficient method of achieving this.

5   As to which, see **15.3ff**.

6   *Coutts & Co v Browne-Lecky* [1947] KB 104; *Swan v Bank of Scotland* (1836) 10 Bligh NS 627; *Brown v Blaine* (1884) 1 TLR 158; *Coutts & Co v Stock* [2000] 2 All ER 56; *Lloyds and Scottish Trust Ltd v Britten* (1982) 44 P&CR 249; *Heald v O'Connor* [1971] 2 All ER 1105; *Anglo Petroleum Ltd v TFB (Mortgages) Ltd* [2003] EWHC 3125 at para 23.

7   *Rees v Berrington* (1795) 2 Ves Jun 540; *Samuell v Howarth* (1817) 3 Mer 272; *Petty v Cooke* (1871) LR 6 QB 790 at 794–795 per Blackburn J; *Bolton v Buckenham* [1891] 1 QB 278; *Rouse v Bradford Banking Co Ltd* [1894] AC 586; *Polak v Everett* (1876) 1 QBD 669 at 673–674 per Blackburn J; *Overend, Gurney & Co Ltd v Oriental Financial Corporation Ltd* (1874) LR 7 HL 348; *Mahant Singh v U Ba Yi* [1939] AC 601 at 606; *Creighton v Rankin* (1840) 7 Cl & Fin 325 at 346-347; *Clarke v Birley* (1889) LR 41 ChD 422; *Holme v Brunskill* (1878) LR 3 QBD 495 at 505–506 per Blackburn J; *Ward v National Bank of New Zealand Ltd* (1883) LR 8 App Cas 755 at 763; *Moschi v Lep Air Services Ltd* [1973] AC 331 at 348 per Lord Diplock. There must, however, be a binding agreement between creditor and borrower to extend time, and not merely delay: *Clarke v Birley* (1889) 41 ChD 422; *Carter v White* (1883) 25 ChD 666; *Mahant Singh v U Ba Yi* [1939] AC 601 at 606.

8   Known as the rule in *Holme v Brunskill* (1878) LR 3 QBD 495. A variation of the principal contract that has the effect of altering the guarantor's rights will discharge the guarantor unless it is unsubstantial and clearly does not prejudice the guarantor (*Holme v Brunskill* (1878) LR 3 QBD 495 at 505 per Cotton LJ; *Egbert v National Crown Bank* [1918] AC 903 at 908–909; *Credit Suisse v Borough Council of Allerdale* [1995] 1 Lloyd's Rep 315 at 361, 365–366 (upheld [1997] QB 306); *Bolton v Salmon* [1891] 2 Ch 48 at 54; *National Bank of Nigeria Ltd v Awolesi* [1964] 1 WLR 1311; *Rees v Berrington* (1795) 2 Ves 540 at 543 per Lord Loughborough LC; *Re Darwen and Pearce* [1927] 1 Ch 176 at 183. For examples of amendments which were not prejudicial to the guarantor, see *Sanderson v Aston* (1873) LR 8 Exch 73; *Frank v Edwards* (1852) 8 Exch 214; *Egbert v National Crown Bank* [1918] AC 903.

9   *Carter v White* (1883) 25 ChD 666 at 670 per Cotton LJ; *Mahant Singh v U Ba Yi* [1939] AC 601 at 606; *Commercial Bank of Tasmania v Jones* [1893] AC 313; *Webb v Hewitt* (1857) 3 K&J 438; *Perry v National Provincial Bank of England* [1910] 1 Ch 464 at 471 per Cozens-Hardy MR.

borrower.[10] Under an indemnity, though, the indemnifier undertakes the obligation itself and agrees to be liable whether or not the borrower is also liable. The liability is primary and does not depend on the borrower's obligation, nor on its default.[11] The distinction is important not just in defining the extent of the 'guarantor's' liability but also because, by s 4 of the Statute of Frauds (1677), a guarantee is unenforceable by action unless the agreement or some memorandum or note thereof is in writing and signed by the guarantor or his authorised agent.[12] However, there is no similar requirement for indemnities.

11.3   Whether a contract is a guarantee or an indemnity is a matter of construction, with the substance of the agreement being determinative rather than any particular labels used.[13] Provisions to the effect that the 'guarantor' is liable 'as a principal debtor and not merely as a surety' and is liable notwithstanding any time, indulgence or release granted to the borrower will obviously point to the arrangement being an indemnity.[14] If the arrangement gives rise to the lender having potentially greater rights against the 'guarantor' than against the borrower, this will point to it being an indemnity.[15]

11.4   Guarantees may themselves be subdivided into two main types, often referred to as 'pure guarantees' and 'conditional payment

---

10 *Bechervaise v Lewis* (1872) LR 7 CP 372; *Murphy v Glass* (1869) LR 2 PC 408; *Trafalgar House Construction (Regions) Ltd v General Surety and Guarantee Co Ltd* [1996] AC 199; *Thornton v Maynard* (1875) LR 10 CP 695; *Hyundai Shipbuilding and Heavy Industries Co Ltd v Pournaras* [1978] 2 Lloyd's Rep 502 at 508 per Roskill LJ (upheld [1980] 2 All ER 29); *BOC Group plc v Centeon LLC* [1999] 1 All ER (Comm) 53 (upheld [1999] 1 All ER (Comm) 970).

11 'An indemnity is a contract by one party to keep the other harmless against loss, but a contract of guarantee is a contract to answer for the debt, default or miscarriage of another who is to be primarily liable to the promisee': *Yeoman Credit Ltd v Latter* [1961] 2 All ER 294 at 296 per Holroyd Pearce LJ; see also *Heald v O'Connor* [1971] 2 All ER 1105; *Moschi v Lep Air Services Ltd* [1973] AC 331; *Argo Caribbean Group Ltd v Lewis* [1976] 2 Lloyd's Rep 289; *General Produce Co v United Bank Ltd* [1979] 2 Lloyd's Rep 255; *The Anemone* [1987] 1 Lloyd's Rep 546 at 555; *Clement v Clement* (1996) 71 P&CR D19; *Goulston Discount Co Ltd v Clark* [1967] 2 QB 493; *Western Credit Ltd v Alberry* [1964] 2 All ER 938; *Stadium Finance Co Ltd v Helm* (1965) 109 Sol Jo 471; *Davys v Buswell* [1913] 2 KB 47 at 53–55 per Vaughan Williams LJ; *Harburg India Rubber Comb Co v Martin* [1902] 1 KB 778 at 784–785 per Vaughan Williams LJ; *General Surety & Guarantee Co Ltd v Francis Parker Ltd* (1977) 6 BLR 16 at 21.

12 See **11.13**.

13 See, eg, *Moschi v Lep Air Services Ltd* [1973] AC 331 at 349 per Lord Diplock; *Western Credit Ltd v Alberry* [1964] 2 All ER 938 at 940–941 per Davies LJ; *Yeoman Credit Ltd v Latter* [1961] 2 All ER 294 at 296 per Holroyd Pearce LJ; *Trafalgar House Construction (Regions) Ltd v General Surety & Guarantee Co Ltd* [1996] 1 AC 199 at 208 per Lord Jauncey; *Perry v National Provincial Bank of England* [1910] 1 Ch 464; *MS Fashions Ltd v Bank of Credit and Commerce International SA* [1993] Ch 425 at 436 per Hoffmann LJ; *Stadium Finance Co Ltd v Helm* (1965) 109 Sol Jo 471; *Harburg India Rubber Comb Co v Martin* [1902] 1 KB 778 at 784–785 per Vaughan Williams LJ. However, outside the banking context, there is a presumption that, in the absence of clear words indicating a primary liability, a contract will be construed as a guarantee rather than an indemnity (*Marubeni Hong Kong and South China Ltd v Mongolian Govt* [2005] 1 WLR 2497; *Canmer International Inc v UK Mutual Steamship Assurance Association (Bermuda) Ltd* [2005] 2 Lloyd's Rep 479).

14 But do not automatically convert it into an indemnity: *Heald v O'Connor* [1971] 2 All ER 1105 at 1110; *General Produce Co v United Bank Ltd* [1979] 2 Lloyd's Rep 255 at 259; *State Bank of India v Kaur* [1996] 5 Bank LR 158; cf *Goulston Discount Co Ltd v Clark* [1967] 2 QB 493; *MS Fashions Ltd v Bank of Credit and Commerce International SA* [1993] Ch 425.

15 See *Yeoman Credit Ltd v Latter* [1961] 2 All ER 294.

guarantees'.[16] A pure guarantee is an undertaking to procure that the principal debtor performs his obligations, and breach gives rise to an action for damages (with a duty on the part of the creditor to mitigate his loss), whereas a conditional payment guarantee is an undertaking that, if the principal debtor fails to pay, the guarantor will pay the amount instead. In that case, the creditor has a debt claim against the guarantor and thus no duty to mitigate.

11.5 Whether the remedy for breach of an indemnity is a debt or a damages claim will depend on the nature of the indemnity obligation. As a general rule, an indemnity in the wide sense of the term (ie an obligation to hold a person harmless against loss) is not a debt; but the type of indemnity relevant here is an obligation that serves the same function as a conditional payment guarantee but involves a primary liability rather than an ancillary liability. If it is drafted as an obligation to pay the principal and interest if the borrower fails to pay, then the creditor's claim should lie in debt, as with a conditional payment guarantee.

11.6 Most guarantees of bond issues and syndicated loans contain both a pure guarantee and a conditional payment guarantee (so that the holders/lenders have both debt and damages claims). In addition, most guarantees of syndicated loans also contain an indemnity obligation in respect of any loss suffered as a result of either the pure guarantee or the conditional payment guarantee being unenforceable, invalid or illegal.[17]

DIFFERENCES FROM OTHER TYPES OF CREDIT SUPPORT

Keepwell agreements

11.7 Guarantees should be distinguished from keepwell agreements. A keepwell agreement, which is usually only seen when the borrower is not the parent company of the group, usually takes the form of an agreement between the borrower and the parent, with, in essence, three basic undertakings by the parent:

(a)   to keep the borrower as a subsidiary;
(b)   to ensure that the borrower has a positive net worth at all times; and
(c)   to ensure that the borrower has sufficient funds to meet its commitments on time.

---

[16]   See the description by Lord Reid in *Moschi v Lep Air Services Ltd* [1973] AC 331 at 344–345. The distinction was neatly illustrated in *Hampton v Minns* [2002] 1 WLR 1, which considered whether a guarantee was, on its proper construction, a pure guarantee or a conditional payment guarantee.

[17]   As this is an indemnity in the wide sense (ie in respect of losses rather than fixed amounts), the lender's remedy would lie in damages rather than debt.

11.8   Keepwell agreements are sometimes used as an alternative to a full guarantee from the parent. The principal drawback from the lender's point of view, though, was (prior to the Contracts (Rights of Third Parties) Act 1999 coming into force) one of enforcement, since the lender, not being a party to the agreement, had no privity of contract with the parent and thus could not enforce the agreement against the parent. Now, however, as a result of that Act, he may enforce the agreement against the parent if it purports to confer a benefit on him (which a normal keepwell agreement clearly does), unless it is clear from the agreement that the parties did not intend that the lender be able to enforce the agreement.

11.9   Even where the lenders cannot enforce the agreement against the parent, the ways in which their position is sometimes strengthened include the insertion in the terms of the borrowing contract of an obligation on the part of the borrower to enforce the keepwell agreement against the parent, with failure to do so, or breach by the parent of the keepwell agreement, being provided to be events of default, entitling the lenders to demand immediate repayment from the borrower. Furthermore, some of the ordinary events of default are occasionally extended to cover events happening to the parent. However, in each case, the fact remains that the lenders have no right to demand repayment from the parent if the borrower fails to pay, and merely a claim for damages for breach of contract, with the lenders having a duty to mitigate their loss (which could involve seeking the liquidation of the borrower).

Comfort letters

11.10   Guarantees should also be distinguished from comfort letters. These are commonly taken where the 'guarantor' is not willing to accept a legal commitment, and are expressed usually as indications of intention to give financial support to the borrower. For a comfort letter to create a binding legal commitment there will need to be consideration, certainty as to terms and intention to create legal relations. In commercial transactions, the intention to create legal relations will be presumed, and the onus is on the provider of the comfort letter to prove the absence of such intention.[18] Relevant factors in proving such absence may include whether or not the issue of the letter has been approved by a board resolution, or whether the provision of the letter is a condition precedent to the borrowing, as well as the terms of the letter itself. A letter will not be regarded as legally binding if it is stated to be binding in honour only,[19] or to be 'an expression of present

---

[18]   *Rose and Frank Co v J R Crompton and Brothers Ltd* [1923] 2 KB 261; *Edwards v Skyways Ltd* [1964] 1 All ER 494, approved in *Kleinwort Benson Ltd v Malaysia Mining Corp Bhd* [1989] 1 All ER 785.
[19]   *Jones v Vernon's Pools Ltd* [1938] 2 All ER 626.

intention by way of comfort only',[20] or is framed in terms that 'it is our policy that . . .'.[21]

11.11 Even if the letter is legally binding, it, like a keepwell agreement, will not give rise to a debt claim, but instead a claim for damages for breach of contract, with a duty on the claimants to mitigate their loss.

CAPACITY AND COMMERCIAL BENEFIT

11.12 Issues relating to the guarantor's corporate capacity and the authority of its officers are considered in **Chapter 9**. The duty of a company's directors to act in the best interests of the company is of particular importance in relation to 'upstream' and 'cross-stream' guarantees (ie guarantees of debts of the company's parent or of a sister subsidiary): this is considered at **9.11ff**.

THE NEED FOR WRITING

11.13 As has been seen, s 4 of the Statute of Frauds (1677) provides that a guarantee (but not an indemnity)[22] is unenforceable by action unless the agreement or some memorandum or note thereof is in writing and signed by the guarantor or his authorised agent. The writing must evidence 'with reasonable certainty' the parties (by name or description), the promise and the subject-matter, but not necessarily the consideration, which may be proved by oral evidence.[23] It is possible for the writing to consist of two or more documents, so long as the document containing the guarantor's signature refers, expressly or impliedly, to the others.[24]

11.14 Section 4 has been disapplied in relation to any 'financial collateral arrangement' within the meaning of the Financial Collateral Arrangements

---

[20]   *Re Atlantic Computers plc* [1995] BCC 696.
[21]   *Kleinwort Benson Ltd v Malaysia Mining Corp Bhd* [1989] 1 All ER 785. For an example of where the wording in a comfort letter was sufficiently unequivocal to be binding, see *Chemco Leasing SpA v Rediffusion* [1987] 1 FTLR 201.
[22]   See eg *Harburg India Rubber Comb Co v Martin* [1902] 1 KB 778 at 784–785 per Vaughan Williams LJ; *Davys v Buswell* [1913] 2 KB 47 at 54–55 per Vaughan Williams LJ; *Re Hoyle* [1893] 1 Ch 84; *Lakeman v Mountstephen* (1874) LR 7 HL 17.
[23]   *Holmes v Mitchell* (1859) 7 CB 361; *Sheers v Thimbleby & Son* (1897) 13 TLR 451; *State Bank of India v Kaur* [1995] NPC 43. See also the Mercantile Law Amendment Act 1856, s 3. Extrinsic evidence is, however, admissible to explain the construction of the written terms in accordance with normal rules, notwithstanding the Statute of Frauds: *Perrylease Ltd v Imecar AG* [1987] 2 All ER 373; *Bank of Scotland v Wright* [1991] BCLC 244 at 251.
[24]   *Timmins v Moreland Street Property Co Ltd* [1958] Ch 110 (on s 40 of the Law of Property Act 1925); *Elias v George Sahely & Co (Barbados) Ltd* [1983] 1 AC 646; *The Anemone* [1987] 1 Lloyd's Rep 546 (three telexes read together held to constitute a sufficient note: only the last was signed, but references in it could be traced to the other two); see also *Elpis Maritime Co Ltd v Marti Chartering Co Inc* [1992] 1 AC 21. As regards the extent to which electronic requirements satisfy the requirements of 'writing' and 'signature', see **19.94ff**.

(No 2) Regulations 2003.[25] For a financial collateral arrangement to fall within the Regulations, it must be evidenced in writing[26] – but it does not have to be signed by the collateral giver.

CONSIDERATION

11.15 Like any other contract, a guarantee or an indemnity must be supported by consideration, unless it is executed as a deed. Usually the consideration moving from the lender is the agreement of the lender to lend the money to the borrower if the 'guarantor' gives his guarantee or indemnity. However, past consideration is no consideration,[27] and thus if a guarantee or indemnity (assuming that it is not executed as a deed) is expressed to be granted in consideration of the lender making the loan, but is only given after the loan has been made or after the lender is already committed, the guarantee or indemnity may fail for lack of consideration. Whereas the consideration need not be stated,[28] if it is it must be correctly stated, since fulfilment of the stated consideration may be construed as a condition precedent to the 'guarantor's' liability.[29]

TRANSACTIONS AT AN UNDERVALUE

11.16 Under s 238 of the Insolvency Act 1986, a company enters into a 'transaction at an undervalue' if, inter alia, it enters into a transaction with a person for a consideration the value of which, in money or money's-worth, is significantly less than the value, in money or money's-worth, of the consideration provided by the company.[30] If the transaction was entered into at a 'relevant time', a liquidator or administrator of the company may apply to the court for an order restoring the position to what it would otherwise have been.[31] A 'relevant time'[32] for this purpose is any time in the period of two years before the 'onset of insolvency' (defined as, broadly, the commencement of the liquidation or the administration)[33] if, at that time, the company either was unable to pay its debts within the meaning of s 123 of the Insolvency Act 1986 or became unable to pay its debts in consequence of the transaction. However, the court shall not make an order if it is satisfied that the company entered into the transaction in good faith and for the purpose of carrying on its business and that at the time it did so there were

---

25   SI 2003/3226, reg 4(1).
26   Regulation 3.
27   See *Chitty on Contracts* (29th edn, 2004), paras 3–026 to 3–035.
28   See **11.13**.
29   *Burton v Gray* (1873) 8 Ch App 932.
30   Subsection (4).
31   Subsections (2) and (3). This can include the release or discharge of security: s 241(1)(c).
32   Defined in s 240.
33   In relation to administration, different points in time apply depending on the method of appointment of the administrator.

reasonable grounds for believing that the transaction would benefit the company.[34]

11.17 In assessing whether the giving of a guarantee or indemnity is a transaction at an undervalue, the test[35] is whether (from the guarantor's point of view) the present value of the contingent liability borne by the guarantor is significantly greater than the present value of the contingent benefit obtained by the guarantor (either directly, eg as a result of a fee received by it, or indirectly, eg as a result of the borrower borrowing the money). This will largely depend upon the financial condition of the borrower and the likelihood of the guarantee or indemnity being called. The practical problems involved in determining and comparing these values mean that in normal circumstances a guarantee or indemnity is unlikely to be a transaction at an undervalue, unless there is a strong risk of default or there is little or no benefit to the 'guarantor' (eg where the guarantee or indemnity is in respect of an advance already made).

11.18 Where there is any risk of the transaction being a transaction at an undervalue, it is prudent practice on the part of the lenders to require the company to deliver a certified copy of the board resolution approving the giving of the guarantee or indemnity, with the board resolution recording:

(a) that the company is and notwithstanding the transaction will remain able to pay its debts within the meaning of s 123 of the Insolvency Act 1986;

(b) that the guarantee or indemnity will be for the purposes of the company carrying out its business and for its commercial benefit; and

(c) the grounds for believing that the guarantee or indemnity will be for the company's commercial benefit (so that the lenders can satisfy themselves that they are 'reasonable').

11.19 Sometimes, a directors' certificate is also required, which is occasionally supported by an auditor's report that they are not aware of anything to suggest that the directors' opinion is unreasonable. Although the provision of such documents will not prevent the guarantee or indemnity being set aside if the company actually is or becomes unable to pay its debts, it is at least helpful comfort.

---

[34] Section 238(5). It is only the good faith of the guarantor that is considered, and it is not necessary for the other parties to the transaction to be acting in good faith.

[35] Applying the approach laid down in *Re M C Bacon Ltd* [1990] BCC 78. Where the guarantee forms part of a series of interconnected agreements or transactions, the court will generally analyse the transactions and the benefits flowing from them in their totality: see eg *Phillips v Brewin Dolphin Bell Lawrie Ltd* [2001] 1 All ER 673.

PROTECTIVE PROVISIONS

11.20 It was seen earlier[36] that under a guarantee (as opposed to an indemnity) the guarantor's liability will be extinguished by alterations to the borrower's liability which could prejudice the guarantor. It is therefore very common for lenders to insert protective provisions in a guarantee to prevent this and in effect to turn the guarantee into an indemnity. Typically, a 'guarantee' will provide that the lender's rights against the 'guarantor' will not be affected by any time, indulgence or release granted to the borrower, any amendment to the terms of the underlying debt or any set-off, counterclaim or defence available to the borrower.[37]

11.21 It is also common to express the guarantee as a 'continuing' guarantee and/or as applying to the 'ultimate balance' of money owing by the borrower. These provisions are designed to exclude the effect of the rule in *Clayton's Case*,[38] as a result of which repayments by the borrower of subsequent, unguaranteed borrowings would, if not specifically appropriated by the borrower or the creditor[39] to the later borrowings, operate in discharge of the earlier, guaranteed borrowing and thereby reduce the liability of the guarantor. Where either or both of these provisions (or other wording indicating a similar intention) is included, this is effective to prevent the liability of the guarantor being reduced in such circumstances.[40] If the guarantor is unwilling for the guarantee to be unlimited, however, the usual solution is to insert a limit on the amount payable.[41]

11.22 Other protective provisions commonly inserted in a guarantee include:

(a) a 'non-competition' clause, under which the guarantor agrees that, while any amount remains owing to the lender, it will not exercise any right of subrogation against the borrower in respect of amounts already

---

[36] See **11.2**.
[37] Such provisions are, in principle, effective (see, eg, *Perry v National Provincial Bank of England* [1910] 1 Ch 464; *British Motor Trust Company Ltd v Hyams* (1934) 50 TLR 230; *Continental Illinois Bank & Trust Co of Chicago v Papanicolaou* [1986] 2 Lloyd's Rep 441). However, a provision that the lender's rights will not be affected by any 'amendment or variation' of the underlying loan facility will not protect the lender where the underlying loan facility is replaced by a new facility (*Triodos Bank NV v Dobbs* [2005] 2 Lloyd's Rep 588).
[38] *Devaynes v Noble* (1816) 1 Mer 572.
[39] As, eg, in *Re Sherry* (1884) 25 ChD 692.
[40] See, eg, *Westminster Bank Ltd v Cond* (1940) 46 Com Cas 60; *Merle v Wells* (1810) 2 Camp 413; *Wood & Priestner* (1866) LR 2 Ex 66, affd (1866) LR 2 Ex 282; *Laurie v Scholefield* (1869) LR 4 CP 622; *Mason v Pritchard* (1810) 2 Camp 436.
[41] As in each of the cases cited in the previous footnote.

paid by the guarantor under the guarantee or prove in a liquidation of the borrower in competition with the lender[42]; and

(b) a suspense account provision, allowing the lender to hold any partial payments[43] by the guarantor in a separate 'suspense' account until the full amount due has been paid. The amount in the suspense account is stated not to reduce the amount due, so that the lender can prove for the full amount in a liquidation of the borrower and thereby potentially increase the liquidation dividend receivable.[44]

EXAMPLE 'GUARANTEE'

11.23 By way of example, a typical 'guarantee'[45] clause in a syndicated loan facility would read as follows:

(1) Guarantee

The Guarantor irrevocably and unconditionally:

(a) as principal obligor guarantees to each Finance Party prompt performance by the Borrower of all its obligations under the Finance Documents;

(b) undertakes with each Finance Party that, whenever the Borrower does not pay any amount when due under or in connection with any Finance Document, the Guarantor shall forthwith on demand by the Agent pay that amount as if the Guarantor instead of the Borrower were expressed to be the principal obligor; and

(c) indemnifies each Finance Party on demand against any loss or liability suffered by it if any obligation guaranteed by the Guarantor is or becomes unenforceable, invalid or illegal.

(2) Continuing guarantee

This guarantee is a continuing guarantee and will extend to the ultimate balance of all sums payable by the Borrower under the Finance Documents, regardless of any intermediate payment or discharge in whole or in part.

---

[42] Waivers and limitations of the right of subrogation are valid (see eg *Midland Banking Co v Chambers* (1869) LR 4 Ch App 398; *Re Rees* (1881) LR 17 ChD 98; *Barclays Bank Ltd v TOSG Trust Fund Ltd* [1984] AC 626 at 644 per Oliver LJ (upheld HL); *Re Butler's Wharf Ltd* [1995] 2 BCLC 43 at 50; *Liberty Mutual Insurance Co (UK) Ltd v HSBC Bank plc* [2002] EWCA Civ 691). However, clear words are required (see eg *Re Butler's Wharf Ltd* [1995] 2 BCLC 43; *Liberty Mutual Insurance (UK) Ltd v HSBC Bank plc* [2002] EWCA Civ 691).

[43] Or even a payment in full, if the guarantee is of only part of a debt.

[44] *Commercial Bank of Australia Ltd v Wilson* [1893] AC 181; *Ulster Bank Ltd v Lambe* [1966] NI 161 (Northern Ireland); *Re Butler's Wharf Ltd* [1995] 2 BCLC 43 at 49. There appears to be a suggestion by Dillon LJ in *MS Fashions Ltd v Bank of Credit and Commerce International SA* [1993] Ch 425 at 448 that suspense accounts are ineffective ('A creditor cannot sue the principal debtor for an amount of the debt which the creditor has already received from a guarantor'): however, the guarantees in that case did not contain suspense account provisions, and accordingly the statement can be distinguished as being authority merely for the position that applies in the absence of a suspense account provision.

[45] Ie in reality combining elements of a pure guarantee, a conditional payment guarantee and an indemnity.

(3) Reinstatement

(a)   Where any discharge (whether in respect of the obligations of the Borrower or any security for those obligations or otherwise) is made in whole or in part or any arrangement is made on the faith of any payment, security or other disposition which is avoided or must be restored on insolvency, liquidation or otherwise without limitation, the liability of the Guarantor under this Clause shall continue as if the discharge or arrangement had not occurred.

(b)   Each Finance Party may concede or compromise any claim that any payment, security or other disposition is liable to avoidance or restoration.

(4) Waiver of defences

The obligations of the Guarantor under this Clause will not be affected by an act, omission, matter or thing which, but for this provision, would reduce, release or prejudice any of its obligations under this Clause or prejudice or diminish those obligations in whole or in part, including (whether or not known to it or any Finance Party):

(a)   any time or waiver granted to, or composition with, the Borrower or any other person;

(b)   the taking, variation, compromise, exchange, renewal or release of, or refusal or neglect to perfect, take up or enforce, any rights against, or security over assets of, the Borrower or any other person or any non-presentation or non-observance of any formality or other requirement in respect of any instrument or any failure to realise the full value of any security;

(c)   any incapacity or lack of powers, authority or legal personality of or dissolution or change in the members or status of the Borrower or any other person;

(d)   any variation (however fundamental) or replacement of a Finance Document or any other document or security so that references to that Finance Document in this Clause shall include each variation or replacement;

(e)   any unenforceability, illegality or invalidity of any obligation of any person under any Finance Document or any other document or security, to the intent that the Guarantor's obligations under this Clause shall remain in full force and its guarantee be construed accordingly, as if there were no unenforceability, illegality or invalidity; or

(f)   any postponement, discharge, reduction, non-provability or other similar circumstance affecting any obligation of the Borrower under a Finance Document resulting from any insolvency, liquidation or dissolution proceedings or from any law, regulation or order so that each such obligation shall for the purposes of the Guarantor's obligations under this Clause be construed as if there were no such circumstance.

(5) Immediate recourse

The Guarantor waives any right it may have of first requiring any Finance Party (or any trustee or agent on its behalf) to proceed against or enforce any other rights or security or claim payment from any person before claiming from the Guarantor under this Clause.

(6)   Appropriations

Until all amounts which may be or become payable by the Borrower under or in connection with the Finance Documents have been irrevocably paid in full, each Finance Party (or any trustee or agent on its behalf) may:

(a)   refrain from applying or enforcing any other moneys, security or rights held or received by that Finance Party (or any trustee or agent on its behalf) in respect of those amounts, or apply and enforce the same in such manner and order as it sees fit (whether against those amounts or otherwise), and the Guarantor shall not be entitled to the benefit of the same; and

(b)   hold in a suspense account any moneys received from the Guarantor or on account of the Guarantor's liability under this Clause, without liability to pay interest on those moneys.

(7)   Non-competition

Until all amounts which may be or become payable by the Borrower under or in connection with the Finance Documents have been irrevocably paid in full, the Guarantor shall not, after a claim has been made or by virtue of any payment or performance by it under this Clause:

(a)   be subrogated to any rights, security or moneys held, received or receivable by any Finance Party (or any trustee or agent on its behalf) or be entitled to any right of contribution or indemnity in respect of any payment made or moneys received on account of the Guarantor's liability under this Clause;

(b)   claim, rank, prove or vote as a creditor of the Borrower or its estate in competition with any Finance Party (or any trustee or agent on its behalf); or

(c)   receive, claim or have the benefit of any payment, distribution or security from or on account of the Borrower, or exercise any right of set-off as against the Borrower,

unless the Agent otherwise directs. The Guarantor shall hold in trust for and forthwith pay or transfer to the Agent for the Finance Parties any payment or distribution or benefit of security received by it contrary to this sub-clause (7) or as directed by the Agent.

(8)   Additional security

This guarantee is in addition to and is not in any way prejudiced by any other security now or subsequently held by any Finance Party.

Related definitions:

'**Finance Document**' means this Loan Agreement, the Fee Letter, a Novation Certificate[46] or any other document designated as such by the Agent and the Borrower.

'**Finance Party**' means the Arranger, a Bank or the Agent.

---

[46]   See further **15.31**.

Chapter Twelve

THE ROLE OF TRUSTEES

INTRODUCTION

12.1 As has been seen,[1] it is common for borrowers to appoint trustees in relation to issues of debt securities. The primary (in the case of eurobonds) or only (in the case of stock) covenant to pay is given to the trustee, and the trustee holds the benefit of that covenant (together with the benefit of any accompanying security) on trust for the holders and is responsible for its enforcement.

12.2 Trustees should not be confused with fiscal agents, which are usually appointed in relation to bearer eurobond issues where there is no trustee, and are commonly (and inaccurately) spoken of as the alternative to trustees. In most bearer eurobond issues, a group of banks is appointed by the issuer as 'paying agents' to make payments to the holders on the issuer's behalf. One of the paying agents is responsible for receiving the amounts due from the issuer, reimbursing the other paying agents as and when they make payments to holders, and carrying out other administrative functions on behalf of the issuer: it is traditionally known as the 'principal paying agent' where there is also a trustee and as the 'fiscal agent' where there is no trustee. Whereas the trustee is a representative of the holders, with a duty to safeguard their interests, the fiscal agent, like a principal paying agent, is thus merely an agent of the issuer and is usually expressly stated not to assume any relationship of agency or trust with the holders.

WHY ARE TRUSTEES APPOINTED?[2]

Advantages for holders

12.3 Since the basic contract to repay and to pay interest is between the issuer and the trustee, enforcement proceedings are taken in one unified

---

1   See **Chapter 3**.
2   See further Wood, *International Loans, Bonds and Securities Regulation* (1995), pp 164–168; Tennekoon, *The Law and Regulation of International Finance* (1991), pp 246–248; Herbert [1987] JIBL 48; Pergam, *Studies in Transnational Economic Law* (Horn, ed), vol III, p 337; Smart, IFLR, December 1982, p 18; Marsden, Euromoney, April 1983, p 145; Goodall, IFLR, February 1983, p 19; Duffett, (1992) 1 JITCP 23.

action on behalf of all the holders by the trustee, the legal and financial advice which it obtains being for the benefit of all the holders. By contrast, individual actions by holders are generally less practicable due to the expense, the general disparity of the holders, the difficulties in organising them and, in the case of bearer securities, the wish of many holders to remain anonymous. The trustee may have a stronger negotiating position than individual holders in any discussions with the issuer, since it represents a larger amount of debt, and any monies recovered by it are required by the trust deed to be distributed to all the holders pro rata, thereby avoiding the risk that some holders recover and others do not. Furthermore, the trustee is usually given certain rights to obtain information from the issuer and is therefore likely to be in a better position to monitor the issuer's compliance with covenants, to identify a breach, and to take appropriate action earlier rather than later.

12.4 The perceived disadvantages for holders are that they lose absolute control over whether their securities are accelerated or not and (since, as will be seen below, the trustee has powers to agree to certain modifications without the consent of the holders) whether the terms of their securities are modified in certain respects, and that they are generally precluded from being personally involved in negotiations with the issuer. How relevant these concerns are will obviously depend on the interests of the holders in question.

Advantages for the issuer

12.5 The trustee is usually given powers to agree to waivers, modifications, substitutions of debtor, etc[3] if in its opinion they are 'not materially prejudicial' to the interests of the holders; this can be an important flexibility for the issuer, especially in long-term issues or issues with detailed covenants, since the alternative would be approval by a resolution at a meeting of the holders.[4] If enforcement proceedings are taken against the issuer, it only has to defend one action, rather than a multiplicity of actions. Furthermore, many events of default do not arise unless the trustee certifies that the event in question is in its opinion materially prejudicial to the interests of the holders, thus protecting the issuer against acceleration or enforcement by maverick holders, who, in an issue without a trustee (and thus no requirement of certification), might take unreasonable opportunistic advantage of a technical default.[5]

---

3   See **12.8**.
4   As to which, see **Chapter 16**.
5   A dramatic example was in relation to Dome Petroleum: see Carr, IFLR, March 1987, p 15. By contrast, in the Adela rescheduling of 1981, the presence of a trustee facilitated the formulation of the rescheduling (see Anderson, *Euromoney*, Sep 1981, p 10; Watkins, *Euromoney*, Jan 1983, p 103).

12.6 The perceived disadvantages for the issuer are the increase in cost[6] and the 'diminution in status' that may be perceived by certain types of borrower. This is in practice not a concern for UK corporate issuers, who traditionally almost always appoint a trustee in relation to their debt security issues, but is in practice the determining factor in relation to other borrowers: borrowers with a high credit-standing, such as governments and governmental bodies, would not generally expect the risk of default to be a concern to holders and would not generally expect to undertake detailed covenants that may require waivers or modifications in the years to come. Consequently, in the case of a borrower other than a UK company, the higher its credit-standing, the less likely it generally is that a trustee will be appointed (unless it is appropriate for one of the reasons mentioned below).[7]

Circumstances of the issue

12.7 For example, in the case of a secured issue, it is generally not practicable to grant security to each individual holder, since specific assets will in most cases[8] need to be allocated to each security interest, and each transfer by a holder will need to be accompanied by a valid transfer of the benefit of his security interest. If a trustee is appointed, however, only one security interest over the whole pool of assets need be granted to the trustee.

TRUSTEES' FUNCTIONS

12.8 The principal functions of the trustee are as follows:

(a) As seen above,[9] the trustee, rather than the holders, is responsible for enforcing the obligations of the issuer, although if the trustee defaults the holders have a residual equitable right to do so. In the case of bearer eurobonds, where a covenant to pay the holder is incorporated on the face of the bond, the terms provide that the holder may not enforce against the issuer unless the trustee has been directed by the holders[10] to enforce (and has been indemnified to its satisfaction[11]) and has failed to

---

6   In practice, this is minimal: in the Court of Appeal judgment in *Concord Trust v Law Debenture Trust Corporation plc* [2005] 1 Lloyd's Rep 113 at 119, for example, it was reported that the trustee's remuneration consisted of an initial acceptance fee of £2,000 and an annual management fee of £2,500.

7   This approach may be changing, though: in 2003, the UK government used a trustee for one of its international bond issues for the first time, in order to encourage the use of a 'collective action' approach by other sovereign issuers in line with recommendations by the G10 Working Group on Contractual Clauses (Bank of England press release, 23 June 2003).

8   Since, if the asset secured is land, legal security cannot be granted to more than four co-mortgagees (Law of Property Act 1925, ss 34–36), and, even where the asset secured is personalty, the pooling of security may result in the issue being a collective investment scheme, and therefore regulated under Part XVII of the Financial Services and Markets Act 2000.

9   See **Chapter 3**.

10 Either by a resolution at a meeting of holders or in writing by a specified proportion of the holders.

11 As to the meaning of the phrase 'indemnified to its satisfaction' see footnote 14 below.

take action.[12] A typical provision to this effect (in this example, in a eurobond issue) would read as follows:

(A)   The Trustee shall not be bound to take any action in relation to the Trust Deed, the Bonds or the Coupons (including but without limitation, enforcement proceedings) unless (a) it shall have been so directed by an Extraordinary Resolution of the Bondholders or so requested in writing by the holders of at least one-fifth in principal amount of the Bonds then outstanding and (b) it shall have been indemnified to its satisfaction.

(B)   Only the Trustee may enforce the provisions of the Trust Deed, the Bonds and the Coupons. No Bondholder or Couponholder shall be entitled to proceed directly against the Issuer to enforce the performance of any of the provisions of the Trust Deed, the Bonds or the Coupons unless the Trustee, having become bound as aforesaid to take proceedings, fails to do so within a reasonable period and such failure is continuing.

(b)   The terms invariably provide that only the trustee may accelerate the securities on the occurrence of an event of default. It is common to provide[13] that the trustee may accelerate in its discretion, and shall accelerate if directed by the holders and indemnified to its satisfaction.[14]

(c)   Most events (other than failure to pay and winding up) are usually provided not to be events of default unless the trustee has certified that the event is in its opinion 'materially prejudicial' to the interests of the holders.[15] Since this involves the opinion of the trustee, it is not open to the holders to direct the trustee to issue such a certificate.[16]

---

12   Such a provision is valid: *Rogers & Co v British & Colonial Colliery Supply Assocn* (1898) 68 LJQB 14. See also *Pethybridge v Unibifocal Co Ltd* [1918] WN 278 (provision restraining a holder from taking action without the consent of a specified number of the holders held valid); *Highberry Ltd v Colt Telecom Group plc (No 2)* [2002] EWHC 2815 (English public policy did not invalidate a 'no-action' clause governed by New York law).

13   For an example provision, see **5.19**.

14   Such a clause is valid (*Concord Trust v Law Debenture Trust Corporation plc* [2005] 1 WLR 1591). The meaning of the phrase 'indemnified to its satisfaction' in this context was considered by the House of Lords in *Concord Trust*, supra. Their Lordships held that: in identifying a risk of liability, the trustee does not have to demonstrate that it would actually incur that liability, merely that it is 'reasonably arguable' that it may do so; once such a risk has been identified the trustee is entitled to be indemnified for the consequences on a 'worst case scenario' basis; under English law, an acceleration notice given when no event of default has actually occurred does not expose the trustee to potential liability to the issuer, but is merely an ineffective notice (and therefore the trustee is not entitled to be indemnified in respect of that risk); the position may well be different, though, under an applicable foreign law; in that case the trustee has to show sufficient differences between the foreign law and English law to give 'some substance' to the fear of liability.

15   The 'interests' of the holders in this context are their contractual entitlements under the securities to be paid in full and on time, together with any ancillary rights designed to provide protection for their entitlement to receive timely payment (such as security or, in the *Acciona* case, the right to appoint a representative to the issuer's board to control the issuer's expenditure), but not extraneous factors (such as market price, ratings, etc): *Law Debenture Trust Corporation plc v Acciona SA* [2004] EWHC 270.

16   Subject, it would seem, to the duty of the trustee at least to consider whether to issue the certificate: see **12.19**. For an example provision, see **5.19**.

(d)   Any funds received by the trustee after acceleration or enforcement are held on trust, the terms usually providing that the trustee may deduct any remuneration and expenses that remain unpaid by the issuer (the right of 'top-slicing') before payment to the holders. A typical provision to this effect (in this example, in a eurobond trust deed) would read as follows:

> All moneys received by the Trustee under this Trust Deed (including any moneys which represent principal, premium or interest in respect of Bonds or Coupons which have become void under Condition [ ] (*Prescription*)) shall be held by the Trustee upon trust to apply them (subject to Clause [ ] (*Investment of de minimis amounts*)):
>
> FIRST in payment or satisfaction of all remuneration, costs, charges, expenses and liabilities then due and unpaid under Clauses [ ] (*Remuneration*) and [ ] (*Indemnity*) to the Trustee;
>
> SECONDLY in or towards payment *pari passu* and rateably of all principal, premium (if any) and interest then due and unpaid in respect of the Bonds and the Coupons; and
>
> THIRDLY in payment of the balance (if any) to the Issuer (without prejudice to, or liability in respect of, any question as to how such payment to the Issuer shall be dealt with as between the Issuer and any other person).

(e)   Various covenants are given by the issuer to the trustee, primarily regarding the keeping of accounts and the provision of certificates and financial information to the trustee. However, it is usual to provide that the trustee is entitled to assume that no event of default or breach of covenant has occurred until it has express notice thereof.[17] Once the trustee has notice, it is obviously under a duty to investigate the alleged event of default or breach and to decide whether or not it is in the holders' interests to take enforcement action. Until it has notice, though, the normal practice is for the trustee to obtain from the issuer annually a directors' certificate that the issuer has complied with all its obligations,[18] to review the annual accounts and other documents sent out to its shareholders or creditors (all of which the issuer will have covenanted to supply to the trustee) and to monitor the financial press. If the terms include financial covenants, such as a borrowing limit or restriction on disposal of assets,[19] an annual report as to compliance with those covenants will also be obtained. In the case of first mortgage debenture stocks, in which capital and income cover requirements are normally included, valuers' and auditors' reports as to compliance with such requirements will also be obtained periodically.

---

[17]   For an example provision, see **12.28**.

[18]   Unless there is specific provision to the contrary, the directors, in giving such a certificate, are acting as agents of the issuer. Accordingly, although the directors owe a personal duty to the trustee to exercise reasonable care and skill in preparing the certificates, the issuer will be vicariously liable for their negligence in so doing: *New Zealand Guardian Trust Co Ltd v Brooks* [1995] 1 WLR 96.

[19]   As to which, see **9.17ff**.

(f) The trustee is usually given power to agree with the issuer certain modifications without the consent of the holders. These are usually of three types: those which in the opinion of the trustee (i) are 'not materially prejudicial' to the interests of the holders (subject, in the case of eurobond issues, to certain exceptions, known as 'entrenched provisions'), (ii) are to correct a manifest or proven error, or (iii) are of a formal, minor or technical nature.[20] The entrenched provisions (which may nevertheless usually be modified under powers (ii) and (iii)) are usually the basic commercial terms of the issue, such as payment dates, amounts of principal and interest, currency etc. In the absence of such a power, or other special provisions, modifications could only be made binding on all holders if either all agree or a majority resolution is validly passed.[21]

(g) The trustee is also usually given power, without the consent of the holders, to waive breaches by the issuer or to determine that an event shall not be treated as an event of default, in each case if this is in its opinion 'not materially prejudicial' to the interests of the holders.[22] A typical provision to this effect (in this example, in a eurobond issue), dealing also with the power of modification referred to in para (f) above, would read as follows:

> (1) The Trustee may agree, without the consent of the Bondholders or Couponholders, to any modification (subject to certain exceptions set out in the Trust Deed) of, or to the waiver or authorisation of any breach or proposed breach of, any of these Conditions or any of the provisions of the Trust Deed, or determine, without any such consent as aforesaid, that any Event of Default or Potential Event of Default (as defined in the Trust Deed) shall not be treated as such, which in any such case is not, in the opinion of the Trustee, materially prejudicial to the interests of the Bondholders, or may agree, without any such consent as aforesaid, to any modification which is of a formal, minor or technical nature or to correct a manifest error.
>
> (2) Any modification, waiver, or authorisation or determination shall be binding on the Bondholders and the Couponholders and, unless the Trustee agrees otherwise, any modification shall be notified by the Issuer to the Bondholders as soon as practicable thereafter in accordance with Condition [ ] (*Notices*).

(h) In eurobond (but not, usually, stock) issues, the trustee is often given power, without the consent of the holders, to agree to a substitution of another entity as the debtor in place of the issuer (ie a novation), again

---

[20] For an example provision, see para (g) below.

[21] As to which, see **Chapter 16**.

[22] A trustee also has residual power under s 15(f) of the Trustee Act 1925 to 'compromise, compound, abandon, submit to arbitration, or otherwise settle any debt, account, claim, or thing whatever relating to . . . the trust'.

if this is in its opinion 'not materially prejudicial' to the interests of the holders. A typical provision to this effect would read as follows:

> The Trustee may, without the consent of the Bondholders or Couponholders, agree with the Issuer to the substitution in place of the Issuer (or of any previous substitute under this Condition) as the principal debtor under the Bonds, the Coupons and the Trust Deed of another company, subject to (a) the Bonds and the Coupons being unconditionally and irrevocably guaranteed by the Issuer, (b) the Trustee being satisfied that the interests of the Bondholders will not be materially prejudiced by the substitution, and (c) certain other conditions set out in the Trust Deed being complied with.

(i) In first mortgage debenture stock issues, the trustee is usually given power to agree to substitutions of fresh assets in place of the assets secured, provided that it is satisfied that the capital and income cover requirements are complied with.

TRUSTEES' LIABILITY FOR BREACH OF TRUST

12.9   A breach of trust is a breach of an obligation owed by the trustee to its beneficiaries. A trustee's obligations to beneficiaries can, broadly, be divided into two types: its duty to act with care and skill in the administration of the trust; and its fiduciary duties.

Duty of care and skill

(i) Standard of care

12.10   Whereas the standard of care required of an individual trustee in the exercise of his duties is that 'which an ordinary prudent man of business would take in managing similar affairs of his own',[23] the standard required of a professional trustee is higher. The leading formulation is that by Brightman J in *Bartlett v Barclays Bank Trust Co Ltd*:[24]

> 'Just as, under the law of contract, a professional person possessed of a particular skill is liable for breach of contract if he neglects to use the skill and experience which he professes, so I think that a professional corporate trustee is liable for breach of trust if loss is caused to the trust fund because it neglects to exercise the special care and skill which it professes to have ... Trust corporations ... hold themselves out as possessing a superior ability for the conduct of trust business, and in any event I would take judicial notice of that fact.'

12.11   In addition to the above equitable duty, a statutory duty of care has been introduced by the Trustee Act 2000. This duty of care requires the

---

[23]   *Speight v Gaunt* (1883) 9 App Cas 1 at 19 per Lord Blackburn.
[24]   [1980] 1 All ER 139 at 152.

trustee to 'exercise such care and skill as is reasonable in the circumstances', having regard in particular to (i) any special knowledge or experience that the trustee has or holds itself out as having and (ii) where it is acting in the course of a business or profession, any special knowledge or experience that it is reasonable to expect of a person acting in the course of that kind of business or profession.[25] However, the duty only applies in the circumstances listed in Sch 1 of the Act. The most relevant of these for corporate trustees are the exercise by a trustee of a power to invest trust property[26] or to appoint an agent, nominee or custodian:[27] but the duty of care does not apply, for example, where the trustee is using its general power to agree modifications to a trust deed.

(ii) Attempts to reduce the duty of care

12.12   The statutory duty of care may be excluded or restricted in the trust deed.[28]

12.13   Attempts in the trust deed to reduce the general equitable duty of care, though, may be void if they go too far. Section 192(1) of the Companies Act 1985 provides:

> 'Subject to this section, any provision contained –
>
> (a)   in a trust deed for securing an issue of debentures,[29] or
> (b)   in any contract with the holders of debentures secured by a trust deed,
>
> is void in so far as it would have the effect of exempting a trustee of the deed from, or indemnifying him against, liability for breach of trust where he fails to show the degree of care and diligence required of him as trustee, having regard to the provisions of the trust deed conferring on him any powers, authorities or discretions.'

12.14   The exact meaning of this subsection is not immediately apparent. One interpretation[30] is that any exemption or indemnity clause is void to the extent that it would protect the trustee where it has failed to show the care and diligence required of it as trustee. But this interpretation ignores the last words of the subsection from 'having regard . . .' onwards. The subsection re-enacts what was originally s 75(1) of the Companies Act 1947, which was enacted on the recommendation in 1945 of the Cohen Committee on

---

25   Trustee Act 2000, s 1(1). The test is thus both subjective (in that para (a) looks to the circumstances of the trustee in question) and objective (in that para (b) looks to standards which can reasonably be expected).
26   Trustee Act 2000, Sch 1, para 1. Note that the duty only applies to a trustee 'when exercising' the investment powers, and thus a failure to exercise investment powers would not constitute a breach of the statutory duty of care.
27   Trustee Act 2000, Sch 1, para 3.
28   Trustee Act 2000, Sch 1, para 7.
29   As to what constitutes a debenture, see **Chapter 17**.
30   See, eg, *Palmer's Company Law*, para 13.151.

Company Law Amendment.[31] The Committee, in advising that the power of trustees to escape liability should be limited, recommended[32] that a general exemption from, or indemnification against, liability should be prohibited, but that 'enabling' clauses (ie clauses enabling the trustee to rely on opinions or evidence or act upon advice upon which it might not otherwise be entitled to rely) should be permitted. It is submitted that therein lies the explanation of the last limb of the subsection, and that the trustee's level of responsibility in the light of s 192(1) is the *Bartlett* level of professed 'special care and skill', *after* taking into account the 'enabling' clauses in the trust deed (but *not* any exemption or indemnity clauses).[33]

12.15 Though the subsection is only applicable to issues by companies incorporated in Great Britain, it is normal practice to include wording to similar effect in all trust deeds for issues of international securities (irrespective of the issuer's place of incorporation).

12.16 It is possible that clauses purporting to limit or reduce the trustee's equitable duty of care may also be subject to a test of reasonableness by virtue of s 2(2) of the Unfair Contract Terms Act 1977. The subsection applies to clauses intended to exclude or restrict liability for negligence. However, there are two reasons why s 2(2) is thought not to apply to trust deeds for debt securities. First, negligence is defined in s 1(1) as a duty arising from the terms of a contract or from a 'common law duty to take reasonable care or exercise reasonable skill'. Since a trustee's duty arises in equity, it is probably outside the ambit of s 2(2).[34] Secondly, s 2 of the Act does not apply to 'any contract so far as it relates to the creation or transfer of securities or of any right or interest in securities'. A trust deed for an issue of debt securities clearly relates to the creation of securities or rights or interests in them, and so there seems little doubt that it is not subject to s 2(2).[35]

12.17 Where a protective clause has not been struck down by a statutory provision,[36] it is effective, except to the extent that it purports to exempt the trustee from liability for its own actual fraud.[37] 'Actual fraud' has been held

---

[31] Cmd 6659.

[32] At para 64.

[33] For an example of exculpatory wording designed to comply with s 192, see **12.28**. For a different interpretation of s 192, see Tennekoon, *The Law and Regulation of International Finance* (1991), pp 237–238.

[34] See the Law Commission's discussion of this point in its Consultation Paper No 171 (*Trustee Exemption Clauses*), paras 2.57–2.64.

[35] Unfair Contract Terms Act 1977, Sch 1, para 1(e).

[36] In addition to the above two provisions, other statutory controls include s 33 of the Pensions Act 1995 (re pension fund trusts) and s 253 of the Financial Services and Markets Act 2000 (re authorised unit trusts).

[37] *Armitage v Nurse* [1998] Ch 241; *Walker v Stones* [2000] 4 All ER 412. See also Panesar (1998) 19(1) Bus LR 8; Kessler (1998) 6(2) PTPR 137; McCormack (1998) 62 Conv 100; Hayton (2000) J Int P 8(2), pp 71–83; Vos, T & ELJ (Oct 2000), pp 22–24.

to mean simply dishonesty,[38] and thus (subject to the provisions described above) it is possible to exclude liability for conduct which is negligent, grossly negligent, imprudent or unreasonable, so long as it is not dishonest.[39] In the words of Millett LJ:[40]

> 'I accept . . . that there is an irreducible core of obligations owed by the trustees to the beneficiaries and enforceable by them which is fundamental to the concept of a trust. If the beneficiaries have no rights enforceable against the trustees there are no trusts. But I do not accept . . . that these core obligations include the duties of skill and care, prudence and diligence. The duty of the trustees to perform the trusts honestly and in good faith for the benefit of the beneficiaries is the minimum necessary to give substance to the trusts, but in my opinion it is sufficient.'

Where, however, there is a doubt as to the exact extent of a protective clause, the doubt will be resolved against the trustee.[41]

(iii) Relief by the court

12.18   Even where a protective clause has failed to protect the trustee, though, the trustee may still be relieved by the court under s 61 of the Trustee Act 1925, if it 'has acted honestly and reasonably, and ought fairly to be excused'.[42] However, the court will be more reluctant to relieve a professional trustee than it will a gratuitous trustee, because of the higher standard of care and skill expected.[43]

(iv) Reliance on certificates, etc

12.19   As seen earlier,[44] the normal practice of trustees, until they have notice of a breach of covenant or event of default, is to obtain from the issuer an annual directors' certificate (and other reports, if appropriate), to review the annual accounts and other documents sent to shareholders and creditors, and to monitor the financial press. It is generally accepted that, unless it appears that something requires further inquiry, the trustee is then

---

38   *Armitage v Nurse* supra at p 251 per Millett LJ; but see the next footnote.
39   In the case of a solicitor-trustee, though, a deliberate breach of trust which the trustee honestly believed to be in the best interests of the beneficiaries but which no reasonable solicitor-trustee could have thought was for the benefit of the beneficiaries was held to constitute 'dishonesty' for this purpose: *Walker v Stones* [2001] QB 902.
40   *Armitage v Nurse* supra at p 253.
41   *Midland Bank Trustee (Jersey) Ltd v Federated Pension Services Ltd* [1996] PLR 179 at 192; *Armitage v Nurse* [1998] Ch 241 at 255 per Millett LJ; *Bogg v Raper* (1998/99) 1 ITELR 267 at 280 per Millett LJ; *Wight v Olswang (No 1)* (1999) 1 ITELR 783.
42   See *Snell's Equity* (31st edn, 2005), pp 682–683; Goldsworth and André (1997) 3(10) T&T, pp 22–26.
43   See, eg, National Trustees Company of Australasia Ltd v General Finance Company of Australasia Ltd [1905] AC 373 at 381; Re Windsor Steam Coal Co (1901) Ltd [1929] 1 Ch 151 at 164–165 per Lawrence LJ.
44   See **12.8**.

entitled to rely on the provision that it may assume that no breach or event of default has occurred, and in particular does not need to seek random certificates or information. However, in examining the documents which it receives, and in particular the accounts, the trustee must, in the light of the *Bartlett* decision,[45] show the standard of special care and skill which it claims to have and which can reasonably be expected from experienced professional trustees.

(v) Exercise of discretions

12.20   In relation to the various discretions conferred on the trustee by the trust deed, the trustee is usually stated to have 'absolute and uncontrolled discretion' as to their exercise.[46] In such circumstances, the trustee, so long as it is acting bona fide, cannot be compelled to exercise them except to the extent provided in the trust deed[47] (or as may be specifically required under the Trustee Act 2000)[48] but, it would seem, must at least always consider whether to exercise them.[49] Unless there is a requirement in the trust deed to do so (and there usually is not), the trustee is not obliged to consult the holders before exercising any of its discretions (though, in practice, most trustees will consult if the matter is a serious one and it is practicable to do so), to accede to their wishes,[50] or to give reasons for the exercise or non-exercise of any of its discretions.[51] Where the trustee does exercise a discretion, the court has a residual right to interfere with the exercise if the

---

[45]   And the duty of care under the Trustee Act 2000, if that has not been excluded.

[46]   For an example provision, see **12.28**.

[47]   *Tempest v Lord Camoys* (1882) 21 ChD 571; *Prendergast v Prendergast* (1850) 3 HLC 195; *Re Brockbank* [1948] Ch 206; *Re George Whichelow Ltd* [1954] 1 WLR 5; *Re 90 Thornhill Road, Tolworth, Surrey* [1970] Ch 261.

[48]   See further **12.27**.

[49]   *Klug v Klug* [1918] 2 Ch 67; *Re Manisty's Settlement* [1974] Ch 17 at 25; *Re Gresham Life Assurance Society* (1872) LR 8 Ch App 446 at 450 per James LJ.

[50]   See, eg, *Re Brockbank* [1948] Ch 206.

[51]   *Re Beloved Wilkes's Charity* (1851) 3 Mac&G 440; *Re Gresham Life Assurance Society* (1872) LR 8 Ch App 446; *Re Londonderry's Settlement* [1965] Ch 918 at 928 per Harman LJ; *Wilson v The Law Debenture Trust Corporation plc* [1995] 2 All ER 337; although if the trustee does give reasons, they may justify the court interfering (*Klug v Klug* [1918] 2 Ch 67; *Re Londonderry's Settlement*, ibid at 928–929 per Harman LJ). See also Thomas [1997] JBL 514.

trustee's decision is 'unreasonable', in a similar sense to the *Wednesbury* principle applicable to public bodies.[52]

Fiduciary duties

12.21   A trustee's fiduciary duties can broadly be summarised as follows:

(a) it must act in good faith;

(b) it must not place itself in a position where its duty and interest conflict; and

(c) it must not make an unauthorised profit or act for its own benefit or for the benefit of a third party without authority.

12.22   Since the business of corporate trustees involves accepting multiple trusteeships, and many corporate trustees are part of international banking groups, the rule against conflicts of interest is particularly relevant in the context of securities issues.

(i) Duty to avoid conflict of interest and duty

12.23   The trustee, like other fiduciaries, must not put itself in a position in which its interest and its duty may be in conflict.[53] The duty is not merely to avoid existing conflicts but also to avoid engagements which may

52   See in particular *Concord Trust v Law Debenture Trust Corporation plc* at first instance [2004] EWHC 1216 at paras 30–34 per Sir Andrew Morritt VC (reversed on appeal but without any criticism of this point): 'provided that the discretion is exercised honestly and in good faith for the purposes for which it was conferred, and provided also that it was a true exercise of discretion in the sense that it was not capricious or arbitrary or so outrageous in its defiance of reason that it can properly be categorised as perverse, the courts will not intervene' (para 32). The onus is not on the trustee to prove reasonableness but on the person challenging to prove unreasonableness (para 33). See also *Indofood International Finance Ltd v JP Morgan Chase NA (No 1)* [2005] EWHC 973 at para 39 per Etherton J (the trustee's decision cannot be challenged provided it 'has asked itself the correct question, has adopted a correct interpretation of the Conditions, has taken into account all the relevant factors and ignored irrelevant factors, and has not arrived at a perverse decision, that is to say a decision at which no reasonable person in the position of the [trustee] could arrive'). Other formulations include: *Dundee General Hospitals Board of Management v Walker* [1952] 1 All ER 896 at 905 per Lord Reid (exercise of discretion impugnable not only on the basis of bad faith but also on the basis of a failure to appreciate the issue); *Re Manisty's Settlement* [1974] Ch 17 at 26 (discretion impugnable if it amounts to misconduct or is 'capricious'); *Re Tuck's Settlement Trusts* [1978] Ch 49 at 62 per Lord Denning MR (discretion not impugnable if the person in whom it is vested does not 'misconduct himself or come to a decision which is wholly unreasonable'); *Mettoy Pension Trustees Ltd v Evans* [1990] 1 WLR 1587 (the court can interfere if it is shown that the trustee did not have a proper understanding of the effect of its act and it is clear that, had it had a proper understanding, it would not have acted as it did); *Scott v National Trust* [1998] 2 All ER 705 (court can interfere if the trustee does not act responsibly and reasonably or if it does not inform itself of relevant matters); *Edge v Pensions Ombudsman* [2000] Ch 602 (court can interfere if the trustee has misdirected itself or reached an irrational decision). See also Hinks, T&ELJ, May 2000, p 22.
53   See *Aberdeen Rail Co v Blaikie Brothers* [1843–60] All ER Rep 249 per Lord Cranworth LC; *Imperial Mercantile Credit Association v Coleman* (1873) 6 HL 189; *Bray v Ford* [1896] AC 44; *Parker v McKenna* (1874) 10 Ch App 96; *Moody v Cox and Hatt* [1917] 2 Ch 71; *Regal (Hastings) Ltd v Gulliver* [1942] 1 All ER 378; *Boardman v Phipps* [1967] 2 AC 46. The prohibition appears, however, to have been relaxed somewhat, as a result of *Kelly v Cooper* [1992] 3 WLR 936.

potentially give rise to a conflict. But this does not extend to all possible conflicts which may arise:[54]

'In my view it means that the reasonable man looking at the relevant facts and circumstances of the particular case would think that there was a real sensible possibility of conflict.'

12.24 The situations which can most commonly give rise to an actual or potential conflict of interest include: where the trustee is also a private lender to the issuer;[55] where the trustee has invested in the issuer, either for its own account or through a trustee investment department; where the trustee has a corporate finance department which advises the issuer; where the trustee, or an entity affiliated with it, fulfils other roles in relation to the issue that involve it owing duties to the issuer (eg paying agent, custodian, etc); where there are common directors; and where the trustee acts as trustee under more than one issue by the issuer. In the last case, the potential conflict is obviously greater if the issues do not rank pari passu, eg where one is secured and the other unsecured, or one subordinated and the other unsubordinated.[56] In practice professional trustees will generally accept trusteeships of such issues (if each trusteeship is authorised by the other trust deed, which it usually is),[57] the rationale being that, so long as the issuer is not in any danger of insolvency, the risk of actual as opposed to potential conflict is assessed to be sufficiently remote as not to prevent the common trusteeships.[58]

(ii) Where conflict of interest and duty permissible

12.25 There are two situations where the trustee may legitimately place itself in a position where its interest and its duty may be in conflict:

(a) where the holders consent, so long as they are given full information on all the material circumstances and of the exact nature and extent of the trustee's interest;[59] or

(b) where the conflict is authorised by the trust deed.[60] The holding of investments in the issuer, the entry into other business transactions with

---

[54] *Boardman v Phipps* [1967] 2 AC 46 at 124 per Lord Upjohn.

[55] As in *Re Dorman, Long and Co Ltd* [1934] Ch 635.

[56] Since the trustee may be under a duty to the unsecured or subordinated holders to challenge the validity of the security or the subordination.

[57] For an example provision, see **12.28**.

[58] As to the course of action to be followed if the risk subsequently becomes greater, see below.

[59] See especially *Boardman v Phipps* [1967] 2 AC 46; *Lindgren v L & P Estates Ltd* [1968] Ch 572; *North and South Trust Co v Berkeley* [1971] 1 WLR 470 at 484–485; *New Zealand Netherlands Society 'Oranje' Incorporated v Kuys* [1973] 2 All ER 1222; *Fullwood v Hurley* [1928] 1 KB 498. The trustee cannot merely disclose that it has an interest: *Imperial Mercantile Credit Association v Coleman* (1873) 6 HL 189; *Dunne v English* (1874) 18 Eq 524; *Costa Rica Railway Co Ltd v Forwood* [1901] 1 Ch 746 at 761 per Vaughan Williams LJ. As to obtaining such consent by majority resolution of the holders, see **Chapter 16**.

the issuer and the holding of trusteeships under other issues of the issuer are all usually expressly authorised,[61] but there are a number of limits on the effectiveness of such authorisations:

(i)   notwithstanding the authorisation, the presence of the conflict may make it more difficult for the trustee to prove that it acted with the requisite standard of care;[62]

(ii)   the authorisation itself may be struck down, particularly as it is in effect 'imposed' on investors who may be relatively unsophisticated and usually do not have an opportunity to participate in its preparation;[63] and

(iii)   notwithstanding the authorisation, the presence of the conflict may make a court less willing to relieve the trustee from liability for breach of trust under s 61 of the Trustee Act 1925.[64]

(iii) Trustees' options where conflict arises

12.26   Where a conflict has arisen, there are generally four alternatives open to the trustee: first, to seek the consent of the holders by means of a resolution;[65] secondly, to resign as trustee (but the trust deed usually expressly provides that the resignation is not effective until a successor trustee has been appointed and approved by the holders); thirdly, to appoint an additional trustee to carry out its functions, if this is permitted by the trust deed; and, fourthly, to delegate its powers and duties, if this is permitted by the trust deed[66] and any applicable provisions of the Trustee Act 2000 are complied with.[67]

---

60   See *Re Llewellin's Will Trusts* [1949] Ch 225; *Boardman v Phipps* [1967] 2 AC 46; *Brown v IRC* [1965] AC 244; *New Zealand Netherlands Society 'Oranje' Incorporated v Kuys* [1973] 2 All ER 1222; *Space Investments Ltd v Canadian Imperial Bank of Commerce Trust Co (Bahamas) Ltd* [1986] 3 All ER 75. See also Mowbray (1996) 10(2) TruLI, pp 49 to 50. Cf *Re Drexel Burnham Lambert UK Pension Plan* [1995] 1 WLR 32 at 43.

61   For an example provision, see **12.28**.

62   See *Re Dorman, Long and Co Ltd* [1934] 1 Ch 635; the trustee was a bank that had lent to the company; as trustee it recommended to the holders a scheme of arrangement which benefited it as lender. 'It is idle, I think, to suggest that it is possible for a bank which is owed about one and a half million pounds . . . to act impartially in considering such a scheme': per Maugham J at 671.

63   See *Re Dorman, Long and Co Ltd* [1934] 1 Ch 635; a provision permitting the trustee to act as banker to the company was described by Maugham J (at 671) as 'a most undesirable clause' and 'one which I myself would never have approved, nor, I believe, would the stockholders if they had been told it was to be inserted or had any idea how it might operate'. As a precautionary measure, the authorisations to the trustee are now usually disclosed in general terms in the offering circular. Section 192(1) of the Companies Act 1985 may also be relevant: see earlier.

64   See, eg, *Re Pauling's Settlement Trusts* [1964] Ch 303 at 339 per Willmer LJ.

65   As to which, see **Chapter 16**.

66   Trustees may not, as a general rule, delegate in the absence of authorisation to do so (but see Trustee Act 1925, ss 23 and 25 and Trustee Delegation Act 1999): see *Snell's Equity* (30th edn, 2000), pp 301–305. Delegation was the solution adopted in 1990 by the trustee of the various issues by members of the British & Commonwealth Group (*Financial Times*, 9 May 1990, p 27; *Re British & Commonwealth Holdings plc (No 3)* [1992] 1 WLR 672 at 674–675). For an example delegation provision, see **12.28**.

67   See further below.

Specific duties under the Trustee Act 2000

12.27 In addition to the general duty of care referred to above,[68] the Trustee Act 2000 imposes specific duties in particular circumstances. Of these, the most relevant for corporate trustees are the following:

(a) Whenever the trustee is exercising a power of investment (whether the general power of investment under the Act or a power under the trust deed), it must: have regard to the 'standard investment criteria';[69] review the investments from time to time;[70] and obtain and consider 'proper advice'.[71] These duties cannot be excluded or restricted.[72]

(b) There are restrictions on the terms of appointment of an agent[73] and the delegation of asset management functions.[74] Though it is not totally clear, it is thought that these restrictions do not apply to appointments and delegations under powers in the trust deed (as opposed to those made under the powers in the Act).

(c) The trustee must keep under review all appointments that it has made of agents, nominees and custodians (and, if it considers it necessary, intervene).[75] However, this duty may be excluded or restricted in the trust deed.[76]

EXAMPLE PROTECTIVE PROVISIONS

12.28 Typical provisions in a trust deed (in this example, for a eurobond issue) to increase the trustee's protection from liability and to deal with the other matters discussed above would read as follows:

1. **Provisions supplemental to the Trustee Acts**

   Where there are any inconsistencies between the Trustee Acts[77] and the provisions of this Trust Deed, the provisions of this Trust Deed shall prevail to the extent allowed by law. In the case of an inconsistency with the Trustee Act 2000 of Great Britain, the provisions of this Trust Deed shall take effect as a restriction or exclusion for the purposes of that Act. The Trustee shall have all the powers conferred upon trustees by the Trustee Acts and the benefit of the following additional provisions:

   (A)   The Trustee may act on the advice or opinion of or any information obtained from any lawyer, valuer, accountant,

---

68 At **12.11**.

69 Trustee Act 2000, s 4(1). The 'standard investment criteria' are set out in s 4(3).

70 Trustee Act 2000, s 4(2).

71 Trustee Act 2000, s 5.

72 But the general power of investment under the Act may: ibid, s 6(1).

73 Trustee Act 2000, s 14.

74 Trustee Act 2000, s 15.

75 Trustee Act 2000, s 22(1).

76 Trustee Act 2000, s 26.

77 Defined as the Trustee Act 1925 and the Trustee Act 2000.

surveyor, banker, broker, auctioneer or other expert (whether obtained by the Issuer, the Trustee or otherwise, whether or not addressed to the Trustee, and whether or not the advice, opinion or information, or any engagement letter or other related document, contains a monetary or other limit on liability). The Trustee will not be responsible to anyone for any Liability[78] occasioned by so acting.

(B)　　Any such advice, opinion or information may be sent or obtained by letter, telex or fax and the Trustee shall not be liable for acting in good faith on any advice, opinion or information purporting to be conveyed by such means even if it contains an error or is not authentic.

(C)　　If the Trustee, in the exercise of its functions, requires to be satisfied or to have information as to any fact or the expediency of any act, it may call for and accept as sufficient evidence of that fact or the expediency of that act a certificate signed by any two Directors of the Issuer. The Trustee need not call for further evidence and will not be responsible for any Liability that may be occasioned by acting on such a certificate.

(D)　　The Trustee may hold this Trust Deed and any related documents or deposit them with any bank or any entity whose business includes the safe custody of documents or with any lawyer or firm of lawyers believed by the Trustee to be of good repute. The Trustee will not be responsible for, and need not insure against, any Liability incurred in connection with any such holding or deposit, and may pay all sums due in respect of any such deposit.

(E)　　The Trustee will not be responsible for the receipt or application by the Issuer of the proceeds of the issue of the Notes, the exchange of any Global Note for another Global Note or definitive Notes or the delivery of any Global Note or definitive Notes to the person(s) entitled to it or them.

(F)　　The Trustee need not notify anyone of the execution of this Trust Deed or any related documents or take any steps to find out whether an Event of Default or Potential Event of Default has happened. Until it has actual knowledge or express notice pursuant to this Trust Deed to the contrary, the Trustee may assume that no Event of Default or Potential Event of Default has happened and that the Issuer is performing all its obligations under this Trust Deed, the Notes and the Coupons.

(G)　　Unless expressly provided otherwise in this Trust Deed:

(i)　　the Trustee will have absolute and uncontrolled discretion as to the exercise or non-exercise of its functions under this Trust Deed;

(ii)　　any such exercise or non-exercise will, as between the Trustee and the Noteholders and Couponholders, be

---

[78] Normally defined as 'any loss, damage, cost, charge, claim, demand, expense, judgment, action, proceeding or other liability whatsoever (including, without limitation, in respect of taxes, duties, levies, imposts and other charges)'.

conclusive and binding on the Noteholders and Couponholders;

(iii)   the Trustee shall not be responsible for any Liability which may result from any such exercise or non-exercise; and

(iv)   in particular, the Trustee shall not be obliged to act at the request or direction of the Noteholders or otherwise under this Trust Deed or to take any other action under this Trust Deed unless it has first been indemnified to its satisfaction against all Liabilities to which it may render itself liable or which it may incur by so doing.

(H)   The Trustee will not be liable to anyone for having acted in good faith on a direction, request or Written Resolution of Noteholders purporting to have been given or signed by the requisite number of Noteholders or a resolution purporting to have been passed at a meeting of the Noteholders in respect of which minutes have been made and signed, even if it is later found that the request, direction or Written Resolution was not given or signed by the requisite number of Noteholders, that there was a defect in the constitution of the meeting or the passing of the resolution, or that for any reason the resolution, direction or request was not valid or binding upon the Noteholders and Couponholders.

(I)   The Trustee will not be liable to anyone by reason of having accepted as valid or not having rejected any Note or Coupon purporting to be such and later found to be forged or not authentic.

(J)   Without prejudice to the right of indemnity given by law to trustees, the Issuer will indemnify the Trustee and every Appointee[79] against all Liabilities to which it or he may be or become subject or which may be incurred by it or him in carrying out any of its or his functions under this Trust Deed or the appointment or in any other way arising out of or in connection with this Trust Deed or the appointment (including, without limitation, Liabilities incurred in disputing or defending any of the foregoing).

(K)   Any consent or approval given by the Trustee for the purposes of this Trust Deed may be given on such terms and subject to such conditions (if any) as the Trustee thinks fit and may be given retrospectively.

(L)   Unless ordered to do so by a court of competent jurisdiction, the Trustee shall not be required to disclose to any Noteholder or Couponholder any information (including, without limitation, information of a confidential, financial or price sensitive nature) made available to the Trustee by the Issuer or any other person in connection with this Trust Deed.

(M)   Where it is necessary or desirable to convert any sum from one currency to another it shall (unless otherwise provided by this Trust Deed or required by law) be converted at such rate or rates,

---

[79] Normally defined as 'any attorney, manager, agent, delegate, nominee, custodian or other person appointed by the Trustee under this Trust Deed'.

in accordance with such method and as at such date as may be
specified by the Trustee (having regard to current rates of
exchange, if available). Any rate, method and date so specified
will be binding on the Issuer, the Noteholders and the
Couponholders.

(N)	In relation to an event set out in Condition [*Events of Default*] that
does not become an Event of Default unless the Trustee issues a
certificate that such event is, in its opinion, materially prejudicial
to the interests of the Noteholders, the Trustee shall have absolute
and uncontrolled discretion as to whether to issue that certificate
and may treat the event as including the circumstances leading to it
and the consequences resulting from it. Any such certificate will be
conclusive and will bind the Issuer, the Noteholders and the
Couponholders.

(O)	As between itself and the Noteholders and Couponholders, the
Trustee may determine all questions and doubts arising in relation
to any of the provisions of this Trust Deed, the Notes or the
Coupons. Each such determination, whether or not relating in
whole or in part to the acts or proceedings of the Trustee, will be
conclusive and will bind the Trustee, the Noteholders and the
Couponholders.

(P)	In connection with the exercise by it of any of its functions under
this Trust Deed (including, without limitation, any modification,
waiver, authorisation, determination or substitution), the Trustee
shall have regard to the general interests of the Noteholders as a
class and shall not have regard to any interests arising from
circumstances particular to individual Noteholders or
Couponholders (whatever their number). In particular, but without
limitation, the Trustee shall not have regard to the consequences of
any such exercise for individual Noteholders or Couponholders
(whatever their number) resulting from their being for any purpose
domiciled or resident in, or otherwise connected with, or subject to
the jurisdiction of, any particular territory or any political subdivision thereof, and the Trustee shall not be entitled to require,
nor shall any Noteholder or Couponholder be entitled to claim,
from the Issuer, the Trustee or any other person any
indemnification or payment in respect of any tax consequence of
any such exercise upon individual Noteholders or Couponholders
except to the extent already provided for in Condition [*Tax gross-
up*] and/or any additional or substitute undertaking given under
this Trust Deed.

(Q)	Any Trustee that is a lawyer, accountant, broker or other person
engaged in a profession or business may charge and be paid all
usual professional and other charges and disbursements for work
and business done and time spent by him or his firm in relation to
matters arising in connection with this Trust Deed.

(R)	Whenever it thinks fit, the Trustee may delegate (by power of
attorney or otherwise) to any person (whether a joint Trustee or
not) all or any of its functions under this Trust Deed. The

delegation may be made on such terms (including power to sub-delegate) and subject to such conditions and regulations as the Trustee may think fit in the interests of the Noteholders. The Trustee will not be obliged to supervise the proceedings or acts of the delegate or sub-delegate and will not be responsible to anyone for any Liability incurred as a result of any misconduct or default by the delegate or sub-delegate. The Trustee will give notice to the Issuer of any such delegation or any renewal, extension or termination thereof as soon as reasonably practicable.

(S) The Trustee may in the conduct of its functions, instead of acting personally, employ and pay an agent (whether or not a lawyer or other professional person) to transact or conduct, or concur in transacting or conducting, any business and to do, or concur in doing, all acts required to be done in connection with this Trust Deed (including the receipt and payment of money). The Trustee will not be obliged to supervise the proceedings or acts of the agent and will not be responsible to anyone for any Liability incurred as a result of any misconduct or default by the agent.

(T) The Trustee may appoint and pay a custodian or nominee on any terms in relation to assets of the trusts constituted by this Trust Deed. The Trustee will not be obliged to supervise the proceedings or acts of the custodian or nominee and will not be responsible to anyone for any Liability incurred as a result of any misconduct or default by the custodian or nominee.

(U) The Trustee will not be responsible to anyone for the execution, delivery, legality, effectiveness, adequacy, genuineness, validity, performance, enforceability or admissibility in evidence of this Trust Deed or any related document and will not be liable for any failure to obtain any relevant licence, consent or other authority.

(V) The Trustee will not be responsible to anyone for failing to request, require or receive any legal opinion relating to this Trust Deed, the Notes or the Coupons or for checking or commenting upon the content of any such legal opinion.

(W) No provision of this Trust Deed requires the Trustee to do anything which:

(i) may be illegal or contrary to applicable law or regulation; or

(ii) may cause it to expend or risk its own funds or otherwise incur any Liability in the performance of its functions, if it has reasonable grounds for believing that repayment of the funds or adequate indemnity against the risk or Liability is not assured to it.

(X) The Trustee will not be responsible to anyone for the maintenance of or failure to maintain any rating of the Notes by any rating agency.

(Y) The Trustee will not be responsible to anyone for, or for investigating any matter which is the subject of, any recital, statement, representation, warranty or covenant of anyone in this Trust Deed or any related agreement or document.

2.   Trustee's liability

If the Trustee fails to show the degree of care and diligence required of it as trustee, having regard to the provisions of this Trust Deed conferring on it any trusts, powers, authorities or discretions, nothing in this Trust Deed will exempt the Trustee from or indemnify it against any liability for breach of trust which would otherwise attach to it.[80]

3.   Trustee contracting with the Issuer

Neither the Trustee nor any director, officer, holding company, subsidiary or associated company of a corporation acting as Trustee shall, by reason of its or his fiduciary position, be precluded from:

> (i)   entering into or having an interest in any contract or financial or other transaction or arrangement with the Issuer or any associated person (including without limitation acquiring, holding or dealing with, or acting as paying or calculation agent in respect of, the Notes or any other securities of the Issuer or any associated person); or
>
> (ii) acting as trustee in relation to any other securities issued by or relating to the Issuer or any associated person or holding any other office of profit under the Issuer or any associated person.

The Trustee and each director, officer, holding company, subsidiary and associated company will be entitled to exercise their rights and perform their duties in relation thereto without regard to the interests of the Noteholders (even if contrary or prejudicial to the interests of the Noteholders), will not be responsible for any resultant Liability occasioned to the Noteholders, and may retain any profit or other benefit received by them.

Where any holding company, subsidiary or associated company of the Trustee, or any director or officer of the Trustee acting other than in his capacity as such a director or officer, has any information, the Trustee shall not as a result be deemed also to have knowledge of that information. Unless it has actual knowledge of that information, the Trustee will not be responsible for any loss suffered by Noteholders resulting from the Trustee failing to take that information into account in acting or refraining from acting under this Trust Deed.

---

[80]   This wording reflects the effect of s 192(1) of the Companies Act 1985: see further **12.13ff**.

Chapter Thirteen

ATTRACTING LENDERS

INTRODUCTION

13.1 The purpose of this chapter is to describe the main ways in which lenders may be solicited (whether publicly or privately), both for bank lending and for the issue of debt securities, and to highlight the main UK statutory provisions regarding invitational material. US restrictions on invitational material are described in **Chapter 14**.

METHODS OF SOLICITATION

Syndicated loans

13.2 In the case of syndicated loans, the syndication process has two principal phases. The first is the pre-mandate phase, during which the company discusses with potential arrangers the type and amount of facility which it requires and then appoints, or 'mandates', one (or more) bank(s) to act as arranger (or co-arrangers). The second phase is the post-mandate phase, during which the syndication itself takes place and the facility agreements are negotiated. The post-mandate phase normally lasts about six to eight weeks, and culminates in the signing of the agreements. The arranger's role usually involves (a) selecting, in consultation with the company, the other banks to form the syndicate and the size of their involvement, (b) soliciting commitments (on a 'subject to satisfactory documentation' basis) from the selected banks to form the syndicate (known as 'running the syndicate book'), (c) if an information memorandum giving information regarding the company is considered appropriate (eg because the company is not well known), preparing this in conjunction with the company and circulating it to the banks, (d) preparing and negotiating with both the company and the other syndicate members the facility documents, and (e) organising the signing arrangements.[1] Where, however, the facility has to be put in place quickly (eg in the case of an acquisition financing), the

---

[1]   On the syndication process, see further Rhodes, *Syndicated Lending* (4th edn, 2004), Chapter 4; Terry, *International Finance and Investment – Multinational Corporate Banking* (3rd edn, 1994), Chapter 7; Fight, *Syndicated Lending* (2nd edn, 2000), Module 2; Cranston, *Principles of Banking Law* (2nd edn, 2002), pp 54-62.

agreement may well be signed only by a core group of banks (or maybe only one bank), with syndication taking place after signing.

Domestic stock

13.3   The three main ways in which domestic stock is issued are by means of a placing, a rights issue to existing shareholders, and takeover offer consideration. The most common is probably the placing.[2] The process is initiated by the company appointing a bank or broker (usually its existing financial adviser) to act as its arranger. However, instead of commitments being solicited over a period of time, as with a syndicated loan, the placing takes place during the course of one day, known as 'impact day'. The normal procedure is for the arranger to agree to underwrite the issue at or before 8 am on impact day (by signing the placing agreement),[3] and then to despatch provisional invitation letters (known as 'pre-placing letters') and preliminary offering circulars to the targeted placees at 8 am. The stock is normally offered on the basis of a stated margin over a comparable gilt-edged security, with the issue yield, rate of interest and issue price being determined later in the day (usually at 3 pm), by reference to the then market price of that gilt, once provisional acceptances have been received from the placees. Formal placing letters and final offering circulars are sent the following morning for formal acceptance to those placees who have provisionally accepted. The trust deed will then usually be executed within the next two weeks (but in any event prior to formal allotment).

Eurobonds

13.4   In the case of eurobonds, the issue procedure differs according to whether the issue is in the traditional 'stand-alone' format (ie where the documents are negotiated specifically for that issue) or under an EMTN programme (where most of the documentation has already been negotiated when the programme was established). The majority of issues are now made under EMTN programmes.

(a)   Stand-alone issues

13.5   The issue procedure for a traditional 'stand-alone' eurobond issue has three principal phases. The first, as with a syndicated loan, is the pre-mandate phase, during which the company discusses with potential lead managers the type and amount of issue required and then awards the

---

2   Stock issued pursuant to a rights issue or a takeover offer is usually ULS or CULS (as to which terms, see **Chapter 3**) rather than secured stock.

3   In practice, the placing agreement is usually signed the evening before impact day and held 'in escrow' overnight.

mandate to one particular bank to act as the lead manager.[4] The second phase, the pre-signing phase, involves the lead manager soliciting commitments (on a 'subject to signing of the subscription agreement' basis) from selected financial institutions to form the management group and to underwrite the issue, preparing and negotiating with the company (and, occasionally, the other managers) the subscription agreement and the offering circular, and organising the signing meeting. At the signing meeting, the subscription agreement (which contains the managers' underwriting commitments)[5] is signed and immediately after the signing the offering circular is formally published. The management commitments are solicited during the course of one day, known as the 'launch date'. On the launch date, the lead manager usually contacts by telephone the proposed managers, and then sends invitation telexes or faxes to those institutions which have expressed interest, confirming the oral invitation. Replies are normally required by telex or fax within 24 hours. During the pre-signing phase, also known as the 'selling period', the managers sell the eurobonds to investors, on a preliminary basis subject to allocation by the lead manager and also subject to signing of the subscription agreement. The eurobonds are allocated among the managers by the lead manager immediately before the signing of the subscription agreement.

13.6 The issue structure of a 'stand-alone' eurobond issue used to involve the formation of a management group (who were to 'subscribe or procure subscribers'), an underwriting group (who in effect sub-underwrote the managers' underwriting obligations) and a selling group (who were obliged to assist in the distribution to the ultimate investors, but did not undertake an underwriting obligation). Nowadays, underwriting and selling groups are rare, with the management group obliged to take up the issue to the extent that other investors cannot be found.

13.7 The third phase of the issue procedure is the post-signing phase, during which the managers will confirm sales to investors on the basis of the eurobonds allocated to each manager, and the lead manager, the company, the paying agents and, if applicable, the trustee will negotiate and settle the final detailed terms of the issue. The post-signing phase culminates with the closing, usually one, or sometimes two, weeks after the signing, at which the

---

4   It used to be the case that the interest rate and issue price would be agreed between the company and the lead manager immediately prior to the launch date (described below). Such a structure (known as an 'open-priced deal') has now been almost completely replaced by the 'pre-priced deal', in which the interest rate and issue price are agreed as part of the terms of the mandate. A variant of the pre-priced deal is the 'bought deal', in which the lead manager 'commits' to the company as part of the terms of the mandate to purchase all the eurobonds to be issued, irrespective of whether other managers are found.

5   The practice is that these commitments are undertaken by the managers on a joint and several basis. Cf the position regarding syndicated loans, where the banks contract on a several basis: see **2.17**.

net proceeds of the issue are paid to the company by the lead manager and the eurobonds are formally issued by the company.[6]

13.8   Alternatively, the issue may take the form of a private placement. In such a case, the above procedure can be greatly simplified, with the whole issue being taken up by a small number of investors targeted in advance by the lead manager, and either no or only a small management group.

(b)   Issues under EMTN programmes

13.9   On the establishment of an EMTN programme, the issuer signs a programme agreement with a selected panel of financial institutions (referred to as 'dealers') and issues a prospectus in relation to the programme. Under the programme agreement, each dealer agrees, on an uncommitted basis, to subscribe for bonds as and when the issuer and that dealer so agree. The prospectus is usually applicable to issues to be made within one year from its date of publication (subject to an obligation on the part of the issuer to update it for any material developments relating to the issuer). After the year has elapsed, an updated prospectus is published, and the issuer and dealers sign a fresh programme agreement, valid for a further year. Listing is obtained on the establishment, and each annual update, of the programme in respect of bonds to be issued under the programme during the coming year.

13.10   The only substantive documents needed, therefore, for an individual issue are: a short supplemental document that records the specific terms of the issue agreed between the issuer and the relevant dealer and which is submitted to the listing authority in order to obtain the listing for that issue;[7] and the global bond representing the bonds being issued.[8]

13.11   It is still possible under an EMTN programme, however, to issue bonds through a syndicate of managers, in a similar way to the syndication of a 'stand-alone' issue. In such a case, one dealer is appointed as lead manager with the responsibility of forming the syndicate. A subscription agreement, in a form scheduled to the programme agreement, is signed between the issuer and the syndicate.

---

[6]   On the eurobond distribution and marketing process, see further Terry, *International Finance and Investment – Multinational Corporate Banking* (3rd edn, 1994), pp 591–599; Lee, *Euromoney*, March 1995, pp 30–36; Fisher, *Eurosecurities and Their Related Derivatives* (1997), pp 65–85, 279–285.

[7]   Usually referred to as 'final terms' where the programme is listed on a regulated market and as a 'pricing supplement' otherwise. In the case of a programme listed on a regulated market, if the terms of the issue are materially different from those envisaged in the programme prospectus, further documentation may be required, in the form of either a 'supplement' (pursuant to FSMA 2000, s 87G) or a 'unitary prospectus' (technically, a new prospectus but incorporating the existing programme prospectus by reference: it is a means of avoiding triggering the 'cooling off period' described at **13.38**).

[8]   On global bonds, see further **3.3**.

13.12   Three particular features of the flexibility of EMTN programmes are worth mentioning. First, the initiative for a new issue does not always come from the issuer. Dealers can approach the issuer, through a process known as 'reverse enquiry', with suggestions for new issues based on investor demand that the dealer has identified. Secondly, further dealers can be added by the issuer without the consent of the existing dealers, either to the programme panel or just for the purpose of a specific issue (the 'dealer for a day' concept). And, thirdly, programmes can cater for more than one issuer. These 'multi-issuer' programmes are most relevant where the corporate group may wish to raise funds through a variety of subsidiaries. Usually, though, the group's parent would act as guarantor.

UK RESTRICTIONS ON PROMOTIONAL MATERIAL

13.13   The main UK statutory provisions regulating the contents of invitational material are contained in the Financial Services and Markets Act 2000 ('FSMA 2000'), as amended to implement the EU Prospectus Directive.

Overview

13.14   Prior to the implementation on 1 July 2005 of the EU Prospectus Directive,[9] the applicable legal restrictions in relation to offers of securities depended on whether the securities were to be offered to the public and whether they were to be listed.[10] As a result of the amendments to Part VI of the FSMA 2000 (and the resultant rules made by the Financial Services Authority (the 'FSA')), in order to implement the Prospectus Directive, the applicable restrictions now depend on: (i) whether the securities are to be offered to the public (with a revised definition); (ii) whether the securities are to be admitted to official listing; and (iii) if they are to be listed, whether the market on which they are to be admitted to trading is a regulated market or not. The restrictions are, in summary, as follows:

(a)   if the securities are to be offered to the public in the UK or admitted to trading on a regulated market situated or operating in the UK, an approved prospectus must be made available to the public before the offer or the request for admission is made;[11]

(b)   if the securities are otherwise to be admitted to official listing (ie involving admission to trading on an unregulated market), listing particulars must first be approved by the FSA and published;[12] and

---

9   2003/71/EC.
10   Part VI of the FSMA 2000 in the case of securities to be listed and the Public Offers of Securities Regulations 1995 in the case of public offers of other securities.
11   FSMA 2000, ss 85(1), 85(2).
12   FSMA 2000, s 79(1).

(c) promotional material in other circumstances is regulated as financial
     promotion under s 21 of the FSMA 2000.

13.15 The main functions of the FSA, in the context of a new issue of
securities, are the maintenance of the official list,[13] the admission of
securities to the official list[14] and the making of rules for the purposes of
Part VI.[15] The rules that have been made by the FSA consist of:

(i)   listing rules[16] – which relate to the official list;
(ii) prospectus rules[17] – which deal with the contents, validity, etc, of
      prospectuses relating to transferable securities;[18] and
(iii) disclosure rules[19] – which relate to disclosure of information in respect
      of financial instruments which have been admitted to trading on a
      regulated market[20] or for which a request for admission to trading on
      such market has been made.

13.16 In order to be admitted to the official list, securities must be
admitted to trading on the London Stock Exchange's market for listed
securities.[21] The introduction of the concept of a regulated market into
Part VI of the FSMA 2000 has led to the development by the London Stock
Exchange of two separate markets for listed debt securities: the Gilt Edged
and Fixed Interest Market and the Professional Securities Market. The
former serves as the UK's regulated market, while the latter is unregulated.

WHEN IS AN APPROVED PROSPECTUS REQUIRED?

13.17 If transferable securities are to be offered to the public in the UK or
admitted to trading on a regulated market situated or operating in the UK
(ie the Gilt Edged and Fixed Interest Market of the London Stock
Exchange), an approved prospectus must be made available to the public
before the offer or request for admission is made.[22] Failure to do so is an

---

13   FSMA 2000, s 74(1).
14   FSMA 2000, s 74(2).
15   FSMA 2000, s 73A(1).
16   Made pursuant to FSMA 2000, s 73A(2).
17   Made pursuant to FMSA 2000, ss 73A(4) and 84.
18   Transferable securities in this context include anything which is a transferable security for the
     purposes of the Investment Services Directive 93/22/EC, other than money-market instruments for
     the purposes of that Directive which have a maturity of less than 12 months, those listed in Sch 11A
     to the FSMA 2000 and such other transferable securities as may be specified in the prospectus rules
     (FSMA 2000, ss 85(5), 85(6) and 102A(3)). The definition of securities will differ slightly once the
     Markets in Financial Instruments Directive 2004/39/EC repeals the current Investment Services
     Directive (which is to have effect from 31 January 2007).
19   Made pursuant to FSMA 2000, s 73A(3).
20   As defined in Art 1(13) of the Investment Services Directive 93/22/EC.
21   Listing rules, para 2.2.3.
22   FSMA 2000, ss 85(1) and 85(2).

offence punishable by a fine or, on conviction on indictment, imprisonment for up to two years.[23]

An 'offer of transferable securities to the public'

13.18 'Offer of transferable securities to the public' is defined in s 102B of the FSMA 2000 as:

> 'a communication to any person which presents sufficient information on –
>
> (a) the transferable securities to be offered, and
> (b) the terms on which they are offered,
>
> to enable an investor to decide to buy or subscribe for the securities in question.'

Specifically excluded from this definition are communications made in connection with trading on a regulated market.[24] This exclusion was incorporated to address concerns that normal secondary market communications would be caught.

13.19 Where the offer is made to a person in the UK, it is an offer to the public in the UK.

13.20 This very broad definition, on which the FSA has declined to provide formal binding guidance,[25] is qualified by a number of exemptions. Exempt offers to the public include the following.

Qualified investor

13.21 Offers made or directed at qualified investors only are exempt offers to the public.[26] The definition of qualified investor is much broader than the concept of professional investors under the old regime and includes:

(a) legal entities that are authorised or regulated to operate in the financial markets or, if not so authorised or regulated, whose corporate purpose is solely to invest in securities;
(b) national and regional governments, central banks and international and supranational institutions;
(c) legal entities that have two or more of (1) an average of at least 250 employees during the last financial year, (2) a total balance sheet of more than €43,000,000 and (3) an annual net return of more than €50,000,000, as shown in its last annual or consolidated account;

---

23 FSMA 2000, s 85(3).
24 FSMA 2000, s 102B(5).
25 See FSA Newsletter *List!*, Issue No 10.
26 FSMA 2000, s 86(1)(a).

(d) individual and corporate investors who fulfil the relevant criteria set out in s 87R of the FSMA 2000 and who are entered on the register of the FSA; and

(e) investors authorised by an EEA State other than the UK to be considered as a qualified investor for the purposes of the Prospectus Directive.

No more than 100 offerees

13.22 An offer is exempt if it is made to or directed at fewer than 100 persons, other than qualified investors, per EEA State.[27] Any offers to trustees of a trust, to members of a partnership in their capacity as such and to two or more persons jointly are specifically stated as being treated as the making of an offer to a single person.[28]

Large offers

13.23 Certain offers are exempt by virtue of being large in value,[29] ie if the minimum consideration which may be paid by any person for transferable securities acquired by him is at least €50,000 (or an equivalent amount).

Small offers

13.24 An offer will be exempt if the total consideration for the securities being offered cannot exceed €100,000 (or an equivalent amount).[30]

13.25 Where an offer falls within one of these exemptions and no application for the securities to be admitted to trading on a regulated market is sought, the prospectus rules will not apply.

Admission to trading on a regulated market

13.26 In relation to debt securities, as mentioned earlier, the Gilt Edged and Fixed Interest Market serves as the UK's regulated market while the Professional Securities Market is unregulated. Consequently, where debt securities are to be officially listed, it is only applications for securities to be admitted to trading on the Gilt Edged and Fixed Interest Market that trigger the need for an approved prospectus within the prospectus rules; applications to the Professional Securities Market instead require the publication of listing particulars under the listing rules.[31] Admission to trading on the Professional Securities Market is only available for 'specialist securities' (defined in the listing rules as 'securities which, because of their

---

[27] FSMA 2000, s 86(1)(b).
[28] FSMA 2000, s 86(3).
[29] FSMA 2000, s 86(1)(c).
[30] FSMA 2000, s 86(1)(d).
[31] Provided that there is also no offer to the public.

nature, are normally bought and traded by a limited number of investors who are particularly knowledgeable in investment matters') and certain other limited categories of securities.[32]

Election under s 87H

13.27 Certain issuers that are otherwise exempt from the requirement to produce and make available an approved prospectus, by virtue of their status and/or the type of securities to be offered to the public or admitted to trading on a regulated market, may elect to have a prospectus in relation to such securities. These issuers and securities include:

(i) non-equity transferable securities issued by governments and local or regional authorities of an EEA State, public international bodies of which an EEA State is a member, the European Central Bank and the central bank of an EEA State;
(ii) transferable securities unconditionally and irrevocably guaranteed by the government, or a local or regional authority, of an EEA State;
(iii) non-equity transferable securities, issued in a continuous or repeated manner by a credit institution, where the total consideration for the offer is less than €50,000 (or an equivalent amount) and the securities are not subordinated, convertible or exchangeable, do not give a right to subscribe to or acquire other types of securities and are not linked to a derivative instrument; and
(iv) transferable securities included in an offer where the total consideration of the offer is less than €2,500,000 (or an equivalent amount).

If such an election is made the prospectus rules would apply as if an approved prospectus would be required.

WHAT DO THE PROSPECTUS RULES REQUIRE?

13.28 Where the prospectus rules apply, an approved prospectus must be made available to the public prior to an offer to the public or an application for admission to trading on the Gilt Edged and Fixed Interest Market.

Approved prospectus

13.29 An approved prospectus is a prospectus approved by the competent authority of the home State in relation to the issuer of the securities, ie the FSA where the home State is the UK.

13.30 The 'home State' of an issuer is dependent on the place of incorporation of the issuer and the type and denomination of the securities.[33]

---

[32] Listing rules, para 4.1.1.

Broadly, the UK is the home State, and the FSA is therefore the competent authority by which a prospectus must be approved, in respect of the following:

(i) issues of equity securities or low denomination debt securities (ie non-equity securities with a minimum denomination of less than €1,000 (or equivalent in another currency)) by non-EU issuers where such securities were first intended to be offered to the public or admitted to trading on a regulated market after 31 December 2003 in the UK and by UK registered issuers; and

(ii) issues of high denomination debt securities where the issuer elects the UK as its home State.

13.31 Once the FSA is satisfied that the UK is the home State of the issuer, it must be satisfied that the prospectus contains all necessary information and that all other requirements of Part VI of the FSMA 2000 and the Prospectus Directive have been complied with.[34] A prospectus will contain all necessary information if it contains:

'the information necessary to enable investors to make an informed assessment of:

(a) the assets and liabilities, financial position, profits and losses, and prospects of the issuer of the transferable securities and of any guarantor; and

(b) the rights attaching to the securities.'[35]

13.32 This is a similar overall disclosure standard as was required under the previous regime although a number of changes have been introduced to the detailed content required in a prospectus. This is now assessed by reference to the relevant schedules and building blocks contained in the FSA Handbook.[36]

13.33 Which building blocks apply in relation to a particular issue will depend on the status of the issuer[37] and the nature of the securities.[38] More onerous disclosure is required in relation to retail issues, a concept that has been simplified under the current regulations, than for wholesale issues. The distinction is now based on the minimum denomination of the issue; retail issues being those with a minimum denomination of less than €50,000 (or

---

[33] FSMA 2000, s 102C.

[34] FSMA 2000, s 87A(1).

[35] FSMA 2000, s 87A(2).

[36] Appendix 3 of the prospectus rules. These have been incorporated, without amendment, from Commission Regulation (EC) No 809/2004 (the Prospectus Regulation).

[37] Special Building Blocks apply in relation to: Banks; Member States, third countries and their regional and local authorities; and Public International Bodies and OECD Member State guarantors.

[38] For example, whether these are debt/derivative/asset-backed and whether they fall within the retail or wholesale regime.

equivalent in another currency) and wholesale issues being those with a minimum denomination of at least €50,000 (or equivalent in another currency).

13.34 In addition to regulating the content of a prospectus, the prospectus rules also regulate the form of the prospectus and the order in which the contents must appear.[39] A prospectus may be made up of a single document, a tripartite document containing a registration document, a securities note and a summary or (in the case of a non-equity securities issued under an offering programme) a base prospectus and (for each issue under the programme) final terms. Information filed with the FSA may also be incorporated by reference.

13.35 The obligation to make the approved prospectus available to the public is satisfied by publication as soon as practicable, and in any case, at a reasonable time in advance of, and at the latest at the beginning of, the offer to the public or admission to trading on the regulated market, in accordance with the prospectus rules, ie by printing in a national newspaper; making available to the public, in printed form, free of charge from the registered office of the issuer and the offices of any financial intermediaries; in electronic form on the issuer's and any financial intermediaries' websites; or in electronic form on the website of the regulated market.[40] There is no longer an obligation to deliver a copy of the prospectus to the Registrar of Companies or to publish a formal notice relating to the admission of securities to trading.

Mutual recognition

13.36 Once a prospectus is approved in the home State it may be used for public offers and admissions to trading on regulated markets in other EEA States, subject to the prospectus being 'passported'.[41] Passporting a prospectus involves the provision of a certificate of approval and a copy of the prospectus from the competent authority of the home State to the competent authority of the host State[42] and a translation of the summary of the prospectus if required by the host State.[43] However, the effectiveness of such passporting is limited due to the failure of some EEA States fully to implement the Prospectus Directive.[44]

---

[39] Prospectus rules, section 2.2.
[40] FSMA 2000, s 84(2)(e) and prospectus rules, section 3.2.
[41] Articles 17 and 18 of the Prospectus Directive and s 87H of the FSMA 2000.
[42] FSMA 2000, s 87I.
[43] The FSA has stated that, as the host State in relation to the passporting of a prospectus into the UK, it will only require a translation of the summary into English where the prospectus is to be used for public offers (see FSA Policy Statement 05/7).
[44] At the time of writing (May 2006), Italy and Belgium had yet to implement the Prospectus Directive into national legislation.

Supplementary prospectuses

13.37 If, during the period between the approval of the prospectus and the end of the offer period or when trading of the securities on the regulated market begins,[45] there has been a significant new factor, material mistake or inaccuracy relating to the information included in the prospectus, the person on whose application the prospectus was approved must prepare, submit for approval and publish a supplementary prospectus containing the details of such.[46]

13.38 Where any such supplement is published and, prior to its publication, an investor has agreed to buy or subscribe for the securities to which it relates, he may withdraw his acceptance before the period of two working days beginning with the first working day after the date of publication.[47]

13.39 Much debate has been raised in relation to the introduction of this 'cooling off period', primarily in respect of who can exercise this right and how to determine the end of the offer period. It is unclear whether s 87Q is intended to give rights to dealers when acting as intermediaries or merely to the end investor. As market practice is still evolving, many take the cautious view that s 87Q does not give such rights to dealers and thus make contractual provision to address this point.

Advertisements

13.40 Announcements relating to a specific offer to the public or admission to trading on a regulated market of securities that aim to promote the potential subscription or acquisition of such securities are now regulated by the prospectus rules.[48] Such an announcement must not be issued unless it states that a prospectus has been or will be published, indicates where investors can, or will be able to, obtain a copy and contains a bold statement to the effect that it is not a prospectus but an advertisement and that any decision to invest in the relevant securities must be based on information contained in the prospectus. Additionally, it must be clearly recognisable as an advertisement, must not be inaccurate or misleading and must be consistent with the prospectus that has been or will be published.[49]

13.41 In addition, the rules against financial promotion will need to be borne in mind as advertisements are specifically carved out of the exemption

---

45 The FSA is of the view that, where there is an offer to the public and admission to trading on a regulated market sought in respect of the same securities, the relevant period during which a supplementary prospectus may be required under s 87G of the FSMA 2000 will end at the later of the closure of the offer period or when trading begins (see FSA Newsletter, *List!*, Issue No 11).
46 FSMA 2000, s 87G.
47 FSMA 2000, s 87Q(4).
48 Prospectus rules, section 3.3.
49 Prospectus rules, paras 3.3.2, 3.3.3.

in relation to documents required or permitted to be published under the prospectus rules.[50]

Annual disclosure

13.42 Issuers of securities[51] admitted to trading on the regulated market are required to provide an annual statement that refers to or contains all information that has been published or made available to the public over the previous 12 months in EEA States or third countries in compliance with Community and national securities laws.[52] This annual statement must be submitted to the FSA within 20 working days of the publication of the annual financial statements of the issuer.

Responsibility

13.43 Responsibility for the contents of a prospectus relating to non-equity securities lies with the following parties:

(i)   the issuer of the securities;
(ii) each person who accepts, and is stated in the prospectus as accepting, responsibility;
(iii) the offeror, if this is not the issuer;
(iv) the person requesting the admission to trading of the securities, if this is not the issuer;
(v)   the guarantor, in relation to information containing in the prospectus relating to the guarantor or the guarantee; and
(vi) each other person who has authorised the contents of the prospectus.

This contrasts with the responsibility for corporate issuers or offerors of equity securities. In the latter case, responsibility also lies with each of the directors of the issuer or offeror at the time the prospectus is published.

SECURITIES TO BE ADMITTED TO TRADING ON AN UNREGULATED MARKET

13.44 The listing rules apply to all applications for the admission of securities to the official list of the FSA. Where securities are to be admitted to official listing but a prospectus is not required to be produced under the Prospectus Directive (ie where the securities are to be admitted to trading on

---

[50]   Article 70(1)(d) of the Financial Services and Markets Act 2000 (Financial Promotion) Order 2005, SI 2005/1529. See further 'Financial promotion' below.

[51]   Issuers of non-equity securities with a denomination of at least €50,000 (or equivalent amount) are excluded from this requirement (prospectus rules, para 5.2.2).

[52]   Prospectus rules, para 5.2.1.

the Professional Securities Market[53] and there is no offer to the public), the listing rules require that listing particulars be approved by the FSA and published.[54]

Listing particulars

13.45 The overriding general duty of disclosure applicable to listing particulars is substantially similar to the general disclosure requirement under the prospectus rules.[55] The duty is to disclose:

> 'all such information as investors and their professional advisors would reasonably require, and reasonably expect to find there, for the purpose of making an informed assessment of:
>
> (a) the assets and liabilities, financial position, profits and losses, and prospects of the issuer of the securities; and
> (b) the rights attaching to the securities.'[56]

13.46 The obligation is imposed on persons responsible for the document, but only extends to the disclosure of information 'within the knowledge of any person responsible for the listing particulars … or … which it would be reasonable for him to obtain by making enquiries'.[57] It is also provided that in determining what information is required regard should be had to a number of factors, including: the nature of the securities and of the issuer; the nature of the persons likely to consider acquiring them; and the fact that certain matters may reasonably be expected to be within the knowledge of professional advisers whom the persons may reasonably be expected to consult.[58]

13.47 The main difference between the requirements for listing particulars and those for a prospectus is that there is no distinction between the disclosure required for retail issues and wholesale issues of non-equity securities. All non-equity securities for which listing particulars are required must comply with the disclosure requirements of the wholesale regime of the prospectus rules irrespective of their denomination.

Supplementary listing particulars

13.48 An obligation to produce, and to submit to the FSA for approval, supplementary listing particulars arises[59] if, after the listing particulars were

---

53   As seen earlier, available only if the securities are 'specialist securities' or fall within certain other limited categories.
54   Listing rules, para 2.2.11 and section 4.1.
55   See above.
56   FSMA 2000, s 80(1).
57   FSMA 2000, s 80(3).
58   FSMA 2000, s 80(4).
59   FSMA 2000, s 81(1).

prepared but before the commencement of dealing in the securities,[60] there is a significant[61] change affecting any matter required to be included in the listing particulars or a significant new matter arises that would have been required to be disclosed had it arisen when the listing particulars were prepared.

Responsibility

13.49 Regulation 6 of the Financial Services and Markets Act 2000 (Official Listing of Securities) Regulations 2001 defines persons responsible as being:

(i)   the issuer;
(ii) where the issuer is a body corporate, each director and each person authorising himself to be named as a director or having agreed to become a director;
(iii) each person who accepts and is stated as accepting responsibility for the particulars or the relevant part thereof; and
(iv) each other person who has authorised the contents of the particulars or the relevant part thereof. This formulation is wide: it would certainly cover accountants who verify the financial figures and, possibly, the managers of an issue whose names appear on the front of the listing particulars. It does not cover, however, those giving advice as to the contents in a professional capacity (eg solicitors).[62]

13.50 This list is reduced, however, if (as will be the case in most situations) the securities are 'specialist securities'.[63] In that case, reg 9 provides that persons falling within categories (i) and (ii) above (ie issuers and directors) are not responsible unless they fall within category (iii) above (ie they accept responsibility). Under para 4.2.13 of the listing rules, the issuer must accept responsibility for the listing particulars, and the directors may, but need not, do so. The net effect is that, in the context of specialist securities, directors of the issuer will not be 'responsible' for the listing particulars unless they accept, and are stated as accepting, responsibility.

---

[60]   After the commencement of dealings, the extent to which the disclosure will be required will be determined by the issuer's continuing obligations (see the listing rules, **Chapter 9**).
[61]   'Significant' means significant for the purpose of making an informed assessment of the matters required to be disclosed under s 80(1) (see s 81(2)).
[62]   Regulation 6(4).
[63]   See above.

LIABILITY UNDER SECTION 90

13.51 In addition to the common law remedies,[64] s 90 of the FSMA 2000 creates civil liability for false or misleading prospectuses or listing particulars. Each person responsible for a prospectus, supplementary prospectus, listing particulars or supplementary listing particulars 'is liable to pay compensation to a person who has ... acquired securities to which the particulars apply ... and ... suffered loss in respect of them as a result of ... any untrue or misleading statement in the particulars ... or ... the omission from the particulars of any matter required to be included in section 80 or 81'.[65]

13.52 Section 90(12) of the FSMA 2000 carves out civil liability that would be solely based on a summary (or any translation of it) in a prospectus unless the summary is misleading, inaccurate or inconsistent when read with the rest of the prospectus.[66]

13.53 A number of points can be made:

(i) The person acquiring the securities need not have relied on the statement or omission, merely suffered loss as a result of it. Thus a person who did not even read the prospectus or listing particulars but suffered loss due to a fall in market price once the misstatement became known would prima facie be entitled to compensation.

(ii) The section gives no guidance as to whether the level of compensation should be assessed on the 'tort' basis (ie out-of-pocket losses) or on the 'contractual' basis (ie loss of expectation of bargain).

(iii) The compensation is payable to a person who has 'acquired' the securities. Acquisition is defined[67] as including contracting to acquire the securities or an interest in them. However, there is no reference to the acquisition being from the issuer, and therefore any subsequent purchaser of the securities or an interest in them (eg an option) who suffers loss as a result of the statement or omission can presumably recover.[68]

(iv) A number of defences are set out in s 90(2) and Sch 10. The principal defence is that the person responsible satisfies the court that he reasonably believed, having made such enquiries (if any) as were reasonable, that the statement was true and not misleading or that the omission was proper, and that: (a) he continued in that belief until the

---

[64] Such as rescission for misrepresentation or an action for damages for misrepresentation, deceit or negligent misstatement.

[65] FSMA 2000, ss 90(1) and (10). Section 90(11) extends this section to prospectuses and, in relation to such, matters required to be included by ss 87A, 87G and 87B.

[66] This implements Art 6(2) of the Prospectus Directive.

[67] FSMA 2000, s 90(7).

[68] This interpretation is borne out by the wording of Sch 10, para 1(3)(d) which implies that liability may occur after the commencement of dealings.

securities were acquired; or (b) the securities were acquired before it was reasonably practicable to bring a correction to the attention of persons likely to acquire them; or (c) before the securities were acquired, he had taken all steps that it was reasonable for him to take to bring a correction to the attention of those persons; or (d) he continued in that belief until after the commencement of dealings and the securities were acquired after such a lapse of time that he ought in the circumstances to be reasonably excused.

PENALTIES UNDER SECTION 91

13.54 If the FSA considers that:

(i)   an issuer of listed securities or an applicant for listing has contravened any provision of the Part VI rules;

(ii) an issuer of transferable securities, a person offering transferable securities to the public or requesting their admission to trading on a regulated market, an applicant for the approval of a prospectus or any other person to who a provision of the Prospectus Directive applies, has contravened a provision of the Part VI rules, the prospectus rules or any provision of or requirement imposed under the Prospectus Directive; or

(iii) another person who was at the material time a director of the issuer of listed or transferable securities was knowingly concerned in the relevant contravention,

it may impose on him a penalty of such amount as it considers appropriate,[69] or publish a statement censuring him.[70]

There is a two-year time limit for the taking of proceedings by the FSA from the date on which the FSA knew of the contravention.[71]

FINANCIAL PROMOTION

13.55 Section 21 of the FSMA 2000 (restrictions on financial promotion) provides that a person must not, in the course of business, communicate[72] an invitation or inducement to engage in investment activity, unless that person is an authorised person or the content of the communication is approved for the purposes of s 21 by an authorised person. It should be noted that the restriction will still apply if the communication is made by an exempt person.

---

69   FSMA 2000, ss 91(1), 91(1A) and 91(2).
70   FSMA 2000, s 91(3).
71   FSMA 2000, s 91(6).
72   Which includes causing a communication to be made: s 21(13).

13.56   Section 21(8) defines 'engaging in investment activity' as 'entering or offering to enter into an agreement the making or performance of which by either party constitutes a controlled activity ... or ... exercising any rights conferred by a controlled investment to acquire, dispose of, underwrite or convert a controlled investment'.

13.57   An activity is a 'controlled activity'[73] if it is an activity of a specified kind or one which falls within a specified class of activity, and it relates of an investment of a specified kind, or one which falls within a specified class of investment. An investment is a 'controlled investment'[74] if it is an investment of a specified kind, or one which falls within a specified class of investment. The specified activities and investments are listed in Sch 1 to the Financial Services and Markets Act 2000 (Financial Promotion) Order 2005[75] (the FP Order).

13.58   The controlled activities are listed in paragraphs 1 to 11 of Sch 1, and include accepting deposits, dealing in securities and contractually based investments, arranging deals in investments, managing investments, safeguarding and administering investments, and advising on investments. The controlled investments are listed in paragraphs 12 to 27, and include deposits, shares or stock (with certain exceptions), debentures, debenture stock, loan stock, bonds, certificates of deposit, any other instrument creating or acknowledging indebtedness, instruments giving entitlement to investments (such as warrants), options, futures and contracts for differences.

13.59   The FP Order provides that 'communication' includes verbal and written communications, television broadcasts and information on web sites.[76] The FP Order also distinguishes 'real time communications' (those made in the course of a personal visit, telephone conversation or other interactive dialogue)[77] from 'non-real time communications' (all other communications, including written communications and e-mails).[78] In addition, a real time communication is treated as 'solicited' if the call, visit or dialogue was initiated or requested by the recipient,[79] but otherwise is treated as 'unsolicited'.[80] These distinctions are relevant (inter alia) for the exemptions described below.

13.60   Even if the communication of the relevant invitational material is prima facie restricted by s 21, a number of exemptions are available (each of

---

[73]   FSMA 2000, s 21(9).
[74]   FSMA 2000, s 21(10).
[75]   SI 2005/1529.
[76]   Article 6.
[77]   Article 7(1).
[78]   Article 7(2).
[79]   Article 8(1).
[80]   Article 8(2).

which can be relied on in combination with others). Some of the most relevant in the context of issues of debt securities are listed below:[81]

(i) The restriction in s 21 does not apply to any non-real time communication included in listing particulars, supplementary listing particulars, a prospectus approved under Part VI of the FSMA 2000, a supplementary prospectus approved under Part VI of the FSMA 2000 or any other document required or permitted to be published by the listing rules or the prospectus rules under Part VI of the FSMA 2000 except advertisements within the meaning of the Prospectus Directive.[82] Consequently, where the securities are to be listed on the London Stock Exchange, the prospectus or listing particulars (once it has been approved by the FSA) may be distributed without causing a breach of s 21.

(ii) In addition, the restriction in s 21 does not apply to any non-real time communication relating to a prospectus or supplementary prospectus where the only reason for considering it to be an invitation or inducement is that it: (a) states the name and address of the person by whom the transferable securities to which the prospectus or supplementary prospectus relates are to be offered; (b) it gives other details for contacting such person; (c) it states the nature and nominal value of the transferable securities to which the prospectus or supplementary prospectus relates, the number offered and the price; (d) it states that a prospectus or supplementary prospectus is or will be available (and, if not yet available, when it is to be expected to be); and/or (e) it gives instructions for obtaining a copy of the prospectus or supplementary prospectus.[83]

(iii) Certain communications to overseas recipients are exempt. Under art 12 of the FP Order, the restriction in s 21 does not apply to any communication which is either (a) made to a person who receives it outside the UK or (b) directed only at persons outside the UK. However, if the communication is an unsolicited real time communication, this exemption will not apply unless it is made from a place outside the UK and for the purpose of a business carried on wholly outside the UK.[84]

In relation to the test in (b), two 'safe harbour' provisions are available. A communication from inside the UK is to be regarded as directed only at persons outside the UK if the conditions set out in

---

[81] The exemptions in paras (1), (2), and (5) do not apply to communications relating to 'deposits': FP Order, art 11 and 27. However, if the debt securities have a maturity of one year or more, or satisfy the requirements for the 'commercial paper' exclusion (as to which, see **10.12**), they are not deposits, and the exemptions in (1), (2) and (5) therefore do apply.

[82] FP Order, art 70(1).

[83] Article 71.

[84] Article 12(2).

art 12(4)(a) to (d) are satisfied;[85] and a communication from outside the UK is to be regarded as directed only at persons outside the UK if the conditions set out in art 12(4)(c) and (d) are satisfied.[86] However, these conditions are not exclusive: a communication may still be regarded as directed only at persons outside the UK even if none of these conditions are satisfied.[87]

(iv) Certain communications to investment professionals are exempt. Under art 19 of the FP Order, the restriction in s 21 does not apply to a communication which either (a) is made only to recipients whom the maker of the communication believes on reasonable grounds to be investment professionals or (b) may reasonably be regarded as directly only at investment professionals. 'Investment professionals' includes an authorised person, an exempt person in certain circumstances, and a person 'whose ordinary activities involve him in carrying on the controlled activity to which the communication relates for the purpose of a business carried on by him ... or ... who it is reasonable to expect will carry on such activity for the purposes of a business carried on by him'.[88]

As with reg 12, there is a non-exclusive 'safe harbour' for the test in (b). If all the conditions set out in art 19(4) are satisfied, a communication is to be regarded as directed only at investment professionals[89] (but can still be so regarded even if none of those conditions are satisfied).[90]

(v) Certain communications to high net worth institutions are also exempt. Under art 49 of the FP Order, the restriction in s 21 does not apply to a communication which either (a) is made only to recipients whom the maker of the communication believes on reasonable grounds to fall within art 49(2) or (b) may reasonably be regarded as directed only at persons falling within art 49(2). The list in art 49(2) includes companies, unincorporated associations and partnerships with called-up share capital or net assets of not less than £5 million. A non-exclusive 'safe harbour' provision is available for the test in (b) in similar terms to that available under art 19.[91]

---

85   Article 12(3)(a).
86   Article 12(3)(b).
87   Article 12(3)(c).
88   Article 19(5).
89   Article 19(2).
90   Article 19(3).
91   Articles 19(3) and (4). Whereas arts 12 and 19 contain a specific provision to the effect that a communication can be treated as falling within the relevant exemption even if it is also made or directed to other persons to whom it can lawfully be communicated, art 49 does not contain such a provision. This is thought to be an oversight, however, since art 11 makes it clear that multiple exemptions can be relied on, and art 12(5) also clearly contemplates a combination of arts 12, 19 and 49.

COMPANIES ACT 1985

13.61   Although many provisions of the Companies Act 1985 in relation to prospectuses and the issue of securities have been repealed, a small number of these remain in force.

13.62   The provisions now remaining in force are ss 81 (for certain purposes described below), 82 (for certain purposes), 83 (for certain purposes), 84, 85 and 97, and (in order to define terms used in those provisions) s 58 and Sch 3, para 2. Of these, the most important is s 81, under which a company may not offer 'debentures'[92] to the public (whether for cash or otherwise) or allot or agree to allot them with a view to all or any of them being offered for sale to the public if it is a private company (other than one limited by guarantee and not having a share capital). 'Offer to the public' is to be construed in accordance with the old provisions (outside the scope of this chapter), which differ in several respects from the definitions in Part VI of the FSMA 2000. Therefore, a private company may still be restricted by s 81 from offering its debentures, even though the offer may be exempt under Part VI of the FSMA 2000.

UK SELLING AND DISTRIBUTION RESTRICTIONS

13.63   As a result of the above provisions, invitational material will usually contain restrictions on the types of people to whom it can be distributed. These only operate as contractual restrictions, and therefore cannot negate a breach of the relevant laws. However, by focusing the minds of the parties, they make a breach less likely; and, if a breach does occur, they give the innocent parties a contractual remedy against the party at fault.

13.64   In the case of a syndicated loan, the information memorandum will usually be circulated on a confidential basis only to banks specifically selected by the arranger. A typical distribution restriction might read:

> The information contained herein is submitted to each recipient on a strictly private and confidential basis. By accepting a copy of this confidential memorandum, each recipient agrees that neither it nor any of its employees or advisers will use the information contained herein for any purpose other than evaluating the specific transactions described herein or will divulge to any other party any such information. This confidential memorandum must not be photocopied, reproduced or distributed to any person other than the recipient without the prior written consent of the Borrower or the Arranger. If the recipient of this confidential memorandum decides not to participate in the financing of this transaction, it agrees promptly to return all material received in connection herewith (including this confidential memorandum) without retaining any copies.

---

[92]   As to which, see **Chapter 17**.

13.65　In the case of debt securities, typical selling restrictions in relation to the Prospectus Directive[93] (in this case, in an EMTN programme) read as follows:

> **European Economic Area**
> In relation to each Member State of the European Economic Area which has implemented the Prospectus Directive (each, a **Relevant Member State**), each Dealer has represented and agreed, and each further Dealer appointed under the Programme will be required to represent and agree, that with effect from and including the date on which the Prospectus Directive is implemented in that Relevant Member State (the **Relevant Implementation Date**) it has not made and will not make an offer of Notes to the public in that Relevant Member State, except that it may, with effect from and including the Relevant Implementation Date, make an offer of Notes to the public in that Relevant Member State:
>
> (a)　　in (or in Germany, where the offer starts within) the period beginning on the date of publication of a prospectus in relation to those Notes which has been approved by the competent authority in that Relevant Member State or, where appropriate, approved in another Relevant Member State and notified to the competent authority in that Relevant Member State, all in accordance with the Prospectus Directive and ending on the date which is 12 months after the date of such publication;
>
> (b)　　at any time to legal entities which are authorised or regulated to operate in the financial markets or, if not so authorised or regulated, whose corporate purpose is solely to invest in securities;
>
> (c)　　at any time to any legal entity which has two or more of (1) an average of at least 250 employees during the last financial year; (2) a total balance sheet of more than €43,000,000 and (3) an annual net turnover of more than €50,000,000, as shown in its last annual or consolidated accounts; or
>
> (d)　　at any time in any other circumstances which do not require the publication by the Issuer of a prospectus pursuant to Article 3 of the Prospectus Directive.
>
> For the purposes of this provision, the expression an 'offer of Notes to the public' in relation to any Notes in any Relevant Member State means the communication in any form and by any means of sufficient information on the terms of the offer and the Notes to be offered so as to enable an investor to decide to purchase or subscribe the Notes, as the same may be varied in that Member State by any measure implementing the Prospectus Directive in that Member State and the expression **Prospectus Directive** means Directive 2003/71/EC and includes any relevant implementing measure in each Relevant Member State.
>
> **United Kingdom**
> Each Dealer has represented and agreed, and each further Dealer appointed under the Programme will be required to represent and agree, that:

---

[93]　For typical US selling restrictions, see **14.36ff**. The extent to which selling restrictions in relation to other jurisdictions are included will depend on where the securities are marketed.

(a)   in relation to any Notes which have a maturity of less than one year, (i) it is a person whose ordinary activities involve it in acquiring, holding, managing or disposing of investments (as principal or agent) for the purposes of its business and (ii) it has not offered or sold and will not offer or sell any Notes other than to persons whose ordinary activities involve them in acquiring, holding, managing or disposing of investments (as principal or as agent) for the purposes of their businesses or who it is reasonable to expect will acquire, hold, manage or dispose of investments (as principal or agent) for the purposes of their businesses where the issue of the Notes would otherwise constitute a contravention of Section 19 of the Financial Services and Markets Act 2000 (the **FSMA**) by the Issuer;

(b)   it has only communicated or caused to be communicated and will only communicate or cause to be communicated an invitation or inducement to engage in investment activity (within the meaning of Section 21 of the FSMA) received by it in connection with the issue or sale of any Notes in circumstances in which Section 21(1) of the FSMA does not apply to the Issuer; and

(c)   it has complied and will comply with all applicable provisions of the FSMA with respect to anything done by it in relation to any Notes in, from or otherwise involving the United Kingdom.

General

Each Dealer has agreed and each further Dealer appointed under the Programme will be required to agree that it will (to the best of its knowledge and belief) comply with all applicable securities laws and regulations in force in any jurisdiction in which it purchases, offers, sells or delivers Notes or possesses or distributes this Offering Circular and will obtain any consent, approval or permission required by it for the purchase, offer, sale or delivery by it of Notes under the laws and regulations in force in any jurisdiction to which it is subject or in which it makes such purchases, offers, sales or deliveries and neither the Issuer, the Trustee nor any of the other Dealers shall have any responsibility therefor.

None of the Issuer, the Trustee and the Dealers represents that Notes may at any time lawfully be sold in compliance with any applicable registration or other requirements in any jurisdiction, or pursuant to any exemption available thereunder, or assumes any responsibility for facilitating such sale. With regard to each Tranche, the relevant Dealer will be required to comply with such other restrictions as the Issuer and the relevant Dealer shall agree and as shall be set out in the applicable Final Terms.

STABILISATION

13.66   One aspect of international capital markets activity that is capable of giving rise to serious disclosure problems is stabilisation. This is the term used to describe the practice (common in the case of eurobonds but not in the case of domestically issued securities) whereby the lead manager may effect transactions in the market with a view to ensuring that, during the immediate post-launch period, the price volatility of the securities is kept to a minimum and that an orderly market in the securities is maintained.

13.67 The most common example of stabilisation is 'over-allotment'. If the lead manager decides that it may need to support the price of the issue immediately after it has been launched (perhaps because the co-managers are likely to sell the bonds allotted to them in the market and so depress the price), it will over-allot bonds to the co-managers, so that the aggregate amount allotted exceeds the amount to be issued. No co-manager will be aware of the extent (if any) to which over-allotment has occurred. To ensure that the issuer will not be required to issue more than the intended amount on the closing date, the lead manager will buy back the 'extra' bonds in the market before the closing date, thereby supporting the price by creating artificial demand.

13.68 Stabilisation could constitute market manipulation (under s 397 of the FSMA 2000), insider dealing (under Part V of the Criminal Justice Act 1993) and/or market abuse (under s 118 of the FSMA 2000). However, in each case,[94] there is a defence for acts done in compliance with the Price Stabilising Rules published by the FSA under s 144 of the FSMA 2000 or with the relevant provisions of Commission Regulation (EC) No 2273/2003 implementing Directive 2003/6/EC (the Buy-back and Stabilisation Regulation).[95]

Safe harbours

13.69 There are two formal safe harbours for the offences referred to above. Stabilisation or ancillary stabilisation may be carried out in relation to a significant distribution[96] of securities if:

(i)   they are relevant securities that have been admitted to trading on a regulated market or a request for their admission to trading has been made, and the stabilisation is carried out in accordance with the Buy-back and Stabilisation Regulation (the regulated market safe harbour); or

(ii) they are securities other than relevant securities and they are admitted to trading on a market, exchange or other institution included in the annex to the Price Stabilising Rules, a request for such admission to trading has been made or they are or may be traded under the rules of the International Capital Market Association, and the stabilising is

---

94   FSMA 2000, s 397(5), Criminal Justice Act 1993, s 53(4) and Sch 1, para 5, and FSMA 2000, s 118A(5), respectively.

95   Set out in Chapter 2 of the Market Conduct Sourcebook of the FSA Handbook. The International Capital Market Association has also published recommendations to its members (the relevant one in relation to issues of debt instruments being Recommendation 1.7) regarding stabilisation activity.

96   An initial or secondary offer of relevant securities, publicly announced and distinct from ordinary trading both in terms of the amount in value of the securities offered and the selling methods employed.

carried out in accordance with section 2.4 of the Price Stabilising Rules (the non-regulated market safe harbour).[97]

13.70 Relevant securities, for these purposes, includes shares, debentures, government and public securities, warrants and certificates representing certain securities.[98]

Regulated market safe harbour

13.71 To benefit from the regulated market safe harbour in respect of bonds and other forms of securitised debt the stabilisation must be carried out only for a limited time period starting on the date of adequate disclosure of the terms of the offer and ending no later than the earliest of 30 calendar days after the date on which the issuer receives the proceeds of the issue and 60 calendar days after the date of allotment of the securities.

13.72 Stabilisation of such debt securities must not be executed above the market price of the securities at the time of the public disclosure[99] and adequate disclosure of any such stabilisation must be given.[100] The FSA must also be notified of the stabilisation activities.

13.73 Any ancillary stabilisation must be done within the specified limits of Article 11, for example, any overallotment not covered by the greenshoe option[101] may not exceed 5 per cent of the original offer and any overallotment covered by the greenshoe facility may not amount to more than 15 per cent of the original offer.

Non-regulated market safe harbour

13.74 The requirements for use of the non-regulated market safe harbour are narrower than those for the regulated market safe harbour.[102] These are based on the same articles of the Buy-back and Stabilisation Regulations as modified by section 2.4 of the Price Stabilising Rules. In particular, section 2.4 modifies references to 'adequate public disclosure'; for the purposes of stabilisation in relation to the non-regulated market safe harbour this includes any public announcement which provides adequate disclosure of the fact that stabilisation may take place in relation to the offer. Rule 2.4.4 of the Market Conduct Sourcebook of the FSA Handbook sets

---

[97] Rule 2.2.1 of the Market Conduct Sourcebook of the FSA Handbook.

[98] See Glossary of the FSA Handbook.

[99] Article 10.

[100] Article 9.

[101] An option granted by the offeror in favour of the investment firm(s) or credit institution(s) involved in the offer for the purpose of covering overallotments, under the terms of which such firm(s) or institution(s) may purchase up to a certain amount of relevant securities at the offer price for a certain period of time after the offer of the relevant securities.

[102] Section 2.4 of the Market Conduct Sourcebook of the FSA Handbook.

out examples of wording to be included in both screen-based announcements and offering documents.

Chapter Fourteen

US SECURITIES LAWS

OVERVIEW

14.1   US securities (and tax) laws are relevant to an issue of debt securities if either:

(a)   the issue is targeted at US investors; or

(b)   it is not so targeted, but there is a risk that the securities might subsequently be bought by US investors.

14.2   The legislation could also potentially apply to the syndication of loans, but only if the loan constitutes a 'security': generally, a commercial loan will not be regarded as a 'security' for these purposes. Accordingly, this chapter deals only with the applicability of the legislation to non-US issuers of debt securities.

14.3   The legislation purports to have extraterritorial effect, in the sense that it applies to offers or sales to a US person even if that person is outside the USA.[1] Regardless of whether non-US jurisdictions would recognise this extraterritorial effect, the importance of the US market and the desirability of avoiding civil (and/or, in certain circumstances, criminal) liability in the USA, where many Euromarket participants have significant assets and operations, make it prudent to include appropriate restrictions in a Euro offering, even where there is no apparent US connection. These restrictions are usually in a standard form, and are described at **14.36ff**.

14.4   The two principal statutes that are applicable to the offer and sale of securities in the USA or to US persons are the Securities Act of 1933 (the 'Securities Act') and the Tax Equity and Fiscal Responsibility Act of 1982 ('TEFRA').

Securities Act

14.5   The Securities Act is a federal statute, administered by the US Securities and Exchange Commission (the 'SEC') in Washington. The Securities Act controls the primary offering of securities to the public (ie new issues and not, in principle, secondary market dealings), and it does this

---

[1]   But only if 'jurisdictional means' (eg the US mail or telephone systems) are used.

by requiring that publicly offered issues must be registered with the SEC, unless an appropriate exemption applies. The Securities Act is considered at **14.8ff**.

TEFRA

14.6   TEFRA is a federal statute, introduced, inter alia, to limit tax evasion by US taxpayers. One of the principal purposes of the legislation is to discourage the issue of bearer bonds in the USA and to encourage US investors to hold bonds in registered form. The legislation (as supplemented by regulations issued by the US Internal Revenue Service (the 'IRS')) may be enforced by the IRS by the imposition of sanctions on the issuer and the holders of bearer bonds. TEFRA is considered at **14.26ff**.

Other statutes and laws

14.7   The following may also be relevant:

(i)   Securities Exchange Act of 1934

This is generally concerned with the public securities markets in the USA. It regulates the US securities exchanges and broker-dealers, specifies periodic reporting requirements for public companies, imposes liability for manipulative and deceptive practices, and establishes the rules for proxies and tender offers.

(ii)   Investment Company Act of 1940

This regulates the activities of collective investment schemes, including their management, marketing and financing. 'Investment company' is broadly defined and can include many entities that bear little resemblance to conventional mutual funds and investment companies.

(iii)   Investment Advisers Act of 1940

This regulates persons who give advice about securities, other than as an incident to a brokerage business (which is regulated by the Securities Exchange Act).

(iv)   Blue sky laws

In addition to the above, which are all federal statutes, offers and sales within the USA will be subject to the state securities (or 'blue sky') laws of the states in which such offers and sales are made.[2]

---

2   The term 'blue sky' came into being, so it is said, because the laws were necessary to curb fraudulent promoters who were so barefaced that they would be prepared to sell building lots in the blue sky in fee simple: *Hall v Gieger-Jones Co* 242 US 539 (1917).

SECURITIES ACT

14.8   As mentioned earlier, the Securities Act requires that publicly offered issues must be either registered with the SEC or exempt from the registration requirements.[3]

14.9   Registration under the Securities Act is a time-consuming and expensive process, that subjects an issuer to ongoing SEC regulation, including the obligation to prepare financial statements in accordance with, or reconciled to, US GAAP (Generally Accepted Accounting Principles), and exposes an issuer to potential litigation in the USA by disappointed investors. Accordingly, where practicable, a non-US issuer will generally seek to ensure that an offering of its securities falls within an exemption from the registration requirements.

14.10   Where an issuer is not directly targeting US investors but wishes to protect itself against an inadvertent breach, Regulation S provides a 'safe harbour' from the registration requirements. Where an issuer is directly targeting US investors, but does not wish to register under the Securities Act, the two most important exemptions are Rule 144A and Section 4(2). Regulation S and Rule 144A are rules adopted and enforced by the SEC under its rulemaking powers.

Regulation S

14.11   Regulation S provides a 'safe harbour', in the sense that, if its requirements are satisfied, the participants in the offering, including the issuer, will be protected from liability even though an inadvertent breach of the Securities Act registration requirements occurs.[4]

(a)   Requirements

14.12   The two fundamental requirements of Regulation S are that the offering be an 'offshore transaction' and that there be no 'directed selling efforts' in the USA[5]. There may be additional requirements depending on the 'category'[6] into which the offering falls.

(i)   Offshore transactions

A sale will qualify as an 'offshore transaction' if:

---

[3]   Section 5. Sales in violation of s 5 are subject to a right of rescission by the purchaser (s 12(a)) as well as a fine of up to US $10,000 and five years' imprisonment (s 24).

[4]   However, the Regulation S safe harbour will not be available if the offering, although in technical compliance with Regulation S, is part of a plan or scheme to evade the registration requirements of the Securities Act.

[5]   The term 'United States' is defined in Regulation S to include the United States of America, its territories and possessions, any State of the United States and the District of Columbia.

[6]   See para (b) below.

(x) the offer is made outside the USA (or is made to US professional
     fiduciaries in the USA acting on a discretionary basis for non-US
     persons), and
(y) either:
     (A)   the buyer is outside the USA when the buy order originated; or
     (B)   the transaction is executed on the physical trading floor of a
           foreign securities exchange.[7]

(ii)   Directed selling efforts

These are activities undertaken for the purpose, or that reasonably could be
expected to have the effect, of conditioning the US market for the securities
being offered. This includes mailing printed material to US investors,
conducting promotional seminars in the USA, or advertising in publications
with general circulation in the USA.[8]

(iii)   Additional requirements

As will be seen in paragraph (b) below, Regulation S divides offerings into
three categories.

If Category 1 applies, there are no requirements other than the two
mentioned above.

If Category 2 applies, two further restrictions must be observed, namely
'offering restrictions' and 'transaction restrictions':

(x) *Offering restrictions.* These require that:
     (A)   each distributor must agree in writing that all offers and sales of
           the securities during the 'distribution compliance period'
           (defined as the period of 40 days beginning on the later of the
           closing date and the commencement of the offering) shall be
           made only (i) in accordance with Regulation S, (ii) pursuant to
           registration of the securities under the Securities Act, or (iii)
           pursuant to an available exemption from registration (such as
           Rule 144A or Section 4(2)); and
     (B)   the offer documents must include certain prescribed selling
           restrictions and warnings.
(y) *Transaction restrictions.* These require that, during the 40–day
     distribution compliance period:
     (A)   offers and sales cannot be made to a US person or for the
           account or benefit of a US person (other than to a distributor);
           and

---

[7] In addition, certain offers and sales to designated entities are deemed to be 'offshore transactions':
     see Rule 902(i)(3).
[8] Preliminary Note 7 to Regulation S and Rule 135e under the Securities Act (which provides a 'safe
     harbour' for certain offshore press contacts) give guidance as to certain types of press briefings that
     will not constitute 'directed selling efforts'.

(B)   participants in the offering selling to a distributor, dealer or other person receiving a selling concession or fee must send a confirmation to the purchaser stating that the US selling restrictions apply.

If Category 3 applies, the Category 2 restrictions must be observed as well as certain additional restrictions.[9]

(b)   Categories

14.13   As mentioned above, Regulation S divides offerings into three categories,[10] on the basis of which the restrictions that will apply are determined. Which category is applicable in any case depends upon the type of securities being sold and the likelihood of them being resold into the USA. In the case of a guaranteed issue where the guarantor is the parent of the issuer, the status of the guarantor determines the applicable category. If the guarantor is not the issuer's parent, the relevant category is the most restrictive category applicable to either the issuer or the guarantor.[11]

(i)   Category 1

This applies to offerings by a non-US non-governmental issuer which reasonably believes that there is no 'substantial US market interest' ('SUSMI') in respect of its debt securities.[12] There will be SUSMI in respect of its debt securities only if all three of the following statements are true:

(x)   the issuer's debt securities[13] are held by 300 or more US persons;

(y)   US $1 billion or more in nominal amount of its debt securities is held by US persons; and

(z)   20 per cent or more in nominal amount of its debt securities is held by US persons.

If any one of the above statements is not true, then there is no SUSMI in respect of the issuer's debt securities, and it is therefore a Category 1 issuer. If all three are true, there is SUSMI, and it is a Category 2 issuer. However, even if an issuer is a Category 1 issuer, it is permissible to adopt Category 2 selling restrictions as well. In fact, this is the normal approach, particularly where there is any doubt as to whether or not SUSMI exists or where the Regulation S offering will be combined with a placement with US investors under Rule 144A or Section 4(2).

---

9   These are not considered in detail here, since issues by non-US issuers of non-convertible debt securities will fall into either Category 1 or Category 2.

10   Rule 903(c) of Regulation S.

11   The situation is different though if the guarantor is a sovereign: in that case the issue will always fall in Category 1, regardless of SUSMI.

12   It also applies to non-US governmental issuers and non-US issuers guaranteed by a sovereign, whether or not there is SUSMI.

13   For these purposes, 'debt securities' includes non-participating preferred stock and asset-backed securities but not US commercial paper and other securities issued under the exemption in Section 3(a)(3) of the Securities Act.

(ii)   Category 2

This applies to foreign issuers where there is SUSMI.

(iii)   Category 3

This is a residual category that applies to any offering that does not fall within either Category 1 or Category 2. In practice, therefore, in relation to offerings of non-convertible debt securities it only applies to US issuers.

Rule 144A

14.14   Rule 144A exempts from the registration requirements of the Securities Act certain resales (not original sales by the issuer) of securities to US institutional investors where certain conditions are met. Since Rule 144A only exempts resales and not original sales by the issuer, a private placement to US investors relying on Rule 144A is typically structured as a two-stage transaction: the securities are issued to the managers in reliance on Section 4(2);[14] and the managers then resell the securities in reliance on Rule 144A.

(a)   Conditions

14.15   To fall within Rule 144A, five conditions must be met:

(i)   Eligible securities

To be eligible, the securities must not be, at the time of issue, of the same 'class' as securities listed on a national US exchange, or quoted in a US automated inter-dealer quotation system such as NASDAQ. Securities issued by an open-end investment company, unit investment trust or face amount certificate company that is or is required to be registered under Section B of the Investment Company Act of 1940[15] are not eligible for Rule 144A resales.

(ii)   Sale to QIBs

The securities may only be offered and sold to 'qualified institutional buyers' ('QIBs'), or to persons that the seller and anyone acting on its behalf reasonably believe to be QIBs. QIBs include certain institutions that own or invest on a discretionary basis in securities of issuers that are not affiliated with the QIBs in an amount of at least US $100 million and certain registered broker-dealers.

(iii)   Information furnishing

Subject to certain exceptions, the issuer must agree to make 'reasonably current' financial information and certain other information available upon

---

[14]   Considered at **14.17ff**.
[15]   Ie not falling within an exemption to the Investment Company Act.

request to the holders of the securities and prospective purchasers from those holders.

(iv)   Notice of reliance

The seller must notify the QIB purchaser at the time of the sale that the sale is being made on the basis of Rule 144A.

(v)   No general solicitation or advertising

There must be no 'general solicitation or advertising' of the offering in the USA. Solicitations which are limited to QIBs are permissible, but press releases and general contacts with the media are not, even though only QIBs are eligible to purchase the securities.

(b)   Other considerations

14.16   Certain other considerations should be borne in mind in connection with a Rule 144A placement:

(i)   Registered form

Because of TEFRA (considered at **14.26ff**), the securities sold under Rule 144A must be in registered form.

(ii)   Blue sky laws

The state securities (or 'blue sky') laws must be considered in each state in which placements will be made or in which prospective QIB purchasers are resident.

Section 4(2)

14.17   Section 4(2) of the Securities Act exempts 'transactions by an issuer not involving a public offering'. 'Public offering' is generally construed as a public offering in the USA or to US residents or nationals. What constitutes such an offering, however, has been the subject of much debate over the years.

14.18   To clarify the applicability of Section 4(2), the SEC adopted Regulation D, which provides a non-exclusive 'safe harbour' for private placements under Section 4(2). In other words, an offering in compliance with Regulation D is deemed to fall within the Section 4(2) exemption; but an offering can still fall within the Section 4(2) exemption if it does not satisfy Regulation D.[16]

14.19   Regulation D is available only to issuers and their agents. Consequently, private placements falling within Regulation D are structured

---

[16]   But in practice an offering in reliance on Section 4(2) rather than Regulation D will still follow the general principles of Regulation D, with many issuers electing to omit only the filing of a Form D with the SEC.

on an agency basis (ie, with all sales being made into the USA by the managers on behalf of the issuer).

(a) Requirements of Regulation D

14.20 Five requirements must be satisfied in order to fall within Regulation D:

(i) No general solicitation or advertising

Neither the issuer nor any person acting on its behalf may offer or sell the securities by any form of solicitation or advertising. What will constitute general soliciting or advertising will depend on the circumstances. The SEC takes the view, for example, that there is no general solicitation or advertising if the offeror and offeree have a sufficiently important pre-existing relationship.

(ii) Accredited investors

Sales may only be made to 'accredited investors' or up to 35 other persons, provided that the issuer reasonably believes that each purchaser that is not an accredited investor (either alone or with his purchaser representative(s)) 'has such knowledge and experience in financial and business matters that he is capable of evaluating the merits and risks of the prospective investment'.[17] 'Accredited investor' is defined in Regulation D as including most major institutions such as banks, insurance companies and investment companies and also certain wealthy individuals.

(iii) Information furnishing

Prospective purchasers who are not accredited investors must receive certain specified information prior to the sale (similar to that which must be included in an offering registered under the Securities Act). In practice, however, most Regulation D placements are made only to accredited investors.

(iv) Not underwriters

The issuer must exercise reasonable care to ensure that prospective purchasers are not underwriters – persons acquiring securities with a view to, or offering or selling for the issuer in connection with, a distribution of the securities.[18] This is normally satisfied by: placing an appropriate legend regarding the transfer restrictions on the securities; requiring purchasers to sign investment letters (see para (b)(ii) below);

---

17 Securities Act Rule 506(b)(2)(ii).

18 This requirement can still be satisfied where the Section 4(2) placement is the first stage of a Rule 144A offering (see **14.14**), since Preliminary Note 7 to Rule 144A provides: 'The fact that purchasers of securities from the issuer thereof may purchase such securities with a view to reselling such securities pursuant to this section will not affect the availability to such issuer of an exemption under section 4(2) of the Act, or Regulation D under the Act, from the registration requirements of the Act'.

instituting 'stop-transfer orders' to enforce the transfer restrictions; requiring a legal opinion in relation to any proposed transfer; and permitting transfers only in large amounts in order to ensure that only sophisticated investors will be purchasing.

(v)   *Form D*

A notice of sale of securities (known as Form D) must be filed with the SEC no later than 15 days after the first sale of securities.[19]

(b)   *Other considerations regarding Section 4(2)*

14.21

(i)   *Interaction with Regulation D.* As mentioned earlier, an offering can still fall within Section 4(2) even if it does not satisfy Regulation D (although it will in practice still follow the general principles of Regulation D). The usual practice in relation to such an offering is to comply with the requirements in paras (a)(i) to (iv) above, but to omit the filing of a Form D with the SEC.

(ii)   *Investment letters.* Purchasers buying securities under Regulation D or Section 4(2) are generally required to sign an investment letter in which the purchaser: acknowledges that the securities have not been registered under the Securities Act and cannot be resold except pursuant to registration or an exemption therefrom; certifies that it is a sophisticated investor, has had an opportunity to investigate the issuer and has received all the information it has requested regarding the proposed investment; and certifies that it is purchasing the securities for its own account for investment purposes and not with a view to any resale or distribution.

(iii) *Integration.* In analysing whether an offering of securities falls within the exemption in Section 4(2), the SEC will also consider other offerings (whether registered or exempt) by the same issuer or by related issuers and may aggregate them together. Offerings more than six months apart, however, generally will not be integrated.

(iv) *Registered form.* Because of TEFRA (considered at **14.26ff**), the securities sold under Section 4(2) must be in registered form.

(v)   *Blue sky laws.* The application of state securities (or 'blue sky') laws will also need to be considered depending on where in the USA the investors are located.

Other exemptions

14.22   A number of other exemptions from the Securities Act restrictions are also available, of which the most important are:

---

[19]   In practice, many issuers relying on Section 4(2) do not file this notice, as the information required in it is relatively onerous: this illustrates the non-exclusive nature of Regulation D.

(a)   Section 4 (1–$^1/_2$)

14.23   Section 4(2) applies only to private sales by issuers. Section 4(1) of the Securities Act exempts 'transactions by any person other than an issuer, underwriter or dealer', and Section 4(3) exempts 'transactions by a dealer not acting as an underwriter'. These three provisions have been read together to permit investors (including dealers) to resell the securities, in accordance with certain procedures, to other investors who would have been eligible to purchase the securities from the issuer in the original private placement. This is the so-called Section 4(1–$^1/_2$) exemption, which does not actually appear in the Securities Act but has developed as a result of market practices.

(b)   Rule 144

14.24   In essence, Rule 144 under the Securities Act generally permits certain limited public resales of privately placed securities without registration one year after the issue date, and unlimited public resales two years after the issue date. Different rules apply to affiliates of the issuer looking to effect resales under Rule 144.

(c)   Commercial paper

14.25   Section 3(a)(3) of the Securities Act, as interpreted by the SEC, exempts 'prime quality'[20] negotiable commercial paper which (i) is of a type not ordinarily purchased by the general public, (ii) has a maturity not exceeding nine months, and (iii) is issued to facilitate 'current transactions'.

TEFRA

14.26   As mentioned earlier, TEFRA is intended to reduce tax evasion by US taxpayers. It does this by discouraging the issue of bearer debt securities in the USA and encouraging US investors to hold debt securities in registered form.

14.27   The TEFRA rules require that bearer securities with a maturity of more than one year:

(x)   must be sold pursuant to 'arrangements reasonably designed' to ensure that the securities will not be sold to US persons;

(y)   must not pay interest in the USA; and

(z)   must bear a specified legend[21] (except where TEFRA C applies).

---

[20]   Ie rated A-3 or better by Standard & Poor's or P-3 or better by Moodys'.
[21]   For the text of this legend, see **14.44**.

'TEFRA C' and 'TEFRA D' are alternative sets of rules adopted by the IRS, compliance with which ensures that an issue of bearer debt securities satisfies the 'reasonable arrangements' requirements. These rules are sometimes respectively referred to as the 'C Rules' and the 'D Rules'.

TEFRA C

14.28 TEFRA C applies to an issue if the securities are only issued outside the USA and its possessions by an issuer that does not significantly engage in 'interstate commerce' with respect to the issue either directly or through an agent, a manager, an underwriter or a member of a selling group.

14.29 The term 'interstate commerce' is defined (at some length) in the TEFRA rules and means essentially any contacts with the USA before or after closing in connection with the primary offering of an issue, including negotiation or any other communication between participants in the issue while one of those participants is in the USA. Genuine secondary market sales to US investors following the primary offering do not constitute 'interstate commerce'.

14.30 Because of the restriction on 'interstate commerce', TEFRA C can only be used where there is no intention to place securities in the USA and it is unlikely that there will be any interest in the USA in such securities. It can never be used in connection with a Rule 144A offering or other private placement into the USA. In addition, while TEFRA D provides a 'safe harbour', so that if its requirements are satisfied inadvertent sales to US persons will not result in the imposition of sanctions on the issuer, TEFRA C provides no such protection. Accordingly, even in situations where TEFRA C is available, issuers may choose to comply with the D Rules instead.

TEFRA D

14.31 TEFRA D is used in most straightforward issues of bearer debt securities in the euromarkets. It provides for a restricted period of 40 days from the closing date of the issue and (except in limited circumstances involving Swiss and German issues) requires that certification of non-US beneficial ownership be obtained before definitive notes can be issued or interest paid to noteholders. It also requires that notes be made available to investors in definitive form within a reasonable period following the end of the restricted period.

14.32 The main reason for preferring TEFRA D to TEFRA C (despite the restricted period and certification requirements of the former) is that TEFRA D provides a 'safe harbour' for the issuer whereas TEFRA C does not (see **14.30**). TEFRA D selling restrictions are in general not difficult to comply with, and indeed are regarded as standard in the euromarkets.[22]

Comparison with Regulation S

14.33 The restricted periods and prohibitions on sales to US persons under Regulation S and TEFRA D are similar and were generally intended to conform to each other. However, the provisions of TEFRA D are more restrictive than those of Regulation S in two respects:

(a)   Certification

Although both TEFRA D and Regulation S prohibit sales to US persons during the restricted period, Regulation S (except where the issuer is in Category 3) does not require certification by purchasers of non-US status.

(b)   US person

The definition of 'US person' under TEFRA is broader than that under Regulation S. The Regulation S definition adopts a territorial approach and includes persons resident and entities organised in the USA. The TEFRA definition is broader in that it includes US citizens resident abroad who are subject to US taxation on their worldwide income. Accordingly, offers to such persons may satisfy the requirements of Regulation S, but will not meet the 'arrangements reasonably designed' test of TEFRA.

Exclusions

14.34   TEFRA does not apply to:

(a) registered debt securities;
(b) debt securities with a maturity of one year or less (ie commercial paper); or
(c) genuine secondary market transactions.

Sanctions

14.35   The sanctions imposed by the IRS for failure to comply with the TEFRA rules are severe and are imposed both on the issuer of the securities and on the holders.

(a)   Issuer sanctions

Issuers who violate the TEFRA rules will:

(i)   be denied the interest deduction with respect to the securities;
(ii) be liable for an excise tax equal to one per cent of the aggregate principal amount issued multiplied by the number of years to maturity; and

---

[22]   For the text of these selling restrictions, see **14.36ff**.

(iii) be disqualified from the portfolio interest exemption from the 30 per cent withholding tax with respect to the securities.

(b)   *Holder sanctions*

Holders will be denied the deduction for loss incurred on the securities, and any gain realised on the securities will be treated as ordinary income rather than capital gain.

SELLING RESTRICTIONS

14.36   The selling restrictions contained in eurobond offerings to ensure compliance with the Securities Act and TEFRA are in a standardised form.

14.37   The wording set out below is for a straightforward issue of bearer notes by a corporate issuer (without a guarantee) to non-US persons, which accordingly is intended to fall within Regulation S. The wording assumes that the notes are initially represented by a temporary global note which is to be exchanged for definitive notes. Different and/or additional wording will be required if some or all of the notes are in registered form, or if the notes have the benefit of a guarantee or are intended to be placed under Rule 144A or Section 4(2).

Invitation telex

14.38   For Category 1 and Category 2 issues (using TEFRA C or TEFRA D):

> The Notes have not been and will not be registered under the United States Securities Act of 1933 (the 'US Securities Act') and include Notes in bearer form that are subject to United States tax law requirements. Accordingly, the Notes may not be offered, sold or delivered within the United States or to US persons except to the extent permitted by the Subscription Agreement. The Notes are not eligible for sale under Rule 144A under the US Securities Act.

Alternatively (and more commonly):[23]

> Sales Restrictions: US: Not 144A Eligible, Reg S [1/2], TEFRA [D/C].

Offering circular

(a) Front cover

14.39

(i)   If TEFRA D applies:

---

[23]   As recommended by the International Capital Market Association (ICMA).

The temporary Global Note will be exchangeable for definitive Notes not earlier than the 40th day after the Closing Date, upon certification as to non-US beneficial ownership.

(ii)   If TEFRA C applies:

The temporary Global Note will be exchangeable for definitive Notes not earlier than the 40th day after the Closing Date.

(b) Inside front cover

14.40   For Category 1 and Category 2 issues (using TEFRA C or TEFRA D):

The Notes have not been and will not be registered under the US Securities Act of 1933 and include Notes in bearer form that are subject to US tax law requirements. Subject to certain exceptions, Notes may not be offered, sold or delivered within the United States or to US persons.

(c) 'Subscription and sale' section or equivalent

14.41

(i)   For Category 1 issues (using TEFRA C or TEFRA D):

The Notes have not been and will not be registered under the US Securities Act of 1933 (the 'Securities Act') and include Notes in bearer form that are subject to US tax law requirements. Subject to certain exceptions, Notes may not be offered, sold or delivered within the United States or to US persons. Each Manager has agreed that it will not offer, sell or deliver a Note within the United States or to US persons except as permitted by the Subscription Agreement.

In addition, until 40 days after the commencement of the offering, an offer or sale of Notes within the United States by any dealer (whether or not participating in the offering) may violate the registration requirements of the Securities Act.

(ii)   For Category 2 issues (using TEFRA C or TEFRA D):

The Notes have not been and will not be registered under the US Securities Act of 1933 (the 'Securities Act') and may not be offered or sold within the United States or to, or for the account or benefit of, US persons except in certain transactions exempt from the registration requirements of the Securities Act. Terms used in this paragraph have the meanings given to them by Regulation S under the Securities Act.

The Notes are subject to US tax law requirements and may not be offered, sold or delivered within the United States or its possessions or to a United States person, except in certain transactions permitted by US tax regulations. Terms used in this paragraph have the meanings given to them by the US Internal Revenue Code and regulations thereunder.

Each Manager has agreed that, except as permitted by the Subscription Agreement, it will not offer, sell or deliver the Notes, (i) as part of their distribution at any time or (ii) otherwise until 40 days after the later of the commencement of the offering and the closing date, within the United States or to, or for the account or benefit of, US persons, and it will have sent to each dealer to which it sells Notes during the distribution compliance period a confirmation or other notice setting forth the restrictions on offers and sales of the Notes within the United States or to, or for the account or benefit of, US persons.

In addition, until 40 days after the commencement of the offering, an offer or sale of Notes within the United States by a dealer that is not participating in the offering may violate the registration requirements of the Securities Act.

Subscription agreement

(a) Representations and agreements of the issuer

14.42 Whether TEFRA C or TEFRA D applies has no effect on the representations and agreements of the issuer.

(i) For all issues:

Neither the Issuer, its affiliates (as defined in Rule 251 under the US Securities Act of 1933 (the 'Securities Act')) nor any persons (other than the Managers) acting on its or their behalf have engaged or will engage in any directed selling efforts (as defined in Regulation S under the Securities Act) in respect of the Notes.

(ii) For a Category 1 issue:

The Issuer reasonably believes that there is no substantial US market interest (as defined in Regulation S under the Securities Act) in the debt securities of the Issuer.

(iii) For a Category 2 issue:

The Issuer, its affiliates and any person (other than any Manager) acting on its or their behalf have complied with and will comply with the offering restrictions requirement of Regulation S under the Securities Act.

(b) Representations and agreements of the managers

14.43

(i) For a Category 1 issue (whether TEFRA C or TEFRA D applies):

Each Manager understands that the Notes have not been and will not be registered under the Securities Act and may not be offered or sold within the

United States except pursuant to an exemption from, or in a transaction not subject to, the registration requirements of the Securities Act. Each Manager represents and agrees that it has not offered or sold, and will not offer or sell, any Notes constituting part of its allotment within the United States except in accordance with Rule 903 of Regulation S. Accordingly, each Manager represents and agrees that neither it, its affiliates nor any persons acting on its or their behalf have engaged or will engage in any directed selling efforts with respect to the Notes. Terms used in this paragraph have the meanings given to them by Regulation S.

(ii) For a Category 2 issue (whether TEFRA C or TEFRA D applies):

Each Manager understands that the Notes have not been and will not be registered under the Securities Act and may not be offered or sold within the United States or to, or for the account or benefit of, US persons except in accordance with Regulation S under the Securities Act or pursuant to an exemption from the registration requirements of the Securities Act. Each Manager represents and agrees that it has offered and sold the Notes, and will offer and sell the Notes (i) as part of their distribution at any time and (ii) otherwise until 40 days after the later of the commencement of the offering and the Closing Date, only in accordance with Rule 903 of Regulation S. Accordingly, each Manager further represents and agrees that neither it, its affiliates nor any persons acting on its or their behalf have engaged or will engage in any directed selling efforts with respect to the Notes, and it and they have complied and will comply with the offering restrictions requirement of Regulation S. Each Manager agrees that, at or prior to confirmation of sale of Notes, it will have sent to each distributor, dealer or person receiving a selling concession, fee or other remuneration that purchases Notes from it during the distribution compliance period a confirmation or notice to substantially the following effect:

'The Securities covered hereby have not been registered under the US Securities Act of 1933 (the 'Securities Act') and may not be offered and sold within the United States or to, or for the account or benefit of, US persons (i) as part of their distribution at any time or (ii) otherwise until 40 days after the later of the commencement of the offering and the closing date, except in either case in accordance with Regulation S under the Securities Act. Terms used above have the meaning given to them by Regulation S.'

Terms used in this paragraph have the meanings given to them by Regulation S.

(iii) If TEFRA C applies to the issue:

Each Manager understands that under US Treas Reg Section 1.163–5(c)(2)(i)(C) (the 'C Rules'), Notes must be issued and delivered outside the United States and its possessions in connection with their original issuance. Each Manager represents and agrees that it has not offered, sold or delivered, and will not offer, sell or deliver, directly or indirectly, Notes within the United States or its possessions in connection with their original issuance. Further, in connection with the original issuance of Notes, the Manager has not communicated, and will not communicate, directly or indirectly, with a prospective purchaser if either the Manager or the prospective purchaser is within the United States or its possessions or otherwise involve a US office of the Manager in the offer or sale of Notes. Terms used in this subparagraph have the meanings given to them by the US Internal Revenue Code and regulations thereunder, including the C Rules.

(iv) If TEFRA D applies to the issue:

(1) Each Manager agrees that, except to the extent permitted under US Treas Reg Section 1.163–5(c)(2)(i)(D) (the 'D Rules'), (i) it has not offered or sold, and during the restricted period will not offer or sell, Notes to a person who is within the United States or its possessions or to a United States person, and (ii) it has not delivered and will not deliver within the United States or its possessions definitive Notes that are sold during the restricted period;

(2) each Manager represents and agrees that it has and throughout the restricted period will have in effect procedures reasonably designed to ensure that its employees or agents who are directly engaged in selling Notes are aware that such Notes may not be offered or sold during the restricted period to a person who is within the United States or its possessions or to a United States person, except as permitted by the D Rules;

(3) each Manager which is a United States person represents that it is acquiring the Notes for the purposes of resale in connection with their original issuance and that, if it retains Notes for its own account, it will only do so in accordance with the requirements of US Treas Reg Section 1.163–5(c)(2)(i)(D)(6); and

(4) each Manager agrees that, with respect to each affiliate that acquires from it Notes for the purpose of offering or selling such Notes during the restricted period, it either (i) repeats and confirms the representations and agreements contained in clauses (1), (2) and (3) above on its behalf or (ii) will obtain from such affiliate for the benefit of the Issuer the representations and agreements contained in clauses (1), (2) and (3) above.

Terms used in this paragraph have the meanings given to them by the US Internal Revenue Code and regulations thereunder, including the D Rules.

Definitive notes

14.44 In the case of TEFRA D (but not TEFRA C) issues, the following legend should appear on the face of the definitive notes:

Any United States person who holds this obligation will be subject to limitations under the United States income tax laws, including the limitations provided in Sections 165(j) and 1287(a) of the Internal Revenue Code.

Chapter Fifteen

TRANSFERS OF LENDERS' INTERESTS

INTRODUCTION

15.1 Debt securities are by their nature transferable. However, a notable development since the mid-1980s has been the growth in the transfer of lenders' interests under loan agreements, and consequently the structuring of loan agreements so as to ensure ready transferability. There are various reasons why a lender, whether under a debt security or a straightforward loan, may want to sell his interest: to make a profit, to avoid over-exposure to a particular borrower or type of borrower, to improve capital adequacy ratios, to avoid adverse tax consequences, to get rid of a loan or a debt security where the borrower is in default, or to free up lending limits to enable fresh loans to be made on a more competitive basis.

15.2 There are four main methods of achieving a transfer (or the commercial equivalent thereof) of a lender's interest, the availability of each of which depends upon both the nature of the interest and the terms of the documentation. The methods are: transfer by delivery (in the case of bearer debt securities); assignment (in the case of registered debt securities and interests under loan agreements); and novation and participation (in the case of interests under loan agreements).[1]

TRANSFER BY DELIVERY

Meaning of 'negotiable instrument'

15.3 The essence of a bearer security is that transfer may be effected by mere delivery of the security to the transferee. The consequences of such a

---

[1]   In relation to transfers of interests under loan agreements, see further the Financial Law Panel report 'Legal Uncertainties in the Secondary Debt Market' (January 1997); Hughes [1997] *Butterworths' JIBFL* 75 and 160; Barratt [1998] JIBL 50; Ellinger, Lomnicka and Hooley, *Ellinger's Modern Banking Law* (4th edn, 2006), pp 722–724; Cranston, *Principles of Banking Law* (2nd edn, 2002), pp 354-368; *Encyclopaedia of Banking Law*, paras F (5005)–F (5305); Hughes [1987] 1 JIBL 5.

transfer depend, however, upon whether the security is a negotiable instrument.[2] A negotiable instrument has three essential characteristics:[3]

(a)   it is transferable by mere delivery, with no notice needing to be given to the borrower;

(b)   a full legal title to the instrument passes to the transferee, who may sue the borrower in his own name without joining the transferor as a party; and

(c)   the title passes free from all equities between the borrower and any prior holder[4] and all defects in title (including an absence of title altogether) if the transferee takes in good faith for value and without notice[5] of the equities or defects (a 'holder in due course'). A negotiable instrument is thus an exception to the general rule of English law that no one can transfer a better title than he himself possesses: *nemo dat quod non habet*.[6]

15.4   Not all bearer instruments are negotiable, and negotiability should be contrasted with both 'transferability' and 'assignability'. An instrument which is merely 'transferable' has characteristics (a) and (b), but not (c). Examples include bills of lading[7] and postal orders.[8] An instrument which is merely 'assignable' can have characteristic (b)[9] (but not (a) or (c)). Assignment is considered below:[10] examples of assignable instruments include registered shares, life policies, government stock, registered bonds and notes and registered stock.

---

2   On negotiable instruments generally, see Milnes Holden, *The History of Negotiable Instruments in English Law* (1955); *Byles on Bills of Exchange* (27th edn, 2002); *Chalmers and Guest on Bills of Exchange, Cheques and Promissory Notes* (16th edn, 2005); Hedley and Hedley, *Bills of Exchange and Bankers' Documentary Credits* (4th edn, 2001); *Richardson's Guide to Negotiable Instruments* (8th edn, 1991); Sealy and Hooley, *Commercial Law* (3rd edn, 2003), Chapter 15; Goode, *Commercial Law* (3rd edn, 2004), Chapter 18 and pp 570–574; Holdsworth (1915) 31 LQR 12, 173 and 376 and (1916) 32 LQR 20; Jenks (1893) 9 LQR 70.

3   See, eg, *Crouch v The Credit Foncier of England Ltd* (1873) 8 QB 374 at 381 per Blackburn J; *The London and County Banking Co Ltd v The London and River Plate Bank Ltd* (1887) 20 QBD 232 at 238–239 per Manisty J.

4   In practice, most bearer debt securities provide, as a contractual matter, that the holder's title shall be free of all equities between the company and the holder himself (to similar effect to the provision described at **3.7** in relation to registered stock). Such a provision is valid (see the cases cited at **3.7**), subject to (inter alia) the mandatory set-off in a winding up of the company in respect of mutual dealings (see **3.7** and *Hankey v Smith* (1789) 3 TR 507; *Collins v Jones* (1830) 10 B&C 777; *Forster v Wilson* (1843) 12 M&W 191).

5   Notice for this purpose means actual notice or a means of notice wilfully disregarded: see *Raphael v The Governor and Co of the Bank of England* (1855) 17 CB 161; *Re Gomersall* (1875) 1 ChD 137 at 146 per Baggallay JA; *Jones v Gordon* (1877) 2 App Cas 616 at 627 per Lord Blackburn; *The London Joint Stock Bank v Simmons* [1892] AC 201 at 217 per Lord Herschell; *Venables v Baring Brothers & Co* [1892] 3 Ch 527 at 542 to 543 per Kekewich J.

6   See cases cited at **3.7**.

7   See, eg, *Gurney v Behrend* (1854) 3 El&Bl 622; *Kum v Wah Tat Bank Ltd* [1971] 1 Lloyd's Rep 439 at 446.

8   *The Fine Art Society Ltd v The Union Bank of London Ltd* (1886) 17 QBD 705.

9   See **15.13ff**.

10   At **15.13ff**.

15.5   The presence of characteristics (a) and (b) depends upon the terms of the instrument itself. However, an instrument can only acquire characteristic (c), and consequently negotiability, by statute or by mercantile usage in the English mercantile world (the 'law merchant'),[11] and not merely by agreement between the parties.[12] The Bills of Exchange Act 1882 recognises the negotiability of bills of exchange, cheques and promissory notes. However, since these are defined[13] as unconditional orders or promises to pay a sum certain on demand or at a fixed or determinable future time, most bearer debt securities will not come within that Act because of, for example, exceptions to the gross-up obligation and early redemption provisions, and can therefore only acquire negotiability by mercantile usage.

15.6   The list of instruments negotiable by mercantile usage 'is not a closed book, nor is it fixed or stereotyped',[14] and accordingly new types of instrument can acquire (but not, it would appear, lose)[15] negotiability as practice changes, notwithstanding that the practice may be of recent origin.[16] 'More depends on the number of transactions which help to create [the usage] than on the time over which the transactions are spread'.[17] The usage must be one in existence in England: the mere fact that an instrument is regarded as negotiable in a foreign country will not make it a negotiable instrument under English law.[18] However, usage cannot override the actual words contained in an instrument. An instrument cannot be negotiable if expressed in a manner incompatible with negotiability, even though it is of a type normally regarded as negotiable – eg a bond expressed to be transferable 'only in person or by attorney on the books of the said company'.[19]

---

11   As to how the law merchant came to be regarded as part of common law, see Milnes Holden, *The History of Negotiable Instruments in English Law* (1955), pp 33–36; Cockburn CJ's judgment in *Goodwin v Robarts* (1875) 10 Ex 337; Rogers, *The Early History of the Law of Bills and Notes* (1995); Carter (1901) 17 LQR 232; Tudsbery (1918) 34 LQR 392; Bosanquet (1899) 15 LQR 130.

12   See, eg, *Bechuanaland Exploration Co v London Trading Bank Ltd* [1898] 2 QB 658 at 665–667; *Edelstein v Schuler & Co* [1902] 2 KB 144 at 154. However, a representation of negotiability either by the borrower in the security itself or by the transferor may give rise to an estoppel, and thus might allow the security to be treated as if it were negotiable as between the person making the representation and the transferee. This is the doctrine of 'negotiability by estoppel'; see further *Paget's Law of Banking* (12th edn, 2002), pp 654–656.

13   In ss 3(1), 73 and 83(1) respectively.

14   *Bank of Baroda Ltd v Punjab National Bank Ltd* [1944] AC 176 at 183 per Lord Wright.

15   *Goodwin v Robarts* (1875) 10 Ex 337 at 357; *Bechuanaland Exploration Co v London Trading Bank Ltd* [1898] 2 QB 658 at 674–675. Cf *Manbre Saccharine Co Ltd v Corn Products Co Ltd* [1919] 1 KB 198 at 206.

16   *Goodwin v Robarts* (1875) 10 Ex 337 at 355–356; *Bechuanaland Exploration Co v London Trading Bank Ltd* [1898] 2 QB 658 at 672–678; *Edelstein v Schuler & Co* [1902] 2 KB 144 at 154; *Venables v Baring Brothers & Co* [1892] 3 Ch 527 at 539–540.

17   *Edelstein v Schuler & Co* [1902] 2 KB 144 at 154 per Bigham J.

18   *Picker v The London and County Banking Co Ltd* (1887) 18 QBD 515; *Venables v Baring Brothers & Co* [1892] 3 Ch 527 at 539.

19   *The London and County Banking Co Ltd v The London and River Plate Bank Ltd* (1889) 20 QBD 232.

Bearer bonds and notes, etc

15.7 Bearer bonds and notes have long been recognised as negotiable. Bonds of a foreign government were recognised as negotiable in 1824[20] and those of a foreign corporation in 1892.[21] An attempt was initially made to distinguish between such bonds and those issued by an English company in England, but the principle that there is no difference was established in 1898.[22] Indeed, it is so well established that bearer bonds and notes are negotiable that proof of mercantile usage will not be required by the court:[23]

> 'the very expression "bearer bond" connotes the idea of negotiability, so that the moment such bonds are issued to the public they rank themselves among the class of negotiable securities.'

15.8 It is immaterial that the bonds or notes are constituted by a trust deed,[24] provided that it is clear from the terms of the bonds or notes and the trust deed read together that the bonds or notes are intended to create obligations to the bearers and not merely obligations to the trustee[25] – hence the duality of obligations in issues constituted by trust deeds: the covenant in the trust deed to pay the trustee and the promises on the bonds or notes to pay the bearers. It is thought immaterial that the holder's rights to sue the borrower on these promises are normally limited to where the trustee is obliged to sue and has failed to do so: what matters is not an unconditional right to sue but that, in circumstances where the holder can sue, he need not sue in the name of a prior holder. Consequently, subordination, being a limitation on the right to sue, should not prevent a bond or note being regarded as negotiable.

15.9 It is also immaterial that the bonds or notes are secured.[26] Decisions in various cases [27] also illustrate that the fact that the bonds or notes contain provisions for early redemption or for payment of uncertain amounts or amounts on uncertain dates does not affect their negotiability. It is on this basis that, for example, floating rate, zero coupon, index-linked and perpetual bonds and notes may be regarded as negotiable. It appears to be immaterial that the instrument, rather than containing a promise by the

---

[20] *Gorgier v Mieville* (1824) 3 B&C 45.

[21] *Venables v Baring Brothers & Co* [1892] 3 Ch 527.

[22] *Bechuanaland Exploration Co v London Trading Bank Ltd* [1898] 2 QB 658. Bearer scrip certificates (ie share warrants) of an English company had already been held to be negotiable: *Rumball v The Metropolitan Bank* (1877) 2 QBD 194.

[23] *Edelstein v Schuler & Co* [1902] 2 KB 144 at 155 per Bigham J.

[24] *Venables v Baring Brothers & Co* [1892] 3 Ch 527; *Re Olathe Silver Mining Co* (1884) 27 ChD 278.

[25] *Re Olathe Silver Mining Co* (1884) 27 ChD 278 at 283.

[26] *Re Olathe Silver Mining Co* (1884) 27 ChD 278; *Venables v Baring Brothers & Co* [1892] 3 Ch 527; *Bechuanaland Exploration Co v London Trading Bank Ltd* [1898] 2 QB 658; *Edelstein v Schuler & Co* [1902] 2 KB 144.

[27] See, eg, the cases cited in the previous footnote.

borrower to pay, instead certifies that the bearer is entitled to the amount payable in respect of a related deposit (ie a certificate of deposit).[28]

15.10   There do not appear to be any decided cases on the negotiability of euro-commercial paper. In conceptual terms, it is indistinguishable from bonds and notes and therefore, assuming, as is presumably likely, that sufficient mercantile usage in England could be proved, there would seem to be no reason why it should not be regarded as negotiable.

Bearer global securities

15.11   Nor have there been any decided cases on the negotiability of bearer global securities, by which the definitive securities are often represented.[29] It could be argued that global securities (as opposed to the interests in them) are so rarely transferred that there is not the necessary mercantile usage for them to be considered negotiable. However, the better argument, it is thought, is that mercantile usage in relation specifically to global securities is not necessary: what matters is that they belong to a class of instruments considered negotiable in mercantile usage, ie bearer bonds and notes. A global security is in essence merely one type of bearer bond or note and, as seen above, anything that can properly be described as a bearer bond or note will be presumed to be negotiable unless it contains provisions incompatible with negotiability (which a normal global security does not). If a global security is not negotiable, the risk for the borrower is that, if the bearer who presents it for payment is not the true owner, the borrower will remain liable to the true owner. Consequently, out of caution, a number of global securities contain exculpatory language to protect the borrower, to the effect that payment to any bearer of the global security discharges the borrower's liability.

15.12   Whether or not a global security is negotiable, the rights of the underlying holders cannot be so, nor can the rights of the accountholders at Euroclear or Clearstream (the European clearing systems) in cases where the definitive securities have been issued but are held in Euroclear or Clearstream. In many cases, such holders will have rights only against Euroclear or Clearstream. Where, as is common in issues with no trustee, the global security is executed as a deed and takes effect as a deed poll, the underlying holders may also have certain rights of enforcement against the borrower. In either case, their rights depend upon entry in the records of Euroclear or Clearstream, and are not transferable by delivery, and therefore

---

[28]   *Customs and Excise Commissioners v Guy Butler (International) Ltd* [1977] QB 377 at 382. See also *Libyan Arab Foreign Bank v Bankers Trust Co* [1988] 1 Lloyd's Rep 259 at 276. The statements indicating the contrary in *Akbar Khan v Attar Singh* [1936] 2 All ER 545 at 550 and *Claydon v Bradley* [1987] 1 All ER 522 at 526 and 528 can perhaps be distinguished either as relating only to promissory notes and not negotiable instruments generally or on the basis that the documents in question were not of a type in relation to which sufficient mercantile usage existed.

[29]   As to which, see further **3.3**.

cannot be negotiable.[30] For the same reason, registered securities cannot be negotiable, since they cannot be transferred by delivery.

ASSIGNMENT[31]

15.13   The two primary considerations in relation to any assignment are: is it legal or equitable, and has notice been given to the obligor?

Distinction between legal and equitable assignments

15.14   A legal assignment is one which satisfies the requirements of s 136(1) of the Law of Property Act 1925, which states:

> 'Any absolute assignment by writing under the hand of the assignor (not purporting to be by way of charge only) of any debt or other legal thing in action, of which express notice in writing has been given to the debtor, trustee or other person from whom the assignor would have been entitled to claim such debt or thing in action, is effectual in law (subject to equities having priority over the right of the assignee) to pass and transfer from the date of such notice –
>
> (a)   the legal right to such debt or thing in action;
> (b)   all legal and other remedies for the same; and
> (c)   the power to give a good discharge for the same without the concurrence of the assignor.'

15.15   Accordingly, the following requirements must be satisfied for the assignment to be a legal one:

(a)   it must be of a debt or other legal thing in action. It might be thought that the reference to 'legal thing in action' confines the subsection to legal choses in action, but this is not so. Equitable choses in action are included,[32] and 'legal' should therefore presumably be read as meaning merely 'enforceable in a court of justice';

(b)   the assignment must be in writing under the hand of the assignor (but no special form is necessary).[33] If the assignment is of an equitable

---

30   See also Tennekoon's discussion of this question in *The Law and Regulation of International Finance* (1991), pp 169–176.

31   On assignment generally, see *Chitty on Contracts* (29th edn, 2004), Chapter 19; *Encyclopaedia of Banking Law*, paras F(5005)–F(5139); *Snell's Equity* (31st edn, 2005), pp 27–54.

32   See *Torkington v Magee* [1902] 2 KB 427 at 430–431 (revd on facts: [1903] 1 KB 644); *Tolhurst v The Associated Portland Cement Manufacturers (1900) Ltd* [1903] AC 414 at 424 per Lord Lindley; *Re Pain* [1919] 1 Ch 38 at 44–45; *Compania Colombiana de Seguros v Pacific Steam Navigation Co* [1965] 1 QB 101 at 121; *Chitty on Contracts* (29th edn, 2004), para 19–011; *Snell's Equity* (31st edn, 2005), p 32. Assignments of future debts are capable of falling within the subsection: *Walker v The Bradford Old Bank Ltd* (1884) 12 QBD 511; *G and T Earle Ltd v Hemsworth RDC* (1928) 44 TLR 605 at 609.

33   *Re Westerton* [1919] 2 Ch 104; *Curran v Newpark Cinemas Ltd* [1951] 1 All ER 295; *The Kelo* [1985] 2 Lloyd's Rep 85 at 89.

interest, it must be in writing anyway in order to be valid, irrespective of s 136(1): Law of Property Act 1925, s 53(1)(c);[34]

(c) the assignment must be absolute[35] and not by way of charge only. An assignment by way of security can still be a legal assignment, however, if it is expressed as an absolute assignment subject to a proviso for reassignment;[36]

(d) the assignment must be of the whole of the chose in action, not part only;[37] and

(e) express notice in writing must be given to the obligor. No special form is necessary, so long as the fact of assignment and the identity of the assignee appear with reasonable certainty,[38] and the notice may be given by any person.[39] The notice is deemed given when it is received by the obligor.[40]

An equitable assignment is any assignment which does not comply with the requirements of s 136(1), subject to the requirement of writing mentioned above.[41]

15.16 In practice, however, the distinction between legal and equitable assignments is not significant. Aside from certain differences regarding the need for consideration,[42] the main distinction is procedural, in that an

---

[34] Which applies to personal, as well as real, equitable interests: *Grey v IRC* [1960] AC 1; *Oughtred v IRC* [1960] AC 206; *Vandervell v IRC* [1967] 2 AC 291; and see Green [1984] MLR 385. Section 53(1)(c) does not, however, affect the creation or operation of resulting, implied or constructive trusts: s 53(2). Consequently, if the true effect of the 'assignment' is the creation of a constructive trust, it need not be in writing in order to be effective in equity: *Neville v Wilson* [1996] 3 WLR 460.

[35] As opposed to conditional: see *Re Williams* [1917] 1 Ch 1. However, the fact that a trust of the proceeds of the chose in action is created in favour of the assignor does not prevent the assignment being absolute: *Comfort v Betts* [1891] 1 QB 737.

[36] *Tancred v Delagoa Bay and East Africa Rly Co* (1889) 23 QBD 239; *Durham Brothers v Robertson* [1898] 1 QB 765; *Hughes v Pump House Hotel Co Ltd* [1902] 2 KB 190.

[37] See *Forster v Baker* [1910] 2 KB 636; *Re Steel Wing Co Ltd* [1921] 1 Ch 349; *Bank of Liverpool and Martins Ltd v Holland* (1926) 43 TLR 29; *G and T Earle Ltd v Hemsworth RDC* (1928) 44 TLR 605 at 609; *Williams v Atlantic Assurance Co Ltd* [1933] 1 KB 81; *Walter & Sullivan Ltd v J Murphy & Sons Ltd* [1955] 2 QB 584.

[38] *Van Lynn Developments Ltd v Pelias Construction Co Ltd* [1969] 1 QB 607; *Denny, Gasquet and Metcalfe v Conklin* [1913] 3 KB 177. In particular, the date of the assignment need not be specified (*Van Lynn*, above); however, where it is stated and it is inaccurate, the notice is invalid: *W F Harrison & Co Ltd v Burke* [1956] 2 All ER 169. A misstatement of the amount of debt might also invalidate the notice (see *W F Harrison & Co Ltd v Burke*, above, at 171 per Denning LJ), but an incorrect statement that notice has already been given does not (*Van Lynn*, above).

[39] *Bateman v Hunt* [1904] 2 KB 530 at 538; *Curran v Newpark Cinemas Ltd* [1951] 1 All ER 295 at 299. There is no time-limit for the giving of notice: *Bateman v Hunt* [1904] 2 KB 530 at 538.

[40] *Holt v Heatherfield Trust Ltd* [1942] 2 KB 1.

[41] Which, technically, only applies to assignments of equitable choses in action, not equitable assignments of legal choses in action. The latter may be made in any way, even orally (see, eg, *Tibbits v George* (1836) 5 Ad&E 107; *Gurnell v Gardner* (1863) 4 Giff 626). Even if the assignee relies on an oral assignment of a legal chose in action, any subsequent assignment, however, must be in writing, as the assignee will only have acquired an equitable interest. As to the general requirements of any assignment (intention, identification of chose, communication to assignee, etc), see *Snell's Equity* (31st edn, 2005), pp 33–38; *Chitty on Contracts* (29th edn, 2004), paras 19–020 to 19–041.

[42] As to which, see *Chitty on Contracts* (29th edn, 2004), paras 19–027 and 19–031 et seq.

assignee under a legal assignment can sue the obligor without joining the assignor as a party to the action,[43] whereas, as a general rule, an equitable assignee must join the assignor.[44] However, failure to join the assignor is not now a reason for defeating a cause of action, although the court may direct that the assignor be made a party.[45] The requirement to join the assignor can be waived by the obligor,[46] and will not be insisted on where there is no need, in particular if there is no dispute between assignor and assignee regarding the existence of an assignment and the assignee has acquired the whole of the chose in action.[47]

15.17 In the case of an assignment of a bank's rights under a loan agreement, it may be unavoidable that the assignment takes effect only in equity (because, for example, the bank may not want the borrower to know that it has assigned its interest or because it wishes to assign part only of its interest). In the case of assignments of registered securities where there is a trustee, the assignment will in most cases take effect only in equity (eg because it is an assignment of only part of a holding or because the prescribed assignment procedure48 involves the giving of notice (by sending in the completed stock transfer form) to the issuer's registrar rather than to the trustee).[49] However, so far as enforcement against the issuer is

---

43 See, eg, *Torkington v Magee* [1902] 2 KB 427 at 435 (revd on facts: [1903] 1 KB 644); *Re Westerton* [1919] 2 Ch 104; *Weddell v J A Pearce & Major* [1988] Ch 26.

44 See, eg, *William Brandt's Sons & Co v Dunlop Rubber Co Ltd* [1905] AC 454 at 462 per Lord MacNaghten; *Performing Right Society Ltd v London Theatre of Varieties Ltd* [1924] AC 1; *Williams v Atlantic Assurance Co Ltd* [1933] 1 KB 81; *Holt v Heatherfield Trust Ltd* [1942] 2 KB 1 at 4–5; *Weddell v J A Pearce & Major* [1988] Ch 26; *Central Insurance Co Ltd v Seacalf Shipping Corporation* [1983] 2 Lloyd's Rep 25 at 34 per Oliver LJ; *Three Rivers District Council v Governor and Company of the Bank of England* [1996] QB 292.

45 Civil Procedure Rules, r 19.2(2).

46 *William Brandt's Sons & Co v Dunlop Rubber Co Ltd* [1905] AC 454 at 462 per Lord MacNaghten; *Performing Right Society Ltd v London Theatre of Varieties Ltd* [1924] AC 1 at 14 per Viscount Cave LC.

47 *Raiffeisen Zentralbank Osterreich AG v Five Star Trading LLC* [2001] QB 825 at 850 per Mance LJ; *Central Insurance Co Ltd v Seacalf Shipping Corp* [1983] 2 Lloyd's Rep 25 at 33–34 per Oliver LJ; *Weddell v J A Pearce & Major* [1988] Ch 26 at 40–41; *Cator v Croydon Canal Co* (1841) 4 Y&C Ex 405 at 593–594; *Fulham v M'Carthy* (1848) 1 HLC 703; *Donaldson v Donaldson* (1854) Kay 711; *Re Steel Wing Co Ltd* [1921] 1 Ch 349 at 356–357.

48 If no procedure is prescribed, then, so long as there are not any restrictions on assignment (as to which, see further below), fully paid registered securities of any company within the meaning of Companies Act 1985 (except a company limited by guarantee or an unlimited company) may be transferred by means of a completed stock transfer form as set out in Sch 1 to the Stock Transfer Act 1963.

49 As seen above (in **Chapter 3**), the holder of a registered security where there is a trustee has only an equitable interest. Although, as seen earlier, such an interest is capable of falling within s 136(1), one of the requirements is that the notice be given to the trustee: see Law of Property Act 1925, ss 136(1) and 137; *Re Dallas* [1904] 2 Ch 385 at 399 and 401 per Buckley J. However, the trustee is invariably given a right to inspect the register, and such an inspection would presumably result in notice to the trustee.

concerned, this is, in practice, immaterial, as it is the trustee, rather than the holders, that is responsible for enforcement.[50]

Giving notice of assignment

15.18 More important, however, than the distinction between legal and equitable assignments is the giving of notice of the assignment to the obligor. As seen above, notice is an essential element of a legal assignment. An equitable assignment is valid even if no notice is given to the obligor,[51] but if notice is given it has the following consequences:

(a) until notice is given, the obligor may discharge his obligations by payment to the assignor, without any liability to the assignee.[52] Once notice is given, payment to the assignor does not discharge the obligor, who remains liable to the assignee;[53]

(b) until notice is given, the obligor may raise against the assignee all rights of set-off, counterclaim, etc, arising out of transactions between the obligor and the assignor, that accrue due before the notice is given. Once notice is given, the obligor may not raise any such rights against the assignee if they accrue due after the notice is given (even if arising out of contracts entered into before the date of the notice), unless they arise out of, or are closely connected to, the same contract as that which gives rise to the assigned debt;[54]

(c) notice is necessary to preserve the assignee's priority against subsequent assignees, since if the subsequent assignee is the first to

---

[50] See **Chapter 3**. Where there is no trustee, the holder's rights are against the company direct; in such a case, whether an assignment is legal or equitable is most likely to depend upon whether it is of the whole, or just part, of the assignor's holding. In practice, the distinction is immaterial, since the need for joinder of assignors is invariably waived by the company, by means of the provision that the registered holder will be regarded as absolutely entitled to the benefit of the security in respect of which he is registered.

[51] *Donaldson v Donaldson* (1854) Kay 711; *Gorringe v Irwell India Rubber and Gutta Percha Works* (1886) 34 ChD 128.

[52] *Stocks v Dobson* (1853) 4 De GM&G 11; *Bence v Shearman* [1898] 2 Ch 582.

[53] *Jones v Farrell* (1857) 1 De G&J 208; *Brice v Bannister* (1878) 3 QBD 569; *Yates v Terry* [1902] 1 KB 527; *Walter & Sullivan Ltd v J Murphy & Sons Ltd* [1955] 2 QB 584 at 588. Similarly, in the case of assignment of an option, the assignee is not entitled to exercise the option until notice is given: *Warner Bros Records Inc v Rollgreen Ltd* [1976] QB 430.

[54] *Watson v Mid Wales Ry Co* (1867) LR 2 CP 593; *Young v Kitchin* (1878) LR 3 ExD 127; *Govt of Newfoundland v The Newfoundland Ry Co* (1888) LR 13 App Cas 199; *Christie v Taunton, Delmard, Lane & Co* [1893] 2 Ch 175; *Biggerstaff v Rowatt's Wharf Ltd* [1896] 2 Ch 93; *Re Pinto Leite and Nephews* [1929] 1 Ch 221; *Roxburghe v Cox* (1881) 17 ChD 520; *Edward Nelson & Co Ltd v Faber & Co* [1903] 2 KB 367; *Business Computers Ltd v Anglo-African Leasing Ltd* [1977] 1 WLR 578; *Marathon Electrical Manufacturing Corp v Mashreqbank PSC* [1997] CLC 1090; *Re Pain* [1919] 1 Ch 38; *Lawrence v Hayes* [1927] 2 KB 111; *Rother Iron Works Ltd v Canterbury Precision Engineers Ltd* [1974] QB 1; *The Raven* [1980] 2 Lloyd's Rep 266; *The Khian Captain (No 2)* [1986] 1 Lloyd's Rep 429; *Muscat v Smith* [2003] 1 WLR 2853; Wood, *English and International Set-Off* (1989), paras 16–10 to 16–169.

give notice he will rank ahead,[55] so long as the subsequent assignee did not know of the prior assignment when he took his assignment;[56] and

(d) until notice is given, the obligor and the assignor can modify the terms of the chose in action assigned without the consent of the assignee, but once notice is given they cannot.[57]

15.19 Notice of an equitable assignment may be either written or oral,[58] but, where the chose assigned is equitable and the notice is given to a trustee, it is not effective to regulate priority between competing assignees unless it is in writing.[59] As with notice under s 136, the notice may be given by any person,[60] and no special form is necessary: all that is required is that 'the fact of the assignment is distinctly and clearly brought to the mind and attention' of the obligor.[61] Unlike notice under s 136, however, a mistake as to the date of the assignment does not invalidate the notice.[62]

15.20 In the case of assignments of a bank's rights under a loan agreement, the only reason in practice why notice might not be given to the borrower would be if the assigning bank does not wish the borrower to know that it has assigned its interest. In the case of assignments of registered securities, the prescribed assignment procedure usually involves the giving of notice to the issuer's registrar (acting as agent of the issuer). It is arguable that this does not constitute adequate notice for the above purposes where there is a trustee.[63] However, in most cases this is immaterial, since the terms usually provide, whether or not there is a trustee, that the persons for the time being entered in the register are to be regarded as the holders[64] and that such persons are entitled to payment free from any set-offs or equities.[65]

---

55 *Dearle v Hall* (1828) 3 Russ 1; *Re Brown's Trusts* (1867) 5 Eq 88; *Lloyd v Banks* (1868) 3 Ch App 488; *Ward and Pemberton v Duncombe* [1893] AC 369; *Marchant v Morton, Down & Co* [1901] 2 KB 829; *Kelly v Selwyn* [1905] 2 Ch 117; *The Afrika Hope* [1988] 1 Lloyd's Rep 439;*E Pfeiffer Weinkellerei – Weineinkauf GmbH & Co v Arbuthnot Factors Ltd* [1988] 1 WLR 150 at 163.

56 *Timson v Ramsbottom* (1837) 2 Keen 35; *Newman v Newman* (1885) 28 ChD 674; *Re AD Holmes* (1885) 29 ChD 786. The fact that the subsequent assignee knew of the earlier assignment when he gave notice is irrelevant: *Mutual Life Assurance Society v Langley* (1886) 32 ChD 460.

57 *Brice v Bannister* (1878) 3 QBD 569.

58 *Re Tichener* (1865) 35 Beav 317; *Browne v Savage* (1859) 4 Drewry 635 at 640; *Ex parte Agra Bank* (1868) 3 Ch App 555.

59 Law of Property Act 1925, s 137(3).

60 See, eg, *Lloyd v Banks* (1868) 3 Ch App 488 (notice acquired by reading a newspaper); *Ex parte Agra Bank* (1868) 3 Ch App 555 (notice given by assignor).

61 *Browne v Savage* (1859) 4 Drewry 635 at 640 per Kindersley VC. See also *Smith v Owners of the Steamship 'Zigurds'* [1934] AC 209 (letter stating that the writers had authority to collect freight 'against which we have made payments' effective notice).

62 *Whittingstall v King* (1882) 46 LT 520.

63 See further **15.17**.

64 For the purposes of, eg, payments and agreement to modifications.

65 Thus excluding all equities, not just those arising prior to the giving of notice. Such a provision is valid, subject to certain limitations: see the footnotes to **3.7**.

Non-assignable rights etc

15.21   Obligations cannot be transferred by way of assignment, only rights. Accordingly, where obligations fall to be performed by the lenders (eg obligations to make further advances), the assignor (and not the assignee)[66] will remain liable to perform these, and a novation must be used if the assignor is to be no longer liable.[67] However, not all rights are assignable. Those which are not assignable include the following:

(a)   Rights expressed to be not assignable,[68] or not assignable without the consent of the obligor[69] or not assignable unless in accordance with a prescribed procedure. Such a procedure is almost always prescribed in the case of registered debt securities, and usually involves completion of a form of transfer and delivery of it to the issuer's registrar.[70] However, if a purported assignment is ineffective as a result of a prohibition on assignment, it may well take effect instead as a

---

[66]   For an example, see *Pan Ocean Shipping Co Ltd v Creditcorp Ltd* [1994] 1 WLR 161 (obligation to repay advance hire payments on ground of failure of consideration did not pass to assignee).

[67]   This problem is sometimes addressed by the assignee agreeing with the assignor to pay amounts equal to the further advances direct to the borrower in return for a deemed assignment by the assignor of the benefit of the resultant new loan (such an assignment being expressed to occur automatically with no fresh instrument of assignment requiring to be executed). There is thus no contractual nexus between borrower and assignee until the payment has been made by the assignee, and the assignor remains liable to make the further advances if the assignee defaults.

[68]   *Helstan Securities Ltd v Hertfordshire County Council* [1978] 3 All ER 262; *Linden Gardens Trust Ltd v Lenesta Sludge Disposals Ltd* [1994] 1 AC 85; *Flood v Shand* [1996] NPC 185; *R v Chester and North Wales Legal Aid Area Office (No.12)* [1998] 1 WLR 1496; *Bawejem Ltd v MC Fabrications Ltd* [1999] 1 All ER (Comm) 377. See further Cartwright (1993) 9 Const LJ 281; Berg [1994] JBL 129. A mere restriction on 'assignment' will not, however, prevent a declaration of trust of the right: *Re Turcan* (1888) 40 ChD 5; *Safeguard Industrial Investments Ltd v National Westminster Bank Ltd* [1982] 1 All ER 449; *Don King Productions Inc v Warren* [1999] 2 All ER 218. The reasoning behind this interpretation, though, has been criticised by a number of academic commentators: see eg Tettenborn [1998] LMCLQ 498 and [1999] LMCLQ 353; McCormack [2000] JBL 422; McMeel [2004] LMCLQ 483. Curiously, it would appear that a prohibition on assignment does not prevent an assignment where the assignment predates the contract containing the prohibition and operates as a contract to assign future property (*Foamcrete (UK) Ltd v Thrust Engineering Ltd* [2002] BCC 221).

[69]   *Hendry v Chartsearch Ltd* [1998] CLC 1382. Even where the contract provides that the consent may not be unreasonably withheld, and it is unreasonably withheld (or it would be unreasonable for it to be withheld if it were asked for), there can be no valid assignment until after (i) consent has been granted or (ii) the consent has been asked for and the court has declared that the consent has been unreasonably withheld: *Hendry v Chartsearch*, ibid. See also *British Gas Trading Ltd v Eastern Electricity* (1996) *The Times*, 29 November (upheld on appeal (unreported), 18 December 1996, CA). The standard form of loan agreement recommended by the Loan Market Association provides that assignments and transfers are (subject to certain exceptions) not effective without the consent of the borrower, such consent not to be unreasonably withheld or delayed: for an example of the wording, see the specimen clause at **15.33**.

[70]   In any event, where the debt security constitutes a debenture (as to which, see **Chapter 17**), the issuer may not register a transfer of it unless a proper instrument of transfer has been delivered to it: Companies Act 1985, s 183(1). The requirement does not apply to an exempt transfer within the Stock Transfer Act 1982 (s 183(1)) or a transmission by operation of law (s 183(2)).

declaration of trust, so long as there is nothing in the contract prohibiting such a declaration.[71]

(b) Rights which, if assigned, result in an increase in the obligor's burden. These are not assignable unless the contract contemplates assignment.[72] This is particularly relevant in relation to tax gross-up or increased costs clauses in loan agreements,[73] and if it is intended that the lenders' interests be assignable the agreement should provide that an assignee can take the full benefit of such clauses.

(c) Rights which are intended to be personal to the assignor. Again, these are not assignable unless the contract contemplates assignment.[74] Rights arising under indemnities (such as tax gross-up or increased costs clauses) may well be held to be personal to the assignor,[75] and therefore if it is intended that the benefit of such clauses be assignable it is advisable to provide to that effect expressly.

(d) Maintenance or champerty. A chose in action is not assignable if the assignment involves or savours of maintenance or champerty.[76] The modern test involves considering whether the facts of the particular case 'suggest that the agreement in question might tempt the allegedly champertous maintainer for his personal gain to inflame the damages, to suppress evidence, to suborn witnesses or otherwise to undermine the ends of justice'.[77]

The impact of CREST

15.22 In the case of debt securities traded through CREST (the UK's electronic settlement system for shares and certain other securities), an assignment can be effected by means of electronic instructions, without any need for an instrument in writing.

---

71 *Don King Productions Inc v Warren* [1999] 2 All ER 218. As mentioned above, a mere restriction on 'assignment' will not be construed as restricting declarations of trust (though this reasoning has been criticised by academic commentators).

72 *Tolhurst v The Associated Portland Cement Manufacturers* (1900) Ltd [1903] AC 414 at 423 per Lord Lindley; *Dawson v Great Northern and City Railway Co* [1905] 1 KB 260 at 272 per Stirling LJ; *J Miller Ltd v Laurence and Bardsley* [1966] 1 Lloyd's Rep 90.

73 See **2.11ff**.

74 *Tolhurst v The Associated Portland Cement Manufacturers* (1900) Ltd [1903] AC 414; *Kemp v Baerselman* [1906] 2 KB 604; *Davies v Davies* (1887) 36 ChD 359; *Nokes v Doncaster Amalgamated Collieries Ltd* [1940] AC 1014; *Southway Group Ltd v Esther Wolff* (1991) 57 BLR 33.

75 See, eg *Peters v General Accident Fire & Life Assurance Corporation Ltd* [1938] 2 All ER 267. Cf *British Union and National Insurance Co v Rawson* [1916] 2 Ch 476.

76 See eg *Martell v Consett Iron Co Ltd* [1955] Ch 363; *Re Trepca Mines Ltd (No 2)* [1963] Ch 199; *Laurent v Sale & Co* [1963] 1 WLR 829; *Trendtex Trading Corporation v Credit Suisse* [1982] AC 679; *Giles v Thompson* [1994] 1 AC 142; *R (Factortame Ltd) v Transport Secretary (No 8)* [2003] QB 381. 'A person is guilty of maintenance if he supports litigation in which he has no legitimate concern without just cause or excuse', and champerty 'occurs when the person maintaining another stipulates for a share of the proceeds of the action or suit': *R (Factortame Ltd) v Transport Secretary* (No 8) [2003] QB 381 at 399 per Lord Phillips MR, approving the definitions in *Chitty on Contracts*.

77 *R (Factortame Ltd) v Transport Secretary (No 8)* [2003] QB 381 at 400 per Lord Phillips MR.

(a) Background

15.23 CREST,[78] which was introduced in July 1996, is operated by CRESTCo Limited ('CRESTCo')[79] in accordance with the Uncertificated Securities Regulations 2001[80] (the 'Regulations'). Its purpose is to 'enable title to units of a security to be evidenced otherwise than by a certificate and transferred otherwise than by a written instrument'.[81]

15.24 The Regulations are not specific to CREST but instead provide in generic terms for a 'relevant system'[82] run by an 'Operator'[83] approved by HM Treasury (which has delegated its powers of approval to the Financial Services Authority (the 'FSA'[84])). To be approved, the Operator and its relevant system must satisfy the approval criteria specified in Sch 1 to the Regulations. CRESTCo has been approved as an Operator, and is supervised on an ongoing basis[85] by the FSA.

15.25 Securities held in CREST are 'uncertificated', ie they are recorded in CREST in electronic form (with no certificates being issued for such securities) and may only be transferred by means of secure electronic instructions. In addition to allowing for existing certificated securities to be admitted to CREST and traded in uncertificated form ('partially dematerialised securities'), the Regulations also allow for securities to be issued in wholly dematerialised form ('wholly dematerialised securities'), ie transferable only in electronic form through CREST. In the case of partially dematerialised securities, the use of CREST is voluntary, in the sense that the issuer can choose whether or not to have the securities admitted to CREST and, once they have been admitted, a holder can either hold his securities in uncertificated form through CREST (if he is a CREST participant) or in certificated form outside CREST. Partially or wholly dematerialised securities that are admitted to CREST are referred to as 'participating securities'.[86]

---

[78] Which is not an acronym but merely the generic name used to describe the CREST system.

[79] A private limited company owned by Euroclear, the European securities settlement organisation.

[80] SI 2001/3755 (as amended), made pursuant to Companies Act 1989, s 207, and replacing the Uncertificated Securities Regulations 1995.

[81] Regulation 2(1).

[82] Defined as 'a computer-based system, and procedures, which enable title to units of a security to be evidenced and transferred without a written instrument, and which facilitate supplementary and incidental matters': reg 2(1).

[83] Defined as 'a person approved by the Treasury under these Regulations as Operator of a relevant system': reg 3(1).

[84] Pursuant to reg 11.

[85] Since the approval may be withdrawn at any time for failure to comply with the approval criteria: reg 7(1).

[86] Defined as securities 'title to units of which is permitted by an Operator to be transferred by means of a relevant system': reg 3(1).

(b) Participating securities

15.26 For a partially dematerialised debt security to be eligible to be a 'participating security', it must (i) fall within the definition of 'securities' in reg 3(1), (ii) not contain any terms inconsistent with the matters referred to in reg 19(2), and (iii) satisfy the requirements of CREST Rule 7. For a wholly dematerialised debt security to be eligible for admission to CREST, it must be a participating security whose terms of issue 'provide that its units may only be held in uncertificated form and title to them may only be transferred by means of a relevant system'.[87]

(i) Definition of securities

The term 'securities' is very widely defined[88] and encompasses not just debt securities in registered form but also those in bearer form. [89]

(ii) Regulation 19(2)

This has the effect that the debt security will not be eligible for admission to CREST if the law under which it is constituted is not English, Northern Ireland or Scots law, or if any term of the debt security is inconsistent with it being held in uncertificated form or transferred by means of CREST or is otherwise inconsistent with the Regulations.

Most domestic stock issues, unless specifically drafted with a view to them being settled through CREST, will contain provisions inconsistent with being held and transferred through CREST (eg provisions to the effect that the stock may only be transferred by a form of transfer lodged with the registrar). In such cases, therefore, modification of the terms of the stock will be necessary in order to make it eligible for admission to CREST.

Since most domestic stock issues have a trustee for the holders,[90] this process is usually straightforward. The trustee is ordinarily given by the trust deed a power to agree to modifications, without the consent of the holders, if, inter alia, it is of the opinion that to do so will not be materially prejudicial to their interests.[91] In practice, most trustees are prepared to take the view that modifications to permit holding and trading through CREST are not materially prejudicial. In addition, the modification is usually effected in such a way that the trustee can rely on reg 40(2). This provides

---

[87] See the definition of 'eligible debt security' in reg 3(1). Under that definition, the security must also be 'constituted by an order, promise, engagement or acknowledgement to pay on demand, or at a determinable future time, a sum in money to, or to the order of, the holder of one or more units of the security'.

[88] 'Shares, stock, debentures, debenture stock, loan stock, bonds . . . and other securities of any description . . . ': reg 3(1).

[89] The Regulations are drafted so that bearer bonds can be settled through CREST, by requiring that CREST maintain a register of the holders of the bonds in uncertificated form (reg 22(3)): entries in that register are prima facie evidence that the person whose name is entered has such title as he would have had if he had held the bonds in certificated form (reg 24(7)).

[90] As to which, see **Chapter 12**.

[91] See further **12.8**.

that a trustee will not be liable for breach of trust by reason only of the fact that he has assented to an amendment of the trust deed *only* for the purposes of allowing the holding of the stock in uncertificated form, the exercise of rights by means of CREST and transfer of title by means of CREST, provided he has given (or caused to be given) notice of the amendment in accordance with the trust deed. The notice must be given, not less than 30 days prior to the amendment becoming effective, to all persons registered as holding the stock on a date not more than 21 days before the despatch of the notice.[92]

(iii)   CREST Rule 7

This sets out certain detailed requirements in relation to both the issuer and the securities. The two most important requirements are that the securities must be fungible (ie identical in all respects) with the other securities of the same issue and must be freely transferable. Accordingly, securities containing a provision under which a transfer of title may be refused in certain circumstances may not be admitted to CREST unless they are modified so as to delete that provision.

(c)   Title and transfer

15.27   Under the 1995 Regulations (which preceded the 2001 Regulations), CREST itself did not maintain a register of holders, but instead generated, upon settlement of the transfer, a request to the issuer to update the register maintained by it. This has changed with the 2001 Regulations, which provide for the electronic transfer of title to participating securities.

15.28   In the case of partially dematerialised debt securities, registers are now required to be maintained in two parts. One part relates to securities held in certificated form outside CREST, and is still required to be maintained by the issuer (the 'issuer register'). The other part relates to securities held in uncertificated form through CREST, and is maintained by CREST (the 'CREST register').[93] The entries in the CREST register constitute the same evidence of title to the securities as if they had been entries in the issuer register.[94] The issuer must, though, maintain a 'record'

---

[92]   There are 'grandfathering' provisions for securities which were already participating securities when the Regulations came into force. As described below (at **15.27ff**), the principal new feature introduced by the Regulations is electronic transfer of title. A security which was a participating security immediately before the Regulations came into force remains a participating security (reg 19(4)(a)) and any of its current terms that are inconsistent with the Regulations shall cease to apply (reg 19(3)), with the result that no further modification to the terms is necessary to reflect electronic transfer of title.

[93]   In the context of corporate debt securities, the relevant provisions are reg 22(2) and Sch 4, para 14.

[94]   Regulation 24(6).

of the entries in the CREST register,[95] and that record must be 'regularly reconciled' with the CREST register.[96]

15.29 In the case of a wholly dematerialised debt security, there is only one register, maintained by CREST.[97] The entries in that register constitute prima facie evidence of title.[98]

15.30 A transfer between CREST participants is initiated by both participants sending electronic instructions to CREST, which must satisfy certain security criteria. If the instructions match, CREST will settle the transaction by simultaneously debiting and crediting the transferor's and transferee's stock and cash accounts accordingly and, 'upon settlement', must register the transfer in the CREST register.[99]

NOVATION

15.31 Novation is the 'substitution of a new contract for an old by the agreement of all parties to the old and the new'.[100] Its advantage is the fact that the 'transferee' is substituted for the 'transferor' as regards obligations as well as rights. It is thus appropriate for loan agreements where the lenders are still under obligations to make further advances, although not appropriate in the case of debt securities, since the holders would not normally be subject to obligations to the issuer. The disadvantage of novation is that it can be unwieldy and cumbersome, since it requires the agreement of all the parties, which may be difficult to obtain. In order to render novation procedures less cumbersome, the practice has developed of providing in loan agreements for novation to be effected by the execution and delivery of a novation certificate.[101] The process operates on the basis of a standing offer by all existing parties to novate (which, on the principle of *Carlill v Carbolic Smoke Ball Co*,[102] can be accepted by execution of the certificate by the 'transferor' and the 'transferee' and delivery to the agent

---

95 Regulation 22(2)(b)(ii).
96 Regulation 22(2)(b)(iii) and Sch 4, para 15(2). In practice, the reconciliations are done at the end of each working day. In addition, immediately upon registration of a transfer in the CREST register, CREST must inform the issuer of the registration: reg 27(7). Certain provisions of s 191 of the Companies Act 1985 (relating to inspection and provision of copies of registers of debenture holders) apply to the issuer's record in the same way as to the register: see further **17.1**.
97 Regulation 22(3A).
98 Regulation 24(8).
99 Regulation 27(1). Regulation 28 deals with a transfer of a partially dematerialised security from a CREST participant to a non-participant (ie involving conversion into certificated form), and reg 33 deals with a transfer from a non-participant (ie involving conversion into uncertificated form).
100 *Tito v Waddell (No 2)* [1977] Ch 106 at 287 per Megarry VC; see also *Nokes v Doncaster Amalgamated Collieries Ltd* [1940] AC 1014 at 1039 per Lord Romer (who dissented on another point); *Argo Fund Ltd v Essar Steel Ltd* [2005] 2 Lloyd's Rep 203 at 214 per Aikens J (affd, CA [2006] EWCA 241).
101 Originally known as transferable loan certificates, or TLCs, when they were first introduced.
102 [1893] 1 QB 256.

bank).[103] Consequently, the need to obtain the consent of all the parties at the time of novation is obviated.

15.32 While novation has the advantage that it can 'transfer' obligations (such as obligations to make fresh advances or to indemnify the agent bank) and, by incorporating the novation certificate structure in the loan agreement, is relatively simple to effect, there are certain disadvantages flowing from the fact that the novation creates a new debt in favour of a new lender. It may be that fresh corporate authorisations on the part of the borrower are required; the new debt may contravene a borrowing limit to which the borrower is subject[104] (ie if the limit restricts merely the 'creation' as opposed to the 'permitting to subsist', of borrowings and the borrower has used up any remaining headroom in the period since the borrowing was first incurred); and where the loan is secured, fresh registration of the security may be required, and priority may be lost (though these would not be relevant concerns where the security has been granted to a trustee for the lenders).

15.33 The following is an example of a standard loan agreement clause (based on the form recommended by the Loan Market Association) for assignments and novations:

24.   **CHANGES TO THE LENDERS**

24.1   **Assignments and transfers by the Lenders**

Subject to this Clause 24, a Lender (the '**Existing Lender**') may:
(a)   assign any of its rights; or
(b)   transfer by novation any of its rights and obligations,
to another bank or financial institution[105] or to a trust, fund or other entity which is regularly engaged or established for the purpose of making, purchasing or investing in loans, securities or other financial assets (the '**New Lender**').

24.2   **Conditions of assignment or transfer**

(a)   The consent of the Company is required for an assignment or transfer by an Existing Lender, unless the assignment or transfer is to another Lender or an Affiliate of a Lender.

(b)   The consent of the Company to an assignment or transfer must not be unreasonably withheld or delayed. The Company will be deemed to have given its consent five Business Days after the Existing Lender has requested it

---

[103] *Argo Fund Ltd v Essar Steel Ltd* [2005] 2 Lloyd's Rep 203 at 212–213 (affd, CA [2006] EWCA 241); Ellinger, Lomnicka and Hooley, *Ellinger's Modern Banking Law* (4th edn, 2006), p 723; Hughes [1987] 1 JIBL 5.

[104] As to which, see **9.17ff**.

[105] As to the meaning of the term 'bank or financial institution' see *Argo Fund Ltd v Essar Steel Ltd* [2006] EWCA 241.

unless consent is expressly refused by the Company within that time.

(c)   The consent of the Company to an assignment or transfer must not be withheld solely because the assignment or transfer may result in an increase to the Mandatory Cost.

(d)   An assignment will only be effective on:

(i)   receipt by the Agent of written confirmation from the New Lender (in form and substance satisfactory to the Agent) that the New Lender will assume the same obligations to the other Finance Parties as it would have been under if it was an Original Lender; and

(ii)   performance by the Agent of all necessary 'know your customer' or other similar checks under all applicable laws and regulations in relation to such assignment to a New Lender, the completion of which the Agent shall promptly notify to the Existing Lender and the New Lender.

(e)   A transfer will only be effective if the procedure set out in Clause 24.5 (*Procedure for transfer*) is complied with.

(f)   If:

(i)   a Lender assigns or transfers any of its rights or obligations under the Finance Documents or changes its Facility Office; and

(ii)   as a result of circumstances existing at the date the assignment, transfer or change occurs, an Obligor would be obliged to make a payment to the New Lender or Lender acting through its new Facility Office under Clause [ ] (*Tax gross-up and indemnities*) or Clause [ ] (*Increased Costs*),

then the New Lender or Lender acting through its new Facility Office is only entitled to receive payment under those Clauses to the same extent as the Existing Lender or Lender acting through its previous Facility Office would have been if the assignment, transfer or change had not occurred.

24.3   **Assignment or transfer fee**

The New Lender shall, on the date upon which an assignment or transfer takes effect, pay to the Agent (for its own account) a fee of [   ].

24.4   **Limitation of responsibility of Existing Lenders**

(a)   Unless expressly agreed to the contrary, an Existing Lender makes no representation or warranty and assumes no responsibility to a New Lender for:

(i)   the legality, validity, effectiveness, adequacy or enforceability of the Finance Documents or any other documents;

(ii)   the financial condition of any Obligor;

(iii)   the performance and observance by any Obligor of its obligations under the Finance Documents or any other documents; or

(iv)   the accuracy of any statements (whether written or oral) made in or in connection with any Finance Document or any other document,

and any representations or warranties implied by law are excluded.

(b)   Each New Lender confirms to the Existing Lender and the other Finance Parties that it:

(i)   has made (and shall continue to make) its own independent investigation and assessment of the financial condition and affairs of each Obligor and its related entities in connection with its participation in this Agreement and has not relied exclusively on any information provided to it by the Existing Lender in connection with any Finance Document, and

(ii)   will continue to make its own independent appraisal of the creditworthiness of each Obligor and its related entities whilst any amount is or may be outstanding under the Finance Documents or any Commitment is in force.

(c)   Nothing in any Finance Documents obliges an Existing Lender to:

(i)   accept a re-transfer from a New Lender of any of the rights and obligations assigned or transferred under this Clause 24; or

(ii)   support any losses directly or indirectly incurred by the New Lender by reason of the non-performance by any Obligor of its obligations under the Finance Documents or otherwise.

24.5   **Procedure for transfer**

(a)   Subject to the conditions set out in Clause 24.2 (*Conditions of assignment or transfer*) a transfer is effected in accordance with paragraph (c) below when the Agent executes an otherwise duly completed Transfer Certificate delivered to it by the Existing Lender and the New Lender. The Agent shall, subject to paragraph (b) below, as soon as reasonably practicable after receipt by it of a duly completed Transfer Certificate appearing on its face to comply with the terms of this Agreement and delivered in accordance with the terms of this Agreement, execute that Transfer Certificate.

(b)   The Agent shall only be obliged to execute a Transfer Certificate delivered to it by the Existing Lender and the New Lender once it is satisfied it has complied with all necessary 'know your customer' or other similar checks under all applicable laws and regulations in relation to the transfer to such New Lender.

(c)   On the Transfer Date:

(i)   to the extent that in the Transfer Certificate the Existing Lender seeks to transfer by novation its rights and obligations under the Finance Documents each of the Obligors and the Existing Lender shall be released from further obligations towards one another under the Finance Documents and their respective rights against one another under the Finance Documents shall be cancelled (being the '**Discharged Rights and Obligations**');

(ii)   each of the Obligors and the New Lender shall assume obligations towards one another and/or acquire rights against one another which differ from the Discharged Rights and Obligations only insofar as that Obligor and the New Lender have assumed and/or acquired the same in place of that Obligor and the Existing Lender;

(iii)   the Agent, the Arranger, the New Lender and other Lenders shall acquire the same rights and assume the same obligations between themselves as they would have acquired and assumed had the New Lender been an Original Lender with the rights and/or obligations acquired or assumed by it as a result of the transfer and to that extent the Agent, the Arranger and the Existing Lender shall each be released from further obligations to each other under the Finance Documents; and

(iv)   the New Lender shall become a Party as a 'Lender'.

24.6   **Copy of Transfer Certificate to Company**

The Agent shall, as soon as reasonably practicable after it has executed a Transfer Certificate, send to the Company a copy of that Transfer Certificate.

24.7   **Disclosure of Information**

Any Lender may disclose to any of its Affiliates and any other person:

(a)   to (or through) whom that Lender assigns or transfers (or may potentially assign or transfer) all or any of its rights and obligations under this Agreement;

(b)   with (or though) whom that Lender enters into (or may potentially enter into) any sub-participation in relation to, or any other transaction under which payments are to be made by reference to, this Agreement or any Obligor; or

(c)   to whom, and to the extent that, information is required to
        be disclosed by any applicable law or regulation,

any information about any Obligor, the Group and the Finance
Documents as that Lender shall consider appropriate if, in relation
to paragraphs (a) and (b) above, the person to whom the
information is to be given has entered into a Confidentiality
Undertaking.

PARTICIPATION

15.34 The terms 'participation' and 'sub-participation', which are used interchangeably, have no technical meanings under English law[106] but are normally used to describe arrangements between the 'transferor' and the participant which are entirely separate from the underlying loan agreement and therefore involve no contractual nexus between the participant and the borrower. There are two types: funded participations and risk participations. In a funded participation, the participant lends funds to the 'transferor' on terms that the 'transferor' will repay those funds together with interest thereon as and when corresponding amounts are received from the borrower under the underlying loan agreement. The participation is thus 'limited recourse' to the 'transferor', since its obligations are conditional upon receipt of sums from the borrower. The participant is only a creditor of the 'transferor', with no direct claim against the borrower and no proprietary interest in any monies paid by the borrower. It is thus taking a double credit risk – that of the borrower and that of the 'transferor'.[107]

15.35 A risk participation, on the other hand, is merely a guarantee by the participant to the 'transferor', in return for a fee, of a specified proportion of the borrower's obligations. The participant receives no payments from the 'transferor' (apart from the fee), and is only obliged to provide funds to the 'transferor' if and when the guarantee is called. Again, there is no direct contractual nexus between borrower and participant, though, once the participant has paid under its guarantee, it will acquire rights against the borrower by means of subrogation. Risk participations, though, are now rarely seen, and have largely been replaced by the use of credit derivatives.

15.36 In both types of participation, the 'transferor' remains liable to perform its obligations to the borrower. Nevertheless, participations are common in relation to bank loan facilities, their purpose being to transfer the commercial risk in the loan from the 'transferor' to the participant

---

[106] *Lloyds TSB Bank plc v Clarke* [2002] 2 All ER (Comm) 992, in which the Privy Council held that the term 'sub-participation agreement' is not a legal term of art and the legal rights and duties created by such an agreement are a matter of construction for the court.

[107] This risk could be lessened by the 'transferor' charging the benefit of the loan agreement to the 'transferee', but this is not generally acceptable to bank transferors and is extremely rare in normal London practice.

without the need for an assignment or novation.[108] Assignment or novation might not be possible under the terms of the loan agreement, or may have adverse tax consequences, or the 'transferor' may wish to remain the beneficial owner of the loan (eg to obtain tax credits) but to transfer the commercial risk.

PROBLEM AREAS

Stamp duty

15.37   This is considered at **18.20ff**.

Capital adequacy

15.38   One of the main considerations for a bank lender wishing to transfer its interest in a loan is to avoid having to maintain capital in respect of that interest. The capital adequacy position in relation to UK banks is set out by the Financial Services Authority (the 'Authority') in its Interim Prudential Sourcebook for Banks.[109] The basic principle is that the exposure will be excluded from the transferor's risk asset ratio and included in the transferee's if the transfer can be regarded as 'clean', ie leaving the transferor free from any residual exposure. Specific rules apply to certain special structures, but in general the following consequences will apply if the conditions in the Authority's Sourcebook are satisfied:

(a)   a transfer by novation will be regarded as a 'clean' transfer;[110]

(b)   a transfer by assignment with notice to the borrower will be regarded as a 'clean' transfer so long as the buyer takes reasonable precautions to ensure that his rights are not impaired, eg by a right of set-off between the seller and the borrower;[111]

(c)   a transfer by silent assignment (ie no notice to the borrower) will also usually be regarded as a 'clean' transfer, provided that the volume of loans sold by the seller on a silent assignment basis is subject to appropriate internal controls and the seller keeps under careful review the risks that follow on from this position;[112]

(d)   a declaration of trust will be regarded as a 'clean' transfer equivalent to a silent assignment, so long as the conditions for silent assignments are

---

108   These European types of participation should not be confused with US-style participations. Under a US-style participation, a beneficial interest in the loan is transferred to the participant, so that, if the transferor becomes insolvent, the participant will have a proprietary claim to sums received by the transferor from the borrower.

109   FSA Handbook, IPRU (Banks), Chapter SE.

110   Chapter SE, para 5.2 and section 6.

111   Chapter SE, para 5.3 and section 6.

112   Chapter SE, para 5.3 and section 6.

fulfilled and the seller receives a legal opinion confirming that the trust is effective to transfer the beneficial interest;[113]

(e)   a funded participation will be treated as a 'clean' transfer if the seller has no undrawn commitments to lend;[114]

(f)   where the seller transfers an undrawn commitment to lend, this will only be regarded as a 'clean' transfer if it is by a novation or by an assignment accompanied by an acknowledgment of the transfer and a release of the seller by the borrower. If it is by way of assignment with no such acknowledgement or by way of funded participation, it will not be regarded as a 'clean' transfer;[115]

(g)   risk participations are not dealt with in the Sourcebook , but since they are no more than guarantees their effect, depending upon the identity of the participant in question, will in most cases be to reduce the percentage of the seller's interest in respect of which it must maintain capital; and

(h)   transfers by delivery are not dealt with either, but these must be regarded as one of the 'cleanest' transfers possible.

Confidentiality

15.39   Banks owe to their customers a legal duty of confidentiality regarding their customers' affairs.[116] Consequently, any disclosure by a bank lender to a potential transferee without the consent of the borrower of the terms of, or indeed even of the existence of, a loan arrangement may constitute a breach of this duty if the borrower can be regarded as a customer of the bank.[117] Accordingly, care should be taken in appropriate cases to obtain the consent of the borrower, either in advance in the terms of the loan agreement or at the relevant time.[118]

Other securities regulation

15.40   The question arises as to whether the 'transfer' constitutes the carrying on of a 'regulated activity' by the transferor and transferee, and is therefore illegal, by virtue of s 19 of the Financial Services and Markets Act 2000, unless the seller and buyer are authorised or exempted under the FSMA 2000. This largely depends on whether the borrowing in question or

---

113   Chapter SE, para 5.4 and section 6.

114   Chapter SE, para 5.5 and section 6.

115   Chapter SE, para 5.6 and section 6.

116   *Tournier v National Provincial and Union Bank of England* [1924] 1 KB 461. See *Encyclopaedia of Banking Law*, paras C(351)–C(450); Neate, *Bank Confidentiality* (3rd edn, 2003), Chapter 9; Obank [1995] *Butterworths' JIBFL* 113.

117   The duty is clearly not applicable in the case of transfers of publicly issued debt securities, so long as the transferring bank does not disclose any information not already in the public domain.

118   The standard form of loan agreement recommended by the Loan Market Association permits disclosure of confidential information to any potential transferee or sub-participant on receipt of an appropriate confidentiality undertaking: for an example of the wording, see the specimen clause at **15.33**.

a document relating thereto is a 'specified investment'; this is considered at **9.45**.

15.41   Other potentially relevant provisions under the FSMA 2000 include s 397 (misleading statements and practices) and the market abuse regime under s 118 (and related sections).

15.42   If either the seller or the buyer is acting on the basis of unpublished price-sensitive information, a potential offence arises under the insider dealing legislation, contained in Part V of the Criminal Justice Act 1993.

The 'London Approach'

15.43   Where the borrower is in financial difficulties, the so-called 'London Approach' may be relevant to any proposed sale of a lender's interest. The 'London Approach' is a general understanding, between banks who do business in the London market, in relation to borrowers that get into financial difficulties. It is not a body of rules which have the force of law, and as such it does not have any specific provisions. Instead, it is a general approach which the market has perceived should be the best way of dealing with borrowers which are in danger of default. Unfortunately, the 'London Approach' is not written out in a single place but has been generally expounded in speeches by various people, principally officials at the Bank of England.

15.44   The main principles of the 'London Approach' are:

(a)   bank creditors should offer support for borrowers in financial trouble and should not hurry to appoint receivers or to realise security;

(b)   decisions in relation to borrowers in financial trouble should be made on the basis of reliable detailed information about the borrower which is shared among all parties to the work-out;

(c)   banks and other creditors should work together to reach a collective view on whether and how a borrower should be given financial support; and

(d)   pain should be shared amongst lenders on an equitable basis.

15.45   It used to be thought that, once a borrower got into financial difficulties, there should be a moratorium on the trading of its debt. This was thought to facilitate the work-out process in three ways: by ensuring that there was a certain and unchanging group of lenders committed to co-operation; by preventing the so-called 'vulture funds' buying up debt and pressing for a winding-up, in the belief that the break-up value would be greater than the purchase price of the debt; and by avoiding the need for new lenders to familiarise themselves with the progress of the work-out and so delaying the whole process.

15.46 However, the Bank of England's view now appears to be that an active market in 'distressed debt' may actually promote the 'London Approach' rather than obstruct it. This is because it enables lenders who do not wish to spend time and money on the work-out process to sell their debt to others who do.

Chapter Sixteen

VARIATION OF RIGHTS

INTRODUCTION

16.1   It is common to provide in the terms of debt security issues and syndicated loans for variations to be effected without the consent of all the holders or lenders. This may be achieved either by agreement between the company and the trustee (in the case of debt securities where a trustee has been appointed) or by the sanction by a specified majority of the holders or lenders of a variation proposed by the company. Trustees' powers to agree variations have already been considered.[1] Where power is given to a majority to sanction variations, the power is usually exercisable by a resolution passed at a meeting of holders[2] (in the case of debt security issues) or by written approval of the proposed variation by a specified majority of lenders (in the case of syndicated loans).

16.2   The purpose behind majority approval provisions is to protect the majority against unreasonable conduct on the part of the minority and to prevent deadlock and the defeat of an attractive proposal because unanimity cannot be reached. In both loan facilities and debt security issues, the lenders are usually given wide powers of approving variations by a majority, subject usually to the fact that variations of the 'entrenched provisions' referred to earlier[3] require a higher than normal quorum (in the case of eurobond, but not usually domestic stock, issues) or unanimity (in the case of loan facilities). In the absence of majority rule provisions, modifications will not be effective against any objecting holder or lender, who may insist on adherence to the original contract. Unanimous approval of all holders or lenders would thus be necessary.

---

[1]   See **Chapter 12**.

[2]   The manner in which votes are cast at a meeting convened by the company is not confidential information vis-à-vis the company: *Haarhaus & Co GmbH v The Law Debenture Trust Corporation plc* [1988] BCLC 640. If no provision is included for giving notice of a meeting, notice by advertisement is sufficient, and will be deemed to have been given on the day of the advertisement appearing: *Mercantile Investment and General Trust Co v International Company of Mexico* [1893] 1 Ch 484n. A requirement that notice be given 'at least 14 days before the date' of a meeting means that there must be 14 clear days between the giving of the notice and the day of the meeting: *Mercantile Investment and General Trust Co v International Company of Mexico* (above).

[3]   See **12.8(f)**.

16.3   In the case of debt securities, there are a number of additional situations in which the terms of the securities can be varied without needing the agreement of all holders:

(a) in a bond issue without a trustee, the issuer is often given a unilateral right to effect a substitution of the guarantor (if there is one) or a subsidiary as the debtor in place of the issuer (ie a novation), so long as various conditions precedent are satisfied – these provisions are considered further below;[4] and

(b) the issuer is usually given a power to buy back the debt securities from holders, either individually in the market or through a tender offer or exchange offer, thus achieving the same economic effect as an early redemption – these provisions were considered earlier.[5]

CONTRACTUAL POWERS OF A MAJORITY

16.4   There is no doubt that, if properly drafted, the contractual power of a majority to pass resolutions that bind the minority is valid.[6] However, the majority can only bind the minority in respect of matters that are specifically envisaged by the power. This is strikingly illustrated by *Hay v The Swedish and Norwegian Rly Co Ltd*.[7] The trust deed contained meetings provisions, and provided that a resolution passed by the requisite majority should be binding on all holders, but there was no description of the matters to which resolutions could relate. As a result, the court held that the majority had no power to sanction anything that was inconsistent with the rights of the minority, and therefore had no power to sanction a modification of the holders' rights.

16.5   Where powers have been inserted, they will be construed as only permitting changes that can reasonably be considered to have been within

---

4   See **16.12ff**.

5   See **5.21**.

6   See, eg, *Re The Dominion of Canada Freehold Estate and Timber Co Ltd* (1886) 55 LT 347; *Follit v Eddystone Granite Quarries* [1892] 3 Ch 75; *Hay v The Swedish and Norwegian Rly Co Ltd* (1889) 5 TLR 460; *Mercantile Investment and General Trust Co v International Company of Mexico* [1893] 1 Ch 484n; *Mercantile Investment and General Trust Co v River Plate Trust, Loan and Agency Co* [1894] 1 Ch 578; *Sneath v Valley Gold Ltd* [1893] 1 Ch 477; *Walker v Elmore's German and Austro – Hungarian Metal Co Ltd* (1901) 85 LT 767; *Re WH Hutchinson and Sons Ltd* (1915) 31 TLR 324; *Shaw v Royce Ltd* [1911] 1 Ch 138; *Northern Assurance Co Ltd v Farnham United Breweries Ltd* [1912] 2 Ch 125; *Cox Moore v Peruvian Corp Ltd* [1908] 1 Ch 604; *Re Joseph Stocks & Co. Ltd* [1912] 2 Ch 134n; *Meade-King v Usher's Wiltshire Brewery Ltd* (1928) 44 TLR 298; *Re New York Taxicab Co Ltd* [1913] 1 Ch 1; *Re German Potash Syndicate's Trust Deed* (1955) *The Times*, 25 March; *Re The Kent Collieries (Ltd)* (1907) 23 TLR 559; *Finlay v Mexican Investment Corporation* [1897] 1 QB 517; *Wright v Revelstoke* (1914) *The Times*, 7 February; *Re Labuan and Borneo (Ltd)* (1901) 18 TLR 216; *Goodfellow v Nelson Line (Liverpool) Ltd* [1912] 2 Ch 324; *Dey v Rubber and Mercantile Corporation Ltd* [1923] 2 Ch 528; *British America Nickel Corporation Ltd v MJ O'Brien Ltd* [1927] AC 369; *Redwood Master Fund Ltd v TD Bank Europe Ltd* [2002] All ER (D) 141 (Dec).

7   (1889) 5 TLR 460.

the contemplation of the parties at the time of issue,[8] and ambiguities are therefore construed in favour of the minority.[9] For example:

(a) A power to 'compromise' is only applicable where there is a dispute about the holders' rights:

> 'A power to compromise [the holders'] rights presupposes some dispute about them or difficulties in enforcing them, and does not include a power to exchange their debentures for shares in another company, where there is no such dispute or difficulty.'[10]

Actual litigation is not required: 'all that is required is a difficulty which cannot be got over without some arrangement'.[11] Where a dispute or difficulty can be shown, the scope of the arrangements which can be approved by the resolution is wide, and includes, for example, an exchange of the debt for shares.[12] However, there must be an element of

---

[8] See eg *Hole v Garnsey* [1930] AC 472 (the case concerned a purported amendment to the rules of an industrial and provident society, but the judgments of the House of Lords make it clear that their Lordships regard the principle as applicable to all contractual majority provisions): 'if a man enters into association with others for a business venture he commits himself to be bound by the decision of the majority of his associates on matters within the contemplated scope of the venture. But outside that scope he remains dominus, and cannot be bound against his will' (at 493–494 per Lord Atkin); a power of amendment by majority approval is limited 'to matters which are within the scope of the administration of the venture as originally framed' (at 496 per Lord Atkin); one of 'the general principles governing contracts inter partes' is that a power of amendment by majority approval 'must, I think, be confined to such amendments as can reasonably be considered to have been within the contemplation of the parties when the contract was made, having regard to the nature and circumstances of the contract' (at 500 per Lord Tomlin).

[9] See eg *Mercantile Investment and General Trust Co v International Company of Mexico* [1893] 1 Ch 484n at 489 per Lindley LJ ('Powers given to majorities to bind minorities are always liable to abuse; and, whilst full effect ought to be given to them in cases clearly falling within them, ambiguities of language ought not to be taken advantage of to strengthen them and make them applicable to cases not included in those which they were apparently intended to meet'); *Re German Potash Syndicate's Trust Deed* (1955) *The Times*, 25 March per Wynn Parry J ('In the absence of the clearest provision, in the document setting out the rights of members of a class, enabling a majority to alter those rights to the prejudice of a minority, they could not do so').

[10] *Mercantile Investment and General Trust Co v International Company of Mexico* [1893] 1 Ch 484n at 489 per Lindley LJ. See also ibid at 491 per Fry LJ (a 'compromise' 'undoubtedly embraces an agreement between two or more persons for the ascertainment of their rights when there is some question in controversy between them or some difficulty in the enforcement to the uttermost farthing of the rights of the claimant. But, in my opinion, the word is applicable only where there is some such controversy or some such difficulty'); *Northern Assurance Co Ltd v Farnham United Breweries Ltd* [1912] 2 Ch 125 at 133 per Joyce J ('there cannot be a compromise in the absence of any dispute or unless some question or other has arisen'); *Mercantile Investment and General Trust Co v River Plate Trust, Loan and Agency Co* [1894] 1 Ch 578; *Sneath v Valley Gold Ltd* [1893] 1 Ch 477; *Walker v Elmore's German and Austro-Hungarian Metal Co Ltd* (1901) 85 LT 767; *Shaw v Royce Ltd* [1911] 1 Ch 138.

[11] *Sneath v Valley Gold Ltd* [1893] 1 Ch 477 at 494 per Lindley LJ.

[12] *Mercantile Investment and General Trust Co v International Company of Mexico* [1893] 1 Ch 484n; *Mercantile Investment and General Trust Co v River Plate Trust, Loan and Agency Co* [1894] 1 Ch 578; *Sneath v Valley Gold Ltd* [1893] 1 Ch 477.

accommodation on both sides, and not merely a one-way release of liability.[13]

(b) A power to approve 'modifications' (or similar terms such as 'amendments', 'arrangements' or 'alterations') does not permit arrangements which amount to a release or extinction of the holders' rights (such as an exchange of the debt for shares)[14] or which benefit some holders at the expense of others (such as a division of proceeds among some only of the holders).[15] It does, however, permit the approval of the creation of prior-ranking security,[16] the modification of dated bonds into perpetual bonds,[17] and an early redemption of the bonds at a redemption price below par.[18]

(c) A power to release security does not include a power to release the obligor from the obligations secured by the security.[19]

(d) There is no power to appoint a committee to act on behalf of the bondholders unless a specific power to delegate has been included.[20]

16.6   Because of these limitations, it is standard to include a wide range of matters which can be approved by resolution, and in particular to make specific references to 'abrogations' of the holders' rights, exchanges of the

---

13   See eg *Mercantile Investment and General Trust Co v International Company of Mexico* [1893] 1 Ch 484n at 489 per Lindley LJ ('A power to compromise does not include a power to make presents'); *Re NFU Development Trust Ltd* [1973] 1 All ER 135 at 140 per Brightman J ('The word "compromise" implies some element of accommodation on each side. It is not apt to describe total surrender. A claimant who abandons his claim is not compromising it').

14   On the basis that that is not a 'modification' but rather an 'extinction': *Mercantile Investment and General Trust Co v International Company of Mexico* [1893] 1 Ch 484n. 'The power to modify the rights of the debenture-holders against the company does not include a power to relinquish all their rights': ibid at 489 per Lindley LJ. See also *Re NFU Development Trust Ltd* [1973] 1 All ER 135 at 140 per Brightman J ('I think that the word "arrangement" ... implies some element of give and take. Confiscation is not my idea of an arrangement').

15   *Re New York Taxicab Co Ltd* [1913] 1 Ch 1; *Re German Potash Syndicate's Trust Deed* (1955) *The Times* 25 March. See also *Finlay v Mexican Investment Corporation* [1897] 1 QB 517 at 522 per Charles J ('if the true effect of the resolution was to benefit one set of debenture-holders at the expense of another it was ultra vires'). The mere fact that the proposal treats some holders differently from others does not, however, make it ultra vires, so long as there are good reasons for doing so, full disclosure and no unfairness or oppression: *Goodfellow v Nelson Line (Liverpool) Ltd* [1912] 1 Ch 324. There is obviously considerable overlap here with the principle that holders should vote in the interests of the class as a whole (see further below).

16   *Re The Dominion of Canada Freehold Estate and Timber Co Ltd* (1886) 55 LT 347; *Follit v Eddystone Granite Quarries* [1892] 3 Ch 75.

17   *Re Joseph Stocks & Co Ltd* [1912] 2 Ch 134n; *Northern Assurance Co. Ltd v Farnham United Breweries Ltd* [1912] 2 Ch 125.

18   *Meade-King v Usher's Wiltshire Brewery Ltd* (1928) 44 TLR 298.

19   'The power to release the mortgaged premises ... does not include a power to release the Defendant company': *Mercantile Investment and General Trust Co v International Company of Mexico* [1893] 1 Ch 484n at 489 per Lindley LJ.

20   *British America Nickel Corporation Ltd v MJ O'Brien Ltd* [1927] AC 369.

bonds for shares, new debt securities and/or cash,[21] and the appointment of committees to act on behalf of the holders. A typical provision (in this case, in an issue of debt securities without a trustee) reads as follows:

> A meeting of the Noteholders shall, in addition to the powers set out above, have the following powers exercisable only by Extraordinary Resolution:
>
> (a) power to approve any compromise or arrangement proposed to be made between the Issuer and the Noteholders and Couponholders or any of them;
>
> (b) power to approve any abrogation, modification, compromise or arrangement in respect of the rights of the Noteholders and Couponholders against the Issuer or against any of its property whether these rights arise under this Agreement, the Notes or the Coupons or otherwise;
>
> (c) power to agree to any modification of the provisions contained in this Agreement, the Conditions or the Notes which is proposed by the Issuer;
>
> (d) power to give any authority or approval which under the provisions of this Schedule or the Notes is required to be given by Extraordinary Resolution;
>
> (e) power to appoint any persons (whether Noteholders or not) as a committee or committees to represent the interests of the Noteholders and to confer upon any committee or committees any powers or discretions which the Noteholders could themselves exercise by Extraordinary Resolution;
>
> (f) power to approve any scheme or proposal for the exchange or sale of the Notes for, or the conversion of the Notes into, or the cancellation of the Notes in consideration of, shares, stock, notes, bonds, debentures, debenture stock and/or other obligations and/or securities of the Issuer or any other company formed or to be formed, or for or into or in consideration of cash, or partly for or into or in consideration of shares, stock, notes, bonds, debentures, debenture stock and/or other obligations and/or securities as stated above and partly for or into or in consideration of cash; and
>
> (g) power to approve the substitution of any entity in place of the Issuer (or any previous substitute) as the principal debtor in respect of the Notes and the Coupons.

INVALID RESOLUTIONS

16.7 In addition to a majority decision being invalid for exceeding the powers given to the majority (as already described above), it may also be

---

[21] For the validity of such provisions, see eg *Re W H Hutchinson and Sons Ltd* (1915) 31 TLR 324 (the majority had power 'to agree to accept any other property or securities instead of the stock' and 'to sanction any scheme for the reconstruction of the company or for the amalgamation of the company with any other company': it was held that an exchange of the stock for new debenture stock of the company's purchaser fell within those powers); *Wright v Revelstoke* (1914) *The Times*, 7 February (the majority had power to approve an exchange of bonds: it was held that an exchange of interest coupons for interest-bearing notes fell within that power).

invalid if there is fraud or the majority are not acting bona fide.[22] In addition, unless there is something in the terms to indicate the contrary,[23] the power of a majority to bind a minority:

'...must be exercised subject to a general principle, which is applicable to all authorities conferred on majorities of classes enabling them to bind minorities; namely, that the power given must be exercised for the purpose of benefiting the class as a whole, and not merely individual members only.'[24]

16.8　　In practice, of course, the lenders may have widely differing interests and commercial objectives, which can therefore make it difficult, or impossible, to ascertain what is for the benefit of the lenders as a whole. Indeed, one of the purposes of majority voting provisions is to provide a way of resolving conflicts between lenders. In addition, it is clearly impossible to investigate the thoughts and motives of each of the lenders. So what does the concept of 'benefiting the class as a whole' mean in practice?

16.9　　It does not mean that a resolution is invalidated merely because its effect is prejudicial to the minority: what is required is some improper or unfair motive on the part of the majority, such as fraud, bad faith, an intention to oppress the minority or to deprive it of its rights, or the majority

---

[22]　See eg *Goodfellow v Nelson Line (Liverpool) Ltd* [1912] 2 Ch 324 at 333 per Parker J ('the powers conferred by the trust deed on a majority of the debenture-holders must, of course, be exercised bona fide'); *Walker v Elmore's German and Austro-Hungarian Metal Co Ltd* (1901) 85 LT 767 at 771 per Williams LJ ('I start with saying this: I think that where you have got a majority of the debenture-holders passing a resolution, and there is no suggestion of fraud or any definite want of bona fides, you should give every weight to the resolution of the debenture-holders') and at 772 per Romer LJ ('the resolutions are to my mind clearly binding, this not being a case where any fraud or mala fides has been established, or indeed, so far as I am aware, even suggested'); *Northern Assurance Co Ltd v Farnham United Breweries Ltd* [1912] 2 Ch 125 at 134 per Joyce J (the grounds for holding the resolution to be valid included the fact that there was no evidence 'to show that the conduct of the majority was actually or technically fraudulent, or that the vote was otherwise than perfectly bona fide, regular and proper'); *Mercantile Investment and General Trust Co v River Plate Trust, Loan and Agency Co* [1894] 1 Ch 578 at 597 per Romer J (the grounds for holding the resolution to be valid included the fact that the resolution 'was honestly arrived at, and was bona fide passed at the meeting by the necessary majority').

[23]　As in *Redwood Master Fund Ltd v TD Bank Europe Ltd* [2006] 1 BCLC 149, where the lenders were divided into three classes with different terms and potentially differing interests.

[24]　*British America Nickel Corporation Ltd v MJ O'Brien Ltd.* [1927] AC 369 at 371 per Viscount Haldane. See also, eg, ibid at 373 per Viscount Haldane ('while usually a holder of shares or debentures may vote as his interest directs, he is subject to the further principle that where his vote is conferred on him as a member of a class he must conform to the interest of the class itself when seeking to exercise the power conferred on him in his capacity of being a member'); *Mercantile Investment and General Trust Co v River Plate Trust, Loan and Agency Co* [1894] 1 Ch 578 at 597 per Romer J (the grounds for holding the resolution to be valid included the fact that the majority were 'acting solely in what they believed to be the interests of the debenture-holders'); *Walker v Elmore's German and Austro-Hungarian Metal Co Ltd* (1901) 85 LT 767 at 772 per Romer LJ (a resolution is valid 'if the majority of the debenture-holders came to a fair and honest conclusion that it was to the interest of the debenture-holders'); *Goodfellow v Nelson Line (Liverpool) Ltd.* [1912] 2 Ch 324 at 333 per Parker J ('the Court can no doubt interfere to prevent unfairness or oppression').

being motivated by a collateral benefit that is not available to the minority.[25] The position has been described by Rimer J as follows:[26]

'The vice against which control on the exercise of majority power is directed is the potential for a dishonest abuse of that power. The starting point in assessing the validity of its exercise in any case must be to assess, by reference to all available evidence, whether the power is being exercised in good faith for the purpose for which it was conferred. If it is, then the mere fact that it can be shown that a minority of those affected by it have been relatively disadvantaged by it as compared with the majority cannot automatically mean it has been exercised improperly. Of course, if it can be shown that the power has been exercised for the purpose of conferring special collateral benefits on the majority, or if the obtaining of such collateral benefits can be shown to have been the motive for the exercise of the power, that will be likely to lead to a conclusion that the exercise has been bad. It would not have been exercised for the purpose for which it was conferred, and its exercise in those circumstances would or might amount to a fraud on the minority. Equally, if the exercise of the power can be shown to have been motivated by a malicious wish to damage or oppress the interests of the minority adversely affected by it, then that too will vitiate the exercise, since that too will clearly amount to the commission of fraud on the minority, which is also obviously outside the scope and purpose of the power.'

16.10 One of the most obvious situations where a resolution can be invalidated on these grounds would be where an undisclosed consideration is given to members of the majority for voting in favour.[27] Another would be where the issuer, or one of its affiliates, holds bonds and exercises the voting rights in a manner which benefits the issuer.[28] There would also be a risk of a successful challenge where members of the majority also had other relationships with the issuer (eg as bank creditors or as shareholders) and voted in a way which benefited them in those other capacities:[29] a solution, however, in such a case (if permitted by the meetings provisions)[30] might be

---

[25] See eg *Greenhalgh v Arderne Cinemas Ltd* [1951] Ch 286 at 291 per Evershed MR (a shareholder resolution can be impeached 'if the effect of it were to discriminate between the majority shareholders and the minority shareholders, so as to give to the former an advantage of which the latter were deprived': this principle is 'equally capable of applying to the manner in which a majority of a class of lenders conducts itself in relation to matters affecting the whole class' (*Redwood Master Fund Ltd v TD Bank Europe Ltd* [2006] 1 BCLC 149 at 173 per Rimer J)); *Peters' American Delicacy Co Ltd v Heath* (1938–39) 61 CLR 457 (a High Court of Australia case that examined the English authorities at length) at 495 per Rich J ('the purpose of bringing forward the resolution must not be simply the enrichment of the majority at the expense of the minority') and 513 per Dixon J (the resolution was valid because it 'involved no oppression, no appropriation of an unjust or reprehensible nature and did not imply any purpose outside the scope of the power').

[26] *Redwood Master Fund Ltd v TD Bank Europe Ltd* [2006] 1 BCLC 149 at 182.

[27] As in *British America Nickel Corporation Ltd v MJ O'Brien Ltd* [1927] AC 369.

[28] In any event, however, most meetings provisions specifically disenfranchise bonds held by the issuer or other members of its group.

[29] As in *Re Holders Investment Trust Ltd* [1971] 2 All ER 289 (a case concerning modification of preference shareholders' rights).

[30] Such a course is normally possible, as standard meetings provisions confer on the trustee or fiscal agent a power to prescribe further regulations regarding the holding of meetings as it thinks fit.

to split the holders into separate sub-classes and have the resolution approved separately by each sub-class.

16.11   The mere fact, however, that the resolution treats some holders differently from others does not by itself invalidate the resolution, so long as there are good reasons for doing so, full disclosure and no unfairness or oppression.[31] The same analysis must also logically apply where an inducement is offered separately from the resolution in order to encourage holders to vote in favour of the resolution. Such inducements take a number of forms, eg a 'success fee' payable to all holders if the resolution is passed, an 'early response fee' to holders who give voting instructions (whether in favour or against) before a specified deadline, or a 'positive response fee' (in the event that the resolution is passed) to all those who vote in favour. In each case, it would follow that such a fee does not (by itself) invalidate the resolution, so long as it is available equally to all holders (or, in the case of the positive response fee, to all holders who vote in favour) and is fully disclosed.

SUBSTITUTION OF DEBTOR

16.12   As mentioned earlier, it is common in bond issues to include provisions permitting the substitution of a fresh debtor in place of the issuer. There are two principal reasons for including such provisions:

(a)   to enable the issuer to avoid the imposition of a withholding tax which would lead to the issuer being obliged to gross up its payments;[32] and

(b)   to facilitate a merger or reorganisation of the issuer's group.

16.13   Substitution provisions, though common, nevertheless tend only to be incorporated if it is felt that one of the above scenarios is likely to occur. The category of potential substitutes is usually limited to the guarantor (if there is one) or a subsidiary of the issuer (or the guarantor), subject (in the case of an unguaranteed issue) to the issuer guaranteeing the new debtor's obligations. An additional restriction sometimes seen is that the substitute must be incorporated in one of a list of named jurisdictions, in order to reduce investor concerns about unexpected tax consequences, political risk, etc.

---

[31]   See eg *Goodfellow v Nelson Line (Liverpool) Ltd* [1912] 2 Ch 324 at 333–4 per Parker J ('A secret bargain by one debenture-holder for special treatment might be considered as corrupt and in the nature of bribery, but, in my opinion, there can be no question of bribery where a scheme openly provides for the separate treatment of persons with special interests … I think, however, that, where there are diverse interests, and none the less where those diverse interests are specially provided for, the Court ought to consider carefully the fairness of any scheme by which a majority of debenture-holders seeks to bind a minority'), approved by the Privy Council in *British America Nickel Corp Ltd v MJ O'Brien Ltd* [1927] AC 369 at 374.

[32]   See further **3.4** and **18.18**.

16.14 The form of the substitution provision differs according to whether or not there is a trustee. Where there is, the provision takes the form of a discretionary right for the trustee to agree to the substitution without needing the consent of the holders, subject to it being satisfied that the holders' interests will not be materially prejudiced.[33] However, where there is no trustee, it would clearly be inappropriate for an equivalent discretionary right to be given to the fiscal agent (since it is the agent of the issuer and is not generally regarded as owing fiduciary obligations to the holders). Accordingly, in an issue without a trustee, the substitution provision takes the form of a unilateral right for the issuer to effect the substitution, subject to the satisfaction of specified conditions precedent. These include the assumption of liability by the new debtor under a deed poll, the execution (if applicable) of a guarantee by the existing issuer, an amended tax gross up provision from the new debtor if it is resident in a different tax jurisdiction from the existing issuer, and the delivery to the fiscal agent of legal opinions.

---

[33] See further **12.8(h)**.

Chapter Seventeen

DEBENTURES

CONSEQUENCES OF A DOCUMENT BEING A DEBENTURE

17.1 Whether a borrowing or a particular document relating to a borrowing constitutes a 'debenture' is important principally for the following reasons:

(a) Various provisions of the Companies Act 1985 relate to debentures. In addition to those mentioned earlier,[1] these include the following:

    (i) section 185 places the company under a duty to complete and have ready for delivery certificates for shares, debentures and debenture stock within two months of allotment or receipt of a duly stamped and valid transfer, except where the conditions of issue otherwise provide or the shares or debentures are allotted or transferred to a clearing house or investment exchange nominee;

    (ii) there is no obligation to keep a register of debenture-holders, but if one is kept ss 190 and 191 impose certain obligations regarding the maintenance, inspection and provision of copies thereof;[2]

    (iii) section 191(3) obliges the company to forward a copy of any trust deed for securing (ie constituting) an issue of debentures to every holder on request on payment of a fee;[3]

    (iv) under s 195, a contract to take up and pay for debentures may be specifically enforced;[4]

---

[1] See **5.2** (re s 193), **5.21** (re s 194), **6.62** and **6.63** (re ss 396(1)(a), 397), **6.83** (re s 402), **12.13ff** (re s 192(1)), **13.62** (re ss 81 and 82) and **15.21** (re s 183).

[2] If the securities are held in uncertificated form through CREST, the references to 'register' include also the record required to be maintained by the company of entries in CREST's register of holders (Uncertificated Securities Regulations 2001 (SI 2001/3755, as amended), Sch 4, para 15(5)): see further **15.28**. See also Companies Act 1985, ss 722 and 723 (re use of computers, etc).

[3] Prescribed by Companies (Inspection and Copying of Registers, Indices and Documents) Regulations 1991, SI 1991/1998.

[4] This represents an exception to the general rule that a contract for a loan of money is not capable of specific performance (*Rogers v Challis* (1859) 27 Beav 175; *Sichel v Mosenthal* (1862) 30 Beav 371; *The South African Territories Ltd v Wallington* [1898] AC 309). Where, however, a loan has been made to be secured by a mortgage, the agreement to grant the mortgage may be specifically enforced (*Ashton v Corrigan* (1871) 13 Eq 76; *Hermann v Hodges* (1873) 16 Eq 18). Where debentures are issued payable by instalments and under their terms the company forfeits them for non-payment of an instalment, the right to specific performance under s 195 (including specific performance of the obligation to pay the unpaid instalments) is lost: *Kuala Pahi Rubber Estates Ltd v Mowbray* (1914) 111 LT 1072.

(v)   sections 238 and 239 impose certain obligations regarding the provision of copies of the annual accounts, directors' report and auditors' report to debenture-holders;

(vi)   sections 323 and 327 impose restrictions on the ability of a company's directors[5] and their spouses, civil partners and children to deal in options over listed debentures of the company or other members of its group;

(vii)   sections 324 and 328 and Sch 13 oblige a company's directors[6] to disclose certain information to the company regarding their, or their spouses', civil partners' or children's, interests in debentures of the company or other members of its group; and

(viii) section 325 obliges the company to maintain a register of all information notified to it under s 324, and where the debentures are listed in the UK s 329 obliges the company to notify the investment exchange of that information.

(b) A number of provisions of the Financial Services and Markets Act 2000 relate to 'debentures'.[7]

(c) By virtue of s 29(2) of the Insolvency Act 1986, a receiver or manager will only be an administrative receiver if he is appointed by or on behalf of the holders of debentures.[8]

(d) Section 765 of the Income and Corporation Taxes Act 1988 makes it a criminal offence for any body corporate resident in the UK to cause or permit a body corporate not resident in the UK over which it has control to create or issue any shares or debentures, unless the transaction represents a movement of capital within the EU^9 or the Treasury has consented to the transaction.[10]

(e) In relation to the 'loan capital' exemption from stamp duty,[11] the definition of 'loan capital' includes a reference to 'debenture stock'.[12]

(f) In relation to the exemption from capital gains tax for disposals of 'qualifying corporate bonds',[13] the definition of 'corporate bond' includes a reference to certain types of debenture.[14]

MEANING: GENERALLY

17.2   'Debenture' is not defined in the Financial Services and Markets Act 2000 or for the purposes of stamp duty or capital gains legislation, and it

---

[5]   Including shadow directors: ss 323(4) and 327(2)(c).
[6]   Including shadow directors: s 324(6).
[7]   See, eg, **9.42ff** (re carrying on a regulated activity) and **13.55ff** (re financial promotions).
[8]   See further **6.42ff**.
[9]   Income and Corporation Taxes Act 1988, s 765A.
[10] See further **9.49**.
[11] See **18.20**.
[12] Finance Act 1986, ss 78(7), 79(12).
[13] Pursuant to Taxation of Chargeable Gains Act 1992, s 115.
[14] Taxation of Chargeable Gains Act 1992, s 117(6A).

thus bears its common law meaning. The term is given an extended meaning for the purposes of the Companies Act 1985 by s 744: this meaning also applies for the purpose of s 29(2) of the Insolvency Act (Insolvency Act, s 251) and s 765 of the Income and Corporation Taxes Act (Income and Corporation Taxes Act, s 767(5)).

COMMON LAW MEANING[15]

17.3 No precise definition of the term 'debenture' is possible.[16] Chitty J has stated that 'a debenture means a document which either creates a debt or acknowledges it, and any document which fulfils either of these conditions is a "debenture" '.[17] On the face of it, this formulation seems too wide to be practicable, since it embraces many types of documents which clearly should not be regarded as debentures (eg contracts for the purchase of goods, tenancy agreements, bank statements in relation to an account in credit, etc). Nevertheless, the formulation has received judicial approval on various occasions,[18] though dicta in various cases[19] do support a narrower definition, and Lloyd J[20] thought that while 'no doubt it is true . . . in general . . . there is no hard and fast definition'. Whatever formulation one adopts, a number of principles can, however, be ascertained. A grant of security is not necessary,[21] and it does not matter by what name the company calls the document,[22] or that the holder of the document is only entitled to repayment upon satisfaction of a contingency.[23] It does not matter that the document is entered into with several lenders[24] or with only one lender,[25] or that the

---

[15] As to the origins and growth of the term 'debenture', see *Palmer's Company Precedents*, vol 3 (16th edn, 1952), Chapter 1.

[16] See, eg, *The British India Steam Navigation Co v IRC* (1881) 7 QBD 165 at 168–169 (per Grove J) and 172–173 (per Lindley J); *Levy v Abercorris Slate and Slab Co* (1887) 37 ChD 260 at 264; *Knightsbridge Estates Trust Ltd v Byrne* [1940] AC 613 at 621 (per Viscount Maugham) and 627 (per Lord Romer).

[17] *Levy v Abercorris Slate and Slab Co* (1887) 37 ChD 260 at 264; see also *Edmonds v Blaina Furnaces Co* (1887) 36 ChD 215 at 219.

[18] See, eg, *City of London Brewery Co Ltd v IRC* [1899] 1 QB 121 at 139 per Rigby LJ; *Clark v Balm, Hill & Co* [1908] 1 KB 667 at 670; *Lemon v Austin Friars Investment Trust Ltd* [1926] Ch 1; *R v Findlater* [1939] 1 KB 594 at 599.

[19] See, eg, *Topham v Greenside Glazed Fire-Brick Co* (1887) 37 ChD 281 at 290; *Brown, Shipley & Co v IRC* [1895] 2 QB 240 at 244 (per Grantham J) and 245 (per Charles J) (revd on other grounds [1895] 2 QB 598).

[20] *NV Slavenburg's Bank v Intercontinental Natural Resources Ltd* [1980] 1 All ER 955 at 976.

[21] *The British India Steam Navigation Co v IRC* (1881) 7 QBD 165; *Lemon v Austin Friars Investment Trust Ltd* [1926] Ch 1.

[22] *Edmonds v Blaina Furnaces Co* (1887) 36 ChD 215 at 220; *Lemon v Austin Friars Investment Trust Ltd* (above), in which the Court of Appeal held that an 'income stock certificate', which certified that the company was indebted to the registered holder in a specified sum, payable only out of profits, and stated that three-quarters of the net profits of the company each year were to be applied in paying off that sum, was a debenture.

[23] *Lemon v Austin Friars Investment Trust Ltd* (above); *R v Findlater* [1939] 1 KB 594. Thus, the fact that the relevant debt is subordinated (as to which, see **Chapter 8**) will not prevent a document being regarded as a debenture.

[24] *Edmonds v Blaina Furnaces Co* (1887) 36 ChD 215 at 221.

[25] Ibid at 221; *Levy v Abercorris Slate and Slab Co* (1887) 37 ChD 260 at 264.

document is both in a foreign language and governed by a foreign law.[26] An ordinary mortgage of freehold property is (notwithstanding Chitty J's formulation) not a debenture at common law,[27] but (it would seem) a floating charge is.[28] A memorandum of a deposit of title deeds as security for the balance for the time being owing on the company's current account has been held not to be a debenture since it contains no acknowledgement of a debt or covenant to pay.[29]

17.4   Bonds, notes, ECP and stock certificates are all clearly debentures at common law. It is unclear whether loan agreements themselves (either when originally entered into or when novated) constitute debentures,[30] but Lloyd J in the *Slavenburg* case[31] stated that he would be unwilling to hold that a document was not a debenture because the debt to which it related was not quantified at the date of the document, and said that, if it had been necessary for his decision, he would have held that a general credit agreement by which a bank was to provide a company with credit facilities[32] was a debenture.

17.5   A clear and helpful summary of the existing case law can be found in the majority judgment in *Handevel Pty Ltd v Comptroller of Stamps (Vic)*[33] (a High Court of Australia case):

> 'Any discussion of the nature of a debenture must begin with the statement that English judges of great authority have confessed that the term defies accurate definition (*British India Steam Company v Commissioners of Inland Revenue* (1881) 7 QBD 165, at pp 172–173; *Lemon v Austin Friars Investment Trust* [1926] Ch 1, at p 17; *Knightsbridge Estates Trust, Ltd v Byrne* [1940] AC 613, at pp 621-622). However, it has been generally agreed that two characteristics of a debenture are, first, that it is issued by a company and, secondly, that it acknowledges or creates a debt – see *British India Company*; *Edmonds v*

---

26   *NV Slavenburg's Bank v Intercontinental Natural Resources Ltd* [1980] 1 All ER 955 at 976.
27   Though it does fall within the extended definition in the Companies Act: *Knightsbridge Estates Trust Ltd v Byrne* [1940] AC 613.
28   *National Provincial Bank of England Ltd v United Electric Theatres Ltd* [1916] 1 Ch 132. The question in that case (which was not referred to in *Knightsbridge*) was whether the floating charge was a debenture for the purposes of s 107 of the Companies (Consolidation) Act 1908. The term bore its common law meaning in that Act, since, as Viscount Maugham and Lord Romer pointed out in *Knightsbridge*, an extended definition did not appear in the Companies Acts until the Companies Act 1928.
29   *Topham v Greenside Glazed Fire-Brick Co* (1887) 37 ChD 281.
30   Berg, for example, in IFLR, January 1991, p 27, argues that they do. Tennekoon in *The Law and Regulation of International Finance* (1991), pp 124–127, argues that they do not, in that the indebtedness is created by the disbursement of funds to the borrower upon drawdown rather than by the agreement itself, and is not acknowledged by the agreement since at the time of the agreement there is no debt which is capable of acknowledgement. Whereas this is certainly the case at the initial execution of the agreement, it is not so in relation to a novation of the agreement after drawdown has taken place.
31   *NV Slavenburg's Bank v Intercontinental Natural Resources Ltd* [1980] 1 All ER 955 at 976.
32   And also a general agreement of assignment whereby the company agreed to assign to the bank all the company's present and future debts and an assignment to the bank by way of security of the entire business of the company.
33   (1985) 157 CLR 177 at para 20.

Blaina Furnaces Company (1887) 36 ChD 215; *Levy v Abercorris Slate and Slab Company* (1888) 37 ChD 260, at p 264; *Topham v Greenside Glazed Fire-Brick Company* (1888) 37 ChD 281, at p 292; *Broad v Commissioner of Stamp Duties* [1980] 2 NSWLR 40, at pp 48–52. The debt may be secured on the assets of the company but security in this sense is not an essential characteristic of a debenture (*Blaina Furnaces*, at p 219). *In Burns Philp Trustee Company Ltd v Commissioner of Stamp Duties* (NSW) (1983) 83 ATC 4,477 Hunt J stated (at p 4,479) that, in order to constitute a debenture the debt which is acknowledged or created must be an existing, not a future debt. His Honour's view is supported by authority (*Lemon v Austin Friars Investment Trust*; *R v Findlater* [1939] 1 KB 594, at p 599). However, the statement needs to be qualified to allow for a document which makes provision for the repayment of a loan to be made thereafter. On the other hand, not every document creating or acknowledging a debt of a company is a debenture. It has been said that commercial men and lawyers would not use the term when referring to negotiable instruments, deeds of covenant and many other documents in which a company agrees to pay a sum of money (*Palmer's Company Law* (1982) vol 1, p 531). And it has never been suggested that a promise in writing by a company to purchase shares at a future date amounts to a debenture in the ordinary sense of that term (cf *Inland Revenue Commissioners v Henry Ansbacher & Co* [1963] AC 191, at p 205). Nor has it ever been suggested that a specific mortgage of land to secure a future obligation to purchase property amounts to a debenture according to its ordinary meaning (*Knightsbridge Estates Trust*, at pp 620, 629).'

COMPANIES ACT MEANING

17.6   As mentioned earlier, the term debenture is given an extended definition in the Companies Act. Section 744 provides:

'In this Act, unless the contrary intention appears, the following definitions apply –

. . .

"debenture" includes debenture stock, bonds and any other securities of a company, whether constituting a charge on the assets of the company or not.'

17.7   The effect of the definition is that, where the term 'debenture' appears in a section, it applies to:

(a)   any instrument which is a debenture within the common law meaning of the term; and

(b)   unless the contrary intention appears, any other instrument which is or constitutes debenture stock, a bond or a security.

17.8   As regards whether a 'contrary intention' appears, the principle of statutory interpretation 'noscitur a sociis' means that the particular section must not be viewed in isolation, but instead in the context of the Act as a whole. The onus of showing that the contrary intention appears lies with the person claiming that the extended definition does not apply in the particular context.[34]

17.9　　The scope of the definition was considered by the House of Lords in *Knightsbridge Estates Trust Ltd v Byrne*,[35] in which the House held that an ordinary mortgage of freehold land fell within the definition due to the reference to 'any other securities'. Lord Romer,[36] with whose judgment Lords Atkin, Wright and Porter concurred, rejected the argument that 'any other securities' should be construed as referring only to securities eiusdem generis as debentures:

> 'In my opinion the words "any other securities" mean what they say, and include all other securities of any kind whatsoever.'

17.10　　The meaning of the general term 'security' has been considered in **Chapter 3**, but, due to the various references throughout the Companies Act to 'shares or debentures', it is clear that, despite the breadth of Lord Romer's statement, the term when used in s 744 can nevertheless be intended only to embrace debt securities and not shares.

---

[34]　See *Knightsbridge Estates Trust Ltd v Byrne* [1940] AC 613 at 621 per Viscount Maugham; *Floor v Davis* [1980] AC 695 at 708 per Viscount Dilhorne.

[35]　[1940] AC 613.

[36]　Ibid at 630.

Chapter Eighteen

TAXATION

DEDUCTIBILITY OF INTEREST

18.1   The tax implications of borrowings by companies are a specialised subject in themselves. The three principal questions which arise, and which are dealt with in this chapter, are: will the company be able to deduct the interest in computing its taxable profits; will the interest be payable without deduction of tax; and to what extent will stamp duty or stamp duty reserve tax be payable?

18.2   In relation to the first of these questions, the Finance Act 1996 contains a comprehensive set of rules designed to tax and to relieve corporation taxpayers in respect of borrowing and lending activities. The general theme underpinning these rules, known as the loan relationship rules, is that a company's tax treatment in respect of its 'loan relationships' will follow the company's accounting treatment of those loan relationships, provided the accounting treatment is permitted under 'generally accepted accounting practice'. This is defined to include both United Kingdom generally accepted accounting practice (**UK GAAP**) and International Financial Reporting Standards (**IFRS**).

18.3   So, for example, where a company pays interest under a borrowing which qualifies as a loan relationship and the company's accounting treatment of the borrowing is permitted under 'generally accepted accounting practice', a company will, ordinarily, be able to claim tax relief for the interest in accordance with that accounting treatment.

18.4   It is important to note, however, that a company's accounting treatment of a loan relationship will not always determine the company's tax treatment under that loan relationship. For example, as is explained below, a company will not be able to claim tax relief for interest which it pays under a loan relationship where the interest constitutes a distribution for UK tax purposes.[1]

18.5   A company will be treated as being party to a loan relationship wherever it stands in the position of either the creditor or debtor as respects a money debt and the money debt arises from a transaction for the lending of

---

[1]   Finance Act 1996, s 84(7) and Sch 9, para 1.

money.[2] The loan relationship rules can also apply in certain limited respects[3] where a company is party to a money debt which does not arise from a transaction for the lending of money and as a result the company is not party to a loan relationship. This might be relevant to trade debts which a company enters into as either creditor or debtor.

18.6   The following analysis deals with the three questions referred to in the first paragraph above and is based on the loan relationship rules (but assumes that the interest will not be paid to a connected person, in relation to which special rules, outside the scope of this chapter, may apply).

Allowable deductions – debits

18.7   The loan relationship rules do not distinguish between capital and income but allow certain deductions for tax purposes ('debits') in relation to loan relationships, including capital and income losses and certain charges and expenses (see below).[4] The debits which can be brought into account must be computed in accordance with 'generally accepted accounting practice' (which is defined to include UK GAAP and IFRS) and, when considered together with all 'credits' in respect of those loan relationships (including profits, gains and payments received in respect of those loan relationships), must fairly represent:

(a)   all profits, gains and losses, including those of a capital nature, arising to a company from its loan relationships and 'related transactions'[5] ('related transaction' meaning any disposal or acquisition of rights or liabilities under a loan relationship, including cases where such rights or liabilities are transferred or extinguished by any sale, gift, exchange, surrender, redemption or release);[6]

(b)   all interest receivable and payable on loan relationships;[7] and

(c)   all charges and expenses incurred by the company under, or for the purposes of, its loan relationships and related transactions, being charges and expenses incurred directly in:

    (i)   bringing a loan relationship into existence;

    (ii)   entering into or giving effect to a related transaction;

    (iii)   making any payments under a loan relationship or in pursuance of a related transaction;

---

[2]   Finance Act 1996, s 81(2) provides that certain debts which are physically settled, ie through the delivery of property other than cash, can still qualify as money debts for these purposes. Finance Act 1996, s 81(3) provides that where an investment is issued for the purpose of representing security for, or the rights of a creditor in respect of, any money debt, that debt is taken to be a money debt arising from a transaction for the lending of money.

[3]   Finance Act 1996, s 100.

[4]   Finance Act 1996, s 84(1).

[5]   Ibid, s 84(1).

[6]   Ibid, s 84(5) and (6).

[7]   Ibid, s 84(1).

(iv)   taking steps for ensuring the receipt of payments due under a loan relationship or a related transaction; or

(v)   an attempt to bring a loan relationship into existence.[8]

18.8   All debits falling within the above categories will be relieved as income on a trading or non-trading basis within either Case I or Case III of Sch D to the Income and Corporation Taxes Act 1988[9] (which contain the framework for taxing and relieving profits and gains for trading and non-trading activities) as set out briefly in the following paragraphs.[10]

Allowable deductions – trading and non-trading

18.9   All debits arising in an accounting period from loan relationships entered into for the purposes of a company's trade are treated as expenses which are deductible in computing its Sch D, Case I profit or loss for that period.[11] For a company to be treated as a party to a loan relationship for the purposes of its trade as a creditor, the loan relationship must form an integral part of the company's trade.[12] This means that the company must have lent money or acquired a debt security as part of its trade as, for example, a bank or other financial trader where this activity should fall into its trade. On the other hand, for a company to be a party to a loan relationship, for the purposes of its trade as a debtor, the loan relationship does not have to form an integral part of the trade. Accordingly, this treatment (under Sch D, Case I) can extend to loans entered into to finance expenditure on capital assets which are used in the company's trade.

18.10   If a borrowing is entered into partly for trading purposes and partly for non-trading purposes, any income and expenditure is split on a pro rata basis between trading and non-trading purposes.[13]

18.11   Where a company is a party to a loan relationship (as debtor or creditor) otherwise than for the purposes of a trade, all credits arising from that loan relationship are netted against all debits. The net amount is then treated as a Sch D, Case III profit (if it is a positive amount) or a Sch D, Case III 'non-trading deficit' (if it is a negative amount).[14]

18.12   It is important to distinguish Sch D, Case I loan relationships from Sch D, Case III loan relationships because profits and losses fall into different sets of rules. Case I loan relationship profits and losses merge with the general trading profit or loss account.[15] Trading losses, broadly speaking,

---

8   Ibid, s 84(3) and (4).
9   Ibid, s 82.
10   Ibid, s 82.
11   Ibid, s 82(2).
12   Ibid, s 103(2).
13   Ibid, s 82.
14   Ibid, ss 80(3), 82(3)–(6).
15   Ibid, ss 80(2), 82(2).

can be off-set against all other profits and gains arising in the same accounting period or in the previous year.[16] Trading losses can be group relieved or carried forward to off-set profits earned in the same trade in subsequent accounting periods.[17]

18.13   Schedule D, Case III non-trading deficits can be off-set against any other profits or gains arising in the same accounting period, group relieved, carried back for one year and set-off against Case III loan relationship profits, or carried forward to succeeding accounting periods to be set-off against any profits or gains except trading profits chargeable under Case I.[18] An important point to note is that a claim to utilise Case III non-trading deficits must be made within two years of the end of the accounting period in which the deficit arose, otherwise the Inland Revenue has the discretion to reject the claim.[19]

Distributions

18.14   If the interest constitutes a 'distribution' for tax purposes, it will not be allowed as a deduction from the company's profits.[20] Some of the circumstances in which interest can constitute a distribution[21] include the examples set out in (a) to (f) below:

(a)   Where, and to the extent that, the interest represents more than a reasonable commercial return for the use of the principal[22] (this is generally unlikely to occur when the loan has been agreed on arms' length terms).

(b)   Where the interest is in respect of certain types of convertible securities and the securities are not listed on a recognised stock exchange within the meaning of the Income and Corporation Taxes Act 1988, s 841 and do not contain terms which are reasonably comparable to securities which are so listed (the London and Luxembourg stock exchanges are examples of recognised stock exchanges).[23]

(c)   Where the interest is in respect of 'securities'[24] under which the interest payable is dependent to any extent on the results of the company's business,[25] unless either the creditor company is within the charge to UK corporation tax in respect of the interest, or the only reason why

---

[16]   Income and Corporation Taxes Act 1988, s 393A.
[17]   Ibid, s 393.
[18]   Finance Act 1996, s 83 and Sch 8.
[19]   Ibid, s 83(6).
[20]   Ibid, s 84(7) and Sch 9, para 1.
[21]   Set out in the Income and Corporation Taxes Act 1988, s 209(2).
[22]   Ibid, s 209(2)(d).
[23]   Ibid, s 209(2)(e)(ii).
[24]   Ibid, s 254 which extends the meaning of 'securities' for the purposes of s 209 to include circumstances where interest is paid on, or other consideration is given for the use of, money advanced so that it shall be treated as paid in respect of a 'security'.
[25]   Ibid, s 209(2)(e)(iii).

this condition is otherwise satisfied is that, under the terms of the relevant 'securities', the interest reduces if the results of the company's business improve or increases if those results deteriorate.[26] Subject to these exceptions, this category of interest can potentially include securities in respect of which interest is only payable if the company has sufficient profits.

(d)   Where the securities of a company are connected with the shares in the company. This means where the rights attaching to the shares or the securities, in particular rights of transfer, are such that it is necessary or advantageous for the owner of the securities also to be the owner of shares[27] in that company.

(e)   Where the interest (or other distribution) is paid by a company in respect of 'equity notes' and that company is 'associated' with the issuing company or is a 'funded company'.[28] For this purpose, an equity note is a security:

(i)   where no date is set for the redemption of all or part of the principal; or

(ii)   where the date for redemption (or the latest date) falls more than 50 years after the date of issue; or

(iii)   where, if a particular event occurs, redemption is to take place more than 50 years after the date of issue, if that event (judged at the time of issue) is certain or likely to occur; or

(iv)   the issuing company can ensure that redemption can be postponed for more than 50 years or indefinitely.[29]

A company is 'associated' with another company if one of them is a 75 per cent subsidiary of the other, or both are 75 per cent subsidiaries of a third company;[30] and a 'funded company' is one in respect of which there are arrangements for it to be put in funds, directly or indirectly, by the issuing company or a company associated with the issuing company.[31]

WITHHOLDING TAXES

Generally

18.15   'Short' interest (ie interest on a loan which is not capable of being outstanding for a year or more) can always be paid without deduction of UK income tax.[32] Any other interest (ie 'yearly' interest) paid by an English

---

[26]   Ibid, s 209(3B).
[27]   Ibid, s 209(2)(e)(vi).
[28]   Ibid, s 209(2)(e)(vii).
[29]   Ibid, s 209(9).
[30]   Ibid, s 209(10).
[31]   Ibid, s 209(11).
[32]   See, eg, *IRC v Hay* 8 TC 636.

company must in general be paid subject to deduction of lower rate UK income tax.[33] The main circumstances in which that obligation will not apply in respect of interest paid by an English company are set out below:

(a) where the interest is payable on an advance from[34] a bank[35] if at the time the interest is paid the person beneficially entitled to the interest is within the charge to corporation tax as respects the interest[36] (thus ensuring that interest paid to a non-resident bank is paid under deduction of tax unless it is paid to a branch within the charge to corporation tax); or

(b) where the interest is paid by a bank (as defined above) or by a person who is authorised under the Financial Services and Markets Act 2000 and whose business consists wholly or mainly in the dealing of financial instruments (as defined) as principal and in both cases the interest is paid in the ordinary course of the relevant person's business;[37] or

(c) where the company paying the interest reasonably believes that one of the conditions in s 349B of the Income and Corporation Taxes Act 1988 is satisfied (and one of those conditions will be satisfied if the beneficial owner of the interest is either a UK tax resident company or a non-UK resident company which is within the charge to UK corporation tax in

---

[33] Income and Corporation Taxes Act 1988, s 349(2). The obligation does not apply, though, if the interest constitutes a 'distribution' (see **18.14**). This is because the obligation to deduct only applies to interest which either constitutes interest for the purposes of the Income Tax (Trading and Other Income) Act 2005 or which is chargeable to UK corporation tax under Sch D, Case III: if the interest constitutes a 'distribution', it will not fall within these categories.

[34] Ie originally from. Therefore, if the lender's rights are assigned the interest can still be paid without deduction so long as the original lender was a bank and the person beneficially entitled to the interest is within the charge to corporation tax as respects the interest. The position may, however, be different in relation to novation of the lender's rights, since that gives rise to a fresh loan, and therefore the likely position is that the identity of the new lender must be examined to determine whether the exemption applies.

[35] Income and Corporation Taxes Act 1988 s 840A. A 'bank' includes:
   (a) the Bank of England;
   (b) a person who has permission under Part IV of the Financial Services and Markets Act 2000 ('FSMA 2000') to accept deposits other than:
      (i) a building society;
      (ii) a friendly society;
      (iii) a society registered as a credit union; or
      (iv) an insurance company;
   (c) an European Economic Area (EEA) firm which is an institution authorised by the competent authority in another EEA member state and has permission to accept deposits under paragraph 15 of Schedule 3 to FSMA 2000; and
   (d) an international organisation (of which the UK is a member) designated as a "bank" by a HM Treasury order.

[36] Income and Corporation Taxes Act 1988, s 349(3)(a).

[37] Income and Corporation Taxes Act 1988, ss 349(3)(b), 349(3)(i). As to the meaning of 'ordinary course', see the Inland Revenue Statement of Practice of 13 May 1996 (SP4/96) which provides, essentially, that interest is payable in the ordinary course of business if it is neither related to the capital structure of the bank nor whose characteristics are primarily attributable to an intention to avoid UK tax. A borrowing will be treated as related to the capital structure of the bank if it conforms to any of the definitions of tier one, two or three capital adopted by the Bank of England, whether or not the borrowing actually counts towards such capital for regulatory purposes.

respect of the interest on the basis that it receives the interest as part of a trade which it carries on through a UK permanent establishment); or

(d) where the interest is paid to a person resident overseas and there is either a double tax treaty between the UK and the country of residence which provides that interest will be exempt from UK tax, and the debtor company has received an appropriate direction from the HM Revenue & Customs Centre for Non-residents; or

(e) where the interest is in respect of a 'quoted Eurobond', ie a debt instrument which satisfies the requirements of s 349(4) of the Income and Corporation Taxes Act 1988,[38] being that it:

    (i)   is issued by a company;

    (ii)   is listed on a recognised stock exchange (this includes London, Luxembourg and certain other stock exchanges); and

    (iii)   carries a right to interest.

18.16 It will be seen, therefore, that interest payable by an English company under loan agreements or debt securities may in a number of circumstances be paid gross. If for some reason the company is not able to pay gross where this would be expected by the lenders, it may be possible to structure the loan so as to avoid any withholding, although tax avoidance legislation and the terms of any relevant double tax treaty would have to be considered in any restructuring.

Typical provisions

18.17 As seen earlier,[39] it is normal for loan facilities and eurobond issues (but not domestic stock issues) to contain a gross-up provision (requiring the company to pay an increased amount if tax[40] is required to be deducted) and a prepayment option for the company (in the event that it is required to deduct).[41]

18.18 Example gross-up and prepayment provisions for a loan facility are set out at **2.11ff**. An example prepayment provision for a eurobond issue is set out at **5.13**. A typical gross-up provision for a eurobond issue would read as follows:

(1) All payments in respect of the Bonds by or on behalf of the Issuer shall be made without withholding or deduction for, or on account of, any present or

---

38   Income and Corporation Taxes Act 1988, s 349(3)(c).

39   At **2.11ff**, **3.4** and **5.11ff**.

40   In the case of a eurobond issue, this would relate only to tax arising in the company's home jurisdiction; in the case of a loan facility, this would relate sometimes to any tax, but often would be limited to tax arising in the company's home jurisdiction or the jurisdiction through which payments are made.

41   In the case of a eurobond issue, as a result of a change in law or regulation; but, in the case of a loan facility, whatever the reasons (the purpose of the prepayment provision being to permit prepayment (a) more quickly than would be possible under a general prepayment right, and (b) of merely the affected banks, rather than all of them).

future taxes, duties, assessments or governmental charges of whatever nature ('**Taxes**') imposed or levied by or on behalf of [*jurisdiction of issuer*], or any political subdivision of, or any authority in, or of, [*jurisdiction of issuer*] having power to tax, unless the withholding or deduction of the Taxes is required by law. In that event, the Issuer will pay such additional amounts as may be necessary in order that the net amounts received by the Bondholders and Couponholders after the withholding or deduction shall equal the respective amounts which would have been receivable in respect of the Bonds or, as the case may be, Coupons in the absence of the withholding or deduction; except that no additional amounts shall be payable in relation to any payment in respect of any Bond or Coupon:

(a) to, or to a third party on behalf of, a holder who is liable to the Taxes in respect of the Bond or Coupon by reason of his having some connection with [*jurisdiction of issuer*] other than the mere holding of the Bond or Coupon; or

(b) presented for payment by or on behalf of a holder who would be able to avoid such withholding or deduction by presenting the relevant Bond or Coupon to another Paying Agent in a Member State of the European Union; or

(c) where such Bond or Coupon is presented for payment more than 30 days after the Relevant Date except to the extent that the holder would have been entitled to additional amounts on presenting the same for payment on the last day of the period of 30 days; or

(d) where such withholding or deduction is imposed on a payment to an individual and is required to be made pursuant to any European Union Directive on the taxation of savings implementing the conclusions of the ECOFIN Council meeting of 26–27 November 2000, or any law implementing or complying with, or introduced in order to conform to, such Directive.

(2) In these Conditions, '**Relevant Date**' means the date on which the payment first becomes due but, if the full amount of the money payable has not been received by the Principal Paying Agent or the Trustee on or before the due date, it means the date on which, the full amount of the money having been so received, notice to that effect shall have been duly given to the Bondholders by the Issuer in accordance with Condition [   ] (*Notices*).

18.19   Clause (1)(d) of the gross-up clause set out above would be relevant to any withholding tax which was imposed pursuant to the EU Directive on the taxation of savings income (EC Council Directive 2003/48/EC). Under this Directive, Austria, Belgium and Luxembourg are for a transitional period (unless they elect otherwise) required to operate a withholding tax system in relation to payments of interest (or similar income) which persons within their respective jurisdictions pay to individuals resident in another EU Member State.

STAMP DUTY AND STAMP DUTY RESERVE TAX

Stamp duty

18.20 With effect from 1 December 2003, UK stamp duty is only chargeable in respect of stock or marketable securities. As a result, the transfer of interests under a loan agreement should no longer be subject to stamp duty. Transfers of registered securities could, potentially, be subject to stamp duty if documented under an instrument of transfer. However, no such charge to stamp duty would arise if the securities in question qualified as 'loan capital',[42] unless they were loan capital falling within the following categories:

(a) loan capital carrying interest which exceeds a reasonable commercial return on the nominal amount of the loan capital;[43]

(b) loan capital carrying conversion and similar rights;[44]

(c) loan capital carrying a right to interest the amount of which falls to be determined to any extent by reference to the results of, or any part of, a business or to the value of any property,[45] unless the only reason why the interest satisfies this condition is that the interest reduces if the results of a business or part of a business improve or the value of any property increases or the interest increases if the results of a business or part of a business deteriorate or the value of property diminishes[46] (note that this is a wider exception than the similar distribution provision set out at **18.14(c)** as it means the amount of interest to be paid cannot be determined by reference to *any* business or *any* property if it is to fall within the loan capital exemption); and

(d) loan capital carrying a right on repayment to an amount which exceeds the nominal amount of the capital and is not reasonably comparable with what is generally repayable (in respect of a similar nominal amount of capital) under the terms of issue of loan capital listed in the Official List of the London Stock Exchange.[47] In this case, it is believed that the correct approach is not to look for an exactly comparable security, but that one should look at what securities are quoted and

---

[42] Finance Act 1986, s 79(4). 'Loan capital' is referred to in ss 78(7) and 79(12) of the Finance Act 1986, and includes:

(a) any debenture stock, corporation stock or funded debt by whatever name known, issued by a body corporate or other body of persons (which here includes a local authority and any body whether formed or established in the UK or elsewhere);

(b) any capital raised by such a body if the capital is borrowed or has the character of borrowed money, and whether it is in the form of stock or any other form; and

(c) stock or marketable securities issued by the government of any country or territory outside the UK.

[43] Finance Act 1986, s 79(6)(a).

[44] Ibid, s 79(5).

[45] Ibid, s 79(6)(b).

[46] Ibid, s 79(7A).

[47] Finance Act 1986, s 79(6)(c).

adapt and extrapolate the provisions of those securities to see if the security in question has a similar economic effect but merely expressed in a different way.

18.21   In these cases, stamp duty is chargeable at the rate of 0.5% of the amount or value of the consideration.

18.22   Stamp duty can also be chargeable on the issue of securities which are in bearer form[48]. The stamp duty would be chargeable at 1.5% of the value of the securities. This charge to stamp duty (referred to below as bearer duty) would not be relevant if the bearer securities in question qualified as loan capital[49] or were denominated in a currency other than sterling and under the terms of the securities the issuer had no discretion to redeem the securities in sterling.

18.23   If neither of these exclusions were relevant, the issue of bearer securities by a UK company in either the UK or outside the UK would be subject to bearer duty at 1.5% of the value of the securities. The issue of bearer securities by a non-UK company would only be subject to bearer duty if the issue were made into the UK. No bearer duty would be due if such securities were issued outside the UK but stamp duty at 1.5% would arise on the first transfer by delivery of the securities in the UK. For these purposes, a UK company includes any company or body of persons, corporate or unincorporated, formed or established in the UK.

Stamp duty reserve tax

18.24   Stamp duty reserve tax may also be relevant. This is a tax on transactions, rather than documents (as opposed to stamp duty which is a tax on documents rather than transactions), and applies[50] to any agreement for the purchase or sale of 'chargeable securities'. Chargeable securities are (subject to certain exceptions):

(a)   stock, shares or loan capital (which for ease of description are collectively referred to here as 'securities'), and interests in securities (or interests in dividends or other rights arising out of such securities);

(b)   rights to allotment of securities or subscription for such securities;

(c)   options for the acquisition of securities; and

(d)   units under a unit trust scheme.[51]

18.25   Under the exceptions referred to above, chargeable securities would not include securities the transfer of which is exempt from all stamp duties

---

[48]   Finance Act 1999, Sch 15.
[49]   As referred to in s 78(7) of the Finance Act 1986, but free of the limitations in ss 79(5) and (6) described above: see Finance Act 1986, s 79(2).
[50]   Finance Act 1986, s 87.
[51]   Ibid, s 99(3).

(for example, loan capital which does not fall within the exceptions set out in **18.20(a) to (d)**).[52] Furthermore, chargeable securities do not include securities which are issued or raised by a body corporate not incorporated in the UK unless:

(a) they are registered in a register kept in the UK by, or on behalf of, the body corporate by which they are issued or raised; or

(b) in the case of shares, they are paired with shares issued by a body corporate incorporated in the UK.[53]

18.26 If stamp duty reserve tax is payable in respect of an agreement relating to chargeable securities, its payment is subject to cancellation of the tax in a case where a written instrument of transfer completing the transaction is stamped before the tax is paid. Repayment of tax which has been paid may be obtained if the written instrument of transfer completing the transaction is stamped within six years of the date of the agreement giving rise to the charge.[54] Stamp duty reserve tax liabilities will therefore most frequently arise where stamp duty would not normally be paid such as in relation to transfers within an electronic transfer system which is not a clearance service (eg CREST). There are also special rules and specific reliefs and exemptions relating to particular circumstances such as, for example, intermediaries, charities and issues to and transfers by issuers of depositary receipts and clearance services.[55]

---

[52] Ibid, s 99(5).
[53] Ibid, s 99(4).
[54] Ibid, s 92.
[55] For a summary, see *HM Revenue & Customs: Stamp Taxes Manual* (March 2002).

Chapter Nineteen

EXECUTION OF DOCUMENTS

19.1   The law relating to execution of documents is often regarded as tedious and overly technical. That it may be; but it is also of fundamental importance to the validity of agreements, since failure to observe the correct formalities could result in an agreement being void and unenforceable. This chapter deals primarily with execution by English companies, but also with execution by foreign companies as this is often relevant in the context of international borrowings.

THE DISTINCTION BETWEEN DEEDS AND OTHER AGREEMENTS

Types of agreement

19.2   An agreement can be in one of three forms: (i) a deed;[1] (ii) 'under hand' (ie, in writing but not taking effect as a deed); or (iii) oral. Oral agreements (also known as 'parol agreements') and agreements under hand are said to be in 'simple form', and deeds are said to be in 'solemn form'.

(a)   Oral agreements

19.3   Enforceability of an oral agreement depends upon (i) its existence and terms being adequately proven, (ii) the general requirements of contract law (offer and acceptance, consideration, intention to create legal relations, etc) being satisfied, and (iii) it not being for a purpose for which a deed, an agreement under hand or evidence in writing is required.[2]

(b)   Agreements under hand

19.4   An agreement under hand is a written[3] agreement, on any substance, and signed (in some cases merely by or on behalf of the party or parties undertaking obligations, and in other cases by or on behalf of all the

---

[1]   Also often referred to as an agreement 'under seal'. As the Law of Property (Miscellaneous Provisions) Act 1989, s 1, and Companies Act 1989, s 130, have now abolished the need for a seal in certain cases it is now better to use the term 'deed'.

[2]   See **19.15–19.22**.

[3]   A reference in a statute or statutory instrument to writing 'includes typing, printing, lithography, photography and other modes of representing or reproducing words in a visible form': Interpretation Act 1978, ss 5 and 21 and Sch 1. As to electronic contracts, see **19.90ff**.

parties),[4] but not executed in such a way as to take effect as a deed. Enforceability of such an agreement depends upon (i) the relevant execution formalities (described at **19.28ff**) being satisfied, (ii) the general requirements of contract law described above being satisfied, and (iii) it not being for a purpose for which a deed is required.[5]

(c) Deeds

19.5   A deed is a document in writing, on any substance,[6] making it clear on its face that it is intended to be a deed,[7] validly executed as a deed by one or more of the parties (or a person authorised to execute it in the name or on behalf of one or more of the parties),[8] and validly delivered. In addition, it will only be a deed if it passes or confirms an interest, right or property or creates or confirms an obligation binding on some person.[9] Enforceability will still depend on the general requirements of contract law described above being satisfied, with one important exception: there is generally no need for consideration.[10] The execution formalities for a deed are described at **19.48ff**, and the formalities for delivery are described at **19.79ff**.

19.6   Technically, there are two types of deed: a deed inter partes, and a deed poll. A deed inter partes (or 'indenture')[11] is expressed to be made between all the interested persons, whereas a deed poll is a document executed as a deed, expressed to be made only by the person(s) undertaking the obligations, but for the benefit of others (who are not actually parties).

19.7   Prior to the Contracts (Rights of Third Parties) Act 1999 coming into force, the significance of the distinction lay, theoretically at least, in the question of enforceability by a person who was not a party. A deed inter partes was subject to the normal privity of contract rule that no-one could enforce it unless he was expressed to be a party: whereas a deed poll can be

---

4   See **19.28**.
5   See **19.15ff**.
6   Law of Property (Miscellaneous Provisions) Act 1989, s 1(1). As to whether electronic communications can constitute deeds, see **19.90ff**.
7   Whether by describing itself as a deed or expressing itself to be executed as a deed or otherwise: the Law of Property (Miscellaneous Provisions) Act 1989, s 1(2). In relation to documents executed on or after 15 September 2005, the requirement is not satisfied merely by executing the document under seal: s 1(2A) of the Law of Property (Miscellaneous Provisions) Act 1989 (as amended by the Regulatory Reform (Execution of Deeds and Documents) Order 2005, SI 2005/1906). See further **19.48ff**; and Companies Act 1985, s 36A(5).
8   Law of Property (Miscellaneous Provisions) Act 1989, s 1(2).
9   See *R v Morton* (1873) LR 2 CCR 22 at 27 per Bovill CJ; the Law Commission's Report of August 1998 'The Execution of Deeds and Documents by or on behalf of Bodies Corporate', paras 2.4 and 2.5; Norton, *A Treatise on Deeds* (2nd edn, 1928), p 3; *Halsbury's Laws of England* (4th edn Reissue, 2000), Vol 13, para 1.
10   See further **19.9**. Although, technically, offer and acceptance and intention to create legal relations are still required, the fact of execution as a deed will create a strong presumption that these are present.
11   The terms 'deed poll' and 'indenture' derive from the fact that the latter used to be cut in a zigzag, or indented, so that each party could have one part and the two parts could subsequently be married together (an early form of protection against forgery), whereas the former were cut straight, or 'polled'. See further Norton, *A Treatise on Deeds* (2nd edn, 1928), pp 27 and 28.

enforced by any person for whose benefit the deed poll purports to be made, even though not a party and not even named, provided he is sufficiently designated.[12] As a result of the Contracts (Rights of Third Parties) Act 1999, third party beneficiaries can now have direct rights of action under contracts (including deeds inter partes[13]) to which they are not party. However, the distinction between deeds inter partes and deeds poll remains relevant. This is because the rights envisaged by the Act arise where a contract is entered into between two or more parties that is intended to confer a benefit on a third person. Where the intention is for one person to confer rights unilaterally on other persons who are not parties (particularly where the identities of the other persons are not known or fluctuate – eg a guarantee in favour of bondholders), a deed poll remains the most efficient means of achieving this.

19.8   A document which fails to take effect as a deed can still be effective as an agreement under hand if it complies with the relevant requirements, even though it was intended to be a deed,14 and, a fortiori, a document which would usually merely be executed under hand will be equally effective if executed as a deed.[15]

Effects of the distinction

(a)   Consideration

19.9   Whereas consideration is required in the case of contract in simple form, it is not required in the case of a contract contained in a deed.[16] However, if there is no consideration, an order of specific performance will not be available, regardless of whether the contract is contained in a deed.[17]

---

12   *The Sunderland Marine Insurance Co v Kearney* (1851) 16 QB 925. In practice, though, the distinction was of limited significance, since any deed showing an intention to benefit another person and affording that person the opportunity to learn of the deed's significance will be enforced as 'analogous to a deed poll' (*Chelsea and Walham Green Building Society v Armstrong* [1951] Ch 853; *Moody v Condor Insurance Ltd* [2006] EWHC 100).

13   Though it is not entirely clear that an agreement, unsupported by consideration, that is contained in a deed counts as a 'contract' for the purposes of the 1999 Act, the better view, supported by the Law Commission, is that it does (*Chitty on Contracts* (29th edn, 2004), pp 55–56; Law Commission Report No 242 of July 1996, 'Privity of Contract: Contracts for the Benefit of Third Parties', p 69).

14   See, eg, *Ortigosa v Brown* (1878) 38 LT 145 at 147 per Hall VC ('. . . it being clear that a transfer by writing without seal was sufficient, and the addition of a seal not rendering the instrument less effectual than it would have been without a seal'). See also *Re Tahiti Cotton Co* (1874) LR 17 Eq 273; *Re Fireproof Doors Ltd* [1916] 2 Ch 142; *Windsor Refrigerator Co Ltd v Branch Nominees Ltd* [1961] Ch 375; *Rushingdale Limited SA v Byblos Bank SAL* (1986) 2 BCC 99, 509.

15   See, eg, *Ortigosa v Brown* ibid, per Hall VC.

16   *Sharington v Strotton* 1 Plowd 298 at 308; *Morley v Boothby* (1825) 3 Bing 107 at 112; *Cannon v Hartley* [1949] Ch 213 at 217.

17   *Wycherley v Wycherley* (1763) 2 Eden 175 at 177; *Groves v Groves* (1829) 3 Y&J 163; *Jefferys v Jefferys* (1841) Cr&Ph 138 at 141; *Re Ellenborough* [1903] 1 Ch 697; *Cannon v Hartley* [1949] Ch 213 at 217. This is on the basis that 'equity will not assist a volunteer'.

(b)   Limitation period

19.10   Whereas the limitation period for an action for breach of contract is six years in the case of a simple contract,[18] it is 12 years in the case of a contract contained in a deed.[19]

(c)   Enforceability by person not a party

19.11   As seen earlier,[20] a contract between two or more parties that confers a benefit on a third person can be enforced by that person if the requirements of the Contracts (Rights of Third Parties) Act 1999 are satisfied; but the Act does not apply where one person purports unilaterally to grant rights to others who are not parties (eg a fluctuating group). In such a situation, a deed poll (or any deed that is analogous to a deed poll) is the most efficient means of conferring the rights.

(d)   Estoppel

19.12   If the contract is contained in a deed, a person executing the deed is, as a general rule, estopped from claiming that the contents of the deed do not correctly express his intentions or that there are reasons why he should not be obliged to give effect to the deed.[21]

(e)   'Contra proferentum' rule

19.13   Where there is doubt about the construction of a contract, the general rule is that the doubt should be resolved against the party who prepared the document[22] ('*verba fortius accipiuntur contra proferentem*'). Where, however, the contract is contained in a deed, the general rule is instead that the doubt should be resolved against the party undertaking the relevant obligation,[23] irrespective of who prepared the document.

---

[18]   Limitation Act 1980, s 5.

[19]   Limitation Act 1980, s 8. The term used in s 8 is 'specialty', which is generally regarded as synonymous with 'deed' or 'agreement under seal': see, eg, *Aiken v Stewart Wrightson Members Agency Ltd* [1995] 1 WLR 1281 at 1292.

[20]   At **19.7**.

[21]   *Whelpdale's Case* (1604) 5 Co Rep 119; *Goodtitle v Baily* (1777) 2 Cowp 597; *Xenos v Wickham* (1866) LR 2 HL 296; *First National Bank plc v Thompson* [1996] 2 WLR 293 at 298 per Millett LJ. There are exceptions: eg defences of lack of capacity, duress, mistake, illegibility, etc, are still available. See further *Halsbury's Laws of England* (4th edn Reissue, 2000), Vol 13, paras 66–87.

[22]   See eg *Fowkes v The Manchester and London Life Assurance and Loan Association* (1863) 3 B&S 917 at 925 per Cockburn CJ.

[23]   See eg, *Doe d Davies v Williams* (1788) 1 H Bl 25; *Earl of Cardigan v Armitage* (1823) 2 B&C 197; *Bullen v Denning* (1826) 5 B&C 842; *Re Stroud* (1849) 8 CB 502 at 529; *Johnson v The Edgware etc Rly Co* (1866) 35 Beav 480 at 484; *Neill v Duke of Devonshire* (1882) 8 App Cas 135 at 149; *Savill Bros Ltd v Bethell* [1902] 2 Ch 523 at 537; *Gruhn v Balgray Investments Ltd* (1963) 107 Sol Jo 112. The rule is reversed for powers of attorney: see **19.25**.

(f) Achievement of purpose

19.14   Depending on its purpose, an agreement may need to be in writing, evidenced in writing or in the form of a deed.[24] Consequently, failure to draw up the agreement in the correct form will result in it not achieving its intended purpose.

When a deed is necessary

19.15   The following is a list of the principal situations relevant to borrowing and security in which a deed is required:[25]

(a) Under statute

19.16

(i)   A conveyance[26] of land[27] or of any interest in land (subject to certain exceptions)[28] for the purpose of conveying or creating a legal estate.[29]

(ii)   A mortgage of any property which is to incorporate the statutory powers of sale, of insurance and of appointing a receiver.[30]

(iii) A conveyance by a mortgagee exercising the statutory power of sale.[31]

(iv)   A statutory mortgage of freehold or leasehold land in the form set out in Sch 4 to the Law of Property Act 1925.[32]

(v)   Certain instruments intended to be registered under the Land Registration Act 2003 (eg an instrument effecting a transfer or charge, or certain forms of lease, of registered land or a transfer or sub-charge of a registered charge).[33]

(vi)   An appointment of a new trustee if the trust property is to vest automatically in that new trustee.[34]

---

[24]   See **19.15–19.22**.

[25]   See further *Halsbury's Laws of England* (4th edn Reissue, 2000), Vol 13, paras 9–25.

[26]   Which includes a mortgage, charge, lease, assent, vesting declaration, vesting instrument, disclaimer, release and every other assurance of property or of an interest therein by any instrument, except a will: Law of Property Act 1925, s 205(1)(ii).

[27]   Which includes land of any tenure, and mines and minerals, whether or not held apart from the surface, buildings or parts of buildings (whether the division is horizontal, vertical or made in any other way) and any easement, right, privilege or benefit in, over or derived from the land: Law of Property Act 1925, s 205(1)(ix).

[28]   These are set out in s 52(2) of the Law of Property Act 1925 and include: assents by a personal representative; disclaimers made in accordance with ss 178–180 or ss 315–319 of the Insolvency Act 1986, or not required to be in writing; surrenders by operation of law, including surrenders which may, by law, be effected without writing; leases, tenancies or other assurances not required by law to be made in writing (ie certain leases for terms not exceeding three years); vesting orders of the court or other competent authority; and conveyances taking effect by operation of law.

[29]   Law of Property Act 1925, s 52(1).

[30]   Law of Property Act 1925, s 101(1).

[31]   Law of Property Act 1925, s 104(1).

[32]   Law of Property Act 1925, s 117(1).

[33]   Land Registration Act 2002, ss 25 and 27 and the Land Registration Rules 2003 (SI 2003/1417), r 206(3) and Sch 9.

[34]   Trustee Act 1925, s 40.

(vii) A discharge of a trustee if no replacement trustee is appointed (provided that, after the discharge, there remain either a trust corporation or at least two persons to act as trustees).[35]

(viii) A bill of sale[36] of personal chattels made or given by way of security for the payment of money.[37]

(ix) A transfer of a British ship or a mortgage (or a transfer of a registered mortgage) of a British ship.[38]

(x) A power of attorney.[39]

(b) At common law

19.17

(i) A gratuitous promise or release (ie one not supported by consideration).

(ii) An express discharge (without consideration) of any obligation arising from a breach of contract or from a wrong.[40]

(iii) An express release (whether of a right in land, goods or chattels or of an action or claim).[41]

(c) Other situations

19.18

(i) Where the document in question is being executed pursuant to an obligation under another document and is required, by that obligation, to be in the form of a deed.

(ii) A transfer of registered securities issued by an unlimited company or a company limited by guarantee and a transfer of partly paid registered securities must be made by deed if the articles of association of the company so require.[42]

(iii) An amendment to an operative part of a document which was required by statute or common law to be a deed. If a document is not required

---

35 Trustee Act 1925, s 39(1).

36 As to which, see **6.65**.

37 Bills of Sale Act (1878) Amendment Act 1882, s 9.

38 See further **6.71**.

39 Powers of Attorney Act 1971, s 1(1) (as amended by the Law of Property (Miscellaneous Provisions) Act 1989) ('an instrument creating a power of attorney shall be executed as a deed'). Consequently, a document calling itself a power of attorney but not executed as a deed takes effect merely as an appointment of an agent, and not a power of attorney. The distinction is relevant for the purposes of determining the extent of the agent's authority to execute documents on his principal's behalf: see further **19.24**.

40 *Pinnel's Case* (1602) 5 Co Rep 117; *Edwards v Weeks* (1677) 2 Mod 259; *Cross v Sprigg* (1849) 6 Hare 552; *Edwards v Walters* [1986] 2 Ch 157 at 168 per Lindley LJ. This would obviously not, however, prevent an estoppel arising.

41 *Jennor and Hardie's Case* (1587) 1 Leon 283. This would obviously not, however, prevent an estoppel arising. See also *Bank of Credit and Commerce International SA v Ali (No. 1)* [1999] ICR 1068 at 1078.

42 Because s 1 of the Stock Transfer Act 1963 (which permits the transfer of registered securities by an instrument under hand in a prescribed form) does not apply to such transfers.

to be a deed under statute or common law (even though it may have been executed as a deed), an instrument amending it does not have to be a deed, if supported by consideration.

(d) Documents under seal which are not deeds

19.19   Not all documents under seal are deeds. As seen earlier,[43] in order to be a deed, a document must not only comply with the relevant execution formalities but also pass or confirm an interest, right or property or create or confirm an obligation binding on some person. In addition, the execution formalities include the requirement that the document must make it clear on its face that it is intended to be a deed, and s 1(2A) of the Law of Property (Miscellaneous Provisions) Act 1989[44] provides that this requirement is not satisfied merely by executing the document under seal.

19.20   Documents which are not deeds even when executed under seal include:

(i)   Court orders, probates, arbitrators' awards, certificates of admission to learned societies and letters of holy orders.[45] Here the sealing is usually only for the purpose of authentication (or grandeur).

(ii)   A share certificate. Even if sealed by the company, a share certificate is merely evidence of ownership of the relevant shares.[46]

(iii)   A company's memorandum of association.[47]

When an agreement under hand is necessary

19.21   The following is a list of the principal situations relevant to borrowing and security in which an agreement in writing (though not necessarily a deed) is required:[48]

(a)   A contract for the sale or other disposition of an interest in land.[49]

(b)   The creation or disposition of an equitable interest in land.[50]

---

[43]   At **19.5**.

[44]   As amended, in relation to documents executed on or after 15 September 2005, by the Regulatory Reform (Execution of Deeds and Documents) Order 2005 (SI 2005/1906).

[45]   *R v Morton* (1873) LR 2 CCR 22 at 27 per Bovill CJ. It is most unusual these days for an arbitrator's award to be under seal: it would only be so if the parties to the arbitration had required it to be sealed.

[46]   *R v Morton* (1873) LR 2 CCR 22 at 27 per Bovill CJ. Under s 186 of the Companies Act 1985, a certificate under the common seal is prima facie evidence of the title to the shares. However, a certificate executed merely by the signature of officers under s 36A of the Companies Act 1985 is deemed to have been executed under the common seal.

[47]   *Re Whitley Partners Ltd* (1886) 32 ChD 337 at 340 per Cotton LJ. It is now highly unusual for a memorandum to be under seal. In any event, under s 14 of the Companies Act 1985, the memorandum and articles of a company bind the company and its members as if they had been signed and sealed by each member and, under s 80 of the Insolvency Act 1986, a contributory's debt in a winding up is a specialty debt (ie it is treated as a debt created by a deed).

[48]   See further *Halsbury's Laws of England* (4th edn Reissue, 2000), Vol 13, paras 143–153.

[49]   Law of Property (Miscellaneous Provisions) Act 1989, s 2. See further **6.14**. The variation of a term material to such a contract also has to comply with the formalities prescribed by s 2: *McCausland v Duncan Lawrie Ltd* [1996] 4 All ER 995.

(c) A declaration of trust respecting land or any interest therein.[50]

(d) A disposition of an equitable interest or trust.[52]

(e) A legal assignment of a chose in action.[53]

(f) An assignment of copyright.[54]

(g) A bill of sale.[55]

(h) Bills of exchange, cheques and promissory notes.[56]

(i) A loan to a person engaged in business where the rate of interest is to vary with profits, or the lender is to receive a share of profits, and the lender desires not to incur the liabilities of a partner.[57]

When evidence in writing is necessary

19.22 A guarantee (but not an indemnity)[58] is unenforceable unless the guarantee 'or some memorandum or note thereof' is in writing and signed by the guarantor or his authorised agent.[59]

POWERS OF ATTORNEY

Generally

19.23 A power of attorney is 'a document by which one person ('donor') gives another person ('attorney') the power to act on his behalf and in his name'.[60] It may be a general power, entitling the attorney to do anything the donor could do himself, or it may be limited to certain defined purposes.

19.24 As seen earlier,[61] an instrument creating a power of attorney must be executed as a deed.[62] If it is not executed as a deed, it can still have the effect of making the attorney the donor's agent, but it is not a power of attorney. The distinction is relevant for determining what documents the attorney can

---

[50] Law of Property Act 1925, s 53(1)(a). A deed will generally be required if a legal estate is to be conveyed or created: see **19.16**.

[51] Law of Property Act 1925, s 53(1)(b).

[52] Law of Property Act 1925, s 53(1)(c): see further **15.15**. Section 53(1)(c) applies only to subsisting equitable interests (and therefore, for example, not to an agreement to create a charge): *Kinane v Mackie-Conteh* [2005] EWCA 45. Section 53(1)(c) does not apply (if it would otherwise do so) in relation to a financial collateral arrangement (as to which, see further **6.33ff**): Financial Collateral Arrangements (No 2) Regulations 2003, SI 2003/3226, reg 4(2).

[53] Law of Property Act 1925, s 136: see further **15.14ff**.

[54] See further **6.78ff**.

[55] See further **6.65**.

[56] Bills of Exchange Act 1882.

[57] Partnership Act 1890, s 2(3)(d).

[58] As to the distinction, see **11.2ff**.

[59] Statute of Frauds (1677), s 4. See further **11.13**.

[60] Aldridge, *Powers of Attorney* (9th edn, 2000), p 1. See also the Law Commission's Report of August 1998 'The Execution of Deeds and Documents by or on behalf of Bodies Corporate', Glossary of Abbreviations.

[61] At **19.16**.

[62] Powers of Attorney Act 1971 (as amended by the Law of Property (Miscellaneous Provisions) Act 1989), s 1(1).

execute on behalf of the donor. This is because an authority to execute a deed on behalf of another person is generally not valid unless given by deed (ie power of attorney).[63] Consequently, a document expressed to be a power of attorney but not executed as a deed can, as a general rule, confer on the attorney the right to execute only agreements under hand and not deeds.[64] It has been suggested[65] that this requirement has been abolished by s 1(1)(c) of the Law of Property (Miscellaneous Provisions) Act 1989, but this is not correct: s 1(1)(c) has only abolished the rule that authority *to deliver*[66] a deed on behalf of another must itself be given by deed.

19.25   Unlike other deeds,[67] a power of attorney is strictly construed and is interpreted as giving only such authority as it confers expressly or by necessary implication.[68]

Revocation

19.26   The authority of an attorney (and, indeed, of any agent) is revocable by, inter alia, agreement between donor and attorney, notice from the donor, death or mental incapacity of either donor or attorney (in the case of an individual) and winding up or dissolution of either donor or attorney (in the case of a body corporate).[69]

19.27   An important exception is a 'security power of attorney'[70]. If a power of attorney is expressed to be irrevocable and is given to secure a proprietary interest of the attorney, or the performance of an obligation owed to the attorney, it is irrevocable so long as the attorney has that interest or the obligation remains undischarged.[71] Such powers of attorney are most commonly given in relation to the grant of security, to enable the chargee to perfect, or to take other steps in relation to, the security where the chargor fails to do so. A typical clause in a charging document might look as follows:

---

[63]   *Steiglitz v Egginton* (1815) Holt 141; *Berkeley v Hardy* (1826) 5 B&C 355; *Powell v London and Provincial Bank* [1893] 2 Ch 555 at 563 per Bowen LJ and 566 per Kay LJ. This would include the affixing of a facsimile signature: ie the person affixing a facsimile signature to a deed must be authorised to do so by a power of attorney from the person whose signature it is.

[64]   An exception is where the 'attorney' signs the deed at the direction and in the presence of the donor and of two witnesses who each attest the signature: Law of Property (Miscellaneous Provisions) Act 1989, s 1(3). The position is also different in relation to execution on behalf of foreign companies: see **19.61**.

[65]   See *Phoenix Properties Ltd v Wimpole Street Nominees Ltd* [1992] BCLC 737.

[66]   As to which, see **19.79ff**.

[67]   See **19.13**. The construction of powers of attorney differs also from the construction of agency authorities given by instruments other than deeds. In that case, the instrument is construed liberally, with regard to the purpose of the authority and the usages of trade or business : see further *Bowstead and Reynolds on Agency* (17th edn, 2001), pp 99–100.

[68]   See, eg, *Bryant, Powis & Bryant Ltd v La Banque du Peuple* [1893] AC 170 at 177; *Withington v Herring* (1829) 5 Bing. 442 at 458. See further *Bowstead and Reynolds on Agency* (17th edn, 2001), pp 96–99.

[69]   See further *Bowstead and Reynolds on Agency* (17th edn, 2001), Chapter 10.

[70]   Another exception is a power of attorney complying with the Enduring Powers of Attorney Act 1985.

[71]   Powers of Attorney Act 1971, s 4(1).

The Chargor, by way of security, irrevocably and unconditionally appoints the Chargee, each receiver of the Charged Property appointed by it and each of their delegates or subdelegates severally to be its attorney to take any action which it is obliged to take under this Deed, including (without limitation) under Clause [   ] (*Further assurances*). The Chargor ratifies and confirms whatever any attorney does or purports to do pursuant to its appointment under this Clause.

EXECUTION OF AGREEMENTS UNDER HAND

The general requirement of signature

19.28   As a general rule, an agreement under hand must be signed by, or on behalf of, the party or parties undertaking obligations. However, the signature of all parties is required in certain cases (the most notable being a contract for the sale or other disposition of an interest in land).[72] In the case of a corporation, though, its seal may, as a general rule, be affixed instead.[73]

19.29   The place and manner of signature are immaterial, so long as the signature is inserted in such a manner as to authenticate the document[74] and it can be identified as representing the name of the signatory.[75]

19.30   The use of electronic signatures is considered at **19.90ff**.

---

[72]   Law of Property (Miscellaneous Provisions) Act 1989, s 2(3). Other examples include: a loan to a person engaged in business where the rate of interest is to vary with profits or the lender is to receive a share of profits, and the lender desires not to incur the liabilities of a partner (Partnership Act 1890, s 2(3)(d)); and a regulated agreement under the Consumer Credit Act 1974 (s 61(1) of that Act).

[73]   See further **19.34**.

[74]   *Knight v Crockford* (1794) 1 Esp 190; *Schneider v Norris* (1814) 2 M&S 286; *Ogilvie v Foljambe* (1817) 3 Mer 53; *Propert v Parker* (1830) 1 Russ&M 625; *Johnson v Dodgson* (1837) 2 M&W 653; *Lobb v Stanley* (1844) 5 QB 574; *Holmes v Mackrell* (1858) 3 CB(NS) 789; *Durrell v Evans* (1862) 1 H&C 174; *Caton v Caton* (1867) LR 2 HL 127; *Kronheim v Johnson* (1877) 7 Ch D 60 at 67; *Evans v Hoare* [1892] 1 QB 593; *Cohen v Roche* [1927] 1 KB 169 at 174–176; *Behnke v Bede Shipping Co Ltd* [1927] 1 KB 649 at 660; *Hill v Hill* [1947] Ch 231 at 240; *Firstpost Homes Ltd v Johnson* [1995] 1 WLR 1567. A signature merely added as witness of the signature of the other party, therefore, will not be binding: *Gosbell v Archer* (1835) 2 A&E 500.

[75]   By the Law of Property (Miscellaneous Provisions) Act 1989, s 1(4), 'sign' includes 'making one's mark on the instrument'. It used to be the case (and maybe still is) that initials or a mark (or even a rubber stamp) will suffice: *Phillimore v Barry* (1818) 1 Camp 513; *Baker v Dening* (1838) 8 Ad&E 94; *Jenkins v Gaisford* (1863) 3 Sw&Tr 93; *Caton v Caton* (1867) LR 2 HL 127 at 143; *Re Blewitt* (1880) 5 PD 116; *Hill v Hill* [1947] Ch 231 at 240; *Leeman v Stocks* [1951] Ch 941; *McDonald v John Twiname Ltd* [1953] 2 QB 304; *Goodman v J Eban Ltd* [1954] 1 QB 550; *LCC v Agricultural Food Products Ltd* [1955] 2 QB 218. The Court of Appeal, however, in holding that the mere typing of the signatory's name does not constitute signature, has expressed the view that 'signature' (at least for the purposes of s 2 of the Law of Property (Miscellaneous Provisions) Act 1989) should be given its ordinary linguistic meaning, with the result that the signatories must write their names (or, in the case of a deed being executed by an attorney, the name of the donor: see **19.41**) with their own hands upon the document: *Firstpost Homes Ltd v Johnson* [1995] 4 All ER 355. Accordingly, how valid the previous authorities remain is unclear. In relation to deeds, the Law Commission take the view that facsimile signatures applied by a printer or by a person other than the signatory are not sufficient: see their Report of August 1998 'The Execution of Deeds and Documents by or on Behalf of Bodies Corporate', paras 3.58–3.63. The fact that the signature is in pencil is immaterial (*Geary v Physic* (1826) 5 B&C 234; *Importers Co Ltd v Westminster Bank Ltd* [1927] 1 KB 869 at 874 per Mackinnon J (affd CA, [1927] 2 KB 297)).

19.31 Witnessing (or 'attestation') is not generally required. Delivery[76] is not required either (being a concept only applicable to deeds), except that, where an agreement is signed in two or more parts which are intended to be exchanged, the parties are not bound until exchange occurs.[77]

19.32 It is usual to insert a testimonium,[78] but this is not necessary. A typical testimonium for an agreement under hand would read:

> SIGNED by each of the parties (or their authorised representatives) on the date which appears first on page 1.

19.33 A person who is party to an agreement in two (or more) capacities normally signs twice (or more, as the case may be). However (subject to the next sentence), a single signature is effective if it is stated to be in both capacities or there is evidence that the signatory intended it to be a double signature.[79] This position has been amended in relation to documents executed on behalf of companies incorporated under the Companies Act 1985. For such a document (whether a deed or an agreement under hand) to be validly executed, a director or secretary signing in respect of more than one company must sign separately for each company which is a party to the document.[80]

English companies incorporated under the Companies Act

19.34 Execution may be (a) under the common seal, (b) by a director and the secretary, or two directors, signing the agreement, provided it is expressed to be executed by the company, or (c) by a person acting under the company's authority, express or implied, signing the agreement.[81]

Other English companies

19.35 The provisions described at **19.34** have been extended[82] to unregistered companies (as defined in s 718 of the Companies Act 1985),

---

[76] See **19.79ff**.

[77] *Domb v Isoz* [1980] 1 All ER 942; *Commission for the New Towns v Cooper (Great Britain) Ltd* [1995] Ch 259.

[78] At the end of the operative clauses of the agreement, before any schedules and before the execution pages.

[79] *Young v Schuler* (1883) 11 QBD 651.

[80] Companies Act 1985, s 36A(4A), inserted (in relation to documents executed on or after 15 September 2005) by the Regulatory Reform (Execution of Deeds and Documents) Order 2005, SI 2005/1906, Sch 1, para 10.

[81] Companies Act 1985, ss 36 and 36A(4). In favour of a purchaser, an instrument (which includes an agreement under hand) is *deemed* duly executed if a seal purporting to be the company's seal purports to be affixed and attested by two directors or by a director and the secretary (or his deputy) (Law of Property Act 1925, s 74(1)). There is a similar deeming provision in s 36A(6) of the Companies Act 1985 for documents (ie including agreements under hand) purporting to be signed by two directors or by one director and the secretary. On both provisions, see further **19.57**.

[82] By Companies Act 1985, s 718 and Sch 22 (as amended).

which includes those incorporated by Royal Charter or under private Acts of Parliament with a view to making a profit.

19.36   In addition, the Corporate Bodies Contracts Act 1960 provides that a written contract made on behalf of any body corporate[83] will be effective if signed by any person acting under its authority, express or implied, or if made under the seal of the company.[84]

Foreign companies

19.37   Since the Corporate Bodies Contracts Act 1960 (described at **19.36**) applies to any body corporate 'wherever incorporated',[85] signature by a duly authorised person on behalf of the company, or the seal of the company, will suffice.[86]

19.38   In addition, the Foreign Companies (Execution of Documents) Regulations 1994[87] provide that a foreign company may validly make a contract under English law (a) under its common seal (if it has one), (b) in any manner permitted by the laws of the country of incorporation for execution of documents by such a company, or (c) by any person who, in accordance with the laws of the country of incorporation, is acting under the authority (express or implied) of the company.[88]

19.39   For other foreign entities, the mode of execution will depend on the laws of the country of incorporation and on the entity's constitution.

Attorneys and other agents

19.40   The method of execution will depend on whether the agent is an individual or a company.

(a)   Where the agent is an individual

19.41   The common law rule is that the agent should sign the name of the principal rather than his own name.[89] Execution by an agent, though, is not permissible if statute requires personal execution by the principal.[90]

---

[83]   Other than a company incorporated under the Companies Act 1985: s 2.
[84]   Section 1.
[85]   Section 1(1).
[86]   Corporate Bodies Contracts Act 1960, s 1.
[87]   SI 1994/950, as amended.
[88]   Regulations 4 and 5.
[89]   *Combes's Case* (1613) 9 Co Rep 75; *Frontin v Small* (1726) 2 Ld Raym 1418; *White v Cuyler* (1765) 6 TR 176; *R v The Justices of Kent* (1873) LR 8 QB 305; *Re Whitley Partners Ltd* (1886) 32 Ch D 337; *France v Dutton* [1891] 2 QB 208; *Dennison v Jeffs* [1896] 1 Ch 611; *LCC v Agricultural Food Products Ltd* [1955] 2 QB 218; *Tennant v LCC* (1957) 121 JP 428.
[90]   See eg *Hyde v Johnson* (1836) 2 Bing (NC) 776; *Wilson v Wallani* (1880) 5 Ex. D 155; *Re Prince Blucher* [1931] 2 Ch 70.

19.42 Execution by the agent in his own name is, however, permissible in two situations:

(i)   In the case of a guarantee complying with the Statute of Frauds,[91] the signature may be that of an agent 'thereunto lawfully authorised', and this has been held to include signature by the agent in his own name.[92]

(ii)   Where the agent is an attorney, s 7(1) of the Powers of Attorney Act 1971[93] provides that he may execute any instrument with his own signature by the authority of the principal,[94] and that any such instrument will be as effective as if executed by the attorney in any manner which would constitute due execution by the principal.[95]

(b)   Where the agent is a company

19.43 The general rule is that the company should execute the agreement in whatever manner would be appropriate if it were executing as principal.[96]

Suggested execution clauses

(a)   For execution by a company

19.44 Either:

---

[91]   See **11.13**.

[92]   *Graham v Musson* (1839) 5 Bing NC 603.

[93]   As substituted by the Law of Property (Miscellaneous Provisions) Act 1989.

[94]   It is unclear whether, as a result of these words, the power of attorney must specifically authorise the attorney to act in his own name if s 7(1) is to be relied on. *Bowstead and Reynolds on Agency* (17th edn, 2001), p 358 and the Law Commission ('The Execution of Deeds and Documents by or on behalf of Bodies Corporate', August 1998, para 7.14) both take the view that it need not.

[95]   Note that the section only applies where the attorney is an individual. A further method of execution is available where the agent is an attorney executing a conveyance of property owned by a corporation (Law of Property Act 1925, s 74(3)). However, since it involves the attorney signing the name of the corporation in the presence of a witness who attests the signature (and is thus more onerous than the common law requirements for agreements under hand), it is in practice only appropriate for deeds and is therefore considered at **19.67**.

[96]   Ie in the relevant manner described in **19.28–19.39**. See also Companies Act 1985, s 36A(7) (inserted, in relation to documents executed on or after 15 September 2005, by the Regulatory Reform (Execution of Deeds and Documents) Order 2005): s 36A(7) clarifies that the methods of execution by a company provided for by s 36A (ie common seal or signatures of two directors or of director and secretary) apply in the case of a document which is executed in the name or on behalf of another person (whether or not that person is an individual, company or other entity). This means also that the deemed validity of execution in favour of a purchaser (see **19.57**) applies in relation to the execution by one of those methods by a corporate agent of a document on behalf of another person. Similarly, the deemed validity of execution in favour of a purchaser under s 74(1) of the Law of Property Act 1925 (see **19.57**) applies to a corporation aggregate executing an instrument on behalf of another person (s 74(1A)). A further method of execution is available where the agent is an attorney executing a conveyance of property in the name or on behalf of another (ie whether an individual or a company) (Law of Property Act 1925, s 74(4)). However, since it involves execution by a duly appointed officer of the attorney company (and is thus no different from the general rules on execution of agreements under hand by companies) it is in practice only appropriate for deeds and is therefore considered at **19.69**.

SIGNED by [NAME OF AUTHORISED SIGNATORY]   )   [Signature of authorised signatory]
[Director/duly authorised]   )
for and on behalf of   )
[NAME OF COMPANY]   )

or:

[NAME OF COMPANY]   )   [Signature of authorised signatory]
by [NAME OF AUTHORISED SIGNATORY]   )
[Director/duly authorised]   )

(b)   For execution by an agent

19.45   If the agent is an individual and an attorney, and is authorised by the power of attorney to sign in his own name:

SIGNED by [NAME OF ATTORNEY]   )   [Signature of attorney]
as attorney for [NAME OF   )
PRINCIPAL]   )

19.46   In other cases where the agent is an individual:

SIGNED by [NAME OF PRINCIPAL]   )   Agent/attorney to sign '[Name of
acting by its [agent/attorney]   )   principal] by
[NAME OF [AGENT/ATTORNEY]]   )   its [agent/attorney]
)   [Name of [agent/attorney]']

19.47   Where the agent is a company, either:

SIGNED by [NAME OF AUTHORISED SIGNATORY]   )   [Signature of authorised signatory]
[Director/duly authorised]   )
for and on behalf of [NAME OF AGENT COMPANY])
as [agent/attorney] for [NAME OF PRINCIPAL]   )

or:

[NAME OF PRINCIPAL] acting by its duly authorised   )   [Signature of authorised signatory]
[agent/attorney] [NAME OF AGENT COMPANY]   )
acting by [NAME OF AUTHORISED SIGNATORY]   )
[Director/duly authorised]   )

EXECUTION OF DEEDS

Generally

19.48   Before the changes in 1989, the general position was that the deed had to be sealed[97] and delivered[98] (but not witnessed)[99] and, in the case of an individual, signed.[100] This position was modified by the Law of Property (Miscellaneous Provisions) Act 1989, s 130 of the Companies Act 1989, the Companies (Unregistered Companies) Regulations 1985,[101] and the Foreign Companies (Execution of Documents) Regulations 1994.[102] Further changes, to clarify certain aspects and to remove inconsistencies, were made in 2005 by the Regulatory Reform (Execution of Deeds and Documents) Order 2005.[103]

19.49   As a result of s 1(2) of the Law of Property (Miscellaneous Provisions) Act 1989, every deed must make it clear on its face that it is intended to be a deed. This would normally be done by incorporating the word 'deed' in the title of the document, including a reference in the testimonium or the execution clause that it has been executed as a deed, or a combination of these. Merely executing the document under seal is not sufficient for this purpose.[104]

19.50   Section 1(2)(b) of the 1989 Act expressly provides that a deed may be validly executed by a person in the name or on behalf of a party to the deed. It is the person who executes the document (whether or not that person is acting in the name or on behalf of a party to the deed) who must comply with the formalities relevant to him or it.[105] This means that an attorney may validly execute a deed in the name or on behalf of a party to it.[106]

19.51   The deed need not, however, be executed by all parties, unless it constitutes a contract for the sale or other disposition of an interest in land.[107]

---

[97]   *National Provincial Bank of England v Jackson* (1886) 33 ChD 1 at 11 and 14; *Re Balkis Consolidated Co Ltd* (1888) 58 LT 300; *Re Smith* (1892) 67 LT 64; *Stromdale & Ball Ltd v Burden* [1952] Ch 223.

[98]   See **19.79ff**.

[99]   *Goddard's Case* (1584) 2 Co Rep 4 at 5; *Garrett v Lister* (1661) 1 Lev 25; *Keith v Pratt* (1862) 10 WR 296.

[100]   Law of Property Act 1925, s 73(1) (repealed by the Law of Property (Miscellaneous Provisions) Act 1989). See also *Stromdale & Ball Ltd v Burden* [1952] Ch 223 at 230.

[101]   SI 1985/680, as amended.

[102]   SI 1994/950, as amended.

[103]   SI 2005/1906. The Order applies to documents executed on or after 15 September 2005.

[104]   Law of Property (Miscellaneous Provisions) Act 1989, s 1(2A) (inserted by the Regulatory Reform (Execution of Deeds and Documents) Order 2005, SI 2005/1906).

[105]   See Law of Property Act 1925, s 74(1A) (re corporations aggregate), Companies Act 1985, s 36A(7) (re companies), Law of Property (Miscellaneous Provisions) Act 1989, s 1(2)(b) (re all entities) and (4A) (re individuals).

[106]   See **19.63ff**.

[107]   Ie., it falls within Law of Property (Miscellaneous Provisions) Act 1989, s 2.

In other words, a party to a deed who does not undertake obligations under it does not normally need to execute it.

19.52   Nor is it necessary for all the parties who do execute to execute the document as a deed. It is generally accepted[108] that, provided the document makes it clear on its face that it is intended to be a deed, the execution by some parties under hand will not normally prejudice the document being enforced as a deed against those parties who have executed it as a deed.[109] In other words, it is acceptable for some parties to execute the document under hand if they are doing so for an ancillary purpose, eg to acknowledge receipt of an undertaking. Where, however, execution by that party is essential to that part of the document which is required to be by deed, that party should execute as a deed.

19.53   It is usual to insert a testimonium, but this is not essential. A typical testimonium[110] for a deed would read:

> IN WITNESS of which this [title of document] has been executed as a deed and delivered on the date which appears first on page 1.

Delivery is also required: this is dealt with at **19.79ff**. What constitutes 'signature' was dealt with at **19.28ff**.

English companies incorporated under the Companies Act

(a)   In normal circumstances

19.54   Such a company is no longer required by law to have a common seal.[111] However, it may still need to if:

(a)   its articles of association require it to have one;

(b)   it executes documents under a non-UK law which requires execution under seal; or

(c)   it wants greater flexibility in who can execute deeds on its behalf. As will be seen below, s 36A(4) of the Companies Act 1985 requires two directors or a director and the secretary to sign if the common seal is not being affixed, whereas the articles may permit a wider range of signatories to sign when the seal is being affixed, or may even permit the seal to be affixed with no signatories.[112]

---

[108] See eg *Law Society's Gazette*, 8 January 1992, p 31.

[109] See also s 1(2)(b)(ii) of the 1989 Act, which recognises that an instrument executed by 'one or more' parties as a deed may constitute a valid deed provided it makes it clear on its face that it is intended to be a deed.

[110] At the end of the operative clauses of the deed, before any schedules and before the execution pages.

[111] Companies Act 1985, s 36A(3). Where it does have a common seal, though, the company's name must be engraved in legible characters on the seal: Companies Act 1985, s 350(1).

[112] Eg a securities seal.

19.55 Under s 36A of the Companies Act 1985,[113] the deed must be either executed by the company under its seal[114] or signed by two directors or by one director and the secretary and expressed to be executed by the company.[115] If a person signs as a director or the secretary of more than one company, he must sign separately in each capacity.[116]

19.56 If the deed is executed by the company under its seal, the formalities will be as prescribed by the articles of association. Where a company has adopted the 1985 Table A as its articles, the directors may determine who shall sign the instrument to which the seal is affixed.[117] There is no such flexibility, though, if the company has adopted the 1948 Table A, which provides that the instrument must be signed by at least one director.[118]

19.57 In favour of a purchaser,[119] an instrument (which includes a deed) is **deemed** duly executed if a seal purporting to be the company's seal purports to be affixed and attested by two directors or by a director and the secretary (or his deputy).[120] There is a similar deeming provision in s 36A(6) of the Companies Act 1985 for documents purporting to be signed by two directors or one director and the secretary.[121]

---

[113] Inserted by s 130 of the Companies Act 1989.

[114] Which can be its common seal (s 36A(2)) or an official seal maintained under s 39. That section provides that, if a company has a common seal and its objects require or comprise the transaction of business in foreign countries, it may, if authorised by its articles, have an official seal for use outside the UK. The official seal must be a facsimile of the common seal but with the addition on its face of the name of every territory, district or place where it is to be used (s 39(1)). The person affixing it must be authorised under the common seal (s 39(3)); and the seal, when affixed, has the same effect as the common seal (s 39(2)). The company may also have a further official seal under s 40, which, when affixed, has the same effect as the common seal (s 40(1)). In practice, though, this is irrelevant for present purposes, since the seal may only be used for sealing securities, which are unlikely to be deeds.

[115] Section 36A(4). As this method is permitted by statute, it can be used even where the only method given in the company's articles for the execution of deeds is under the common seal.

[116] Section 36A(4A) (inserted by the Regulatory Reform (Execution of Deeds and Documents) Order 2005, SI 2005/1906).

[117] Paragraph 101. There is thus a degree of flexibility as to authorised signatories which is not available under the s 36A(4) execution provisions: see **19.54(c)**.

[118] Paragraph 113.

[119] Defined as a purchaser in good faith for valuable consideration, and including a lessee, mortgagee or other person who for valuable consideration acquires an interest in property: Law of Property Act 1925, s 205(1)(xxi).

[120] Law of Property 1925, s 74(1) (as amended by the Regulatory Reform (Execution of Deeds and Documents) Order 2005, SI 2005/1906); and see *Johnsey Estates (1990) Limited v Newport Marketworld* [1996] NPC 81. Section 74(1B) specifies that, if the officer attesting is in fact a corporation, then the person attesting should be an authorised officer of that corporation. The deeming provision applies not just to companies incorporated under the Companies Act but to any 'corporation aggregate' (ie any body of persons which has a legal personality separate from the particular members of the body for the time being). Note that this deeming provision does not apply if the affixing of the seal is attested by other persons, even though they are permitted to do so by the company's articles. The Land Registry will not require evidence of the authority of the attesting signatories where the deeming provision applies, but may do so where it does not: see Practice Guide 8 (September 2005), p 10.

[121] As with s 74(1) of the Law of Property Act 1925, the deeming is in favour of a 'purchaser', defined as a purchaser in good faith for valuable consideration and including a lessee, mortgagee or other person who for valuable consideration acquires an interest in property: s 36A(6). Both deeming provisions apply to agreements under hand as well as deeds.

(b)   During insolvency, etc

19.58   Where a deed is executed on behalf of a company by a liquidator, administrator or receiver, the position is rather more complicated.

(i)   Liquidator

A liquidator has a statutory power to execute deeds in the name and on behalf of the company, and for that purpose to use when necessary the company's seal.[122] However, he cannot execute under s 36A(4) of the Companies Act 1985,[123] since execution under that section is only available to directors and the secretary. The party to the deed will be the company;[124] the liquidator is also sometimes made a party, but this is not necessary.[125]

The wording of the liquidator's power, which appears to link the power to execute with the power to use the seal ('and for that purpose to use, when necessary, the company's seal'), has caused a concern as to whether the liquidator cannot execute except by using the seal.[126] The prevailing view, though, is that he can,[127] and the usual method of execution where the seal is not being used involves the liquidator signing the deed (in the name of the company) in the presence of a witness who attests the signature.[128]

(ii)   Administrator and administrative receiver

Both an administrator and (provided there is no provision to the contrary in the charging document under which he is appointed) an administrative receiver[129] have statutory powers to execute deeds on

---

[122]   Insolvency Act 1986, ss 165 and 167, and Sch 4, para 7.

[123]   Ie signature by two directors or by one director and the secretary.

[124]   Since its property remains vested in it unless the court makes an order to vest it in the liquidator under s 145(1) of the Insolvency Act 1986.

[125]   See, eg, *Re Wyvern Developments Ltd* [1974] 1 WLR 1097 at 1101.

[126]   See eg the Law Commission's Report of August 1998, 'The Execution of Deeds and Documents by or on behalf of Bodies Corporate', paras 7.66–7.74.

[127]   This is certainly the view of the Land Registry, which will accept deeds executed either under the common seal with the liquidator attesting or by the liquidator signing (in the name of the company) in the presence of a witness who attests (see Practice Guide 35 (Oct 2005)).

[128]   This is specifically permitted (where the purpose of the deed is to convey an interest in property) by Law of Property Act 1925, s 74(3), which applies where the signatory is authorised under a power of attorney or under 'any statutory or other power' to convey an interest in property in the name or on behalf of a corporation sole or aggregate. For other deeds, the normal practice is to use the same method of execution (though there is no specific statutory authorisation, it is difficult to see why such a method of execution would not be valid once one accepts the basic principle that the liquidation can execute without using the company seal).

[129]   Ie a receiver or manager of the whole (or substantially the whole) of a company's property appointed by or on behalf of the holders of any debentures of the company secured by a charge which, as created, was a floating charge, or by such a charge and other securities: Insolvency Act 1986, s 29(2).

behalf of the company and to use the company's seal.[130] The power to execute and the power to use the seal are separate powers, and therefore the potential concern applicable to liquidators as to the power to execute without using the seal does not arise. The usual methods of execution are the same as for a liquidator, ie affixing the company seal with the administrator/administrative receiver attesting or the administrator/administrative receiver signing (in the name of the company) in the presence of a witness who attests the signature.

The charging document under which an administrative receiver is appointed will normally contain a power of attorney in favour of the receiver, in which case he can alternatively execute deeds as attorney of the company.[131]

(iii) Other receiver

A receiver that is not an administrative receiver will not ordinarily be entitled to execute a deed under the seal of the company, as this will not usually be permitted by the company's articles. If he is appointed under a charge, his ability to execute a deed depends on the terms of the charging document and the terms of his appointment: normally, he will have a power of attorney contained in the charging document which will enable him to execute deeds as the company's attorney.[132] Even though he may be appointed under hand, he will still be able to execute deeds under this power of attorney, provided the charge was made by way of deed.[133]

If the receiver is appointed by the court, his ability to execute a deed depends on the terms of the court order. In general, though, it is thought that he may execute a deed on behalf of the company in the same way as a deed is executed by an individual.[134]

---

[130] Insolvency Act 1986, s 8, Sch B1, para 60 and Sch 1, paras 8 and 9 (in the case of an administrator) and s 42(1) and Sch 1, paras 8 and 9 (in the case of an administrative receiver). In relation to administrative receivers, the wording of s 42(1) (to the effect that the powers conferred on the administrative receiver by the charging document 'are deemed to include' the Sch 1 powers) has caused a concern that the administrative receiver's powers to execute and to use the seal are contractual rather than statutory, and therefore would terminate once the company goes into liquidation (as is the case for other receivers: see below): see eg the Law Commission's Report of August 1998, ibid, paras 7.76–7.83. The Land Registry's view is that the powers are statutory, and therefore in accepting deeds executed by administrative receivers (as opposed to other receivers) it does not require evidence that the company has not gone into liquidation (see Practice Guide 36 (Oct 2005)).

[131] Such a power is no longer exercisable once the company goes into liquidation, since the administrative receiver ceases to be the company's agent once the company goes into liquidation (Insolvency Act 1986, s 44(1)).

[132] It has been held, though, that such a power is revoked if the company goes into liquidation, but a separate power (as opposed to a power of attorney) given to the receiver by the terms of the charge to dispose of the charged property and to do so in the name and on behalf of the company survives the liquidation of the company (*Barrows v Chief Land Registrar* (1977) *The Times*, 20 October). The reasoning of the case was criticised by the Law Commission in their Report of August 1998, ibid, para 7.86.

[133] *Phoenix Properties Ltd v Wimpole Street Nominees Ltd* [1992] BCLC 737.

[134] See, eg, *Brooke's Notary* (12th edn, 2002), p 193.

Other English companies

19.59 The provisions of ss 36A and 36AA have been extended[135] to unregistered companies (as defined in s 718 of the Companies Act 1985), which includes those incorporated by Royal Charter or under private Acts of Parliament with a view to making a profit.

19.60 Execution of deeds by other English companies is governed by the common law, unless there are specific statutory provisions applicable to the company. Accordingly, in the absence of such statutory provisions, a deed is executed by affixing the company's seal in accordance with the formalities, if any, prescribed by its constitution.[136]

Foreign companies

19.61 As a result of the Foreign Companies (Execution of Documents) Regulations 1994,[137] a foreign company has the following choices for execution of a deed:

(a) affixing its common seal (if it has one);

(b) executing the deed in any manner permitted by the laws of the country of its incorporation for the execution of documents[138] by such a company; or

(c) having the document signed by a person or persons who, in accordance with the laws of the company's country of incorporation, is or are acting under the authority (express or implied) of that company, with the document being expressed (in whatever form of words) to be executed by the company; or

(d) appointing an attorney by any of the above three methods, who then executes as described in **19.63ff**.

19.62 The 1994 Regulations only apply, though, to foreign companies.[139] For other foreign entities, the common law rule remains that sealing is required. This has particularly caused problems where the entity in question

---

135 By Companies Act 1985, s 718 and Sch 22 (as amended).
136 Accompanied by delivery: dealt with at **19.79ff**.
137 SI 1994/950, as amended.
138 Ie any documents, and not necessarily deeds.
139 'Company' is not defined in the Regulations, nor is there any applicable definition in the Companies Act 1985. The Land Registry treats a foreign body corporate as a company falling within the Regulations if it has characteristics broadly similar to those of a company incorporated under the Companies Act 1985.

does not have its own seal. The solution usually adopted is for the entity to execute under a plain wafer seal.[140]

Attorneys

19.63 As with agreements under hand, the method of execution will depend on whether the agent is an individual or a company.

(a) *Where the attorney is an individual*

19.64 As with an agreement under hand:[141]

(a) the common law rule is that the attorney should sign the name of the principal rather than his own name, although he may add his own signature if he wishes;

(b) execution by an attorney is not permissible if statute requires personal execution by the principal; and

(c) execution by the attorney in his own name is permissible (i) in the case of a guarantee complying with the Statute of Frauds or (ii) in accordance with s 7(1) of the Powers of Attorney Act 1971.

19.65 In all cases, though, the signature should be in the presence of a witness who attests the signature.[142] The witness is required to be physically present at the time of signature (although, presumably, he can sign by way of attestation later).[143] Strictly speaking, it is not sufficient, therefore, for the attorney to acknowledge his signature to the witness subsequently, or for the witness to attest a signature which he knows but has not actually seen being made. However, where the fact that the witness was not physically present at the time of signature is not known to the other parties, the relevant signatory may be estopped from denying the validity of his execution.[144]

---

[140] On the basis that any seal can be adopted for use from time to time: *The Bailiffs, Aldermen, Burgesses and Commonalty of Yarmouth and Cowper's Case* (1630) Godb 439; *Cooch v Goodman* (1842) 2 QB 580. An important question is whether the deed is still valid if such a seal is missing. It will be if, instead of the seal, the letters LS (short for *locus sigilli*, 'the place for the seal') appear where the seal would otherwise have appeared (*First National Securities Ltd v Jones* [1978] Ch 109); and, even where those letters are missing, the relevant party will be estopped from denying the validity of the deed if it contains a statement that it has been sealed by him (*TCB Ltd v Gray* [1986] Ch 621, affd on another point [1987] Ch 458n).

[141] See **19.41ff**.

[142] This is the case irrespective of whether the attorney signs in the name of the principal or in his own name, and is the combined effect of s 7(1A) of the Powers of Attorney Act 1971 and ss 1(3)(a), (4)(a) and (4A) of the Law of Property (Miscellaneous Provisions) Act 1989. Alternatively, the deed may be signed by another person at the attorney's direction and in his presence and the presence of two witnesses who each attest the signature: s 1(3)(a)(ii) of the 1989 Act.

[143] Attestation 'means, as I understand it, that one or more persons are present at the time of the execution for that purpose, and that as evidence thereof they sign the attestation clause, stating such execution': *Wickham v Marquis of Bath* (1865) LR 1 Eq 17 at 24 per Sir J Romilly MR.

[144] As in *Shah v Shah* [2002] QB 35.

19.66 There is no restriction on who may be a witness, except that a party to the deed cannot also be a witness for another party.[145]

19.67 A further method of execution is permitted where the deed is a conveyance[146] of property[147] owned by a corporation: in such a case, s 74(3) of the Law of Property Act 1925 provides that the attorney may execute the conveyance as attorney by signing the name of the corporation in the presence of at least one witness who attests the signature. Such execution is as effective as if the conveyance had been executed by the corporation.

(b) Where the attorney is a company

19.68 As with agreements under hand,[148] the general rule is that the company should execute the deed in whatever manner would be appropriate if it were executing as principal.[149]

19.69 A further method of execution is permitted in the case of a deed or other instrument conveying[150] property:[151] in such a case, s 74(4) of the Law of Property Act 1925 provides that the attorney company may execute the deed or other instrument in the name of the owner by an officer appointed for that purpose by the board of directors, council or other governing body of the attorney company. Where the instrument is a deed, the officer must sign it in the presence of a witness who attests the signature. This method of execution is available whether the owner of the property is an individual or a corporation. Where an instrument appears to have been executed by an officer so appointed, then, in favour of a purchaser,[152] the instrument shall be deemed to have been executed by an officer duly authorised.

---

[145]   *Coles v Trecothick* (1804) 9 Ves Jun 234 at 251; *Freshfield v Reed* (1842) 9 M&W 404; *Wickham v Marquis of Bath* (1865) LR 1 Eq 17 at 25; *Seal v Claridge* (1881) 7 QBD 516 at 519; *Re Parrott* [1891] 2 QB 151.

[146]   As defined in Law of Property Act 1925, s 205(1)(ii).

[147]   As defined in Law of Property Act 1925, s 205(1)(xx).

[148]   See **19.43ff**.

[149]   Section 36A(7) of the Companies Act 1985 (inserted, in relation to documents executed on or after 15 September 2005, by the Regulatory Reform (Execution of Deeds and Documents) Order 2005) clarifies that the methods of execution by a company provided for by s 36A (ie common seal or signature of two directors or of director and secretary) apply in the case of a document which is executed in the name or on behalf of another person (whether or not that person is an individual, company or other entity). This means also that the deemed validity of execution in favour of a purchaser (see **19.57**) and the presumption of delivery (see **19.87**) apply in relation to the execution, by one of those methods, by a corporate attorney of a document on behalf of another person. Similarly, the deemed validity of execution in favour of a purchaser under s 74(1) of the Law of Property Act 1925 (see **19.57**) applies to a corporation aggregate executing an instrument on behalf of another person (s 74 (1A)).

[150]   As defined in Law of Property Act 1925, s 205(1)(ii).

[151]   As defined in Law of Property Act 1925, s 205(1)(xx).

[152]   Defined as a purchaser in good faith for valuable consideration, and including a lessee, mortgagee or other person who for valuable consideration acquires any interest in property: Law of Property Act 1925, s 205(1)(xxi).

Suggested execution clauses[153]

(a) For execution by an English company incorporated under the Companies Act[154]

19.70   Not using the seal:

SIGNED as a deed by [NAME OF COMPANY]	)	
acting by [NAME OF DIRECTOR]	)	....
and [NAME OF DIRECTOR/SECRETARY]	)	Director

....

Director/Secretary

19.71   Using the seal: the precise manner of execution will depend on the company's articles, but the following is common:

The common seal of [NAME OF COMPANY] was	)	[Common seal]
affixed to this deed in the presence of:	)	

..........................……......

Director

..........................……......

Director/Secretary

(b) For execution by a foreign company

19.72   Assuming the company is covered by the Foreign Companies (Execution of Documents) Regulations 1994,[155] the method of execution will need to be a valid method for execution of documents in the company's country of incorporation. However, leaving aside execution by an attorney (which is considered in para (c) below), the following are common:

SIGNED as a deed by [NAME OF COMPANY]	)	[Signatures of authorised
acting by [NAME OF FIRST AUTHORISED	)	signatories]
SIGNATORY] and [NAME OF SECOND AUTHORISED	)	
SIGNATORY], acting under the authority of that company	)	

or:

---

[153]   In relation to registered land, slightly different execution clauses are required in some cases by the Land Registry: see Practice Guide 8 (September 2005).

[154]   In normal circumstances (ie where it is not in liquidation, administration or receivership: if it is, the wording should be adapted accordingly).

[155]   As to which, see **19.61**.

SIGNED as a deed by [NAME OF COMPANY]   )   [Signature of authorised
acting by [NAME OF AUTHORISED SIGNATORY],   )   signatory]
acting under the authority of that company, in the   )
presence of:

Witness's signature ....
Name ....
Address ....

19.73   Where, however, registered land is involved, the form of execution clause recommended by the Land Registry (subject to it being valid in the company's country of incorporation) is as follows:[156]

SIGNED as a deed on behalf of [NAME OF COMPANY],   )   [Signature[s] of
a company incorporated in [COUNTRY OF INCORPORATION],   )   authorised
by [NAME OF AUTHORISED SIGNATORY] [and [NAME OF   )   signator[y/ies]]
SECOND AUTHORISED SIGNATORY]], being [a] person[s]   )
who, in accordance with the laws of that territory, [is/are] acting   )
under the authority of the company   )

(c)   For execution by an attorney

19.74   If the attorney is an individual and is authorised by the power of attorney to sign in his own name:

SIGNED as a deed by [NAME OF ATTORNEY] as attorney   )   [Signature of attorney]
for [NAME OF PRINCIPAL] in the presence of:)   (as attorney for
)   [NAME OF PRINCIPAL])

Witness's signature ....
Name ....
Address ....

19.75   In other cases where the attorney is an individual:

SIGNED as a deed by [NAME OF PRINCIPAL] acting by its   )   [Attorney to sign '[Name of
attorney [NAME OF ATTORNEY] in the presence of:)   principal] by its attorney
)   [Name of attorney]']

Witness's signature ....
Name ....
Address ....

19.76   Where the attorney is an English company incorporated under the Companies Act not using its seal:

---

[156]   See the Land Registry's Practice Guide 8 (September 2005), p 16.

SIIGNED as a deed by [NAME OF ATTORNEY COMPANY]   ) ....

acting by [NAME OF DIRECTOR], Director, and [NAME OF   ) Director of attorney

DIRECTOR/SECRETARY], [Director/Secretary], as attorney for   ) company

[NAME OF PRINCIPAL]   )

) ....

Director/Secretary of

attorney company

19.77 Where the attorney is such a company using its seal, the precise manner of execution will depend on the company's articles, but the following is common:

The common seal of [NAME OF ATTORNEY COMPANY] acting   ) [Common seal of attorney

as attorney for [NAME OF PRINCIPAL] was affixed to this   ) company]

deed in the presence of:)

....

Director

....

Director/Secretary

19.78 Alternatively, where the attorney is executing a deed or other instrument conveying property (and thus within s 74(4) of the Law of Property Act 1925),[157] the following may (but need not) be used:

SIGNED as a deed by [NAME OF PRINCIPAL] acting by   ) [Officer to sign '[Name of

[NAME OF OFFICER OF ATTORNEY COMPANY], duly   ) principal] by [Name of

appointed to execute as an officer of its attorney, [NAME OF   ) officer], duly appointed

ATTORNEY COMPANY], in the presence of:) officer of its attorney,

[Name of attorney

company]']

Witness's signature ....….......

Name ....…...................…......

Address ....….................…......

DELIVERY

Generally

19.79 As seen earlier,[158] delivery is necessary for a deed, but not for an agreement under hand. Originally, delivery involved physically handing the

---

[157] See **19.69**.
[158] At **19.5**.

deed over to the other party or authorising him to take it up. Now, no special action is required, merely words or conduct expressly or impliedly acknowledging the relevant party's intention to be immediately and unconditionally bound by the contents of the deed, irrespective of whether he actually hands over possession or not.[159] The delivery must be at the same time as, or after, (but not before) the signature and/or sealing.[160]

19.80 It used to be the case that the appointment of an agent to deliver a deed on the maker's behalf must itself be made by deed, but this rule has now been abolished.[161]

19.81 In practice, in many transactions, any necessary deed will be executed in advance of the closing or completion, and tabled at the closing/completion meeting by the relevant lawyer. Since the lawyer does not need to be authorised by deed to deliver the deed on the party's behalf, the usual interpretation is that delivery does not occur until the lawyer tables the deed at the closing/completion meeting. Thus the handing back of the deed to the lawyer by the party is of no legal effect, and the deed is merely an undelivered deed, held to the relevant party's order (and therefore recallable by the party at any time prior to closing/completion).[162]

Delivery in escrow

19.82 If a deed is delivered unconditionally, it takes effect immediately. Alternatively, it may be delivered on condition that it should operate only at some future time or on the happening of a specified event or upon some condition being fulfilled. Technically, the deed is not a deed, but rather an escrow, until it becomes effective,[163] but the process is generally referred to as 'delivery in escrow'.

---

[159] See, eg, *Parker v Tenant* (1560) 2 Dyer 192; *Shelton's Case* (1582) Cro Eliz 7; *Chamberlain v Stanton* (1588) Cro Eliz 122; *Thoroughgood's Case* (1612) 9 Co Rep 136; *Doe d Garnons v Knight* (1826) 5 B&C 671; *Exton v Scott* (1833) 6 Sim 31; *R v Longnor Inhabitants* (1833) 4 B&Ad 647; *Grugeon v Gerrard* (1840) 4 Y&C Ex 119 at 130; *Fletcher v Fletcher* (1844) 4 Hare 67 at 79; *Hall v Bainbridge* (1848) 12 QB 699; *Tupper v Foulkes* (1861) 9 CB (NS) 797; *Keith v Pratt* (1862) 10 WR 296; *Xenos v Wickham* (1867) LR 2 HL 296; *London Freehold and Leasehold Property Co v Baron Suffield* [1897] 2 Ch 608; *Re Seymour* [1913] 1 Ch 475; *Macedo v Stroud* [1922] 2 AC 330; *Beesly v Hallwood Estates Ltd* [1960] 2 All ER 314 at 324 (affd [1961] Ch 105); *Vincent v Premo Enterprises (Voucher Sales) Ltd* [1969] 2 QB 609 at 619 per Lord Denning MR.
[160] *Goddard's Case* (1584) 2 Co Rep 4 at 5.
[161] By the Law of Property (Miscellaneous Provisions) Act 1989, s 1(1)(c).
[162] See *Governors and Guardians of the Foundling Hospital v Crane* [1911] 2 KB 367 at 379 per Farwell LJ; *Longman v Viscount Chelsea* (1989) 58 P&CR 189. Cf *Venetian Glass Gallery Ltd v Next Properties Ltd* [1989] 2 EGLR 42. See also the Law Commission's discussion of this issue in their Report of August 1998, 'The Execution of Deeds and Documents by or on behalf of Bodies Corporate', paras 6.4 and 6.5. Prior to the 1989 reforms, since an agent could only deliver a deed on another's behalf if authorised by a deed, the analysis had to be that the handing back of the deed to the lawyer constituted delivery in escrow (dealt with below), with the result that the deed could not then be withdrawn or recalled by the executing party.
[163] *Perryman's Case* (1599) 5 Co Rep 84; *Xenos v Wickham* (1866) LR 2 HL 296 at 323 per Lord Cranworth; *Alan Estates Ltd v WG Stores Ltd* [1982] Ch 511.

19.83 Once the condition is satisfied the deed is treated as taking effect from the date of delivery in escrow (the doctrine of 'relating back'),[164] (but without prejudice to third party dealings that have taken place in the meantime).[165] If the condition is not satisfied, the deed is ineffective and is treated as never having been delivered.

19.84 As with unconditional delivery, delivery in escrow need not be made in any special form, the essential thing being words or conduct from which can be inferred an intention to be bound on satisfaction of the relevant condition.[166]

19.85 Once delivered in escrow, the deed cannot be withdrawn or recalled by the executing party,[167] except where the condition is not satisfied within a reasonable period.[168] Accordingly, if that party wishes to retain the right to do so, he should either make it clear that the delivery is also conditional on him not having revoked it,[169] or, preferably, make it clear that the deed is not being delivered at all (whether as a deed or as an escrow) but, rather, held to his order.

19.86 The term 'escrow' is also in practice often applied to documents other than deeds.[170] Technically, this is incorrect, since escrow, being a form of delivery, is a concept only applicable to deeds. The correct description of

---

164 *Jennings v Bragg* (1595) Cro Eliz 447; *Butler and Baker's Case* (1591) 3 Co Rep 25 at 35; *Perryman's Case* (1599) 5 Co Rep 84; *Graham v Graham* (1791) 1 Ves Jun 272 at 274 and 275; *Coare v Giblett* (1803) 4 East 85 at 94 and 95; *Copeland v Stephens* (1818) 1 B&Ald 593 at 606; *Edmunds v Edmunds* [1904] P 362 at 374; *Alan Estates Ltd v WG Stores Ltd* [1982] Ch 511. The position is different, though, for stamp duty purposes: see **19.100**.

165 *Butler and Baker's Case* (1591) 3 Co Rep 25 at 36; *Thompson v McCullough* [1947] KB 447 at 455; *Security Trust Co v Royal Bank of Canada* [1976] AC 503 at 517; *Alan Estates Ltd v WG Stores Ltd* [1982] Ch 511 at 521 per Lord Denning MR.

166 *Johnson v Baker* (1821) 4 B&Ald 440; *Murray v Earl of Stair* (1823) 2 B&C 82; *Bowker v Burdekin* (1843) 11 M&W 128; *Gudgen v Besset* (1856) 6 El&Bl 986; *Davis v Jones* (1856) 17 CB 625 at 634; *Xenos v Wickham* (1866) LR 2 HL 296 at 323 per Lord Cranworth; *London Freehold and Leasehold Property Co v Baron Suffield* [1897] 2 Ch 608 at 622; *Governors and Guardians of the Foundling Hospital v Crane* [1911] 2 KB 367 at 374 per Vaughan Williams LJ, and 377 per Farwell LJ; *Macedo v Stroud* [1922] 2 AC 330 at 337; *Lady Naas v Westminster Bank Ltd* [1940] AC 366 at 399 per Lord Wright; *Thompson v McCullough* [1947] KB 447; *Beesly v Hallwood Estates Ltd* [1960] 2 All ER 314 at 324 (affd [1961] Ch 105); *Vincent v Premo Enterprises (Voucher Sales) Ltd* [1969] 2 QB 609 at 619 per Lord Denning MR; *D'Silva v Lister House Development Ltd* [1971] Ch 17; *Glessing v Green* [1975] 2 All ER 696; *Alan Estates Ltd v WG Stores Ltd* [1982] Ch 511 at 526 per Sir Denys Buckley; *Longman v Viscount Chelsea* (1989) 58 P&CR 189; *AIB Group (UK) plc v Hennelley Properties Ltd* 2000 WL 664567 at para 33 (affd CA, 2000 WL 1881366).

167 *Beesly v Hallwood Estates Ltd* [1961] Ch 105; *Kingston v Ambrian Investment Co Ltd* [1975] 1 WLR 161 at 166 per Lord Denning MR; *Alan Estates Ltd v WG Stores Ltd* [1982] Ch 511.

168 *Beesly v Hallwood Estates Ltd* [1961] Ch 105 at 118 per Harman LJ; *Kingston v Ambrian Investment Co Ltd* [1975] 1 WLR 161; *Glessing v Green* [1975] 2 All ER 696; *Alan Estates Ltd v WG Stores Ltd* [1982] Ch 511 at 520 per Lord Denning MR.

169 Which arguably means that the deed has not been delivered at all: see *Governors and Guardians of the Foundling Hospital v Crane* [1911] 2 KB 367 at 379 per Farwell LJ; *Beesly v Hallwood Estates Ltd* [1961] Ch 105.

170 A common example is a document (such as a placing agreement in relation to a domestic stock issue: see **13.3**) which has been executed but is to be held by one party's lawyers subject to either the fulfilment of some condition or merely final agreement, is intended to be effective from the date the condition is fulfilled rather than the date of execution, and is treated by the parties as recallable.

such a document would usually be that it has been executed subject to the condition that it becomes binding only when the parties agree.

Presumptions

19.87   Where a document is validly executed by a company[171] as a deed (ie executed under the common seal or by two directors or a director and the secretary), there is a presumption, under s 36AA(2) of the Companies Act 1985,[172] that it is delivered upon its being executed. This presumption may be rebutted if a contrary intention is proved.

19.88   The presumption applies only to deeds executed by companies incorporated under the Companies Acts and to unregistered companies (as defined in s 718 of the Companies Act 1985).[173] A similar presumption, however, applies in relation to a corporation aggregate,[174] pursuant to s 74A(2) of the Law of Property Act 1925.[175]

19.89   Where, in the course of, or in connection with, a transaction, a solicitor, licensed conveyancer or duly certificated notary public, or any agent or employee of them, purports to deliver an instrument as a deed on behalf of a party to the instrument, it is **conclusively** presumed in favour of a purchaser[176] that such person is authorised to deliver the instrument.[177]

---

[171]   Either as a party in its own right or as a person authorised to execute the deed in the name or on behalf of one or more of the parties: this is the combined effect of s 1(2)(b) of the Law of Property (Miscellaneous Provisions) Act 1989 and s 36AA(1) of the Companies Act 1985.

[172]   Inserted, in relation to documents executed on or after 15 September 2005, by the Regulatory Reform (Execution of Deeds and Documents) Order 2005, SI 2005/1906.

[173]   Companies Act 1985, s 718 and Sch 22 (as amended).

[174]   Again, either as a party in its own right or as a person authorised to execute the deed in the name or on behalf of one or more of the parties: this is the combined effect of s 1(2)(b) of the Law of Property (Miscellaneous Provisions) Act 1989 and s 74A(1) of the Law of Property Act 1925. A corporation aggregate is a body of persons which has a legal personality separate from the particular members of the body for the time being.

[175]   Inserted, in relation to documents executed on or after 15 September 2005, by the Regulatory Reform (Execution of Deeds and Documents) Order 2005, SI 2005/1906. The deeming provision in Law of Property Act 1925, s 74(1) (considered at **19.57**) that a deed which has been sealed by a corporation aggregate in accordance with that section is 'deemed to have been executed' does not dispense with the need for delivery of the deed as a separate requirement over and above due execution (*Bolton MBC v Torkington* [2004] Ch 66).

[176]   Defined as a purchaser in good faith for valuable consideration, and including a lessee, mortgagee or other person who for valuable consideration acquires any interest in property: the Law of Property Act 1925, s 205(1)(xxi).

[177]   Law of Property (Miscellaneous Provisions) Act 1989, s 1(5).

ELECTRONIC COMMUNICATIONS AND SIGNATURES[178]

Background

19.90   As a result of EU directives,[179] recent UK legislation has expressly permitted the recognition of electronic communications and signatures. The main implementing measures are the Electronic Communications Act 2000 and the Electronic Signatures Regulations 2002.[180] The Act makes electronic signatures admissible in evidence in legal proceedings (s 7) and enables ministers to amend legislative provisions relating (inter alia) to execution formalities (s 8), and the Regulations deal with digital signature service providers, including (inter alia) their supervision and liability.

19.91   The term 'electronic signature' is a generic description of various electronic methods for 'signing' data. It can include typing one's name at the end of an email, attaching a scanned manuscript signature to an email, clicking on an 'I accept' icon on a website, or using a digital signature. A digital signature is a particular, more secure, form of electronic signature. It relies on encryption and the use of electronic passwords to encode and decode the message, with its authenticity being guaranteed and certified by a third party digital signature service provider.

Admissibility in evidence

19.92   Under s 7 of the Electronic Communications Act 2000, an electronic signature is admissible in evidence for certain purposes. 'Electronic signature' is defined for this purpose as anything in electronic form that is 'incorporated into or otherwise logically associated with' an electronic communication or electronic data, and purports to be so incorporated or associated for the purpose of being used to establish the authenticity and/or integrity of the communication or data.[181] 'Authenticity' relates to whether the communication or data comes from a particular person or other source, whether it is accurately timed and dated and/or whether it is intended to have legal effect;[182] and 'integrity' relates to whether there has been any tampering with, or other modification to, the communication or data.[183] If an electronic

---

[178]   See further Mason, *Electronic Signatures in Law* (2003); Brazell, *Electronic Signatures Law and Regulation* (2004); Anderson and Warner, *Execution of Documents* (2005), Chapter 25; *Encyclopaedia of Forms and Precedents* (5th edn, 2003 Reissue), Vol 12(2), pp 432–455.

[179]   The Electronic Signatures Directive 1999 (1999/93/EC) and the Electronic Commerce Directive 2000 (2000/31/EC). Under art 5 of the Electronic Signatures Directive, member states must ensure that a digital signature satisfies the legal requirements of a signature in relation to electronic data in the same manner as a handwritten signature does in relation to paper-based data, and that an electronic signature is not to be denied legal effectiveness solely on the grounds that it is in electronic form or is not a digital signature. Under art 9(1) of the Electronic Commerce Directive, member states must ensure that their legal systems allow contracts to be concluded by electronic means.

[180]   SI 2002/318.

[181]   Electronic Communications Act 2000, s 7(2).

[182]   Electronic Communications Act 2000, s 15(2)(a).

[183]   Electronic Communications Act 2000, s 15(2)(b).

signature satisfies these requirements, it is admissible in evidence in relation to any question as to the authenticity and/or integrity of the communication or data.[184] The certification by any person of an electronic signature is also admissible for the same purposes.[185]

19.93 A number of points should be noted about s 7:

(a) It is not clear why it was felt necessary to introduce these provisions, as the general position under English law is that any form of evidence is admissible if it is relevant and assists the court in determining the facts.[186]

(b) The section merely provides that the signature and/or certificate shall be admissible, not that they shall be conclusive. The evidential weight to be attached to them will therefore depend on the circumstances, and will be for the court to decide.

(c) The question arises of whether any form of electronic signature is admissible, or only digital signatures. Whereas the Electronic Signatures Directive 1999 (which the Act is implementing) draws a distinction between 'electronic signatures' (in the wide sense described earlier) and 'advanced electronic signatures' (equating, in general, to digital signatures), this distinction is not reflected in the Act. It might be thought, though, that the references to the electronic signature only being admissible if it is used for the purpose of establishing the authenticity and/or integrity of the communication might indicate that some form of digital signature is required.[187] 'Authenticity', however, is defined widely for the purposes of s 7, and (as seen above) relates not only to whether the communication did indeed come from the person it purports to, but also whether it was intended to have legal effect. It must follow, therefore, that any form of electronic signature, if used to signify the relevant intention to have legal effect, is potentially admissible. That said, digital signatures clearly carry considerably more evidential weight.

---

[184] Electronic Communications Act 2000, s 7(1)(a).

[185] Electronic Communications Act 2000, s 7(1)(b). Such a certification must be a statement confirming that the signature, a means of producing, communicating or verifying it, or a procedure applied to it, is a valid means of establishing the authenticity of the communication or data: Electronic Communications Act 2000, s 7(3).

[186] Presumably, the aim was to demonstrate that there was no doubt about the admissibility, in the light of the obligation under art 5 of the Electronic Signatures Directive referred to earlier to ensure that electronic signatures are not denied legal effectiveness. It would be unfortunate, though, if, by prescribing certain purposes for which electronic signatures are admissible, this raised doubts about whether electronic signatures are admissible for other evidential purposes.

[187] 'Authenticity' has at least two potential meanings in the context of electronic communications. One is that the signature is added in order to demonstrate that the communication does originate from the purported signatory and has not been altered since it was signed: this would in practice require some form of digital signature or other advanced signature process. The other is that the signature is added in order to signify approval or intention to be bound, or conferring legal significance on the remainder of the document: in that case, merely typing one's name at the end of an email could potentially satisfy the requirement. As seen below, 'authenticity' when used in s 7 is defined as including both meanings.

(d) Similarly, where certification of an electronic signature is to be admitted, the certification can, technically, be of any person, not just a digital signature service provider (though it will obviously carry more evidential weight if it is of a digital signature service provider).

(e) The admissibility in evidence provided for by s 7 is only as to the authenticity or integrity of the electronic communication or data. Section 7 does not therefore have the effect of deeming the communication itself to be something that satisfies the formality requirements, where they are applicable, of 'writing' and of 'signature'. This is considered below.

Requirements of 'writing' and 'signature'

19.94 The view of the Law Commission[188] is that, where a document is required by law to be in writing and/or to be signed, these requirements can in general be satisfied by certain forms of electronic communication without changes needing to be made to the existing law. In their view: the requirement of 'writing' can be fulfilled by electronic communications that involve visible text[189] (such as electronic mail or web-site trading, but not electronic data interchange);[190] and the requirement of 'signature' can generally be interpreted as meaning conduct of a would-be signatory that indicates to a reasonable person an authenticating intention (and thus, in general, digital signatures, scanned manuscript signatures, typing one's name (or initials) at the end of an email and clicking on a website button are all capable of satisfying a signature requirement).[191]

19.95 On this basis, it must follow that, in general, a deed can be executed in electronic form. As seen earlier,[192] there is no requirement that a deed need

---

[188] Advice to Government, 'Electronic Commerce: Formal Requirements in Commercial Transactions' (2001). See also Beale and Griffiths [2002] LMCLQ 467.

[189] On the basis that the definition of 'writing' in s 5 of the Interpretation Act 1978 includes 'modes of representing or reproducing words in a visible form'.

[190] Paras 3.5–3.23 of their Advice to Government. The view that an email satisfies the requirement of 'writing' (for the purposes of s 4 of the Statute of Frauds) has received judicial approval (*Metha v J Pereira Fernandes SA* [2006] EWHC 813 at para 16).

[191] Paras 3.24–3.40 of their Advice to Government. The view that typing one's name in an email satisfies the requirement of 'signature' (for the purposes of s 4 of the Statute of Frauds) has received judicial approval: *Metha v J Pereira Fernandes SA* [2006] EWHC 813 at para 29 per Judge Pelling QC ('I have no doubt that if a party creates and sends an electronically created document then he will be treated as having signed it to the same extent that he would in law be treated as having signed a hard copy of the same document') and para 31 (having referred with approval to the Law Commission's view, ' . . . if a party or a party's agent sending an email types his or her or his or her principal's name to the extent required or permitted by existing case law in the body of an email, then in my view that would be a sufficient signature for the purposes of Section 4'). In that case, the judge held that the automatic insertion of a person's email address by the internet service provider after the email had been sent did not constitute a signature for the purposes of s 4, as it did not indicate the requisite authenticating intention.

[192] At **19.5**.

be written on paper,[193] and the only requirements for a valid deed are that it is in writing, evidences an intention that it should be a deed, and is executed as a deed. Clearly a seal cannot be affixed electronically, but electronic signature by an appropriately authorised signatory in the presence of a witness, who then also electronically signs the communication by way of attestation, should, on the basis of the Law Commission's view, be generally capable of being a valid means of execution.

19.96 Though a deed is technically capable of being executed in electronic form, there are clearly enormous potential evidential issues regarding the authenticity and integrity of such a deed. And, even if digital signatures were used, there is presumably an issue as to whether both signatory and witness need to apply their separate digital signatures to the same communication in order to satisfy the requirement of attestation. In practice, therefore, until the Land Registry's electronic conveyancing service described below becomes operational, paper-based deeds are likely to remain the norm.

Legislative amendment

19.97 Where existing statutory requirements regarding execution do prevent the use of electronic contracts (eg by requiring paper, a seal or a manual signature), legislative change can be effected by exercise of the power contained in s 8 of the Electronic Communications Act 2000. This authorises the appropriate government minister to issue statutory instruments modifying any primary or subordinate legislation in order to authorise or facilitate the use of electronic communications for a number of purposes. These include doing anything which is: required to be or may be done or evidenced in writing or otherwise using a document, notice or instrument;[194] required to be or may be authorised by a person's signature or seal;[195] or required to be delivered as a deed or witnessed.[196]

---

[193] The common law requirement was that a deed must be written on parchment or paper, but this was abolished by s 1(1) of the Law of Property (Miscellaneous Provisions) Act 1989 (which provided that 'any rule of law which . . . restricts the substances on which a deed may be written . . . is abolished'). Curiously, both the Lord Chancellor's Department (as it then was) and the Land Registry take the view that paper is required. In the Lord Chancellor's Department Consultation Paper on Electronic Conveyancing (March 2001), para 4 states: 'In England and Wales contracts for the sale or creation of interests in land have to be made in writing and signed by the parties. Similarly, deeds must be in writing and the signature of the party or parties making the deed must be witnessed. All conveyances, transfers, leases, mortgages and legal charges must be deeds. Thus, notwithstanding the growing use of electronic communication at all the other stages of a conveyancing transaction, the two key stages of making the contract and completion must be achieved by using paper documents'. And the Land Registry consultation paper on e-conveyancing (May 2002), para 2.3.3 states ' . . . provisions in existing legislation (eg the Law of Property Act 1925 and the Law of Property (Miscellaneous Provisions) Act 1989) . . . require, for example, contracts for the sale of land to be in writing and signed by the parties to the transaction, and transfers and legal charges to be executed on paper as deeds'. In both cases, the references to paper being required clearly result from an assumption that 'writing' and 'signature' do not include electronic documents and signatures (contrary to the Law Commission's view).

[194] Section 8(2)(a).

[195] Section 8(2)(c).

[196] Section 8(2)(c).

19.98   A number of orders have been made under s 8,[197] but these have not made any general amendment to the execution formalities for deeds. Part 8 of the Land Registration Act 2002 has made provision for the ability to transfer and create interests in registered land by electronic means through a network controlled by the Land Registry, but this procedure is not expected to become operational until around 2010.[198]

DATING

19.99   A deed takes effect from the date of delivery, and an agreement under hand from the date of execution, by the last party whose delivery or execution (as the case may be) is essential to its validity.[199] However, in the case of an agreement under hand executed in more than one part and intended to be exchanged, the correct date is that of the exchange.[200]

19.100   Where a deed is delivered in escrow, the correct date is that of the delivery in escrow, not the fulfilment of the condition.[201] However, for stamp duty purposes, it is treated as the date the condition is fulfilled.[202]

19.101   Although the date expressed in a deed or agreement under hand is prima facie to be taken as its effective date, external evidence is admissible to show the correct date, and, if proven, the correct date will prevail.[203] A reference in the document, though, to its date (eg to pay interest from 'the date hereof') is construed as referring to the date stated in the deed.[204] Consequently, if the parties intend the document to be operational either

---

[197]   Many dealing with communications with government. Probably the most relevant in the context of corporate borrowing is the Companies Act 1985 (Electronic Communications) Order 2000 (SI 2000/3373), which authorises and facilitates the use of electronic communications between companies and their members (eg in relation to the electronic transmission of annual reports and accounts and notices of meetings) and between companies and Companies House.

[198]   Pursuant to r 14 of the Land Registration Rules 2003 (SI 2003/1417), the procedure only becomes operational once the Registrar has issued a notice under Sch 2 of the Land Registration Rules that he is satisfied that adequate arrangements have been made or will be in place. The Land Registry's consultation document on e-conveyancing (May 2002) indicates (at para 2.3.3) that an order under s 8 of the Electronic Communications Act 2000 will be required. Though, on the basis of the Law Commission's view described above, deeds can, technically, already be executed in electronic form, the need for legislative change to permit electronic conveyancing seems to derive from (a) a wish to put it beyond doubt that electronic conveyancing documents will be regarded as deeds and (b) the need to lay down a form of electronic conveyancing system that provides the Land Registry with sufficient certainty as to authenticity and integrity of the electronic documents submitted to it.

[199]   *Goddard's Case* (1584) 2 Co Rep 4; *Clayton's Case* (1585) 5 Co Rep 1; *Hall v Cazenove* (1804) 4 East 477; *Steele v Mart* (1825) 4 B&C 272; *Bishop of Crediton v Bishop of Exeter* [1905] 2 Ch 455; *Alan Estates Ltd v WG Stores Ltd* [1982] Ch 511. See also the Stamp Act 1891, s 122.

[200]   *Domb v Isoz* [1980] 1 All ER 942 at 948 per Buckley LJ; *Alan Estates Ltd v WG Stores Ltd* [1982] Ch 511; *Commission for the New Towns v Cooper (Great Britain) Ltd* [1995] Ch 259.

[201]   See further **19.83**.

[202]   Stamp Act 1891, s 122(1A). See also *Terrapin International Ltd v IRC* [1976] 1 WLR 665.

[203]   *Goddard's Case* (1584) 2 Co Rep 4; *Clayton's Case* (1585) 5 Co Rep 1; *Hall v Cazenove* (1804) 4 East 477; *Steele v Mart* (1825) 4 B&C 272; *Morgan v Whitmore* (1851) 6 Exch 716; *Morrell v Studd & Millington* [1913] 2 Ch 648 at 658; *Esberger & Son Ltd v Capital and Counties Bank* [1913] 2 Ch 366.

[204]   *Styles v Wardle* (1825) 4 B&C 908.

from a future date or from a date earlier than its effective date, this should be stated in a commencement clause, rather than post-dating or pre-dating the document.[205]

ALTERATIONS

Alterations before execution

19.102 Deeds and agreements under hand may be altered in any way before being executed, without affecting their validity.[206] No initialling is required, although it is obviously useful evidence. In relation to a deed, any alteration is presumed, in the absence of evidence to the contrary, to have been made before the execution of the deed.[207] In relation to an agreement under hand, though, there is no such presumption, and the party seeking to enforce the agreement must prove the circumstances of the alteration.[208]

Alterations after execution

(a) Immaterial alterations

19.103 Alterations which are not material do not affect the validity of the document, whether made by a party to the document or by someone else.[209] For this purpose, it used to be the case that an alteration was treated as

---

[205] Although to date a document 'as of' the commencement date is becoming more common. Whether or not a contract (or a clause in a contract) is capable of having retrospective (or, by necessary analogy, delayed) effect depends upon the express or implied intention of the parties (*Trollope & Colls Ltd v Atomic Power Constructions Ltd* [1963] 1 WLR 333; *City of Westminster v Clifford Culpin & Partners* [1986] 12 Con LR 117; *Northern & Shell plc v John Laing Construction Ltd* [2003] EWCA 1035). Inserting the wrong date with the intention to deceive may give rise to offences under the Theft Act 1968 (see ss 15, 15A and 16) or the Forgery and Counterfeiting Act 1981 (see ss 1 to 4 and 9(1)(g)).

[206] *Cole v Parkin* (1810) 12 East 471; *Matson v Booth* (1816) 5 M&S 223 at 226; *Doe d Lewis v Bingham* (1821) 4 B&Ald 672; *Hall v Chandless* (1827) 4 Bing 123; *Jones v Jones* (1833) 1 C&M 721.

[207] *Trowel v Castle* (1661) 1 Keble 21; *Fitzgerald v Lord Fauconberge* (1729) Fitz–G 207 at 214, affd (1730) 6 Bro Parl Cas 295; *Doe d Tatum v Catomore* (1851) 16 QB 745; *Simmons v Rudall* (1851) 1 Sim (NS) 115 at 136; *Williams v Ashton* (1860) 1 J&H 115 at 118.

[208] *Henman v Dickinson* (1828) 5 Bing 183; *Knight v Clements* (1838) 8 Ad&E 215; *Cariss v Tattersall* (1841) 2 Man&G 890; *Clifford v Parker* (1841) 2 Man&G 909; *Doe d Tatum v Catomore* (1851) 16 QB 745 at 746.

[209] See, eg *Waugh v Bussell* (1814) 5 Taunt 707 at 711; *Keane v Smallbone* (1855) 17 CB 179; *Adsetts v Hives* (1863) 33 Beav 52; *Aldous v Cornwell* (1868) LR 3 QB 573; *Re Howgate and Osborn's Contract* [1902] 1 Ch 451; *Bishop of Crediton v Bishop of Exeter* [1905] 2 Ch 455; *Lombard Finance Ltd v Brookplain Trading Ltd* [1991] 2 All ER 762. Filling in the (correct) date of a deed after execution is an immaterial alteration (since the deed takes effect from that date anyway, even if undated): *Keane v Smallbone* (1855) 17 CB 179; *Adsetts v Hives* (1863) 33 Beav 52; *Bishop of Crediton v Bishop of Exeter* [1905] 2 Ch 455.

material if it varied the legal position of the parties[210] (even if to the prejudice of the person making the alteration). Now, however, the position is that (with the exception of negotiable instruments), an alteration will only be treated as material if it potentially prejudices the legal rights or obligations under the document of the person seeking to avoid liability as a result of the alteration.[211]

(b) Accidental alterations

19.104 Accidental alterations of, or damage to, a deed or agreement under hand do not invalidate it, and it remains enforceable in its original form.[212]

(c) Material alterations with the consent of all parties

19.105 In this case, the document takes effect as altered,[213] although, if the alteration is sufficiently fundamental that the document is in effect a new instrument, restamping will be necessary. Initialling is not necessary,[214] but it is obviously useful evidence.

---

[210] *Gardner v Walsh* (1855) 5 El&Bl 83 at 89; *Markham v Gonaston* (1598) Cro Eliz 626 at 627; *Eagleton v Gutteridge* (1843) 11 M&W 465; *Burchfield v Moore* (1854) 3 El&Bl 683 at 686; *Aldous v Cornwell* (1868) LR 3 QB 573; *Suffell v Bank of England* (1882) 9 QBD 555; *Bishop of Crediton v Bishop of Exeter* [1905] 2 Ch 455; *Koch v Dicks* [1933] 1 KB 307; *Lombard Finance Ltd v Brookplain Trading Ltd* [1991] 2 All ER 762.

[211] *Raiffeisen Zentralbank Osterreich v Crossseas Shipping Ltd* [2000] 3 All ER 274.

[212] *Doctor Leyfield's Case* (1611) 10 Co Rep 88 at 92; *Clerke d Prin v Heath* (1669) 1 Mod 11; *Read v Brookman* (1789) 3 Term Rep 151; *Master v Miller* (1791) 4 Term Rep 320 at 339; *Bolton v Bishop of Carlisle* (1793) 2 H Bl 259 at 263, 264.

[213] *Zouch v Claye* (1671) 2 Lev 35; *Paget v Paget* (1688) 2 Chan Rep 410; *Bates v Grabham* (1703) 3 Salk 444; *French v Patton* (1808) 9 East 351; *Matson v Booth* (1816) 5 M&S 223 at 227; *Adsetts v Hives* (1863) 33 Beav 52; *Rudd v Bowles* [1912] 2 Ch 60; *Re Danish Bacon Co Ltd Staff Pension Fund* [1971] 1 All ER 486 at 496.

[214] See, eg, *Bowman v Nichol* (1794) 5 Term Rep 537.

(d) Intentional material alterations by one party without the consent of the other

19.106 The document can no longer be enforced by the party making the alteration; but the other party may still enforce the document, in its original form, against him.[215]

(e) Intentional material alterations by someone not a party

19.107 These have the same effect as if they were made by the party responsible for the custody of the document,[216] except, possibly, where made against his will.[217]

NOTARISATION

19.108 Notarisation is 'the act of a notary public,[218] authenticated by his signature and official seal, certifying the due execution in his presence of a deed, contract or other writing, or verifying some fact or thing done in his presence or of which the notary has certain knowledge'.[219] Notarisation is primarily relevant for documents intended to be used in other jurisdictions: under the Commercial Code of Spain, for example, a debt evidenced by a notarial instrument in public form (an 'escritura publica') will rank ahead of ordinary debts in a bankruptcy.

19.109 Notarisation can be in either private or public form. 'Private form' means that the notary appends a form of authentication to the document. This is the form most commonly used by English notaries. 'Public form' means that the notary draws up a narrative, setting out the identity of the

---

[215] *Pigot's Case* (1614) 11 Co Rep 26; *Master v Miller* (1791) 4 Term Rep 320, (1793) 2 HBl 141; *Laird v Robertson* (1791) 4 Bro PC 488; *Weeks v Maillardet* (1811) 14 East 568; *Langhorn v Cologan* (1812) 4 Taunt 330; *Powell v Divett* (1812) 15 East 29; *Fairlie v Christie* (1817) 7 Taunt 416; *Campbell v Christie* (1817) 2 Stark 64; *Forshaw v Chabert* (1821) 3 Brod&B 158; *Davidson v Cooper* (1844) 13 M&W 343; *Mollett v Wackerbarth* (1847) 5 CB 181; *Gardner v Walsh* (1855) 5 El&Bl 83 at 89; *Fazakerly v McKnight* (1856) 6 El&Bl 795; *Croockewit v Fletcher* (1857) 1 H&N 893; *Sellin v Price* (1867) LR 2 Exch 189; *The Bank of Hindustan, China and Japan (Ltd) v Smith* (1867) 36 LJCP 241; *Suffell v Bank of England* (1882) 9 QBD 555; *Lowe v Fox* (1887) 12 App Cas 206 at 214, 216; *Ellesmere Brewery Co v Cooper* [1896] 1 QB 75; *Co-operative Bank plc v Tipper* [1996] 4 All ER 366 at 369, 370; *Raiffeisen Zentralbank Osterreich v Crossseas Shipping Ltd* [2000] 3 All ER 274. As mentioned above, a party seeking to avoid liability on the grounds of an alteration by the other must (except in the case of a negotiable instrument) now be able to demonstrate that the alteration is one which is potentially prejudicial to his legal rights or obligations under the instrument (*Raiffeisen*, ibid). Where, however, the document is printed, typed or written in ink, an amendment in pencil will be presumed not to be an operative alteration: *Co-operative Bank plc v Tipper* [1996] 4 All ER 366.

[216] *Pigot's Case* (1614) 11 Co Rep 26 at 27; *Davidson v Cooper* (1843) 11 M&W 778 at 801, 802, affd (1844) 13 M&W 343; *The Bank of Hindustan, China and Japan (Ltd) v Smith* (1867) 36 LJCP 241; *Robinson v Mollett* (1875) LR 7 HL 802 at 813; *Suffell v Bank of England* (1882) 9 QBD 555.

[217] *Lowe v Fox* (1887) 12 App Cas 206 at 216, 217 per Lord Herschell.

[218] A legal officer appointed by the Court of Faculties.

[219] *Brooke's Notary* (12th edn, 2002), p 65.

parties and the matters which they wish to have recorded. This is the form most commonly used by notaries in civil law jurisdictions.[220]

19.110 If the document is executed before a notary outside the country in which it is to be used, it is usually necessary for the notary's signature to be verified. This can be done in two ways:

(a) by 'legalisation', ie authentication by the embassy or consulate, located in the country of the notary, of the country in which the document is to be used;[221] or

(b) if it is executed in a country which has ratified the Hague Convention of 1961, by an 'apostille' issued by the Foreign Ministry of that country.

---

[220] See further *Brooke's Notary* (12th edn, 2002), pp 65 to 69.

[221] Thus, for example, a document executed in London for use in Sweden would be legalised by the Swedish Consulate in London.

INDEX

References are to paragraph numbers.